Navigating Change

The Management of Innovation and Change Series
Michael L. Tushman and Andrew H. Van de Ven, Series Editors

Navigating Change

Change

[
How CEOs,
Top Teams, and
Boards Steer
Transformation
]

Edited by

Donald C. Hambrick

David A. Nadler

Michael L. Tushman

Harvard Business School Press

Boston, Massachusetts

Copyright © 1998 by the President and Fellows of Harvard College
All rights reserved
Printed in the United States of America
02 01 00 99 98   5 4 3 2 1

Library of Congress Cataloging-in-Publication Data
    Navigating change: how CEOs, top teams, and boards steer
       transformation/edited by Donald C. Hambrick, David A. Nadler,
    Michael L. Tushman.
          p.   cm.
    Includes index.
    ISBN 0-87584-784-6 (alk. paper)
      1. Leadership   2. Executive ability.   3. Organizational change.
    I. Hambrick, Donald C.   II. Nadler, David   III. Tushman, Michael.
    HD57.7.N39   1998   97-19266
    658.4'092—dc21   CIP

The paper used in this publication meets the requirements of the American
National Standard for Permanence of Paper for Printed Library Materials
Z39 49-1984

Contents

[III]
Boards of Directors

[IV]
Senior Leadership and Discontinuous Change

[V]
Integration

Preface

Try to think of a major industry that is *not* experiencing profound upheaval. If you're like us, you will have to think long and hard. In the vast preponderance of business arenas—pharmaceuticals, automobiles, telecommunications, computers, health care, major appliances, food products, financial services, publishing, retailing, advertising, and on and on—the rules of the game have changed radically. But the new "rules" are not rules at all; because they too are transitory, soon to be superseded in the face of new alien conditions brought about by external forces or bypassed by devilish rule breaking on the part of industry upstarts or mavericks. And changes in the business landscape are not going to stop. Making it through one transition simply earns a corporation the chance to try to make it through the next one.

Under these conditions of unrelenting turbulence, the few people at the top of a company make a world of difference to its competitiveness and vitality. Senior leaders centrally influence the form and fate of the enterprise. Through their action or inaction, their boldness or caution, and their cohesion or fragmentation, the upper echelons mediate between external shifts and organizational responses. While the impact of senior leadership has always been felt, it is particularly significant today, as corporate landscapes are continually wrenched by technological, geopolitical, competitive, and marketplace discontinuities—all requiring strategic choices and sweeping organizational transformations.

Successful corporate transformation depends on effective decision making and leadership from three distinct but interconnected entities:

the CEO, the top management team, and the board of directors. The CEO is the executive who has overall responsibility for the conduct and performance of the firm; clearly his or her mindset, imagination, and behavior will have a defining effect on corporate adaptation. Ultimately, however, senior leadership is a shared endeavor, extending beyond the CEO to other top executives. Thus, the senior management group, widely referred to as the top management team, also has a central role in formulating and executing corporate transformation. The top management team is not simply an aggregation of individual executives. Rather, the dynamics and complementarities that exist within the team greatly influence corporate outcomes. Finally, the board of directors has legal responsibility for the governance of the firm. Although not charged with administrative decisions, the board creates the context within which the firm's executives make strategic choices. The board's vigilance, expectations, internal dynamics, and relationships with management can make the difference between corporate stagnation and vitality.

All three of these leadership entities are critically important to effective corporate adaptation under conditions of turbulence. This book examines all three, including their interconnections to one another and, particularly, their roles in designing and navigating effective corporate change.

The importance of top leadership today has brought about a widespread interest in this topic. Academic research has burgeoned; it is now rare to pick up an issue of a scholarly management journal and *not* find technical articles dealing with CEOs, top management teams, or boards of directors.

The popular and business press also cater to a public appetite for stories about executive brilliance and ineptitude, huge CEO pay packages, executive personality clashes, and boardroom coups. Indeed, we now live in an era in which many CEOs are well-known media figures, their names and deeds (or misdeeds) familiar in many households.

But between these two extremes—the technical and the popular—very little literature exists. The purpose of this book is to bridge that gap by providing insights about senior leadership that are thoughtful, analytic, and leading-edge, while at the same time being practical, engaging, and stimulating for executives. Our aim has been to create a volume that will be simultaneously a primary guide for future research on top executives *and* a catalyst for changes in both attitudes about senior leadership and applied organizational policies. We have enlisted as contributors some of the foremost academic experts and consultants on senior leadership, as well as several prominent CEOs and corporate directors.

Navigating Change is distinctive, we hope, not only because of the caliber of the contributors and their ideas, but also because of the breadth of perspectives they represent and their strong desire to exchange and reconcile those perspectives. Indeed, the authors all convened in April 1996 for a conference at Columbia University's executive campus, Arden House, to present, debate, and refine their views. (Throughout the book are numerous instances in which the authors refer to the discussions at the conference, evidencing the fruitful exchanges.) Thus, the book is a rare example of the type of collaboration that is urgently needed between the spheres of management scholarship and management practice.

Our intent is for the book to be highly pertinent for both academics and executives. For scholars, the book establishes a comprehensive new platform for future research on CEOs, top management teams, and boards. This is a scholarly arena currently experiencing explosive but fragmented growth. The book should help coalesce and direct future inquiries into pressing pragmatic issues regarding senior leadership.

For executives, the book addresses an array of difficult and highly sensitive senior-level issues and their effects on corporate adaptation and performance. Top executives; professionals involved in executive search, consulting, and executive compensation and appraisal; and board members who must evaluate top executive performance and capabilities—all will find in this book a considerable stimulus for updating their points of view and practical tools.

Navigating Change is organized into five parts. In Part I, on CEOs, David Nadler and Jeffrey Heilpern (Delta Consulting) set the stage by identifying the set of constituencies, particularly the "hot spots," to which the CEO must respond during times of industry upheaval. They also propose the idea that CEOs evolve during their tenures in ways that affect their abilities to formulate and execute large-scale organizational redesign. James Houghton (Corning) discusses his views on corporate transformation and particularly his vision of what it takes to be an effective CEO in today's corporate environment. Manfred Kets de Vries (INSEAD) addresses psychological factors that contribute to both dysfunctional and highly effective CEO leadership. Focusing on three seemingly very different but highly successful CEOs, Kets de Vries extracts the characteristics they have in common and suggests the leadership qualities that will be needed in the twenty-first century. Christopher Bartlett (Harvard Business School) and Sumantra Ghoshal (London Business School) debunk the Russian doll model of management, in which each successively higher level of the organization is filled by "bigger" versions of the managers just below. The authors argue that each managerial level in contemporary firms has distinctly different types of roles, requiring widely different aptitudes. Only when companies select managers with the required "embedded traits" for *that* level will they achieve effective leadership. Finally, Jeffrey Sonnenfeld (Emory University) synthesizes the first four chapters of Part I, examining the interplay between CEOs and their environment and asking whether society creates the "hero" or whether the hero stamps his or her vision on society.

Part II focuses on executive teams. Paul Allaire (Xerox) discusses in depth the role of the senior management team in bringing about a major transformation at his company. Donald Hambrick (Columbia) argues that companies are under increasing pressure to achieve "corporate coherence," or unity of purpose and action, which in turn requires more coherence within senior management groups. He lays out the detailed characteristics of a coherent executive team, as well as recommendations to CEOs for achieving more teamlike properties at the top of the firm. Kathleen Eisenhardt, Jean Kahwajy (both of Stanford University), and Jay Bourgeois (University of Virginia) address the important role of conflict within top management teams. Based on extensive field research, their chapter examines the levers that can be employed to promote constructive conflict among the senior group. The authors also identify key roles that team members must take in order for such healthy conflict to occur. In a closely related chapter, Charles Raben and Janet Spencer (Delta Consulting) discuss the role of the CEO in confronting conflict within the top management team. They lay out seven alternative models for the CEO, ranging from "the Optimist" to "the Terminator," and they identify the conditions under which each conflict management approach is most warranted and the CEO aptitudes needed to exercise it. Deborah Ancona (MIT) synthesizes Part II with a call to CEOs to pay much more attention to top team design, team processes, and the relationships between teams and the external environment.

Part III examines boards of directors. John Vogelstein (Warburg Pincus), a major investor and a director of numerous companies, discusses how, even after years of calls for reforms, boards are still in great need of improvement. He sets forth several tangible changes he would like to see in corporate boards. Jay Lorsch (Harvard) focuses specifically on the role of the corporate board as an agent of change. Lorsch argues that boards must move beyond reviewing only financial information and should serve as an early warning system, helping to identify and catalyze needed strategic adjustments before financial performance deteriorates. Andrew Pettigrew and Terry McNulty (University of Warwick, England) extend the argument for a more proactive board by asserting that there is great need for creativity in the boardroom, as a complement to the customary emphasis on control. They discuss the chief factors that may enhance board creativity, focusing on board composition, board processes, and the role of the CEO. Edward Zajac (Northwestern University) and James Westphal (University of Texas at Austin) set forth a comprehensive framework for considering CEO–board relationships. This article integrates a wealth of academic and applied literature on corporate governance, helping to sort out the rationales and logics behind various governance models. Part III is synthesized by Gerald Davis (Columbia), who contends that reforms in formal board arrangements may not be sufficient to bring about the changes in behavior that the authors in this section envision. Ultimately, Davis maintains, there must be changes in boardroom cultures as well.

Part IV deals with senior leadership in the context of discontinuous changes. The first two chapters describe the experiences of two CEOs in leading large-scale organizational transformations. David Lawrence (Kaiser Permanente) presents ten lessons he learned in transforming America's largest health care provider. He particularly emphasizes the timing and sequence of initiatives and the role of the top management team and board. Robert Bauman (British Aerospace) chronicles his highly successful efforts as CEO of SmithKline Beecham. Simultaneously integrating two large companies *and* adapting to major environmental shifts, Bauman learned five "fundamentals of implementing change," which he presents in his chapter. Michael Tushman (Columbia), Philip Anderson (Dartmouth College), and Charles O'Reilly (Stanford) discuss the need for companies to be "ambidextrous"—to deal with continuous improvement and efficiency seeking on the one hand, while at the same time engaging in radical innovation and regeneration on the other hand. The authors examine the critical role of technological innovation in this stressful corporate balancing act, and they discuss the role of the senior team in building and managing ambidextrous organizations. Elise Walton (Delta Consulting) synthesizes Part IV, highlighting the joint role of the CEO and senior team as a central information-processing unit and learning device for the firm.

Finally, in Part V, Ralph Biggadike (Columbia) identifies and assesses the common themes that span the scope of the entire book. He particularly builds upon the examples of successful transformations described in individual chapters. One of the themes he identifies captures the central essence of the book: Successful corporate transformation requires vigilance, appetite for change, concerted effort, and clarity of purpose from all three senior leadership entities— the CEO, the top management team as a whole, and the board.

Our indebtedness for help on the book extends in several directions. Foremost, thanks go to the authors who signed on for this venture and then responded so admirably to our constant cajoling. Deep appreciation goes to our colleagues at Columbia Business School and Delta Consulting Group who stimulated and influenced the book in ways they may not have known. Our two organizations co-sponsored the project in a remarkable collaboration. We are thankful to Meyer Feldberg, Dean of Columbia Business School, who provided support. Janet Spencer, Senior Director at Delta, played a major role in pulling the conference together and worked with the three of us as a key collaborator in making it happen. Mark Nadler, Editorial Director at Delta, worked on a number of the chapters and contributed significantly to their readability and coherence. Marjorie Williams, executive editor at Harvard Business School Press, and Nicki Sabin, acquisitions editor at the Press, were of invaluable assistance in helping to craft the overall concept and execution of the book. Finally, Peg Latham and Jay Howland at Colophon provided exceptional assistance in refining and smoothing the diverse chapters into a unified whole.

Navigating Change

[1]

CEOs

[1]

The CEO in the Context of Discontinuous Change

David A. Nadler
and Jeffrey D. Heilpern

THE 1990s have seen an unprecedented increase in the public visibility of corporate and institutional CEOs. The collective anonymity that once enveloped the leaders of our major commercial and not-for-profit institutions has given way to intense public attention. With increasing frequency the men and women who lead important organizations are seeing their names and faces on television, in newspapers, on magazine covers and book jackets.

This barrage of publicity testifies to a growing recognition of CEOs' central role in American life. But heightened visibility can be a mixed blessing. CEOs are alternately portrayed as visionaries, gurus, and saviors—or as villains and even as "killers," to use the term employed on the cover of one newsmagazine. The fact that so many of the depictions amount to nothing more than superficial caricatures does nothing to lessen the importance of this trend.

The question CEOs ought to be asking themselves is, What is behind this profound change in the public's perception of their power and social impact?

The answer, we believe, lies in the increasing rate at which corporate and public institutions are finding themselves forced to undergo massive, fundamental, and inherently disruptive change. Driven by a host of competitive forces, those changes increasingly translate into headlines trumpeting mergers, acquisitions, spin-offs, breakups, and ultimately the job loss and downsizing that so often accompany the pursuit of greater efficiency and productivity. At the same time, the press is awash in stories reporting the impressive results achieved by many of these same companies and the seemingly staggering compensation awarded to those who drive that performance.

To the general public, the result is a confusing and sometimes disturbing picture of economic dislocation accompanied by endless reports of rising profits, booming financial markets, and lavishly paid executives. At the center of this maelstrom is the CEO, the single most pivotal—and visible—individual associated with each new instance of organizational change and disruption.

Some CEOs, through a combination of vision, skill, luck, and smart public relations, are able to emerge as corporate heroes. Bill Gates of Microsoft, Jack Welch of General Electric, and Roberto Goizueta of Coca-Cola are the latest to inherit the mantle of corporate superhero first bestowed upon Lee Iacocca. Less fortunate, but much more common, are the CEOs who either fail to produce the necessary change or fail to meet the critical needs of their key constituencies while implementing change, and end up being either ridiculed or demonized.

Obviously, the determination of success or failure isn't that simple. Any useful assessment of the CEO's role requires a basic understanding both of the nature of the changes being experienced by our major organizations and of the unique and complex world of the CEO.

That's what this book is about. In this chapter we will first provide a perspective on change, one focused on pinpointing exactly why the role of the CEO is so crucial. Second, we will examine the world of the CEO and how it is impacted by change. Third, we will look at the issue of CEO effectiveness in periods of change and identify some of the behaviors required by CEOs as they lead their organizations through change. Fourth, we will turn to the dynamics of the CEO's role by considering how that role evolves over time. Finally, we will consider the implications of periods of major change for the CEO's relationships with his or her key constituencies.

Before proceeding, a few comments about terminology and subject matter. First, while the term *CEO* is typically associated with business firms and corporations, our discussion is equally relevant to the chief executives of any enterprise that operates in the context of market forces, including universities, health care organizations, not-for-profit institutions, and so forth. Second, while many of our observations are aimed at CEOs of public companies, many points also apply to other forms of CEOs—the top executives of autonomous operating companies within a corporation, for instance, or the heads of joint ventures between corporate partners. Additionally, although we address our observations specifically to United States–based corporations, many of the implications also apply to companies based in other countries.

A Perspective on Change

This current period of large-scale change in our major organizations started in the mid-1980s, driven by competitive pressure on U.S. companies to improve quality, increase productivity, and heighten overall efficiency. But what began as a belated and somewhat desperate response to competition from abroad continued unabated through the mid-1990s and seems likely to remain a fact of organizational life into the next century. Basic market forces have converged to ensure a continuing need for constant change.

Briefly, the most important of these forces are:

- *The emergence of global competition.* Producers, suppliers, and capital markets are all competing across traditional national and geographic boundaries.

- *New technology.* The ever increasing pace of technological change, particularly in the area of information technology, is transforming market offerings, production processes, and internal organizational structures and processes.

- *Public policy.* Government deregulation and privatization are reshaping the fundamental nature of competition in a wide range of industries and business sectors from telecommunications to health care.

Additionally, powerful social, economic, and political forces are at work, constantly redefining markets, trade relationships, and the bases of competition.

Of course, change has always been a factor in organizational life. Static periods tend to look that way in hindsight, rather than while they're actually in progress. But the type of change experienced in the past decade is qualitatively different from what we saw in the past.

A Different Kind of Change

We have written elsewhere about the altered nature of change and the environmentally driven "change imperative" that has emerged (Nadler, 1997). Our basic proposition is that industries or product classes typically evolve through relatively predictable patterns of growth over time in a pattern classically described as the "S curve." The curve traces each industry from its earliest days, with a wide variety of competing designs and technologies, to the emergence of dominant designs and a weeding out of competitors, and finally to the mature phase, when product innovation becomes secondary to process innovation.

This perspective argues that at various stages in the development of any industry, there is relative equilibrium among the multitude of factors that shape that particular industry. Periodically, however, each industry experiences a phase of substantial upheaval and disequilibrium, generally precipitated by a destabilizing event or series of events. Such events might include the emergence of a new technology, major judicial or legislative action, or the appearance of a new player who somehow alters the basis of competition.

Unlike the incremental changes that gradually modify the industry during normal periods, these destabilizing events can be likened to mutations, radically reconfiguring the scale, shape, and pace of change. The most recent and dramatic example of a major destabilizing event is the telecommunications reform enacted by Congress in early 1996. Just the anticipation of that event was enough to prompt the largest voluntary corporate breakup in U.S. history, AT&T's spin-off of Lucent Technologies and NCR; and the event's aftermath will bring fundamental and far-reaching change to the telecommunications and entertainment industries for years to come.

It is during such periods of disequilibrium that the change imperative surfaces. That is, companies that make the appropriate fundamental changes in strategy, work, people, formal organization, and operating environment stand a good chance of weathering the storm and emerging as healthy players, well positioned for the next phase of industry development. But companies that fail to make the necessary changes during this crucial period cease to continue in the same form, and often disappear.

These periods of upheaval require what we have described as *discontinuous change* (Nadler, Newman, & Tushman, 1988; Nadler & Tushman, 1995) in an organization—a step function change that affects practically every major variable in the equation of the enterprise. This form of change responds to environmental discontinuity through a carefully designed, deliberately led period of organizational discontinuity.

This view of change implies three basic challenges for top management. The first is the challenge of recognition—the need to understand the environment and recognize at an early stage the massing of forces that are likely to create disequilibrium and require discontinuous change.

Second is the challenge of strategy—the need to make appropriate strategic choices to reposition the organization as a strong competitor in the context of the disequilibrium reshaping the industry.

Third is the challenge of rearchitecting the organization—the need to design creatively and implement deftly the changes that will enable the organization to function successfully in the new environment. In some ways, the process through which the organization designs and puts into place its new architecture is just as important as the actual substance of the design.

The Integrated Change Agenda

The issue of change management is one that merits separate treatment, and we have devoted several other works exclusively to that topic. For our purposes here, it's important to emphasize that in most of the successful change efforts we've seen, the core of the process lies in the CEO's development and ownership of an overall plan. In generic terms, we have described this road map for change as an *integrated change agenda*. The specific content varies from one organization to another, but the basic ingredients are fairly constant. They typically include:

- *Purpose:* A broad statement spelling out a philosophy, vision, or mission for the organization. It articulates, in general terms, the organization's ultimate goals and portrays what kind of organization the change is intended to create.

- *Values:* A description of the core values that the organization considers most important, such as quality, innovation, and service. Values are expressed in axiomatic statements of principles the organization holds to be inherently worthwhile and depict an ideal of what kind of organization its leaders want it to be.

- *Strategies:* A statement of the core strategies, including a definition of businesses, markets, and offerings and a determination of particular bases for competition. These are translated into the specific strategic objectives that will drive the key decisions on how the organization ought to be changed and redesigned.

- *Governance:* A general explanation of the structures and processes used to coordinate management at the enterprise level.

- *Organization:* A broad framework for the architecture of the enterprise—the structures, processes, and systems that will enable people, working in the context of the operating environment, to perform the work required by the strategy and vision.

- *Operating environment:* The patterns of behavior required of people within the organization over time. While the statement of values generally implies a certain kind of operating environment or culture, the change agenda also describes in fairly specific terms the kind of operating environment that will be required in order to achieve the organization's strategic objectives. An envisioned environment might be described, for instance, as customer focused, responsive, and empowering with a new emphasis on speed, front-line decision making, and heightened accountability.

- *Operational performance:* The actions that will be taken to improve the effectiveness of the core operations, including process redesign, quality, cost reduction, and so on.

- *Talent:* A plan for upgrading the organization's talent pool. This may include development of present employees and, if necessary, recruitment of new ones, to ensure that people have the skills and talents required to execute the new strategies.

Typically, the integrated change agenda emerges from a deliberate, disciplined, and participative process involving, at the very least, the CEO and the senior team. Ideally, top leadership develops the agenda through a process involving a significant number of appropriate people—for three reasons. First, participation by people closer to the work tends to improve the content of the planned change. Second, those who participate tend to feel considerably greater personal ownership of the change. Finally, participation is an essential mechanism for managing the politics of change; those who have been involved in developing the change agenda frequently go on to become its most ardent advocates, forming the nucleus of a critical mass of support for the change within the organization.

The change agenda, if it is to succeed, must also be part of a process that pays particular attention to the issue of implementation. In our experience, inadequate participation and poor implementation are the two most common reasons why organizations fail to redesign themselves successfully. Surprisingly often, executives seem to think the change is as good as done when the change agenda is completed. In some ways, that's where the most difficult work—the management of change—actually begins.

The Role of the CEO

Our experience and observation show that without the active personal involvement of the CEO in a central role, successful discontinuous change is simply impossible. The reason is obvious: Fundamental change requires the focused and aggressive exercise of power. And within any organization, the levers of power are uniquely concentrated in the hands of the CEO.

That power, which we define as the ability to influence effectively the behavior of others, flows from different categories of sources (French & Raven, 1959). The first category might be described as the formal sources of power. These include the "legitimate power" automatically associated with a specific job, office, or rank in any commercial, social, political, or military institution. A second source of formal power lies in a leader's ability to extend rewards to those who perform in desired ways. A third source is the ability to impose sanctions upon those who fail to perform as required.

Two informal sources of power are tied more closely to the individual than to his or her official position within an organization. The first is "expert" power; certain individuals are able to wield influence in given settings because others recognize their superior expertise in a critical area. The second is "referent" power, which flows from the desire of others to be like the leader, to be identified and somehow associated with him or her.

Power also is strongly tied to the motive profile of the individual CEO. CEOs typically have strong needs for both achievement and power; simply put, they enjoy the exercise of power. Consequently, they are internally motivated to build and then use the potential power available to them from a variety of formal and informal sources.

And yet, interestingly, there's something of a paradox here. On one hand, the CEO is the person who wields the most power; at the same time, CEOs often admit to a sense of being powerless. We frequently hear CEOs compare their situation to that of a captain on the bridge who issues orders, pushes buttons, and pulls levers, but still gets no response from the engine room. In part, this problem is inherent in the size and complexity of large corporations. But it also has to do with the multiple constituencies—the "world" of constituencies—each CEO is required to serve.

The World of the CEO

Rather than thinking of the CEO as the captain on the bridge, unilaterally setting a course and issuing orders, we ought to consider a more realistic view: the CEO as positioned at the center of a collection of constituencies, each of which acts as a "role sender." In this model, each constituency periodically transmits a set of expectations regarding the behavior and performance they expect from the CEO, whose job is to find the proper balance among those varied, and sometimes conflicting, expectations.

Depending on the size, scope, and nature of the organization, each CEO will have had a varied set of role senders. However, there are some important and fairly universal constituencies that can be mapped with a 360-degree view of the world of the CEO (Figure 1.1). There are two sets of external constituencies. One external group, including the financial community, suppliers, and customers, is clearly related to the organization's "value chain." The other external group, which can be described as the social constituencies—the government and official regulators, communities where the organi-

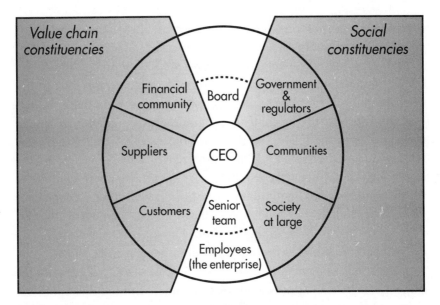

Figure 1.1   The World of the CEO—360° Map

zation operates, and society at large—can, at various times, send equally pressing messages about their expectations of the CEO.

Of most immediate concern are the internal constituencies at the top and bottom of the map. The shareholders—the institutions and individuals with an economic stake in the firm—convey their expectations through their proxy, the board of directors, an infinitely important constituency in itself. Similarly, the CEO manages and regularly interacts with another key constituency, the senior management group, which acts as the linkage between the CEO and the rest of the employees (the enterprise as a whole).

Taken together, the various role senders correspond to what are often referred to as corporate stakeholders. In reality, the organization's stakeholders become the CEO's constituencies (Heilpern, 1995).

Now let's consider how this perspective on the world of the CEO intersects with our view of discontinuous change. During periods of discontinuous or radical change, each constituency experiences seriously heightened uncertainty or lack of clarity about the future. Accordingly, each makes increased demands upon the CEO. Although the demands of all the constituencies are important, we would argue that it is absolutely essential for the CEO to focus his/her personal energy and attention on a limited group of constituencies—those that no one else in the organization can adequately address.

For example, while customers represent an essential constituency for any organization, the CEO's personal involvement is not a truly essential component of customer transactions. In some situations, particularly those involving industrial marketing, customers may like to meet and greet the CEO; but their real business is with the sales and service representatives. So if, during a period of major change, the CEO decides his/her time can better be spent elsewhere and makes fewer customer visits, it's unlikely that business will suffer. In consumer businesses, the CEO's connection to customers is even more abstract; the truth is that most customers neither know nor care who heads up the company that makes their laundry detergent or their VCR.

The same holds true for most of the other external constituencies, where the CEO's personal role is normally limited to ceremonial visits and public rituals. Those activities are an important part of the CEO's role in normal times, but we suggest they should be considered peripheral and secondary during periods of discontinuous change—when the organization's very future may be at stake.

Instead, we believe that during these turbulent periods the CEO must concentrate on the "hot spots"—those critical areas of tension where the CEO, and only the CEO, can play a decisive role. There are three of these hot spots. The first is the board of directors, because no one in the organization but the CEO has the legitimate standing to deal with them. The second is the senior team, because only the CEO, as their immediate supervisor, can shape, manage, and lead this group of top executives. And third are the employees and the enterprise at large, because no one but the CEO can speak to them as the single institutional leader.

Given the pressures of change and the requirements change imposes on the CEO in terms of dealing with his/her key constituencies, we must ask what constitutes effective leadership in the world of the CEO. Let's consider some different perspectives on this question.

CEO Effectiveness: A Static View

If we look at CEO effectiveness in a static sense—as a snapshot in time—it's evident that there are numerous different styles and approaches that work for different individuals. Nevertheless, some common roles are shared by nearly all effective CEO leaders of change, regardless of their stylistic differences (Nadler & Tushman, 1989). These roles fall into three broad categories:

1. *Envisioning.* Successful CEOs share an ability to articulate and communicate a vision of the organization that captures the imagination of the people they lead. Typically, that vision challenges people to meet seemingly unattainable goals by committing themselves to a superior level of performance.

2. *Energizing.* Effective CEOs energize their people by constantly and publicly demonstrating their own sense of personal excitement and total engagement. They consistently convey a sense of absolute confidence in the organization's ability to achieve the most challenging goals. And they actively energize people by highlighting examples of success as a way of building a sense of confidence and accomplishment.

3. *Enabling.* In addition to envisioning a set of goals and energizing people to pursue them, effective CEOs then find realistic ways to give people the confidence, authority, and resources they need to work toward their shared objectives.

At the same time, truly effective CEOs understand the need for strong operational leadership—the development, management, and control of essential structures, systems, and processes. Frequently, a CEO delegates substantial responsibility for operational leadership to one or more senior direct reports; because in practice, it's generally difficult, particularly in change situations, for a CEO to play simultaneous roles as institutional leader and operational manager. Regardless of how those duties are delegated, however, their successful performance is still part of the CEO's ultimate responsibility.

Beyond these major roles, some personal characteristics are particularly central to CEOs' success in building and managing relationships with various constituencies during periods of change. These traits include:

- A particular "towering strength" balanced by other strong capabilities. Typically, CEOs are particularly good at some aspect of the job—such as making bold moves, managing operational performance, or articulating an inspiring vision. But they must be able to do other things well too, so that when change alters the rules and the game no longer plays to their towering strength, they can comfortably switch gears without becoming immobilized or incompetent.

- Emotional strength and perspective. CEOs must possess a groundedness that prevents them from getting rattled by pressure and adversity when dealing with numerous constituencies, all of whom may be anxious, impatient, and demanding. Effective CEOs stay in touch with their own sense of perspective and common sense.

- The ability to convey the sense that the CEO is acting and responding as a genuine human being. Genuineness is practically impossible to fabricate; it requires the CEO, in fact, to open up to people to an unusual degree. Effective CEOs avoid giving the impression that they are cloaking themselves in the role of chief executive to shield their true thoughts and emotions.

- A sense of humor. As obvious as it may seem, a sense of humor—particularly one that allows for occasional mild self-deprecation—plays a key role in helping all concerned maintain perspective during pressure-filled periods.

- A capacity for empathy with a broad range of people. Although President Clinton's phrase "I feel your pain" became a source of mirth among politicians, journalists, and late-night TV show hosts, Clinton succeeds in convincing people in face-to-face situations that he not only understands their problems but somehow shares their experiences and emotions. Particularly in difficult times, members of each key constituency constantly look for signs that the CEO truly understands the depth of their concerns.

- Connectedness. This trait, an ability to make a deeply personal connection with individuals on an emotional or intellectual basis, lets people feel that even a brief exchange is a substantive interaction rather than a perfunctory ritual.

Truly effective CEOs possess these capabilities for managing difficult relationships. It is worth noting that in our discussion of CEOs as great leaders, we have avoided using the term *charisma*. In our experience, the characteristics popularly associated with charismatic leaders have relatively little to do with long-term success in leading complex organizations. Few of the most successful CEOs rely on movie-star looks or celebrity appeal. Instead, their capacity to achieve long-term results rests upon the more subtle and complex traits we've just described.

The preceding discussion, while describing certain elements essential to a CEO's success, provides only a first layer of analysis. Let's turn now to a more dynamic view of how CEO effectiveness is likely to change over a substantial period of time.

CEO Effectiveness: A Dynamic View

A dynamic perspective on CEO effectiveness describes the intersection of two factors: the frequency of discontinuous change and the predictable patterns of the CEO "life cycle." This perspective also assumes that in general—given variations from one industry to another—there is a movement toward greater frequency of periods of disequilibrium and discontinuous change.

Through the mid-1980s, a CEO could easily serve out a normal tenure without ever experiencing a true period of discontinuous change. From the mid-1980s to the early 1990s, with the restructuring of U.S. business and the growing intensity of foreign competition, there was a high probability that a CEO would encounter one cycle of discontinuous change. Now, in the late 1990s, and particularly in industries undergoing fundamental change (such as health care, financial services, and information technology), there is every likelihood that a CEO will have to manage more than one period of discontinuous change.

That fact in itself presents major challenges to CEOs and their organizations. David Kearns, the former chairman of Xerox Corporation, once described the job of managing discontinuous change as "all-consuming." The toll this kind of responsibility takes on CEOs on a very personal level should not be underestimated. In the early 1990s, a Fortune 500 company whose board had just removed a CEO for failing to initiate sufficiently radical change was having great difficulty finding a successor. When asked why the search was taking so long, the CEO of another major corporation told us, "Because of what they're facing, their ideal candidate is somebody who has already managed a major change. But anybody who's done it once doesn't want to go through it again."

A closely associated issue involves the "CEO life cycle" or the "seasons of the CEO." Donald Hambrick and Gregory Fukutomi of Columbia University have studied this area (Hambrick and Fukutomi, 1991). Essentially, they contend there are predictable patterns of activity and behavior that constitute five discernible periods in the normal tenures of most CEOs.

The first period begins with what Hambrick and Fukutomi refer to as "response to mandate." The new CEO embarks on his/her tenure with a commitment to a particular paradigm—a model based on personal assumptions about how an organization ought to be structured and managed—combined with the CEO's personal perspectives on his/her own personal tool kit of strengths and skills. At this stage the CEO seeks out unfiltered information from numerous sources; has relatively little knowledge of, but high interest in, the tasks involved in the job; and possesses a relatively low—but growing—degree of power.

The next phase is one of "experimentation." The CEO's commitment to his/her original paradigm will vary at this point, depending upon the individual's experience and degree of success in the initial stage. Task knowledge is moderate, while interest remains high. The CEO's power has increased somewhat. Information continues to flow from numerous sources, but is increasingly filtered by the time it reaches the CEO.

The CEO's defining phase, to a great extent, comes next: the period characterized by the selection of an "enduring theme." The CEO's commitment to a paradigm is becoming stronger. Knowledge of the tasks required by the job is high, and the rate of learning declines, while interest remains moderately high. Information now comes from fewer, and somewhat filtered, sources. The CEO's power is moderate and continuing to grow.

Hambrick and Fukutomi describe the fourth phase as "convergence," as the CEO pursues a series of incremental actions to reinforce the major changes that have come before. By this point, the CEO's commitment to a certain paradigm has grown strong. Knowledge of tasks, which by this time have become almost routine, is high, while interest in them has started to diminish. Information, highly filtered, now comes from only a few sources. And the CEO's power is strong and increasing.

In the final stage, which Hambrick and Fukutomi have labeled "dysfunction," the CEO's effectiveness is seriously diminished. The CEO's commitment to a given paradigm has hardened, seriously weakening any interest in experimentation. The specific tasks have become habitual; not surprisingly, the CEO's interest in them has weakened considerably. The CEO at this stage depends on only a very few, highly filtered sources of information. And yet, at the same time that interest has waned, energy has ebbed, and the appetite for risky and dramatic change has all but vanished, the CEO's power and ability to lead change are at an all-time high.

This view of the CEO life cycle, when overlaid upon the patterns of industry evolution and the unavoidable periods of disequilibrium, raises some serious issues that should be considered by anyone concerned with organizational governance in times of change.

To begin with, it is common to find discontinuous change taking place during the early stages of a CEO's tenure. Frequently, the new CEO has been hired expressly to initiate and manage the kind of major change the previous CEO, for whatever reason, failed to undertake. Presumably the new CEO was hired because his/her experience, abilities, and organizational perspectives were well suited to the kind of change the board believed was necessary. The CEO enters the job with considerable energy, a genuine desire to be open-minded and inventive, and a compelling drive to put a personal stamp on the organization.

But what happens when the need for discontinuous change develops during the latter phases of the CEO's tenure? As Hambrick and Fukutomi make clear, the CEO's later years are marked by diminished energy and openness; moreover, considering the CEO's huge investment of emotional capital in existing structures, processes, and people, it's unlikely the late-life-cycle CEO will suddenly turn into an agent of radical change.

Similarly, what happens when the need for a *second round* of discontinuous change becomes necessary late in the tenure of a CEO who has already managed a round of major change at an earlier stage? Given the time, energy, and personal commitment the CEO devoted to the first change, it's unreasonable to expect any but a few highly unusual individuals to be enthusiastic about starting all over again.

Clearly, there is a critical relationship between the timing of change and the length of the CEO's tenure. When the need for change coincides with the appropriate phase of the CEO's tenure—

as often happens in the early years—the results are often quite successful. But when the need for change—either a first or a second round—becomes evident late in the CEO's tenure, the situation becomes much more complicated. The responses vary from the truly constructive to the highly dysfunctional. There are four patterns of response, in particular, that we have observed:

1. *Denial.* Convinced that the people, structures, processes, systems, and operating environment he/she put into place are sufficient to meet any challenge, the CEO insists that sufficient change can be accomplished through incremental moves.

2. *Avoidance.* Some CEO's, rather than subject themselves to the arduous task of leading radical change involving every element of the organization, attempt to make dramatic personnel changes among top executives or major structural moves such as spin-offs, in a search for a less painful, quick-hit approach to change.

3. *Bowing out.* Some CEOs, recognizing the situation demands radical change and accepting the fact that they no longer have the interest, energy, or appetite for such change, simply leave. After nineteen years as chairman of Corning Incorporated, for example, Amory Houghton Jr. gave up the job and went on to a successful career in politics, leaving his younger brother, James R. Houghton, to lead the company through a decade of sweeping change beginning in the mid-1980s.

4. *Succession management.* In some situations, where CEOs have recognized both the need for discontinuous change and their own lack of interest in managing it, the change effort has been closely linked to the issue of succession. The CEO supports the change effort, but doesn't lead it with the same degree of personal involvement he or she invested in earlier phases. At the same time, the CEO delegates significant responsibility for directing the change effort to an heir apparent. This paves the way for the heir's ascension to the CEO's job as architect, and now leader, of the newly redesigned organization.

This intersection of times of change with CEO life cycles is far more than a theoretical concern. In some industries waves of severe disequilibrium are occurring as closely as five years apart—an interval considerably shorter than the tenure of many CEOs. In fact, one study done in the late 1980s (Vancil, 1987) found that one out of four Fortune 500 CEOs served for ten years or more. Consequently, as the pace of change in markets, technology, and competition continues to increase, so too does the likelihood that organizations will face multiple periods of turbulence calling for discontinuous change during the tenure of any given CEO.

Implications for Institutional Leaders

We have presented a case for the centrality of the CEO's role in discontinuous change, and we have suggested that the intersection of the demands of change with the CEO life cycle has numerous and profound implictions. In a sense, this book is an attempt to examine these implications from many different perspectives; and ensuing chapters, drawing on both practice and research, will present a collection of insights. At this point, however, we can begin to sketch out a general landscape with some initial observations.

First, there is a set of implications having to do with how the CEO deals with the three hot spots—the board, the senior team, and the institution and employees—during times of change. Second, there are implications for the institution—including the responsibility of the board to ensure effective CEO leadership before and during periods of discontinuous change.

The CEO and the Board

It is imperative that the CEO, in his/her role as chairman, ensures the selection of an active, nonritualistic board: what Millstein describes as a "certifying board" (Millstein, 1993). It is the CEO's responsibility to help shape a board that is truly engaged and involved in the direction of the organization, one that works closely with the executive team. The board should include a sufficient number of people who are currently active (rather than retired) and in possession of a range of experience and expertise in markets, strategy, management, and appropriate technologies to be helpful in dealing with the issues related to change.

Moreover, the board should be brought into the strategic process in an active way, and early enough to play the role of strategic early warning system. The CEO should make sure that board members are provided with comprehensive and continually updated information about the strategic issues facing the organization. That information, when filtered through board members' collective experience and insight, should enable them to recognize and alert the company to the early signs of impending disequilibrium.

Finally, CEOs should recognize the importance of actively and explicitly seeking their board's assessment and feedback regarding their own performance. Only the board, as the CEO's surrogate supervisor, can fulfill this role. As CEOs pass through each phase of their tenure, their performance will tend to improve in certain areas while weakening in others. Yet as CEOs' tenure grows longer and they become more powerful, self-assured, and comfortable in the job, they are less likely to feel the need to seek out the board's assessment of their performance—even though that may be the time when they most need it.

CEOs need to realize that, whether with or without their knowledge and participation, the board will indeed be judging their performance. Consequently, it's infinitely preferable for the CEO to structure a formal appraisal process, one that provides for helpful feedback and affords an opportunity to modify performance. The alternative is the kind of informal hallway talk that board members sometimes engage in as momentum builds toward some drastic action, possibly even toward dismissal of the CEO.

The CEO and the Senior Team

Much as is the case with the board, the CEO's relationship with the senior team during times of change depends on the kind of team the CEO has put together and the nature of the relationship already in place between the CEO and the other senior executives. Particularly in large, complex organizations, it is literally impossible for the CEO to be everywhere, see everything, and manage everyone. The senior team must effectively become an extension of the CEO's personal leadership, a force that projects the CEO's vision, values, objectives, and requirements out into the organization (Nadler, 1997).

Consequently, part of the CEO's responsibility is to build a senior team whose members possess the skills, experience, and personal characteristics to satisfy two needs. First, they must collectively share the technical and managerial expertise required to enable the organization to meet its strategic objectives. Additionally, the mix of individuals in the team should balance and complement the professional skills and personal characteristics of the CEO. One of the most rudimentary rules of managment is that leaders should avoid surrounding themselves with subordinates who replicate their own strengths and weaknesses. At the senior team level, that issue becomes critical to the organization's success. There is no CEO who is equally adept at every aspect of the job; the role of the senior team, in part, is to fill the gaps and offset the weaknesses. In light of the fact that CEOs' energy levels, interests, and areas of emphasis change over the course of their tenure, effective CEOs will periodically take stock and reassess whether the composition of their senior team adequately plays to their own changing strengths and weaknesses.

Second, the CEO can take the initiative in developing the senior team's role as a vehicle for institutional learning. Through the delegation of specific responsibilities and the structuring of both formal and informal activities, the CEO can use the senior team as a sophisticated form of institutional radar, constantly scanning the external environment for evidence of destablizing events or trends that might signal the onset of turbulence and discontinuity. Late in the CEO's tenure, when his/her personal antennae may be less acute than in the past and he/she may be more predisposed to discount evidence indicating the necessity of change, the senior team can be actively engaged in its own search for vital clues.

Once change becomes inevitable, the CEO has the ultimate responsibility for developing an integrated change agenda. But effective CEOs will build that agenda through a process that recognizes the senior team's crucial role in collectively implementing and managing the agenda. To that end, the CEO must promote the senior team's active participation in shaping the agenda in order to create a collective sense of ownership. Ideally, members of the team will become champions of particular aspects of change, taking on aggressive leadership roles. They become partners with the CEO in articulating the team's collective vision and assume the hands-on responsibility for deploying the organization's resources in the service of that vision. Just as they become extensions of the CEO's leadership, they, in turn, project their shared vision and objectives throughout the organization by constructing concentric circles of involvement on the part of lower-level managers and supervisors.

The CEO and the Institution

During periods of turbulent change, the CEO assumes the role of institutional icon. While others on the senior team can and should assume much of the operational responsibility for managing change, it is up to the CEO to lead change. To a great extent, the CEO does that by articulating the change agenda in clear, memorable terms that challenge, inspire, energize, and reassure the people employed by the organization. During these unstable periods, only the CEO has the combination of formal and informal power—of legitimate institutional authority coupled with the character traits of an experienced leader— to slice through the cacophony and deliver a focused message to the entire organization with a clear voice. Only the CEO has the standing to gain a consistent "share of mind" among the employees and to have a ready audience for practically any public utterance.

Given that audience, CEOs should deal with this particular hot spot during times of change through constant repetition of closely related themes—through what Paul O'Neill, chairman of ALCOA, describes as "consistency and connectedness." Successful leaders understand that as instability breeds anxiety, the important messages have to be communicated time and time again before they truly begin to have an impact. Moreover, the messages have to be clearly and closely linked to the change agenda, so that people understand there is a unifying logic to the changes taking place all around them.

James R. Houghton, the recently retired chairman of Corning Incorporated, offers another perspective on the CEO's relationship to the enterprise and its people. Houghton argues that the best CEOs adopt a contrarian emotional perspective in relation to their organizations. In other words, during downturns or periods of change and instability, the CEO's proper role is to be confident, upbeat, and reassuring. When things are going smoothly, the CEO is skeptical and concerned, warning subordinates to remain ever vigilant to the dangers that so often accompany arrogance and complacency. This contrarian posture requires the CEO to walk a sensitive line—neither appearing to be a Pollyanna during rough times nor failing to recognize and celebrate success when times are good.

The Role of the Board

Our discussion in this section has focused on the CEO's role in managing relationships with each of the key constituencies during periods of major change. The underlying assumption has been that the CEO recognizes not only the potential for change, but the likelihood that with the passage of time, he/she may have to draw upon the insights and energy of others to help anticipate and drive the change effort in ways that might not have been quite so necessary early in his/her tenure. But not all CEOs, of course, can make that kind of realistic assessment of their own limitations. In light of our earlier discussion of CEO effectiveness over time, we should consider the board's role in situations in which the need for change is obvious but the CEO's response is inadequate.

The responsibility for ensuring appropriate action by the CEO falls squarely on the board and no one else. The board must have a thorough understanding of the kinds of issues raised here concerning the nature of change and the life cycles of CEOs. It is incumbent upon the board to recognize that the energetic, deeply engaged CEO who eagerly led the organization through an earlier period of change will generally undergo a gradual transformation and cannot realistically be expected to respond precisely the same way the second time around.

One of the board's key roles is to provide the CEO with regular, in-depth appraisals and feedback. Earlier we presented this process as a responsibility of the CEO, but it cannot be assumed that the CEO will always take the lead. If the initiative does not come from the CEO, then it is up to the board to develop a systematic process for regularly assessing the CEO's performance and delivering feedback in timely, constructive ways. In too many situations, boards fail to become actively involved until a crisis has already erupted. At that point, faced with pressing business concerns, the board tends to demand that the CEO make immediate and dramatic changes, usually with unsatisfactory results. Ideally, a board's dissatisfaction with a CEO should never come as a surprise, and performance problems should be recognized and raised early enough for the CEO to have sufficient time to demonstrate improved performance.

As part of that process, it is essential that the board devise a mechanism for discussing these issues in the CEO's absence. Given the CEO's traditional role as chairman of the board, that's not always easy or comfortable. Nevertheless, a candid discussion with the CEO out of the room should be incorporated into the board's routine process, with a committee or one or two board members assigned to discuss the substance of those discussions with the CEO at a later date.

Furthermore, given the implications of the CEO life cycle, it is important for the board to become more actively involved in decisions involving strategic choices and major change in the later years of the CEO's tenure. That's more easily said than done. The need for the board's involvement may be greatest exactly when the CEO is at the height of his/her power and influence. Moreover, with the passage of time, an increasing number of board members will have been selected with the CEO's active participation and are likely to find themselves conflicted by feelings of personal loyalty or friendship.

Yet this is the time when the board must be at its most vigilant in assessing the appropriateness of the CEO's response to the need for change. The board has the responsibility not to accept at face value the CEO's denial of the need for major change, or the CEO's avoidance in the form of structural or personnel moves that fail to address the fundamental issues. Indeed, it may well become the board's duty to decide that the best way to handle change is by managing succession, either gradual or immediate.

Questions for the CEO

A few years ago, we prepared a confidential memo for the CEO of a major corporation whose industry was clearly entering a period of unprecedented upheaval. It was obvious at that point that massive change of one kind or another would soon become unavoidable if the company was to maintain its role as an industry leader. So we posed a number of questions to the CEO, who earlier in his tenure had already led the organization through a series of historic changes. We asked him:

- Do you believe that major change will be required?

- If you are to lead such change, what do you think will be required of you?

- At this point in your life and your career, are you capable of leading this change?

- Do you want to do it?

We would suggest that all CEOs facing the likelihood of major change ought to ask themselves these same questions. Clearly, these are unsettling questions for any CEO to contemplate. To begin with, most CEOs, by their very nature, are oriented toward action rather than toward introspection; their jobs demand the ability to make decisions and then plunge ahead without reservations or self-doubt. Perhaps more importantly, an admission that a person may no longer be up to the challenge carries the implication of professional mortality and a recognition that it may be time to hand over the reins to someone else. And like the rest of us, most CEOs are less than eager to pursue a line of questioning that's likely to arrive at that conclusion. But the awesome responsibility they owe to their various constituents, both within and outside the organization, requires that at some point each CEO give serious consideration to those deeply personal questions.

Summary

Our purpose in this opening chapter has been to raise a series of important issues concerning CEOs in the context of change and to provide some perspectives for thinking about these serious challenges. First, we outlined a pattern of industry evolution that results in periodic phases of fundamental instability requiring organizations to respond with major, discontinuous change. In that context, we examined the set of constituencies to which CEOs must respond and considered how the CEO ought to address the key hot spots in the stakeholder map during times of radical change.

We then explored two views of the CEO as a leader of change, beginning with a static view of the roles CEOs must play and the personal characteristics they need as they guide an organization through discontinuous change. We then moved to a more dynamic view, laying out a theory of how CEOs evolve during their tenures, and we examined the implications for the change process of the relationship between periods of change and phases of the CEO's tenure.

Finally, we considered the need for CEOs and their boards to deal actively with the necessity for change—often at the period in the CEO's career when he/she may be least inclined to acknowledge the need for massive change. And we concluded by urging CEOs to engage in serious, albeit uncomfortable, reflection about their own capacity for leading discontinuous change.

These issues will be examined in considerably greater depth, and from a variety of perspectives, in the chapters that follow. Much of this book is devoted to raising difficult questions and offering some experience-based observations. We hope that this collection of ideas will provide the impetus for additional research that will move beyond case studies and personal reflection to empirical validation of concepts. Such research will be of material assistance to those entrusted with leading and governing our major institutions.

References

French, J. R. P., Jr., & Raven, B. R. (1959). The bases of social power. In D. Cartwright (Ed.), *Studies in Social Power*. Ann Arbor, MI: Institute for Social Research.

Hambrick, D. C., & Fukutomi, G. D. (1991). The seasons of a CEO's tenure. *Academy of Management Review*, 16:719–742.

Heilpern, J. D. (1995). The emerging role of the CEO. In D. A. Nadler, R. B. Shaw, & A. E. Walton, *Discontinuous Change: Leading Organizational Transformation*. San Francisco: Jossey-Bass.

Millstein, I. M. (1993). The evolution of the certifying board. *Business Lawyer*, 48: 1485–1497.

Nadler, D. A. (1996). Managing the team at the top. *Strategy and Business*, 2:42–51.

Nadler, D. A. (1997). *Champions of Change*. San Francisco: Jossey-Bass.

Nadler, D. A., Newman, M. L., & Tushman, M. L. (1988). Executive leadership and organizational evaluation: Managing incremental and discontinuous change. In R. H. Kilman & T. J. Covin (Eds.), *Corporate Transformation: Revitalizing Organizations for a Competitive World*. San Francisco: Jossey-Bass.

Nadler, D. A., & Tushman, M. L. (1989). Leadership for organizational change. In A. M. Mohrman Jr., S. A. Mohrman, G. E. Ledford Jr., T. G. Cummings, & E. E. Lawler III (Eds.), *Large Scale Organizational Change*. San Francisco: Jossey-Bass.

Nadler, D. A., & Tushman, M. L. (1995). Types of organizational change: From incremental improvement to discontinuous transformation. In D. A. Nadler, R. B. Shaw, & A. E. Walton, *Discontinuous Change: Leading Organizational Transformation*. San Francisco: Jossey-Bass.

Vancil, R. F. (1987). *Passing the Baton*. Boston: Harvard Business School Press.

[2]

Corporate Transformation
and Senior Leadership

James R. Houghton

THE WORLD'S NEW EMPHASIS ON INFORMATION has caused major paradigm shifts in the business arena. These shifts have changed not only the rules of the game, but the game itself. In the discussion that follows, I'll first set forth my views on the transformation of corporations in today's world. Then I'll present my vision of what it takes to be a senior leader in the new corporate environment.

The Transformation of Corporations

For much of the nineteenth century, the United States was primarily rural and agrarian. People lived on farms; they worked the fields or toiled in small workshops. Formal education was pretty informal, and for most people education usually ended at an early age. For any given enterprise, markets were local and the workforce was largely homogeneous.

By the start of the 1900s, the Industrial Revolution had changed all that. The body and the soul of America were transformed. Millions of workers and their families migrated to our shores, attracted by opportunities and by jobs. These workers brought a tremendous capacity for work, and they helped this country grow great. However, many of them did not know the language; few had any education. These factors—combined with the prevailing psychology of the day—resulted in the creation of large, hierarchical organizations. Workers were considered little more than cogs. Leaders were expected to be commanding and authoritative, armed with all the answers.

But all of that has changed once more with the advent of the Information Age. I wish to explore the implications for business of the two most important present-day paradigm shifts: globalization and the changing workforce.

Responding to Globalization

Globalization of markets and industries has occurred largely because of access to information, which has made national borders meaningless. This shrinking of the world has increased, by orders of magnitude, the competitive stakes for which businesses play. No market is protected anymore; competitive threats appear daily in the form of new technologies and new global contenders. Today, firms in every region of the world can access any market—bringing to bear the power of new technologies; of low-paid, highly skilled workers; and of large amounts of capital. How do businesses transform themselves so as to respond to global competition? With a continuing thrust toward world-class quality. Corning Incorporated has been involved in Total Quality Management (TQM) since 1983. TQM is an important force in the company, and we believe that much of our business success since 1983 can be attributed to this initiative. Furthermore, I personally am convinced that any company that does not practice some form of TQM will be at a great competitive disadvantage in the global marketplace and may not survive in the long run.

We must always remember that TQM is a journey and not a destination. It is a process aiming at never-ending improvement. Even when we have reached the point where error rates are at the parts-per-million level, I think it's important to keep looking to get more from quality. Beyond production of ever more flawless products and services, what else can TQM give us? I believe that quality will allow us to meet worldwide customers' needs even before they know they have them. And I believe TQM will lead to higher levels of employee involvement and training. At Corning Incorporated, the quality initiative has led to goal sharing and profit sharing, and everybody from senior leaders to the shop floor participates. We've achieved flatter organization with fewer bosses and more teammates. Our plant in Blacksburg, Virginia, for example, has two levels of employment—plant manager and teams. It's a very different way of operating.

I also believe TQM will allow us to develop fully the potential skills and talents of all our employees. There will be no more "Check your brains at the door" as you come to work. I love the phrase I heard once: "When you hire a pair of hands, you get a head for free. Use it."

Building a Skilled Workforce

That leads me to the second paradigm shift occurring in business today. Simply put, in addition to globalization, businesses are facing an unprecedented need for highly skilled labor. In the old days, companies' competitive advantage came from some combination of money, technology, raw materials, and people. Now, three out of these four are less important. Money and technology flow around the world at supersonic speeds—and are broadly available. Also, raw materials are much less critical in the Information Age; products can be made and shipped from almost anywhere.

As to people, I agree with Lester Thurow of MIT. In *Head to Head*, he writes:

> The skills of the workforce are going to be the key competitive weapon in the twenty-first century. Brain power will create new technologies, but skilled labor will be the arms and legs that allow one to employ the new product and process technologies that are being generated. Skilled people become the only sustainable competitive advantage.

Just as capital and technology now flow around the world, conceptual workers—people who primarily use their heads to get a job done—are mobile and enjoy ever increasing choices as to where they live and work. These conceptual workers are ones who have doctorates in highly specialized fields, or who are talented and trained in marketing, finance, information services, or production management.

At Corning, conceptual workers form a growing percentage of our workforce. For example, in 1972 one third of our workforce was made up of conceptual workers while two thirds were people who basically used their hands. Today the ratio is reversed: Two thirds are conceptual workers, and one third use mainly physical skills.

Workers who use mainly physical skills remain very important, and we must do more to continually upgrade their skills. Lifelong training is absolutely essential. But these workers tend to be relatively rooted in their place of employment. Conceptual workers are much more mobile, have many opportunities, and can sell their skills to the highest bidder—whether in money or in the intangibles of the work-place or both. If we're honest with ourselves, individual businesses need this group of mobile workers more than they need us; so we had better pay attention and prove our worth as employers. Moreover, to avail ourselves of the entire pool of talent out there, companies can-not rely only on white males. In the near future, a majority of people entering the U.S. workforce are going to be women and people of color. To attract the best talent, we must therefore demonstrate that we really believe in and practice diversity in the workplace.

If you accept the argument that knowledge or skills may ulti-mately be the only competitive advantage, then you must intensify your efforts to truly "value the individual." Talented individuals will choose a friendly environment where everyone has a chance to suc-ceed to his or her highest potential. Conceptual workers will be drawn to a company that makes them feel appreciated and gives them the independence and flexibility to make decisions at the level where the work is being done. They will be attracted not by hierarchy but by horizontal structure. They will be attracted not by security but by the opportunity for personal growth. They will be attracted not by homogeneity but by cultural diversity. Also, they will be attracted not by work alone but by a perceived balance between work and leisure.

How will traditional businesses need to transform themselves in order to keep pace with these challenges? First, I believe we'll need to adopt a new concept of loyalty and obligation. This concept has been well articulated by Chris Bartlett and Sumantra Ghoshal in ar-ticles in the *Harvard Business Review*. Companies can no longer guar-antee job security—if, in fact, they ever could. What they can and should guarantee is the provision of opportunities for personal and professional growth. In addition, companies must provide the tools by which each individual can attain lifelong training, so that his or her skills are constantly upgraded to meet the requirements of the job at hand. Ultimately, companies should, to quote an executive at

General Electric, strive to "make employees eager to stay, but ready to go."

This is a big shift. It changes the nature of companies' responsibilities, and it demands that individuals be ready to take advantage of opportunities. In the *Harvard Business Review*, Chris Bartlett describes this new concept as a shift from "guarantee of employment to commitment to employability." Making the change will not be easy, because it flies in the face of the old paternalistic, controlling, "cradle-to-grave" thinking.

Second, we must increasingly think of all employees as professionals. With high-performance work teams in both manufacturing and administrative settings, we need to entrust employees with strategic ownership of the business. Without question, this kind of strategic ownership makes for a more inventive company, one that is able to respond to the requirements of a diverse global clientele.

Even investors are beginning to appreciate that a company's real investment today is no longer in machines but in the knowledge of the worker. Workers today—whether they are equipped with conceptual or physical skills—must be capable of thinking for themselves. They must be able to make critical decisions about their customers and their immediate work environment. They must possess "transferable" skills and be able to apply knowledge gained in one situation to very different situations.

Thinking of employees as professionals means that it behooves us to make lifelong training of each and every employee a priority—and not just for basic skills. The new way of working will require new skills such as empathy and listening. Companies can and must give these skills the same level of priority we assign to technical skills.

Third, and perhaps most important, as we turn the corner to the next millennium, companies need to own up to their social obligations and responsibilities to workers. We ignore this responsibility at our peril.

There is great euphoria about "market economies" and "globalization." Corporate strategists proclaim the wisdom of competitive advantage, of leanness and meanness. If one can get software development done in Bangalore as well as and cheaper than in Silicon Valley, so be it. If one has to announce a massive layoff as earnings are rising, well, that's good for shareholders; the stock price almost always goes up with such an announcement. But that kind of game cannot go on forever. Society will not stand for it.

The point is that while bolstering the economy of developing nations is all very well, we cannot forever neglect or ignore our own infrastructure or our own people. If we take a totally free-market view, over time our political institutions will inject themselves into the process—more than they already have; and that would be the worst outcome imaginable. Already questions are being raised about why the real income of average Americans is shrinking when corporate earnings, the stock market, and CEO salaries are all growing. I think that the current bashing of corporations and CEOs is ill advised; the numbers reported by the media are mainly wrong, or taken out of context. Nevertheless, the questions are being raised. And if we in business do not show a sensitivity to this issue, and to the fate of our current workforce—whether it be in France, in the United States, or in Japan—then someone is going to make some rules we won't like. Jobs will be protected, borders will be closed, and we'll be back in the economic Dark Ages. Thus, companies face the task of balancing two needs: the need to be global players, and the need to ensure a healthy workforce where we operate.

In terms of corporate transformation, then, I believe the pursuit of quality and a new emphasis on valuing the individual will become more and more important. Does this sound too soft—too humanistic and liberal? The financial community would answer in the affirmative. From the perspective of the analysts, financial performance is all that counts, and issues like quality and people are viewed as only for the "wine-and-quiche crowd." I totally disagree with this view, however. Pursuing quality is a hard-nosed strategy for survival. So is a focus on people and valuing the individual. Both lead to distinct competitive advantages and long-term shareholder value.

If we accept the principles of corporate transformation outlined above, what are the implications for the senior leadership of these new corporations?

Senior Leadership for the New Corporation

As we move away from command-and-control structures and toward a horizontal, empowered organization, there will be new demands on leadership. This raises some fundamental questions. What is leadership? Who is a leader? Genghis Khan, Stalin, Mao, and Hitler certainly led. So did Nelson, McArthur, and Patton, in a different way.

The first group were despots who led by fear and use of raw power. The second group, though working for supposedly more noble aims, led totally by hierarchical rigidity and focused on one well-defined objective (or enemy).

The leader that interests me is the democratic leader. That person usually heads an institution and drives it to success by the use of power—but it is power that is restricted and subject to many forms of checks and balances. Leaders that come to mind are Pericles and Lincoln (in government); John XXIII, Gandhi, and Martin Luther King Jr. (religion); Hesburgh, Conant, and Matthew Arnold (education); and Watson and Sloan (business).

Narrowing the field this way should make the task of definition easier, but it doesn't. I'm not sure one can describe leadership effectively. Justice Potter Stewart's comment about pornography may apply to leadership: "I'll know it when I see it." But at a deeper level, leadership may have more in common with Justice Learned Hand's wonderful description of liberty. Hand believed that "the spirit of liberty is that spirit which is not too sure it is right." Perhaps the spirit of true leadership is the spirit that is not too sure it is right—at least, not all the time. I believe that leaders who are not totally sure they are right are leaders who show a sensitivity and who listen. And history tells us that those in leadership positions who do not listen eventually fail. Just being a good listener is, of course, no guarantee of success; but I believe that lack of this characteristic will inevitably be a fatal flaw.

What then is leadership? Let me give you some descriptions I have found useful.

- It is enough modesty to constantly doubt, be open, and listen.

- It is performance over time, not charisma.

- It is responsibility, not privilege.

- It is deep-seated belief in the organization's values and goals and the ability to live them, articulate them, and push them forward with constancy over time.

- It is willingness to change everything except those basic values and goals. In relation to goals, the words of Gary Wills are pertinent:

Most literature on leadership is unitarian. But life is trinitarian. One-legged and two-legged stools do not, of themselves, stand. A third leg is needed. Leaders, followers, and goals make up the equally necessary supports for leadership. . . . The leader is the one who mobilizes others toward a goal shared by leader and followers—all three elements are present and indispensable.

- It is personal integrity and instinctively knowing and doing "the right thing."

- It is a strong belief in team play, in the power of horizontal (as opposed to vertical) relationships, in making the most of others' strengths and not knowing all the answers.

- It is understanding that personal success can come only from group success—and that credit should be distributed accordingly.

- It is demanding strong subordinates and potential successors and staying out of their way.

- It is earning people's trust over time.

- It is the willingness to take risks and the strength to have no fear of failure.

- It is the continuing thirst for education: for self-improvement, expansion, and renewal.

- It is continual dissatisfaction with "things as they are" and a drive to change things for the better.

- It is the ability to hear and accept bad news—and then to move on, using the experience as a tool for future improvement.

- It is the talent sometimes to reject the logical and decide because of the instinct and the heart.

- It is creating the perception and the reality that the leader is both visible and touchable.

- It is focus on and attention to the important.

- It is capturing reliable information through a network of sources so that judgments can be formed.

- It is toughness and willingness to use power and pressure, but always after thought and with caution.

- It is the ability to deal comfortably with ambiguity.

- It is an understanding that compromise and muddling through are not weaknesses as long as the basic values and goals remain intact.

- It is the belief that true quality should define all relationships and that success can come only if quality is present.

- It is a shared and contagious sense of optimism even in the darkest hour.

- It is possession of a positive and open sense of humor—and the ability to laugh at life's quirks and especially at oneself.

There are about twenty-five descriptive statements above. I am certain I have captured some of the characteristics of leadership—but I am also certain that the list is hardly exhaustive. So, in conclusion, let's come back to the overall subject—"leadership: a view from 50,000 feet," as it were. From research and experience emerge five key points about leaders:

1. Leaders are good at a lot of things.

2. Leaders emerge from the organizational soup with no particular clues as to their chances of success.

3. Upbringing, schooling, training, job classifications, gender, and race show no particular patterns that can help us identify leaders.

4. Are leaders born? Maybe.

5. Can leaders be trained? Absolutely!

We need leaders desperately in all fields. Present-day senior leadership has the task of identifying potential leaders for the future—and of giving them the chance to fail, either on their way to success or on their way to failure. Remember the saying "Good judgment comes from experience; experience comes from bad judgment." We've got to keep testing and trying; and history says that if we do a good job, we will be able to find that next generation of leaders.

Peter Drucker said that "the first job of leaders is to define reality, the last is to say thank you." I would paraphrase and amplify this a bit. In my mind a leader must, in order:

1. Define reality

2. Enshrine the institutional values

3. Articulate a vision

4. Set the strategic path to that vision

5. Demand performance

6. Empower the people (and get out of their way)

7. Say thank you

To me, the essence of leadership is summarized by Lao Tzu, the ancient Chinese philosopher:

A leader is best when people barely know he exists, not so good when people obey and acclaim him, worst when they despise him. "Fail to honor thy people—they fail to honor you." But of a good leader, who talks little, when his work is done, his aims fulfilled, they will all say, "We did this ourselves."

[3]

Vicissitudes of Leadership

Manfred F. R. Kets de Vries

Et ceux qui ne font rien ne se trompent jamais.
(And those who do nothing never make
mistakes.)
— Théodore Faullain de Banville

*An institution is the lengthened shadow of
one man.*
— Ralph Waldo Emerson

T HIS CHAPTER ADDRESSES various factors that make for both dysfunctional and highly effective leadership. First I will explore the role of narcissism in the development of leadership, drawing a distinction between constructive and reactive narcissism; I'll highlight inner "scripts" that contribute to failure in leadership. Then I will take a close look at three highly successful CEOs, focusing on the interface between their inner theater and their outer behavior: Richard Branson of Virgin, Jack Welch of General Electric, and Percy Barnevik of ABB. I will examine key characteristics of these three leaders' high-performing corporations, and I'll suggest that the way these companies are run can serve as a paradigm of what companies are going to look like in the twenty-first century.

Introduction

The creatures known as *processionary caterpillars* get their name from the peculiar way that leader–follower interaction takes place among them. After one caterpillar sets the direction, all others follow closely behind, taking the same path. Scientists who have observed these caterpillars closely say that the behavior of the followers appears to take on an automatic response pattern; scientists point out, for example, that the eyes of caterpillars in the following mode are half-closed.

An experiment by a French naturalist, Jean-Henri Fabre, investigated the behavior of these insects. Fabre managed to get the lead caterpillar to circle a large flowerpot. Soon after, all the other caterpillars marched in line, eventually encircling the flowerpot completely. As a result, it was impossible to distinguish the beginning of the line from the end. Remarkably enough, no caterpillar decided to break this vicious circle. On the contrary, all the caterpillars continued their dysfunctional activity for a number of days and nights until they eventually died of exhaustion and starvation.

Admittedly, extrapolating behavior from the insect world to *homo sapiens* is a major mental jump. The point, however, is that caterpillars do not have a monopoly on dysfunctional behavior. In the leader-follower interchange of human beings, as with these caterpillars, many mindless scripts can also be discerned. Many leaders, incapable of either generating new rules or changing the existing rules, initiate a game without end, making for vicious circles that all too many followers are willing to consent to. The example of the processionary caterpillar is symbolic, then, of dysfunctional leader–follower interaction patterns in the workplace.

In spite of the intricacies of leader–follower dynamics and their influence on organizational functioning, some organizational observers argue that the importance of leadership is highly overrated (Hannan and Freeman, 1977; Pfeffer, 1977; Pfeffer and Salancik, 1984). These observers see an organization as influenced mainly by the environment in which it operates. According to this "environmental" school of thought, leaders are subject not only to many internal organizational constraints (in the form of structures, procedures, and political processes) but also to numerous external constraints. Immutable organizational and industrial strictures, not leaders, determine which companies survive in the competitive business jungle. Advocates of this point of view reduce the complex person–organization–environment interface to a limited number of simple variables that supposedly influence a firm's strategic direction and performance.

Obviously, the environment plays a major role in what happens to an organization. Socioeconomic, political, and industry-specific factors should be taken into consideration in any assessment of leadership. But to negate the influence of leadership entirely throws out the baby with the bathwater. Nevertheless, the theory of impotent leadership continues to be surprisingly popular. After all, adding a leadership dimension to the business equation does complicate matters: If leaders make a difference, then we have to account for a host of complicated human factors (Bass, 1990)—facets such as emotions, motivation, and irrational action.

Yet, given the power leaders wield—the opportunity they have to externalize their inner script and enact it on the public stage that is the corporation—they can in fact have an enormous impact on a company's strategy, structure, and culture. That can be for the good or for the bad. The Spanish saying "Fish start to smell at the head" is all too often applicable to organizations. Therefore, the leadership dimension warrants further exploration.

The Genesis of Leadership

In the best of all possible worlds, leaders' behavior and actions are compatible with external forces in the environment. Leaders are supposed to develop, articulate, share, and enact a vision. Leaders, it is hoped, possess an adequate capacity for reality testing: They know how to scan the environment and how to make rational decisions. Ideally, there should also be an alignment between a leader's vision of the future and the followers' expectations. But that is not always how it works.

A Clinical Paradigm in Organizational Analysis

Many organizational scholars would like to ban irrationality from organizational analysis. After all, irrational behavior only muddles things up. As many of us have learned the hard way, however, leaders can be completely derailed by their hidden motives—not only making life miserable for their subordinates but disrupting their organization's equilibrium enough to contribute significantly to its decline. Apparently, irrational behavior in organizations is here to stay. The challenge, then, becomes to tease out its hidden rationale and make sense out of it.

Clinical investigation has shown that the reasons a leader has a particular outlook tend to be deeply rooted. Leaders are driven and influenced by a very strong inner theater—a specific "script" that determines their character (Kets de Vries, Miller, and Noel, 1993; Luborsky, Crits-Christoph, Minz, and Auerbach, 1988). This inner theater is what drives leaders to externalize private motives and present these on a public stage (Lasswell, 1930). The inner theater organizes the way a leader processes information and acts upon it in interpersonal situations (Horowitz, 1991); for example, a given leader's problems may derive from rigid, self-defeating communication patterns that create a dysfunctional style.

This rather cluttered perception of human behavior stands in sharp contrast to more simplistic perspectives on human functioning based on the model of the "economic man." Going beyond the model of the economic man—that imagined lightning-fast calculator of pleasures and pains, driven only by rational motives—and instead looking closely at the complex inner theater of the top executive will give us a more realistic perspective on the dynamics of an organization.

But how do we go about it? How do we arrive at insights about this inner theater? How do we decipher a person's character? What I have found is that putting executives on the couch (metaphorically speaking in most cases)—that is, using the clinical approach to organizational analysis—proves to be a good way of analyzing the conflicts and motivations that occur within organizations.

I should explain here that my clinical approach to management rests on three main premises. The first is that *all behavior is somehow determined.* What at first glance may seem completely irrational may on closer inspection reveal an explanation and a deeper rationale. The second premise is that *there is such a thing as unconscious behavior.* We are not always aware of many of our wishes and fantasies. All of us have blind spots, and a considerable amount of our behavior appears to be outside conscious awareness. The third premise is that *intrapsychic and interpersonal processes have a considerable influence on the way we act and make decisions.* In one way or another, we are all prisoners of our previous life history; past patterns of interaction with early caregivers strongly influence how we deal with present and future events. A person's core patterns tend to be quite stable, although specific responses may vary over time (Erikson, 1963; Levinson, 1978, White, 1975).

Over time, through interactions with caregivers, teachers and other influential people, we develop an inner theater characterized by various scripts containing certain themes. We rely on these inner scripts—packages of integrated information, retained in memory—when we interpret and act on the world around us. The core relationship themes contained in these scripts form the essence of an individual's personality (Luborsky, Crits-Christoph, Minz, and Auerbach, 1988). And such scripts play an essential role in the molding of leaders.

Narcissistic Development

So where does this intrapsychic theater start? Where does it all begin? In the first years of life, the foundations are put in place for the kind of person we are going to be; and in this process of growing up, a critical factor is how the child deals with the question of narcissism. Narcissism concerns issues of self-concept and identity: how valuable we feel, how good we feel about ourselves. For many of us, however, the term *narcissism* has a somewhat derogatory connotation. This is because in more general usage it may stand for egotism, self-centeredness, or an exaggerated self-love. Who wants to be compared to that unfortunate young man, the mythological figure Narcissus, who fell in love with his own reflection? But narcissism is much more than common usage suggests. The term also refers to a stage of infantile development during which the growing child derives pleasure from his or her own body and its functions. The kind of treatment a child receives during this critical period of development will very much color the child's (and later the adult's) way of dealing with the world. It will affect the person's self-consciousness and the way he or she responds to approval or to criticism. Narcissism is a double-edged sword: Either too much or too little can create problems. We must remember that narcissistic elements help constitute the base of self-esteem and identity. But when the proper balance is lost, instability in the core of the personality may occur.

Each of us gradually acquires a sense of who we are and what we think we are able to do through interaction with the environment; that is, initially, with our primary caregivers. For normal development, frustration should occur in tolerable doses. Again, too little is as bad as too much: If there is no experience of age-appropriate frustration, the aftereffects may come to haunt us later in life. As a way of coping with the shortcomings of parental care, and in an attempt to ward off frustration, children in their early years create both a grandiose, exhibitionistic image of themselves and an all-powerful, idealized image of their parents (as saviors and protectors). Psychologists call these two narcissistic configurations the "grandiose self" and the "idealized parent image" (Kohut, 1971, 1977). Over time, in an ideal scenario, these two images will be tamed by the forces of reality. Parents, siblings, and other important figures will modify the child's exhibitionistic displays, channeling grandiose fantasies of power and glory in proper directions, thus laying the foundation for well-grounded ambition, stable values, well-defined career interests, and a secure sense of self-esteem and identity.

Unfortunately, the ideal scenario does not always match reality. Children may be exposed to parental overstimulation or understimulation or to nonintegrative, inconsistent interventions (Kets de Vries, 1989; Kohut, 1971; Miller, 1981). They may be exploited unconsciously by caregivers for the maintenance of the caregivers' self-esteem; or they may be turned into proxies in the caregivers' own search for admiration and greatness—thus becoming confused about what kind of life they are supposed to lead. Consequently, they may get stuck in a lifelong compensatory struggle for self-assertion and self-expression. Such children may come to believe that they cannot reliably depend on anyone's love or loyalty. When they become adults, they act according to that expectation. These are people who, in spite of their pretense of self-sufficiency, are continually trying to boost a defective sense of self-esteem and are preoccupied with emotions such as envy, spite, and vengefulness.

In these "reactive" narcissists, a cohesive sense of self is absent. These people chronically need external affirmation to feel internally secure. They tend to have an exaggerated sense of self-importance and self-grandiosity and a concomitant need for admiration. They are preoccupied with fantasies of success, power, brilliance, beauty, and love. They habitually take advantage of others in order to achieve their own ends. They also live under the illusion that their problems are unique. They experience a sense of entitlement; because they feel special, they have the sense that the rules set for others do not apply to them. Furthermore, they are addicted to compliments: they can never get enough. (Granted, in getting what they want, they can be extremely charming!) The achievements of others, on the other hand, evoke strong envious reactions and are belittled (American Psychiatric Association, 1994; Kernberg, 1975; Kets de Vries, 1989; Millon, 1981). Their relationships are based on searching out the kinds of people who can enhance their self-esteem. These people lack empathy, being unable to experience how others feel. Last but certainly not least, their rage, when they are hampered in fulfilling their wishes, can be formidable.

Certain professions tend to attract more narcissists than others. People in organizational leadership positions, for example, make up an important category. Politicians, certain medical specialists, and actors are likewise no strangers to narcissistic behavior. There is a famous anecdote about a movie star who ran into a friend at a party and proceeded to tell the friend about his last film. "The audience loved it, and they loved me in it. The reviewers are calling me the new Laurence Olivier. I see Oscar nominations. And listen to this: I'm going to be on the cover of *Time* magazine next week! But I haven't asked about you. Tell me: What did *you* think of me in the film?"

I should point out that some reactive narcissists eventually overcome their original feelings of bitterness and become motivated by reparation; that is, they try to prevent others from suffering as they have. That is a much more constructive solution to previous hurts than the course of self-centeredness, exploitation, and vindictiveness.

It is important to remember, too, that not all narcissism is necessarily bad. Indeed, without a certain degree of narcissism, it would be very hard for anybody to function. And this is especially true for people in positions of leadership. Narcissism is the engine that drives people to participate in political and organizational life; it is the motivator that makes things happen.

There does exist a positive form of narcissistic behavior based on a secure sense of identity and a good understanding of who one is and what one is able to do. People who develop this positive narcissism were fortunate in having caregivers who knew how to provide age-appropriate frustration. Their caregivers knew how to provide a supportive environment, the kind that leads to feelings of basic trust and the acquisition of a sense of control over one's actions. These "constructive" narcissists are individuals who are well balanced, have a positive self-regard, and possess a secure sense of self-esteem. These people have the capacity for introspection; they radiate a sense of positive vitality and are capable of empathic feeling (Kets de Vries, 1989, 1993; Kets de Vries and Miller, 1985).

Narcissism As a Factor in Failed Leadership

Suppose the negative form of narcissism, reactive narcissism, has paid off in terms of a person's career. Imagine that the drive and ambition that emanate from narcissism have led to organizational success and that a reactive narcissist has finally reached a top position. What comes next? What are some of the psychological pressures that may contribute to a leader's downfall? What can be said about narcissism as a failure factor in leadership?

Many leaders have found out the hard way that being on top is not necessarily a bed of roses. First, trite as it may sound, there is the problem of the loneliness of command. The moment a person becomes the top dog, the network of old relationships is disturbed. Every move that person makes now has a great deal of symbolism attached, and being continually in the public eye results in a lot of pressure for that reason. Everyone is trying to get the new leader's attention, but a leader who has to make critical decisions about people's careers cannot be as close to old colleagues as he or she once was. Whether the new leader likes it or not, some distance must be maintained. And this is not always going to be easy. After all, leaders still have their own dependency needs. Who is going to take care of them? This dilemma may cause more stress and frustration than some leaders are able to handle.

Another troublesome problem concerns envy. Many people will look at the power, status, and perks that come with the leader's job and become quite envious. Others' envy can be very disconcerting to the leader and may awaken dormant paranoid thinking complete with illusions of grandeur and delusions of persecution. Angst about losing the power of office can become a considerable drain on a leader.

Finally, leaders often have to deal with a lack of sincerity among people lower in the hierarchy. A cynic once said that the moment you reach the top is the moment you cease hearing the truth from your sub-ordinates. Remember the child's grandiose self-image and idealized parental image: Each of us has experienced these configurations, and remnants of these early feelings linger on in everybody. If these feelings are reawakened in followers vis-à-vis people in positions of authority, they can have a very negative effect on the leader–follower interchange. That is, followers may not perceive and respond to leaders according to the facts of the situation but as if the leader were a significant fig-ure from the past (such as a parent, other caretaker, or sibling).

Playing out ancient conflicts on the stage of the present may seem like a strange process, but clinical experience demonstrates that fol-lowers often do displace many of their hopes and fantasies onto lead-ers. Some people handle their self-esteem problems by regarding certain others as perfect—and leaders are good candidates for venera-tion; they share in that perfection by identifying with those others. They try to please their leaders in any way they can think of. These ideal-hungry people are likely to find a very receptive response, par-ticularly with narcissistic personalities. And narcissistic leaders, who welcome the outpouring of admiration, may eventually no longer be able to function without this kind of fix.

Of course, the existence of such an interchange of "idealizing" and "mirroring" can create a lot of energy in the system. It can be very use-ful in aligning and energizing subordinates to enact a common vision. The danger of this form of interaction, a corruption that takes place insidiously, is that leaders may eventually find themselves in a hall of mirrors, hearing and seeing only what they want to hear and see. Or, if people do not oblige—if the followers are unwilling to share the lead-ers' view of the world—the leaders may throw tantrums. When lead-ers are troubled by reactive narcissism, they may see noncompliance as a direct attack on the very essence of their personality (given their frag-ile sense of self-esteem) and may give vent to blind rage.

Predictably, such outbursts of rage intimidate the followers and lead to regressive, childlike behavior and a climate of dependency. The leaders' world actually becomes a very simple one; in other words, leaders who are reactive narcissists often consider people to be neither with them or against them. In such an environment there is no place for independent thinkers; people who have a mind of their own can-not survive in the inner circle. Those who do not collaborate quickly turn into "deviants" and are assigned an inferior, subhuman status.

Most people in the organization will quickly fall in line and share the leaders' indignation toward those unwilling to share their outlook. It is much better for one's physical and mental health to toe the line and "identify with the aggressor" (Freud, [1917] 1955). Actually, doing so solves two problems. In the first place, compliance with a leader's way of thinking is what the leader likes to see. Second, identifying with the aggressor is a way of resolving one's sense of helplessness vis-à-vis the leader.

This inducement to participate in a form of groupthink does not come without certain rites of passage. One such rite is the leader's not-so-subtle request to participate in aggression directed toward those unwilling to share the leader's vision of the world. Given the outlook of leaders who are reactive narcissists, there will be a continuous stream of people to be made into villains; the world of this type of leader is filled with "evildoers." Paradoxically, these scapegoats fulfill an important function: They become to others the external stabilizers of identity and inner control. They are a point of reference on which to project everything one is afraid of, everything that is perceived as bad.

This kind of frightening scenario can have various outcomes—all negative. In extreme cases, it can lead to complete self-destruction, meaning the end of the organization. In any case, it is quite likely that the scapegoating process will be accompanied by some kind of bloodbath, because the need for scapegoats accelerates when things do not work out according to the leader's desires.

In such situations, there may come a point when sharing the delusions of the leader is no longer possible. The price of remaining on good terms with the leader becomes too high. The endgame may include a palace revolution whereby the leader is overthrown as the cycle of abrasive behavior becomes unbearable. Followers may come to realize that they may be the next to be sacrificed on the insatiable altar of the leader's wrath. The attempt to remove the leader becomes a desperate way both to save one's neck and to break the magic spell.

Neurotic Organizations

Usually, it is reactive narcissism that is the most salient factor in defective leadership. Careful observation of numerous senior executives reveals that parallels can be drawn between individual pathology—excessive use of one neurotic style, such as reactive narcissism—and organizational pathology, the latter resulting in poorly functioning organizations, or what I have called "neurotic organizations" (Kets de Vries and Miller, 1984, 1987). At the head of a neurotic organization (especially one in which power is highly centralized), one is likely to find a top executive whose rigid, neurotic style is strongly mirrored in inappropriate strategies, structures, and organizational culture in the firm. Good examples of dysfunctional behavior at the helm can be seen in such business leaders as the first Henry Ford, John DeLorean, Harold Geneen, Robert Maxwell, Kenneth Olson, and Bernard Tapie. Because of their increasingly dysfunctional behavior, they maimed or destroyed the organizations they had built up.

In classifying neurotic organizations, I have made distinctions among *dramatic, suspicious, detached, depressive,* and *compulsive* organizations. Each has unique salient features (Kets de Vries and Miller, 1987). Table 3-1 outlines how the leader's personal leadership style and inner script interrelate with the organization's traits, culture, and strategy.

Transformational Leadership: Three Role Models

Fortunately, situations of extreme leadership dysfunctionality are relatively rare. Not only are there quite a few leaders whose inner theater has a constructive narcissistic quality, but many reactive narcissists adopt a more reparative stance toward life. Such people have the capacity for self-reflection and empathy; they do not fall into the narcissistic traps that lead to a hall of mirrors. Even the reparative reactive narcissists, who have struggled since childhood with self-esteem issues, feel good in their skin and are able to accept dissenters; they are not prisoners of their internal demons, having experienced a solid dose of reality testing. These people plan for continuity and try to institutionalize solid values that will outlast their tenure in the organization. Such leaders know how to transform strategic constraints into new challenges.

Three contemporary business leaders who know how to deal with the vicissitudes of narcissism and who regularly grace the front pages of the major business journals are Richard Branson of Virgin, Jack Welch of General Electric, and Percy Barnevik of ASEA Brown Boveri (ABB). These three executives, although quite different in personal philosophy and leadership style, continue to have a major impact on the way we view organizations. The images of their inner theater seem to have been externalized in a particularly effective way (Kets de Vries, 1990).

Table 3-1
Leadership Style and Neurotic Organizations

Executive Style	Inner Script	Corporate Traits	Culture	Strategy
DRAMATIC				
Leader needs attention, excitement, activity, and stimulation; feels a sense of entitlement; has a tendency toward extremes.	Grandiosity: "I want to get attention from and impress the people who count in my life."	Organization is characterized by a structure that is too primitive for its many products and its broad market; by overcentralization that obstructs the development of effective information systems; by second-tier executives who retain too little influence in policy making.	Dependency needs of subordinates complement "strong leader" tendencies of chief executive; leader is idealized by "mirroring" subordinates; leader is catalyst for subordinates' initiative and morale.	Strategy is hyperactive, impulsive, venturesome, and dangerously uninhibited; initiating bold ventures is the executive's prerogative; diversification and growth are rarely consistent or integrated; action is pursued for action's sake; decision making is nonparticipative.

Table 3–1 (con't)

Executive Style	Inner Script	Corporate Traits	Culture	Strategy
SUSPICIOUS Leader is vigilantly prepared to counter any and all attacks and personal threats; exhibits hypersensitivity; seems cold and lacks emotional expression; is suspicious and distrustful, and insists on loyalty; becomes overinvolved in rules and details to secure complete control; craves information; is sometimes vindictive.	"Some menacing force is out to get me; I'd better be on my guard. I can't really trust anybody."	Organization is characterized by elaborate information processing; by abundant analysis of external trends; by centralization of power.	Fight-or-flight atmosphere dominates, characterized by dependency, fear of attack, emphasis on the power of information, intimidation, uniformity, and lack of trust.	Strategy is reactive, and conservative; overly analytical; diversified; secretive.
DETACHED Leader seems withdrawn and uninvolved; lacks interest in present or future; is sometimes indifferent to praise or criticism.	"Reality doesn't offer satisfaction; interactions with others will fail; it's safer to remain distant."	Organization is characterized by an internal focus and insufficient scanning of external environment; by self-imposed barriers to free flow of information.	Warmth and emotional displays are rare; conflicts and jockeying for power are common; insecurity prevails.	Strategy is vacillating, indecisive, inconsistent, the product of narrow, parochial perspectives.

Table 3–1 (con't)

Executive Style	Inner Script	Corporate Traits	Culture	Strategy
DEPRESSIVE				
Leader lacks self-confidence, self-esteem, or initiative; fears success and tolerates mediocrity or failure; depends on messiahs.	"It's hopeless to think about changing the course of events; I'm just not good enough."	Organization is characterized by ritual, bureaucracy, inflexibility, and hierarchy; by poor internal communications; by resistance to change; by impersonality.	Initiative is discouraged; passivity, negativity, and lack of motivation are the order of the day; ign,orance of markets is common; a leadership vacuum is felt.	Strategy is characterized, by "decidiphobia"; by inward-focused attention and a lack of vigilance over changing market conditions; by drifting with no sense of direction; by confinement to antiquated "mature" markets.
COMPULSIVE				
Leader tends to dominate organization from top to bottom; insists that others conform to tightly prescribed procedures and rules, is dogmatic or obstinate; is obsessed with detail, perfectionism, routine, rituals, efficiency, and lockstep organization.	"I don't want to be at the mercy of events; I have to master and control all the things affecting me."	Organization is characterized by rigid formal codes, elaborate information systems, and ritualized evaluation procedures; by thoroughness and exactness; by a hierarchy in which individual managers' status derives directly from specific positions.	The culture is rigid, inward-directed, and insular; subordinates are submissive, uncreative, and insecure.	Strategy is tightly calculated and focused, though slow and maladaptive; exhaustive evaluation is featured; reliance on a narrow established theme is typical, as is an obsession with a single aspect of strategy (e.g., cost cutting or quality) to the exclusion of other factors.

What have these individuals done to change our way of looking at organizations? What is it about their particular way of running their companies that has made them unique? Why have they been so successful?

Virgin is now one of the top five brand names in the United Kingdom. Its chairman and founder, Richard Branson, has become an international celebrity and the subject of numerous profiles in the press and on television. In the United Kingdom he has achieved folk-hero status and is frequently cited as a role model for young people. He became one of Britain's richest people before he turned forty, running an empire that encompasses travel (Virgin Atlantic), communications (book publishing, radio and television stations, computer/video games), retail enterprises (Megastores), financial services, beverages, and hotels. (The highly successful music division was sold.)

Jack Welch, the chairman and CEO of General Electric, runs one of the world's largest corporations. Since taking the reins in 1982, he has rebuilt the company into a $60 billion conglomerate of diverse businesses, including medical systems, aircraft engineering, plastics engineering, major appliances, NBC television, and financial services. During his term as chairman, Jack Welch has succeeded where many other CEOs of large companies fail: He has turned a plodding dinosaur that was increasingly suffering from organizational arteriosclerosis into a lean, sharply focused company that is proving to be a paradigm of a new leadership style.

In 1987 Percy Barnevik surprised the business community by announcing the largest cross-border merger in modern history. In record time, he combined ASEA, a Swedish engineering group, with Brown Boveri, a Swiss competitor. Since then, by adding more than 100 additional companies in Europe and the United States, he has created a $30 billion giant with a portfolio covering global markets for electric power generation and transmission equipment, high-speed trains, automation and robotics, and environmental control systems. At present a cadre of 250 global managers leads 230,000 employees in 1,300 companies (which are divided into 5,000 profit centers in 140 countries around the world).

At first glance there may appear to be few similarities among these three organizations—and even fewer among the three business leaders. Virgin, run by a flamboyant, intuitive, disarmingly friendly entrepreneur, has a corporate culture that highly values creativity and innovation. Richard Branson is regularly featured trying to beat a ballooning or speedboat record or dressed up as a character such as Spiderman or Robin Hood. General Electric is a relatively ancient U.S. company led by a highly technical individual with a doctorate in engineering. For many years, Jack Welch has been featured in *Fortune* magazine as the toughest executive in North America. In comparison, ABB is an assembly of companies with many different nationalities. Its chairman, Percy Barnevik, is a soft-spoken, intense, philosophical Swede, a business school graduate and a specialist in data processing and information systems. These three men differ fundamentally, too, in their predominant operational codes. Richard Branson is a *builder*. He has created an organization completely from scratch. Jack Welch, the high priest of business process reengineering, is a highly regarded *transformer* of organizations. Percy Barnevik has been hailed for assembling the ultimate global organization; he is seen as a highly effective *integrator*.

Despite these basic differences, however, there are many similarities in these leaders' outlook toward organizational design and in the way they view their roles. All three came to leadership dissatisfied with the way organizations had traditionally been run. Consequently, they were motivated to experiment with new ways of making organizations more effective. Searching for alternatives, each one developed a new concept of how a corporation should be run and a vision of where he wanted to take his organization in the future. The beliefs and values of each of these leaders are an integral part of his vision, originating from his inner theater and motivating him to spread his message with passion and conviction. Observing Welch, Barnevik, and Branson in action, we see three people who know how to create the kind of enthusiasm and commitment that inspire others to join them. They recognize the importance of their multifaceted roles as change agent, cheerleader, coach, and mentor. They want to change the way people work in their respective companies by changing people's attitudes. Moreover, these three business leaders want to instill in their employees the kind of pride that goes beyond the numbers game. They want to contribute something to society. These three business leaders fit the contemporary heroic model of what a business leader should be like. That does not mean that they are without weaknesses. But in contrast to those executives who are easily seduced when power's sirens are calling, they make a great effort (as can be seen in the way they have designed their organizations) to retain a sense of reality.

Leaders As Architects

What makes these three men so different from many other executives? First, all three are adamant about releasing the creative energy *at all levels of their organizations*. In other words, they want to get their employees involved. Although their narcissistic needs are substantial, they are willing to let other people shine.

How did they become the leaders they are? It is important to remember that the original model of the organization is the family. Branson, Welch, and Barnevik are very much products of their upbringing. In all three cases, strong family role models and early developmental experiences are reflected in the way they have structured their respective organizations (Elms, 1994).

Jack Welch was the only child in the family. His parents were Irish immigrants who did not finish high school. His father was a railroad conductor—in Welch's own words, "a good man, hard-working, passive" (Sherman, 1989). Welch was close to his mother, who was very domineering. She was the one who pushed him to get an education—a B.S. and a Ph.D. in engineering. Welch's mother told him that he could do anything and that he should control his own destiny, a slogan that would later become Welch's rallying cry at GE. Supported by his mother, Welch demonstrated leadership qualities from the outset. An excavated gravel pit in the neighborhood turned into a park for all kinds of highly competitive games, such as hockey and basketball, with Welch usually taking on a leadership role (Morris, 1995). This formative experience in a "street-fighting" ambiance made for the kind of toughness that can handle any situation.

Percy Barnevik was born to a relatively well-to-do-family in a small town in the south of Sweden. His family later moved to the barren, windswept west coast of Sweden, where Barnevik spent most of his childhood years. The strict Lutheran work ethic of the fishermen and boat builders frowned upon waste, inefficiency, indecisiveness, and disorderly conduct; Barnevik was taught, by word and by example, that we are put on this earth to earn our bread by the sweat of our brow. When his father started his own printing business (in which both parents worked), Barnevik himself worked as a typesetter during his spare time. That job taught him the motivational advantages of working in small units, the value of working long hours, and the need for responsiveness to the customer. His experiences at the printing shop served him later as a model for the design of organizations (Kets de Vries, 1994a, 1994b; Kets de Vries and Morcos, 1994).

Richard Branson was the first child and only son in his family. His father was the son and grandson of eminent lawyers, and he also became a lawyer (albeit reluctantly). Branson's father was not very ambitious, but he was very supportive of his children. The driving force in the family was Branson's mother, who had been a dancer and a flight attendant, traveling to South America when air travel still contained a significant element of adventure and danger. When Branson was born, his mother declared that one day he would be prime minister. His mother had very decided views on child rearing and pushed her children to be self-reliant, competitive, and responsible. To encourage self-reliance, she once put young Branson (aged four at the time) out of the car and told him to find his way home. Through her unconventional methods, she convinced him that he would be able to do whatever he set his mind to. She taught him the value of money, and from early on, she encouraged Branson's entrepreneurial ventures. His need to challenge the established way of doing things, his antiauthoritarian outlook, and his need to play David against the Goliaths of the business world—these must have started in childhood (Kets de Vries, 1995a, 1995b; Kets de Vries and Dick, 1995).

The developmental experiences of these three business leaders set the stage for the kinds of interventions they later employed in their respective organizations. As organizational architects, they have redesigned their corporate culture to inspire people wherever they happen to be positioned in the organization. Decentralization and operational autonomy are a sine qua non for the creative and high-performance atmosphere found in these three companies. These leaders want to foster a sense of *ownership* in their people. It is their strong belief that strategic awareness should not be limited to the top echelons of the organization but should be pushed deep down. Barnevik has pushed authority, responsibility, and accountability far down into the organization, in part by ensuring that there are never more than five people between himself and the shop floor. Welch has been called the master of "delayering"; where once there were nine organizational layers between himself and the shop floor, there are now around five. And the lack of hierarchy at Virgin has become proverbial. Also, all three executives have designed their respective organizations for *simplicity of organizational structure*; they want to minimize the potential for confusion in the decision chain.

Barnevik, Branson, and Welch know that the corporate culture of the postwar generation—typified by the so-called organization man (the loyal individual who strongly identifies with his company and makes a commitment for life)—has become a liability in the current climate of leveraged buyouts, merger mania, corporate downsizing, and business reengineering. These three business leaders are looking for radical formulas to replace outdated concepts such as lifetime employment. Whereas the traditional command-and-control style of management and organization was designed for an unskilled labor base, these three business leaders realize that the future of the high-performance organization lies in *self-managed teams* run by people who do not have to be continually prodded to do things. These executives look for people who set their own high standards and who criticize themselves when they fail to live up to these standards. They want people who are eager to learn, know how to adapt, and possess a high tolerance for ambiguity. Consequently, they pay a lot of attention to the selection process.

All three business leaders know, however, that in creating an exciting working environment, they create a dilemma. Larger corporate size means more possibilities, of course, but it can also become a serious impediment. These executives are very aware that when organizational units become too big, employees sometimes become less involved. They may experience a sense of alienation and depersonalization, with obvious negative repercussions on creativity, innovation, and entrepreneurship. To challenge their employees and give them a sense of ownership, Branson, Welch, and Barnevik have minimized the negative aspects of large organizations by eagerly embracing the *small-is-beautiful* concept. They have gone to great lengths to create in their large corporations a small-business atmosphere in a high-performance workplace. They also realize that *flat structures* are in, and they encourage lateral rather than vertical communication. Furthermore, the decision-making process in each of these firms is facilitated by a *network structure*. Welch talks about the "boundaryless corporation," meaning a structure without the crippling costs of bureaucratic controls and hierarchical authority. The "loose" organizational architectures of Virgin and ABB are of a similar nature. Additionally, all three executives have created a *centralized/decentralized structure*. They strongly believe in decentralization, but at the same time they keep a close watch on key performance indicators to stay informed about what is happening in their various strategic units.

Such an organizational design would have been impossible until recently. Being big and small at the same time—that is, being a large organization broken up into a number of small, loosely connected companies and yet maintaining organizational cohesiveness—has become feasible only with the revolution in information technology. *Sophisticated information systems* have become a major force pulling geographically dispersed employees together. It is now possible for top executives to decentralize without losing control. Modern information and communication technology has made it possible for Barnevik to say, "We want to be centralized and decentralized, big and small, global and local." Similar comments, although not as extreme, have been made by Branson and Welch. Branson has said that when there are more than fifty to seventy-five people in a building, they lose their sense of identity and belonging. When a unit grows beyond that size, it is time to spin off the division, creating a new business in another building. Branson applies his philosophy religiously: His organization consists of numerous *small autonomous units*, continuously dividing and reproducing like an amoeba. Virgin is a subtle network of interrelated companies with a mutuality of interests, all of which can be mystifying to outsiders. To some extent, given the myriad of alliances that make up the company, Virgin is an imaginary organization. In a similar vein, Welch has noted on many occasions that General Electric is a company made up of small companies whose people are very much encouraged to take on "intrapreneurial" challenges.

The design of these organizational structures is very much in line with the realization on the part of Barnevik, Welch, and Branson that the employees of the 1990s want to have some control over their own careers. These three business leaders are also aware that the people who work for them are impatient. These people want responsibility and rewards now. Consequently, they are attracted to organizations in which they will be stretched, in which senior executives are willing to take a gamble on them and give them the room to learn. Because learning and the permission to make mistakes are very closely linked, people are searching for organizations in which employees are given *permission to make mistakes*. After all, people who do not make mistakes have made no decisions!

Consequently, these business leaders have their new recruits go through a carefully planned *socialization process*. They realize the importance of having these high-potential employees acquire a broad exposure to products, services, and the industry early in their careers. If people are to be developed as leaders, they must be given early project responsibility. Being given permission to err does not mean, however, that employees are not held accountable for their performance. *Accountability* is driven deep down in these organizations. This also implies measurability: The statement "If it isn't measured it doesn't get done" is, unfortunately, all too true. Measurement also implies benchmarking both internally and externally. It is impossible to develop a winning institution without making a distinction between excellent and mediocre work. Thus, constructive feedback about performance is very much a part of the culture of these three organizations.

In this new type of organizational structure, large head offices, which were previously needed to exert control over the operating companies, are no longer required. Indeed, one could argue that there is an *inverse* relationship between the size of the head office and the effectiveness of an organization. Branson does not have a head office—at least not under the old definition. His corporate headquarters used to be a houseboat, and currently he works out of a townhouse in London. Barnevik's aversion to large head offices is well known, and according to ABB's policy "bible," the organization's so-called 30 percent rule must be applied when ABB acquires companies with large head offices. This means a cut of 30 percent of personnel at the head office, another 30 percent cut to decentralize certain functions into profit centers, and yet another 30 percent reduction to create new service centers that invoice services at market rates. Full implementation of the 30 percent rule means that only 10 percent of the former staff remains in the acquired company's main office. To illustrate this rule in action, Barnevik held ABB's Zurich head office to a mere 150 people after the merger. Before the merger, Brown Boveri had 4,000 people in Baden, Switzerland, while ASEA had 2,000 people in Västerås, Sweden.

In all three organizations, bureaucracy is a dirty word. The three business leaders make a great effort to avoid turning their organizations into paper factories. Welch introduced the concept of company "workouts" at General Electric: At these workout sessions, all members of an organizational unit, irrespective of position, have an opportunity to review existing procedures, approval systems, measurement systems, and report and meeting requirements, and to decide whether these still add value. If they do not, radical surgery takes place. The executives at Virgin and ABB also use a minimum amount of paper, preferring to use the telephone, e-mail, and fax, or to manage by flying around and seeing people in person.

These three executives try to create a *climate for innovation* by giving not only strong financial but also strong emotional support to getting projects off the ground. Besides being good business, this desire for innovation may be a reflection of these leaders' inner need for continuous stimulation. All three executives will do anything in their power to resist the not-invented-here syndrome. Receptivity to and experimentation with new ideas characterize their companies. These leaders like to see a continuous stream of new projects and products in their portfolio. And this approach pays off for all three firms. Rarely a week goes by without an announcement of yet another project that is off to a flying start. All three business leaders want a considerable part of their product portfolio to be new each year.

The principle behind Barnevik's, Branson's, and Welch's way of designing organizations is that when people have a *sense of control*, they feel better about what they are doing and are therefore more creative. Obviously, a sense of control has a very personal meaning for the leaders themselves. They have discovered over time that only when they feel in control can they function most effectively. And they are not alone in these feelings. Research on stress has shown that when people feel that they have control over their lives—that is, when they do not experience a sense of helplessness—they show fewer stress symptoms (Zaleznik, Kets de Vries, and Howard, 1977). And the absence of stress tends to have a positive effect on people's productivity at work.

When people feel a sense of ownership for a particular part of the organization, they have greater *commitment* to it. Equally important, they have more fun doing their job. Most people who have fun work harder, a connection that Welch, Branson, and Barnevik seem to understand thoroughly. In all too many organizations, top executives seem to have forgotten the importance of fun. Although students of creativity will tell you that playfulness and creativity are closely related, in most organizations a version of Gresham's Law prevails: It is not bad money that drives out good money but noncreative people who drive out creative people.

Another critical characteristic of these organizations is *customer-centeredness*. Close customer contact for everyone in the organization is a major pillar of the business philosophy of each of these three business leaders. Barnevik, growing up as part of the small printing business of his parents, experienced early on how vital a customer orientation can be. Branson saw the same thing in his many early entrepreneurial ventures. Welch, having been given early profit-and-loss responsibility in one of GE's new start-ups (creating a market for a new thermoplastic), quickly recognized the importance of a customer orientation. These three executives realize that only customers can give their organization tenure. They also realize that close customer contact for all employees increases the employees' sense of ownership. And in each firm a process orientation—how best to help the customer—is preferred over a functional orientation. All structures and procedures in these high-performance organizations are directed toward giving the best service possible to customers, who are never merely an abstraction or a distraction. In this, the three executives set the example, devoting a considerable part of their time to dealings with customers. (Here, too, small business size enhances the possibility of contact and improves the feedback loop.)

Another characteristic of these high-performance organizations is *speed*. Again, this is a reflection of the inner world of these executives. These are people who do not like to wait. Extremely impatient, they like things to be done *now*. Although there are probably some deeper reasons for their sense of urgency (including, almost certainly, the roles of their early caregivers), they make the rational argument that product life cycles are growing ever shorter and that speed to market is becoming increasingly important. At General Electric, speed is considered part of the company's core philosophy. Welch himself continually stresses this value. Likewise, Branson says of himself, "I can have an idea in the morning in the bathtub and have it implemented in the evening." Speed has an essential place in Barnevik's management philosophy as well. In ABB's policy bible, Barnevik asserts that "it is better to be roughly right than exactly right with respect to speed." He expects his executives to have about a 70 percent batting average. Barnevik has said that the best thing to do in his organization is to make the right decision; the next best thing to do is to make the wrong decision. Not taking any action at all, however—losing an opportunity because of a reluctance to make a decision—is unacceptable.

An important related component of the corporate culture of Virgin, General Electric, and ABB is *continuous change*. Behind this component may be the leaders' fear that without new stimuli they would get bored or (even worse) depressed. Thus, their inner restlessness ends up having a beneficial effect. Nurturance of a positive attitude toward continuous change is critical in the workplace because of the danger of complacency in the face of external danger signs. As the saying goes, "Nothing kills like success."

Branson, Barnevik, and Welch also realize that the high-performing employees of today, like frogs in a wheelbarrow, can jump out any time. (These leaders surely must have experienced the impulse to flight themselves.) Accordingly, beyond giving employees the opportunity to spread their wings, organizations must also provide attractive material rewards: Today's employees want *rewards according to their contribution*. They prefer organizations that will give them a piece of the action in the form of stock options, bonuses, or gain- or profit-sharing plans. Share ownership plays an important role in retaining the best people in a company. And indeed, Richard Branson is explicit—financially as well as verbally—about the fact that he does not want his high performers to leave Virgin to start their own companies elsewhere. He makes sure that key players have the possibility of becoming millionaires under the Virgin umbrella. Under Jack Welch's rule, General Electric, too, has seen an explosive growth in the number of employees who have been granted stock options. Only at ABB is this dimension of management not fully developed.

Barnevik, Welch, and Branson are aware that the "psychological contract" between an employee and his or her organization is changing. With merger and acquisition mania and the passion for business process reengineering, job loyalty has declined steeply, just as job tenure and security are no longer to be expected. All three executives realize that a new form of security has to be offered to make their organizations attractive, and what these three executives offer is *employability*. They provide their executives with portable skills. If the day comes when the organization no longer needs the services of a particular employee, that person will be better equipped to find a position elsewhere. Paradoxically, doing so makes the employee more valuable to the company.

The implication of this new psychological contract is that there must be a sufficient and appropriate *learning culture* in an organization. All three executives have created organizations that provide world-class learning opportunities for employees at all levels. It is the responsibility of the employees to use these opportunities to their maximum advantage. To observe this notion of employability in action, one has only to look at the number of executives of these organizations who have been poached by competitors. A "graduate" of GE or ABB has an undeniable attraction to headhunters.

What holds together the dynamic but diverse groups of people who make up Virgin, ABB, and General Electric? I have already mentioned one kind of glue: sophisticated information systems. The other kind of glue is provided in the way that Branson, Welch, and Barnevik shape their corporate cultures. A set of *shared common values*—a factor taken seriously by these leaders—goes a long way toward fostering cohesiveness. These three business leaders request, either implicitly or explicitly, that each organizational participant share certain values specific to the particular corporation—values that go beyond national culture. At GE and ABB these key values are summarized in policy bibles. At Virgin these values are more subtly instilled. Everyone at all three firms, however, is expected to be familiar with the corporate culture. New recruits are indoctrinated and trained in these values and are then expected to internalize the values and behave accordingly. The positive payoff is a decreased need for external controls. And, as has been said earlier, many of these key values are very much determined by the upbringing of the corporate leader.

As culture guardians, the three executives profiled here make an enormous effort to let people speak their minds. They encourage *contrarian thinking*; they have taken to heart General Patton's assertion that "when everyone agrees, somebody is not thinking." They realize that when people do not have the confidence to say what they mean, the CEO receives filtered information. One of Welch's cultural rules is, "Be candid with everyone." He is famous for his directness in dealing with his people, and he expects the same directness from them. Barnevik, who acknowledges the risk of not getting enough feedback from coworkers, goes to great lengths to encourage people to speak their minds. Branson has an open-door policy and in some ways, plays the role of ombudsman in his organization. Always prepared to listen (and, more important, to act) when people have legitimate complaints, he welcomes critical comments about ways to improve the operation of his companies.

Branson, Barnevik, and Welch know that the key ingredient for encouraging people to speak their minds and be frank is *trust*. And while these leaders know that factors such as integrity, competence, credibility, consistency, support, respect, and honesty are key to the trust equation, they recognize that the most important factor in creating trust in the organization is *communication*—active listening as well as talking. These leaders know, too, that shooting the messenger of bad news is a sure way to kill trust in the organization.

These three business leaders are trying to make *good internal corporate citizenship* an essential part of each organization's value system, and it seems to be working. One factor that makes their companies so successful is that most employees are prepared to go out of their way to help one another and to preserve the integrity of their organizations. To make this good corporate citizenship happen, organizational leadership must set the example. Barnevik frequently reminds his executives of the need to "walk the talk"; the top executives at Virgin are always ready to give a helping hand where needed; and GE management models a cooperative attitude.

Another factor contributing to the effectiveness of these three organizations is the fact that all three leaders have a considerable knowledge of their own weaknesses, and they find people with corresponding strengths to compensate. At Virgin, Branson has had a series of strong managers. Nik Powell, his first partner, was methodical and cautious. He took on difficult tasks such as cost cutting and staff reduction. Simon Draper, "Mr. Golden Ears" when Virgin Music was part of its portfolio of businesses, forged Virgin's creative direction. Financial management, control systems, and partnerships are managing director Trevor Abbot's strengths. The team is presently rounded out by Branson's brother-in-law, Robert Devereux, whose hands-off relationship with his boss gives him the freedom to bring Branson down to earth when necessary. At ABB, Barnevik, when he was CEO, depended on several colleagues who have been working with him for a long time, some giving him advice on long-term business developments, the others giving him tactical support. At GE, Welch has two vice-chairmen with whom he forms a team; he is also a regular participant in GE's now famous workout sessions.

Leaders As Charismatic Guides

In the context of good leadership, it is important to remember that effective leaders take on a *charismatic* as well as an *architectural* role. The previous discussion highlighted how Percy Barnevik, Jack Welch, and Richard Branson design their respective organizations and set up the proper control and reward systems. In each man's role as an organizational architect, his inner theater dictates much of what he says and does. But the charismatic role, which has to do with the *envisioning*, *empowering*, and *energizing* elements of leadership, is another essential part of what leadership is all about.

What makes these leaders (and their organizations) so successful is that all three have a strong, clear *vision* of what they want to do and where they want to go, and they are able to communicate that vision to their workforce. In other words, they are effective in their charismatic role. These leaders know how to set the direction for the organization and how to build commitment to follow that direction. By pushing responsibility down the line and encouraging dialogue throughout the organization, these three leaders nurture strategic awareness and pride in the organization.

As with the architecture, the relentless quality of their efforts to get their vision across to others in the organization is an externalization of strong inner needs (and the personal history that spawned them). These leaders' inner imagery, which centers in certain core conflictual relationship themes, dramatically colors their behavior on the public stage. And the content of each man's vision is unique. For example, Welch has told everyone at General Electric that he wants every GE unit to be number one or number two in whatever business segment it is in. If a unit is not in one of those top two slots, it should either ask for the resources to get there or simply get out—"disengage," to use his terminology. Branson, on the other hand, is in the business of fostering entrepreneurship. He is looking for people with innovative ideas to start new entities, be it in entertainment, communications, the airline or hotel business, store management, or beverage services. Barnevik, meanwhile, is trying to create the world's number one engineering group.

But the vision of each leader extends beyond bottom-line business success. All three executives reveal a kind of pragmatic idealism: a level of *social concern*. Barnevik has said that he is motivated by a desire to create a better world by providing employment (particularly in Eastern Europe, where he is the largest single investor), clean energy, and transportation. For Branson, too, "doing good works" is an important part of corporate philosophy and of corporate activity. Welch has stated that he wishes to contribute to a better society through the products made by General Electric.

Vision lays out a road map for the future, generates excitement, creates order out of chaos, and provides criteria for success; but it is useless if it is not shared by all members of an organization. Branson, Welch, and Barnevik—each of whom has something of the showman—recognize the importance of *impression management*. For example, Branson (though apparently a rather shy person) has a showy, almost exhibitionistic style and is very cognizant of the importance of public relations. Welch is an aggressive, confrontational "cowboy," while Barnevik appears to be both more rational and more humanistic. But although they differ in style, all three exude enthusiasm and radiate self-confidence when talking about what they are trying to do and where they want to go, and this makes their vision contagious.

I have already described, in discussing the architectural role of leadership, how these three business leaders foster the *empowerment* of people. These executives treat their people as responsible human beings; they keep them informed and minimize secrecy. Although letting go of power may seem difficult in the short run (after all, power has an addictive quality), eventually the whole organization benefits. Employees become more productive; and as a result of the organization's productivity, the CEO becomes more powerful. In this empowerment process, successful leaders set high performance expectations and publicly express confidence in their executives. They know that high expectations are likely to motivate capable people.

Many organizations have depressive and paranoid characteristics, generally rooted in the flawed interpersonal skills of the top executive. Many CEOs, for example, engage in conflict avoidance, adhere to the general rule that garbage goes down and credit goes up, practice micromanagement, and exhibit abrasive behavior. In workplaces where these practices are common, dysfunctional social defenses may come to the fore among employees as a way of dealing with anxiety. Welch, Barnevik, and Branson, however, are skilled at *harnessing the affectionate and aggressive energy* of their people, another critical component of the charismatic leader's "tool kit." They know how to function as an emotional "container." They are aware of the importance of interpersonal and transcultural skills in their corporations. These executives also recognize and value people skills. Charismatic leaders are good at playing the role of psychiatric social worker and expressing affection when needed. Because their caring way of behaving cascades down in the organization, they get the best out of their people. They also recognize the necessity of harnessing aggressive energy. To avoid excessive politicking, turf fights, and lack of teamwork within the organization, they set clear boundaries and at the same time direct people's aggressive energy outward, toward the competition. Having a strong common "enemy" gets the adrenaline flowing in an organization and is an ideal way to give the group a sense of focus. Jack Welch has said that he does not want his people to fight with the person at the next desk; he wants them to fight competitors such as Westinghouse or DuPont. Percy Barnevik constantly reminds his people of competitors such as Siemens and General Electric. And the nemesis of Virgin Atlantic is, of course, British Airways.

Concluding Remarks

The era of the highly structured organization is past. Rigidity in organizational design, hierarchical structure, and power hoarding constitute a recipe for corporate disaster. Organizations that do not consider the individual and maximize the potential of today's high-performing employees will not have the kind of creativity and imagination they need to survive in the global business world of the twenty-first century.

In their architectural and charismatic roles as leaders, Branson, Barnevik, and Welch have constructed the kind of high-performance learning organizations that will become the standard of the future. Many business leaders would do well to follow their example. Some executives, of course, will not be able to deal with the ambiguities that this new kind of networking, "boundaryless" organization entails. Inner boundaries—the boundaries inside people's heads—are difficult to dissolve. Some executives, along with many of their employees, may find it hard to relinquish the old authority, structure, and control. Many organizational leaders, too, waste the creative potential of their people. They do not know how to create the kind of learning culture that proactively transforms itself (as opposed to being changed by outside intervention). But leaders such as Branson, Welch, and Barnevik realize that if people get the opportunity to spread their wings, they often take off. These leaders nurture the creative spirit in their organizations. They go to great lengths to make life in their organizations a meaningful and enjoyable experience.

What we have seen is the extent to which the leadership styles and strategies of these three executives have been influenced by their earlier experiences, especially those in childhood. These developmental experiences resulted in the distinctive scripts that came to dominate each man's inner theater. Although these scripts have been continuously refined and modified over the years (and will continue to be refined and modified throughout the life span), these executives' early attitudes toward power and authority created an organization in the mind—one based on existing family dynamics—that strongly influenced the way they designed, and now run, their organizations.

The poet T. S. Eliot wrote in his *Four Quartets*:

We shall not cease from exploration
And the end of all our exploring
Will be to arrive where we started
And know the place for the first time.

In our efforts to understand the enigma that is leadership, it seems that the end can be found in the beginning.

References

American Psychiatric Association. *Diagnostic and Statistical Manual of Mental Disorders* (4th ed.). Washington, D.C.: American Psychiatric Association, 1994.

Bass, B. M. *Bass and Stogdill Handbook of Leadership: Theory, Research and Managerial Implications* (3rd ed). New York: Free Press, 1990.

Elms A. C. *Uncovering Lives*. New York: Oxford University Press, 1994.

Erikson, E. H. *Childhood and Society* (2nd ed.). New York: W. W. Norton, 1963.

Freud, S. "A Childhood Recollection from *Dichtung und Wahrheit*." In J. Strachey (ed. and trans.), *The Standard Edition of the Complete Psychological Works of Sigmund Freud*, Vol. 17. London: Hogarth Press and the Institute of Psychoanalysis, 1955. (Originally published 1917.)

Hannan, M. T., and Freeman, J. H. "The Population Ecology of Organizations." *American Journal of Sociology*, 1977, *82*, 926–964.

Horowitz, M. J. (ed.). *Person Schemas and Maladaptive Interpersonal Patterns*. Chicago: University of Chicago Press, 1991.

Kernberg, O. *Borderline Conditions and Pathological Narcissism*. New York: Jason Aronson, 1975.

Kets de Vries, M. F. R. *Prisoners of Leadership*. New York: Wiley, 1989.

Kets de Vries, M. F. R. "Leaders on the Couch." *Journal of Applied Behavioral Science*, 1990, *26*(4), 423–431.

Kets de Vries, M. F. R. *Leaders, Fools, and Impostors*. San Francisco: Jossey-Bass, 1993.

Kets de Vries, M. F. R. "Making a Giant Dance." *Across the Board*, Oct. 1994a, pp. 27–32.

Kets de Vries, M. F. R. "Percy Barnevik and ABB: Teaching Note." *INSEAD Case Study* (Fontainebleau, France), 1994b.

Kets de Vries, M. F. R. "Branson's Virgin: Teaching Note." *INSEAD Case Study* (Fontainebleau, France), 1995A.

Kets de Vries, M. F. R. "Richard Branson: The 'Iconoclastic' Entrepreneur: An Interview." *INSEAD Case Study* (Fontainebleau, France), 1995b.

Kets de Vries, M. F. R., and Dick, R. "Branson's Virgin: The Coming of Age of a Counter-Cultural Enterprise," *INSEAD Case Study* (Fontainebleau, France), 1995.

Kets de Vries, M. F. R., and Miller, D. *The Neurotic Organization: Diagnosing and Changing Counterproductive Styles and Management*. San Francisco: Jossey-Bass, 1984.

Kets de Vries, M. F. R., and Miller, D. "Narcissism and Leadership: An Object Relations Perspective." *Human Relations*, 1985, *38*(6), 583–601.

Kets de Vries, M. F. R., and Miller, D. *Unstable at the Top*. New York: New American Library/Penguin, 1987.

Kets de Vries, M. F. R., Miller, D., and Noel, A. "Understanding the Leader–Strategy Interface: The Application of the Strategic Relationship Interview Method." *Human Relations*. 1993, *46*(1), 5–22.

Kets de Vries, M. F. R., and Morcos, R. "Percy Barnevik and ABB." *INSEAD Case Study* (Fontainebleau, France), 1994.

Kohut, H. *The Analysis of the Self*. Madison, Conn.: International Universities Press, 1971.

Kohut, H. *The Restoration of the Self*. Madison, Conn.: International Universities Press, 1977.

Lasswell, H. D. *Psychopathology and Politics*. Chicago: University of Chicago Press, 1930.

Levinson, D. *The Seasons of Man's Life*. New York: Knopf, 1978.

Luborsky, L., Crits-Christoph, P., Minz, J., and Auerbach, A. *Who Will Benefit from Psychotherapy?* New York: Basic Books, 1988.

Miller, A. *Prisoners of Childhood*. New York: Basic Books, 1981.

Millon, T. *Disorders of Personality*. New York: Wiley, 1981.

Morris, B. "Roberto Goizueta and Jack Welch: The Wealth Builders." *Fortune*, Dec. 11, 1995, pp. 38–47.

Pfeffer, J. "The Ambiguity of Leadership." *Academy of Management Review*, 1977, 2, 104–111.

Pfeffer, J., and Salancik, G. R. *The External Control of Organizations: A Resource Dependency Perspective*. New York: HarperCollins, 1984.

Shapiro, D. *Neurotic Styles*. New York: Basic Books, 1965.

Sherman, S. P. "The Mind of Jack Welch." *Fortune*, March 27, 1989, pp. 37–44.

White, R. W. *Lives in Progress* (3rd ed.). Troy, Mo.: Holt, Rinehart & Winston, 1975.

Zaleznik, A., Kets de Vries, M. F. R., Howard, J. H. "Stress Reactions in Organizations: Syndromes, Causes and Consequences." *Behavioral Science*, May 1977, 151–162.

[4]

Beyond the Russian Doll Management Model

New Personal Competencies for New Management Roles

Christopher A. Bartlett
and Sumantra Ghoshal

THE BOSTON CELTICS have won more National Basketball Association championships than any other team in the league. They achieved their winning record through the effectiveness of their organization—the exceptional leadership ability of their general manager, the strong team development skills of coaches, and the outstanding on-court talent of players. And everyone would agree that in an NBA organization that the capable general manager, the savvy coach, and the star player all add value in very different ways. Most business organizations, by contrast, operate on a long-standing and widely shared belief in what might be called a Russian doll model of management. That is, corporations tend to structure management roles as a neatly nested hierarchy of ever expanding responsibilities in which each element focuses on bidding for resources, negotiating objectives, and meeting performance targets. At each level of the hierarchy, a manager supposedly gains the knowledge and expertise required for success at the next level of the larger planning, budgeting, and control process. Thus, frontline managers who demonstrate skill in preparing the inputs to the strategy and budget development process and in implementing

70

approved objectives are assumed to be ready to take on the middle management role of administering the planning process and controlling its implementation; and the most effective of these administrative controllers become the top-level managers who define the strategy, set the objectives, and allocate the resources.

This Russian doll approach, which assumes a generic set of management capabilities, is reflected in hundreds of books and articles on "management skills" and has become deeply embedded in thousands of corporate management development programs. It is even gaining fresh new endorsement in the currently popular management competency models that many companies are embracing.

Over the past decade or so, however, many of these traditional views about management roles and capabilities have come under increasing question and challenge. In many companies the hierarchy of roles bound together by planning and control systems has been overthrown by transformations that have delayered the hierarchic structures, reengineered the organizations' processes, and empowered the frontline managers. And many companies have found their assumptions about generic management skills and competencies to be a major impediment to the development of a new organizational model.

As part of a broader study of companies adjusting to the new strategic, organizational, and managerial imperatives, we have developed a model of management roles as they are being redefined in newly restructured corporations; and we have come up with some hypotheses about the individual competencies required to succeed in these roles. (For a full description of the study and the changes, see our book *The Individualized Corporation*, Harper Business, 1997).

New Organization Model: New Management Roles

To understand the new management roles, we must first recognize the major elements of the emerging organizational framework that is shaping them. In our research we found that companies as diverse as AT&T, Komatsu, ABB, and Corning, despite their considerable differences in fields of activity, national origin, and corporate history, were converging on a similar posttransformational organization model that represented a major change from their traditional authority-based hierarchies. Other companies we studied, such as 3M, Royal Dutch Shell, ISS, and Kao, already shared many of these emerging organizational characteristics and therefore had avoided the worst pathologies of the classic hierarchy. And in many ways this latter group provided both the inspiration and the example for other companies undergoing major transformations.

The clearest and most widespread trend we observed was that companies were rethinking their old approach of dividing the organization from the top down into groups, sectors, and divisions; instead, they were building from the bottom up on a foundation of small frontline operating units. For example, the $30 billion Swiss-based electrotechnical giant ABB divided its operations into 1,300 local operating companies, each of which is a separate legal entity with its own balance sheet and P&L responsibilities. In 3M, the company's $15 billion in sales, generated by a portfolio of more than 60,000 products, is managed by 3,900 entrepreneurial profit centers. And ISS, the Danish-based cleaning services organization, attributes its growth into a $2 billion multinational corporation to its policy of forming, in each of the 17 countries it has expanded into, not one national subsidiary but four or five small autonomous business, each serving a particular client group.

The second common characteristic in the emerging organization model is the portfolio of cross-unit integrative processes designed to break down the insulated, vertically oriented segmentation of the old hierarchy model. In ABB, the tensions inherent in the company's global matrix were resolved through a proliferation of business boards, functional councils, and project teams at every level of the organization. At 3M, the R&D community's carefully developed network of communication channels and decision-making forums became the model for similar relationships linking marketing and manufacturing resources across the company's innovative frontline units. And ISS made extensive use of both training and development and cross-unit meetings and committees to ensure that knowledge and expertise developed in one part of the company was rapidly transferred systemwide.

Finally, these changes to the old structure and processes were supported by a strong commitment to genuine empowerment, a philosophy that represented a powerful challenge to the authority-based culture in most classic hierarchies. In ABB, CEO Percy Barnevik based the company's management practice on the twin principles of radically decentralized responsibility and firmly enforced individual accountability. Known for its core commitment to entrepreneurship and belief in the individual, 3M worked to translate those beliefs into a culture that "stimulates ordinary people to produce extraordinary performance." And in his thirty years at the head of ISS, Poul Andreassen developed a set of guiding principles, central to which was genuine respect for his workers and delegation of responsibility as close to the individual cleaning contract as possible.

This radically decentralized yet horizontally linked organizational model with a strong culture of empowerment required companies to break with the old Russian doll model of management. In these and other companies we studied, operating-level managers had to evolve from being frontline implementers to become innovative entrepreneurs; senior-level managers had to redefine themselves less as administrative controllers and more as developmental coaches; and top-level executives were forced to serve less as their companies' strategic architects and more as their organizational leaders. The implications of such role changes for the distribution of key tasks and responsibilities are profound.

The Operating-Level Entrepreneurial Role

In identifying the new roles and responsibilities of people running business units, national subsidiaries, or other such frontline units, we studied scores of operating-level managers as they struggled to adjust to the demands of the new corporate model. We will focus on a select group of managers at ABB, 3M, and ISS—not as definitive role models, but as illustrations of the framework of management tasks we have developed.

Don Jans headed a relays unit that was part of the troubled power transmission and distribution business Westinghouse sold to ABB in 1989. Westinghouse had long regarded relays as a mature business, and Jans and his team had been encouraged to milk their slowly declining, modestly profitable operation. But when exposed to ABB's decentralized entrepreneurial environment, the same management group turned their mature business into one with the performance profile of a young growth company. Within three years of the ownership change, export sales skyrocketed, new products were introduced, and operating profits doubled. Equally important, the revitalized U.S. relays unit began developing an electronic capability to supplement its traditional electromechanical expertise, thus laying the foundation for long-term expansion into a major new growth area.

In 3M we saw a similar example of frontline entrepreneurship when in 1989 Andy Wong became the leader of a project team that had been struggling for more than a decade to commercialize optical technologies that had never found market applications. Over the next four years, Wong redeployed the unit's resources, refocused its energy and attention, protected the operations from several threats to shut them down, and remotivated the discouraged team. By 1994 Wong's unit had introduced two highly successful new products and had become a showcase within 3M.

And at ISS we watched Theo Buitendijk take over the company's small Dutch commercial cleaning business and double revenues within two years. He moved into the specialized higher-margin specialty of slaughterhouse cleaning, eventually becoming ISS's center of expertise in this sector and supporting its expansion throughout Europe. Like Jans, Buitendijk had previously been a traditional line manager in a classic authoritarian hierarchy (in his case, Exxon); but he found that the different organizational context in ISS not only allowed but encouraged him to redefine his role and change his behavior.

In each of these companies, a similar framework of organizational structure, processes, and culture supported the entrepreneurial activities of frontline managers like Jans, Wong, and Buitendijk. Among the many tasks and responsibilities these managers undertook, we identified three that were central to their role as entrepreneurs rather than just implementers. See Table 4.1.

CREATING AND PURSUING OPPORTUNITIES. First, each manager took the initiative to create and pursue new business opportunities. No longer implementers of programs and priorities pushed down from above, managers like Jans and Buitendijk found that in their new situations they not only were free to initiate new activities but were expected to do so. Jans expanded into export markets in Mexico, Canada, and the Far East and committed his unit to the development of microprocessor-based relays, despite the substantial up-front investment involved. Buitendijk's abattoir cleaning caused a sharp drop in his company's profitability before finally proving to be a much more attractive segment than the highly competitive core office-cleaning business.

Table 4.1
Management Roles and Tasks

	Operating-Level Managers	Senior-Level Managers	Top-Level Managers
Changing role	From operational implementers to aggressive entrepreneurs	From administrative controllers to developmental coaches	From resource allocators to institutional leaders
Primary value added	Driving business performance by focusing on productivity, innovation, and growth within front-line units	Providing the support and coordination to bring large company advantages to the independent frontline units	Creating and embedding a sense of direction, commitment, and challenge to people throughout the organization
Key activities and tasks	Creating and pursuing new growth opportunities for the business Attracting and developing resources and competencies Managing continuous performance improvement within the unit	Developing individuals and supporting their activities Linking dispersed knowledge, skills, and best practices across units Managing the tension between short-term performance and long-term objectives	Challenging embedded assumptions while stretching opportunity horizons and performance standards Institutionalizing a set of norms and values to support cooperation and trust Creating an overarching corporate purpose and ambition

ATTRACTING AND DEVELOPING RESOURCES. Second, these frontline entrepreneurs all expanded the assets, resources, and capabilities of their operating units. Rather than playing the more traditional passive–dependent role defined by corporate processes such as head count authorization and capital budget allocation, these individuals saw it as their responsibility to "do more with less," as one of them described it. Andy Wong's actions in upgrading his unit's existing technological and manufacturing resources were impressive enough, but his creation of an entirely new marketing capability in a resource-constrained operation was truly entrepreneurial. Through persistent negotiations with senior management, creative internal resource reallocations, and persuasive recruiting within the company, he was able to reinforce his struggling unit with an experienced marketing manager and to back him with the distribution support of two other 3M divisions that agreed to help bring his unproven product to market. Don Jans's ability to develop a microprocessor-based product line and his unit's recognition as the benchmark in cycle time management exhibited the same commitment to building on and leveraging existing capabilities; Jans earned recognition as a "giver" rather than a "receiver," as ABB referred to managers who became net developers rather than consumers of the organization's resources.

MANAGING CONTINUOUS IMPROVEMENT. Third, these frontline managers were responsible for ensuring continuous performance improvement in their operating as always, but in the new organizational context, they received considerably more freedom, incentive, and support for this effort than they had had before. Thus, despite the fact that he had long been driven to maximize operating performance in Westinghouse, Don Jans was able to achieve substantial additional expense cuts, inventory and receivables reductions, and operating efficiency improvements within the ABB organization, largely because he was given what Barnevik described as "maximum degrees of freedom to execute."

Improving current performance also became a priority for Andy Wong. He knew that by leveraging the unit's existing assets and resources he could build the credibility and confidence he would need to obtain additional investment and support. Therefore, Wong initially invested a large part of his energy in focusing development attention on only two technologies and reducing manufacturing costs by 50 percent. After building organizational confidence with his operating effectiveness, he won both the freedom to engage in the resource development and the time to implement his unit's entrepreneurial new product launch.

If these three categories of entrepreneurial tasks do not yet describe the actual practice of most frontline managers, it only shows the untapped potential for performance improvement available to most companies. The dramatically changed behavior of managers like Jans and Buitendijk, and Wong's rapid transition from engineer to project team leader, suggest that inside every hierarchy, even the most authoritarian, entrepreneurial hostages are waiting to be unleashed.

The Senior-Level Coaching Role

The risk of redefining the role of operating-level managers as entrepreneurs is that it will fragment the company's resources and capabilities and lead to the kind of undisciplined, localized expansion that conglomerates experienced in the 1960s. To prevent this, senior-level managers—those between the frontline units and the corporate-level management—must redefine their role from one of preoccupation with authority-based control and must focus on support-based management and organization development.

Traditionally, senior managers' power came from their pivotal position in large and complex hierarchies. They played a vital intermediary role, disaggregating corporate objectives into business unit targets and aggregating business unit plans for corporate review. They were the linchpins in the resource allocation process, because corporate management relied on their input in capital budgeting and personnel appointment decisions. And they stood at the crossroads of internal communication, interpreting and broadcasting management's priorities, then channeling and translating frontline feedback.

These classic senior management tasks have been challenged by the new independence of frontline units, the radical decentralization of assets and resources, and the empowerment of operating managers. They have been further undermined by the delayering of middle levels of the organization and the impact of new information technologies on internal communication. Left to fulfill their traditional role, senior managers may find themselves increasingly frustrated by the irrelevance and powerlessness of their position. Consequently, unless there is a radical realignment of their role, this group can become the silent subverters of change; and their invisible yet persistent resistance can derail even the most carefully planned transformation program.

Some companies, however, have succeeded in the crucial redesign of the senior management role. At these companies senior management now plays a key role in supporting frontline units by coordinating their activities and coaching their operating-level entrepreneurs. Ulf Gundemark, Don Jans's boss and the head of ABB's worldwide relays business area, played a central role in managing the tension inherent in ABB's ambition to be "global and local, big and small, radically decentralized with central reporting and control." Similarly, Paul Guehler, vice president of 3M's Safety and Security Systems Division, to which Andy Wong's unit belonged, challenged Wong to define the focus and priorities in his business while simultaneously helping him build the support and obtain the resources he needed. And at ISS, Waldemar Schmidt, head of the European region, supported Theo Buitendijk's new business initiative despite its short-term profit impact and led the effort to leverage the expertise Buitendijk's unit developed into a European business capability.

None of these managers saw themselves in traditional terms as strategic span breakers, administrative controllers, and information relays. Instead, this new generation of senior managers added value to frontline activity through three core tasks (refer to Table 4.1). First, they became a vital source of support and guidance for the frontline entrepreneurs. Second, they took primary responsibility for linking and leveraging the resources and competencies developed in the frontline units. And third, they played a key role in ensuring resolution of the numerous tensions and conflicts built into the management process.

SUPPORTING AND GUIDING. When a company decides to change its dominant management model from one driven by authority to one built on empowerment, the basic orientation of the senior manager's task is turned 180 degrees from direction and control to development and support. ABB not only reflected this change in its cultural norms, it institutionalized it in the way key senior-level jobs were structured. For example, although Ulf Gundemark was the relays business area head, he had a staff of only four to help him run the $250 million worldwide business. As a result, he routinely asked managers in operating units to take on broader responsibilities, stretching their abilities and developing their contacts and support as they did so. To develop the worldwide relays strategy, Gundemark assembled a nine-person team of managers drawn from the front lines of his operating companies; and to guide the ongoing business operations, he created a business area board that included his staff members and four key company presidents, including Don Jans. As Jans put it, "I'm a much broader manager today than I was at Westinghouse. . . . We feel we are rediscovering management."

Paul Guehler at 3M described his job as "to develop the people who can develop the business." He worked intensively with Wong and his team, challenging them to refine their plans; forcing them to commit them to paper; and, most important, encouraging them to communicate and defend the plans in multiple forums in order to build their struggling unit's thin support within 3M. And at ISS, Waldemar Schmidt stated that "the most important thing I can do is show an interest, to show that I care about them and their performance." He backed his words with actions, developing a strongly supportive relationship with his frontline managers and phoning them often to say "Well done" or "How can I help?"

LINKING AND LEVERAGING. The second of the common senior-level tasks we observed was focused more on organization development, as managers took on the job of linking the knowledge and expertise developed in their frontline units and embedding them as organizational capabilities to be leveraged companywide. Gundemark forced his frontline relays companies to rationalize and specialize what had been overlapping structures and responsibilities. He then appointed key specialists from the companies to councils mandated to identify and coordinate best practice in R&D, quality, purchasing, and other functional areas. Waldemar Schmidt achieved similar cross-unit linkages through regular meetings specifically devoted to leveraging the expertise of particular country units. When Theo Buitendijk's unit in Holland showed superior customer retention, for example, Schmidt gave Buitendijk a day at his next European presidents conference to discuss his approach.

MANAGING TENSIONS. Beyond these important developmental tasks, however, senior managers still must accept responsibility for the performance of their frontline units. Each of the three managers played a pivotal role in ensuring that those reporting to him kept operating priorities and strategic objectives in balance. ABB has a global matrix designed to legitimize rather than minimize the tensions and paradoxes inherent in most management decisions. To effect the conflict resolution vital to the organization's smooth operation, senior-level managers like Ulf Gundemark developed and managed communication channels and decision forums such as ABB's worldwide business board, its functional councils, and local steering committees that act as boards for frontline companies. These forums not only serve a development and integration role but become the place where differences are aired and resolutions obtained on the conflicting perspectives and interests created by the matrix.

In 3M, this critical conflict resolution role is so ingrained in the culture that senior-level managers like Paul Guehler have integrated it into their ongoing management approach. For example, in what he terms his "give-and-take management style," Guehler tightened the screws on Wong's team by requiring them to make the cuts necessary to meet their financial objectives, while behind the scenes he was defending against attempts to close the unit down and was lining up backing for Wong's proposed development initiatives.

Senior-level managers are often the forgotten and forsaken group in organizational transformations. Amid rounds of delayering, destaffing, and downsizing, many corporate executives have overlooked the fact that the success of small, empowered frontline units depends on an organization's ability to bring large-company benefits to those units. Organizations that dismantle vertical integration without simultaneously creating horizontal coordination quickly lose potential scale economies and, even more important, the benefits that come from the leveraging of the units' knowledge and capabilities companywide. At the same time, such intense horizontal flows can also paralyze the organization by distracting or overburdening frontline managers. It is the middle managers who can make "inventing the pyramid" operational, not only by developing and supporting the frontline entrepreneurs but by absorbing most of the demands of the cross-business, cross-functional, and cross-geographic integration. In this way they can prevent those at the operating level from becoming overwhelmed by the ambiguity, complexity, and potential conflicts that are often endemic in horizontally networked organizations.

The Top-Level Leadership Role

Those at the apex of many of today's large, complex organizations often find themselves playing out a role they have inherited from their corporate forebears: to be the formulators of strategy, the builders of structure, and the controllers of systems. As strategy, structure, and systems became increasingly sophisticated, there was a growing assumption that these three tools could allow organizations to drive purposefully toward clearly defined goals, largely unaffected by the occasional eccentricities and pathologies of individual employees' behavior. And indeed, to some extent, under the strategy/structure/systems doctrine, most large companies eventually became highly standardized and efficient, with individual employees being treated as inputs in predictable but depersonalized systems.

In entrepreneurial organizations, however, we have seen a rollback of this dehumanizing management paradigm and a rethinking of top management's role—from one grounded in the old strategy, structure, and systems to one focusing on purpose, process, and people. From being the formulators of corporate strategy, the individuals at the top of the most entrepreneurial companies in our study had evolved to become the shapers of a broader corporate purpose to which individual employees could feel commitment. Instead of focusing on formal structures that gave them control over the firm's financial resources, these leaders devoted much effort to building processes that added value by enabling the parts of the organization to work more effectively together. And rather than depending on management systems that isolated them from the organization and treated employees as factors of production, they created a challenging organizational context that let them get in touch with people and focus on affecting individual inputs rather than just monitoring collective outputs.

Let's consider the three key tasks inherent in this new kind of top leadership.

STRETCHING THE OPPORTUNITY HORIZON. First, those at the top had to stretch the opportunity horizon to create a work environment that fostered entrepreneurial initiative rather than compliant implementation. Poul Andreassen, like many of the CEOs we observed, was constantly questioning the past and challenging his organization to achieve more. To overcome ISS's constrained potential as a Danish office-cleaning business, Andreassen began to conceive of the company as a more broadly defined professional service organization. His explicit objective was "to make ISS and service as synonymous as Xerox and photocopying." This objective legitimized the entrepreneurial initiatives of operating-level managers such as Theo Buitendijk as he developed the abattoir-cleaning business in Holland, or the ISS manager in Germany who saw an opportunity to start a business removing building rubble in the former East Germany.

INSTITUTIONALIZING NORMS AND VALUES. The second key task of top management was to replace traditional control-based values with norms of collaboration and trust. Over the years, 3M's top executives have created an organization with such values, allowing resources and expertise to move freely across 3,900 profit centers in 47 divisions and 57 country operations. From the earliest days the 3M leaders developed clear integrating norms; for example, the rule that while products belong to the division, technologies belong to the company. In addition, they carefully developed a framework for collaboration; for example, the mutually supportive relationships within 3M's scientific community had been formed and reinforced through grassroots forums, internal technology fairs, cross-unit transfer practices, and many other elements that the company's leaders had built over the years. But overarching all of these policies and practices was a sense of trust based on the respect with which those at the top treated individuals and their ideas. Current CEO Livio "Desi" DeSimone reminds his managers that they must listen carefully to subordinates and continually ask, "What do you see that I am missing?" It was this environment of trust and respect that allowed entrepreneurs like Andy Wong to take risks and encouraged middle managers like Paul Guehler to back them.

CREATING A SENSE OF PURPOSE. A third vital role of leadership is that of providing a stabilizing and motivating sense of purpose. As ABB Executive Vice President Goran Lindahl explained, "In the end, managers are loyal not to a particular boss or even to a company, but to a set of values they believe in and find satisfying." ABB CEO Percy

Barnevik believed that he had to do more than just develop a clear strategy for his newly merged worldwide entity—he had to create an organizational environment that made people proud to belong to, and motivated to work for, the company. He articulated ABB's overarching mission not in terms of market share, competitive position, or profit objectives but in terms of sustainable economic growth and world development. He emphasized a sensitivity to environmental protection and a commitment to improving living standards worldwide; and he reflected those beliefs not only in ABB's formal mission statement but also in major strategic decisions. The company's pioneering investments in Eastern Europe, its transfer of technology to China and India, and its innovations in environmentally benign processes allowed ABB's employees to feel that they were helping to change the world for the better.

The approach taken by top executives in companies like 3M and ISS reflected the simple belief that an important part of their job was to capture the energy, commitment, and creativity of those within the institution by treating them as valued organizational members. In addition to managing strategy and structure, they took the time to define a corporate purpose and shape the integrating organizational processes. And rather than simply monitoring performance through abstract systems, they focused their attention on the people whose motivations and actions would drive performance.

In part, it was this new focus on the individual as a primary unit of analysis that led to the current fascination with identifying and developing management competencies. But interest was also spurred by the fact that at some redesigned companies, many managers were having serious difficulty adjusting to their changed roles. This finding raised questions about the individual competencies required to succeed in the new roles.

New Management Roles: New Personal Competencies

Over the past few years organizations as diverse as AT&T, British Airways, BP, Siemens, and the World Bank have invested enormous amounts of management time in efforts to profile their ideal future corporate leaders. Siemens, for example, has defined twenty-two desirable management characteristics, categorizing them under five basic competencies of understanding, drive, trust, social competence, and what they call a "sixth sense." The World Bank's ideal profile identifies twenty attributes and groups them into seven quite different categories: intellectual leadership, team leadership, staff development, work program management, communication, interpersonal impact, and client orientation. Pepsico's desired profile has eighteen key dimensions defining how individuals see the world, how they think, and the way they act.

Not surprisingly, this emerging interest in individual competencies has created a cottage industry among consultants. Yet despite consultants' prodigious efforts in designing questionnaires, conducting interviews, and running seminars to define leadership competencies, few of the profiles devised have won the kind of credibility necessary for widespread adoption and application. Furthermore, there is rarely any clarity about what is meant by management competencies, so the profiles generated often inventory personality traits, individual beliefs, acquired skills, and other personal attributes and behaviors on the basis of unclear selection criteria and with little logical linkage. One problem is that these profiles are often based on surveys of current managers or on analysis of the most successful performers in the organization's existing context. Therefore, they risk defining future leadership needs in terms of the capabilities required in old organizational forms.

But in our view, the most important problem with these management competency exercises is that they almost always delineate a single ideal profile. This extension of the old Russian doll model has limited usefulness in the emerging delayered organization built on a differentiated set of management roles and tasks.

As part of our research into posttransformation organizations, we studied managers who were succeeding in adding value in very different ways at each level of the organization. Our observations led us to develop a model that classifies into three categories the broadly defined competencies for roles and tasks at each level (Table 4.2). In the first category we listed deeply embedded characteristics such as attitudes and traits. In the second, we included attributes like knowledge, experience, and understanding that generally could be developed through training and career planning. In the third, we pinpointed acquired skills and abilities directly linked to the job's task requirements and built on the individual's personal characteristics as applied to his or her developed knowledge.

This model enabled us to develop some hypotheses about different management competencies and how they enter into important human resources decisions. In the following sections we will outline those hypotheses and elaborate on their implications.

Selecting for Embedded Traits

The high rate of failure among managers attempting to adapt new kinds of tasks in transformed organizations underscores the importance of redefining selection criteria. In ABB, for example, despite careful selection of those appointed to 300 top and senior management positions when the merged company was created in 1988, more than 40 percent of that group were no longer with the company six years later.

Most of the radically reengineered companies we observed tended to select individuals primarily on the basis of their accumulated knowledge and job experience. These were, after all, the most visible and stable qualifications in an otherwise tumultuous situation. Furthermore, a company could select on this basis by default, simply by requiring existing managers to take on totally redefined job responsibilities. In such situations, however, past experience did not prove to be a good predictor of future success. The most obvious problem was that much of the acquired knowledge and experience was likely to reflect old management models and behavioral norms. Equally problematic were the personal characteristics of those who had succeeded in the old business environment. As many companies discovered, highly task-oriented senior managers who were both comfortable and successful in the well-structured traditional work environment often had great personal difficulty in taking on the coaching and integrating roles that became an important part of their redefined responsibilities.

As a result, many companies have come to believe that it is much more difficult to convince an authoritarian industry expert to adopt a more people-sensitive style than to develop industry expertise in a strong people manager. This belief is leading companies to conclude that intrinsic personal characteristics should take precedence over acquired experience as key selection criteria. And equally importantly, companies are recognizing that because management roles and tasks differ widely at levels of the organization, so too will the attitudes,

Table 4.2
Management Competencies for New Roles

Role/Task	Embedded Attitude/Traits	Developed Knowledge/Experience	Acquired Skills/Abilities
OPERATING-LEVEL ENTREPRENEURS	RESULTS-ORIENTED COMPETITOR	DETAILED OPERATING KNOWLEDGE	FOCUSES ENERGY ON OPPORTUNITIES
Creating and pursuing opportunities	Energetic, intuitive	Knowledge of the business's technical, competitive, and customer characteristics	Ability to recognize potential and make commitments
Attracting and developing resources and competencies	Persuasive, engaging	Knowledge of internal and external resources	Ability to motivate and drive people
Managing continuous performance improvement	Competitive, persistent	Detailed understanding of the business operations	Ability to sustain organizational energy around demanding objectives
SENIOR MANAGEMENT DEVELOPERS	PEOPLE-ORIENTED INTEGRATOR	BROAD ORGANIZATIONAL EXPERIENCE	DEVELOPS PEOPLE AND RELATIONSHIPS
Developing individuals and supporting their activities	Supportive, patient	Knowledge of people as individuals and understanding how to influence them	Ability to delegate, develop, empower
Linking dispersed knowledge, skills, and practices	Integrative, flexible	Understanding of the interpersonal dynamics among diverse groups	Ability to develop relationships and build teams
Managing the tension between short-term performance and long-term objectives	Perceptive, demanding	Understanding the means–ends relationships linking short-term priorities and long-term goals	Ability to reconcile differences while maintaining tension

TOP-LEVEL LEADERS	INSTITUTION-MINDED VISIONARY	UNDERSTANDING OF COMPANY IN ITS CONTEXT	BALANCES ALIGNMENT AND CHALLENGE
Challenging embedded assumptions while stretching opportunity horizons and performance standards	Challenging, stretching	Grounded understanding of the company and its business and operations	Ability to create an exciting, demanding work environment
Institutionalizing norms and values to support cooperation and trust	Open-minded, fair	Understanding of the organization as a system of structures, processes, and cultures	Ability to inspire confidence and belief in the institution and its management
Creating an overarching sense of corporate purpose and ambition	Insightful, inspiring	Broad knowledge of different companies, industries, and societies	Ability to combine conceptual insight with motivational challenges

traits, and values of those most likely to succeed in each position. Recruitment and succession planning thus becomes a sophisticated exercise of identifying the kinds of individuals who can succeed as operating-level entrepreneurs, senior management developers, and top-level leaders.

ISS, for example, had long recognized the vital importance of recruiting individuals who were results-oriented competitors to run their frontline operating units. Although a country manager's job at ISS could be regarded as a low-status position (managing frontline supervisors in the mature and menial office cleaning business), ISS knew that by giving country managers status and autonomy, they could attract the kind of energetic, intuitive, and creative individuals they wanted. Status elements like the "managing director" title and the prestigious company car signaled the importance ISS attached to this position, but entrepreneurial individuals like Theo Buitendijk were even more attracted by the independence of operating their own business behind what ISS called "Chinese walls" to prevent unwanted interference. After seeking out motivated self-starters, ISS had little difficulty in training them in industry knowledge and helping them develop the specific job skills they required to succeed.

The personal profile required at the divisional level of management in ISS was quite different, however. Few of the operating-level entrepreneurs were expected—or indeed had an ambition—to move up to this level; but one who did was Waldemar Schmidt. Schmidt turned around the company's Brazilian business, then was appointed head of the European division. Despite his lack of knowledge of the European market or of experience in that part of the organization, Schmidt impressed Poul Andreassen as a people-oriented integrator who had a genuine interest in developing and supporting others. Indeed, the company's employee training program had originated in Brazil as part of Schmidt's commitment to continual upgrading of his people. Furthermore, Schmidt was recognized as being a very balanced individual who tended to operate more by influence than by authority yet was demanding of himself and others. Andreassen regarded these qualities as vital and felt they far outweighed Schmidt's limited European knowledge or experience.

At the top level of the organization, another set of personal qualities is important. When Poul Andreassen became the president of ISS in 1962, he too was selected primarily on the basis of his personal attributes rather than on the basis of experience or proven leadership skills. Then a young engineer in his mid-thirties, he was frustrated in his job with a traditional large company and was looking for the opportunity to build a very different kind of organization. Andreassen's most appealing characteristic was his willingness to question and challenge everything; and even after thirty years in the job, he still felt that his best days were when he could go into the field, confront his division or business unit mangers, and help "stir up new things."

Only a few individuals will have the breadth of personal traits and the temperamental range to adapt to the very different roles and tasks demanded of them at different organizational levels. At ISS, Waldemar Schmidt progressed from successful operating-level entrepreneur to effective senior management developer; and after Poul Andreassen's retirement, Schmidt was asked to succeed him as top-level corporate leader. One of management's most important challenges is to identify the characteristics that will allow an individual to succeed in a new and often quite different role—and, equally important, to recognize when someone who is successful at one level lacks the personal traits to succeed at the next. For those with the perceived potential, however, the next key challenge is to develop the knowledge and experience that can support and leverage their embedded traits.

Training for Knowledge Acquisition

While training and development activities are rarely very effective in changing deeply embedded personal traits, attitudes, or values, they are extremely appropriate means of fostering the kinds of knowledge and experience that allow an individual to build on and apply those embedded attributes. As a person who is naturally energetic, engaging, and competitive learns more about a particular business and its customers and technologies, for example, he or she becomes a much more effective and focused operating-level entrepreneur. Poul Andreassen understood this well and made training and development one of the few functions that he controlled directly from ISS's small corporate office. Under the corporate philosophy of ensuring that all employees had the opportunity to use their abilities to the fullest, ISS's Five Star development program consisted of five levels of training designed to give frontline supervisors with the appropriate profiles the knowledge and experience they would need in a broader management job.

Because of its strong promote-from-within culture, 3M also had a long-standing commitment to develop its people to their fullest potential. After a new employee joins 3M (within six months for a clerical employee or within three years for a laboratory scientist), management initiates a formal Early Career Assessment process to ensure that the individual is a proper fit with the company. This process includes a program to prepare people for their next career opportunity. For example, a promising accounting clerk might be set the personal education goal of becoming a Certified Public Accountant within three years while being given internal experience in preparing financial statements and participating in audits. This development process continues, albeit in a somewhat less structured format, throughout an individual's career at 3M.

The company provides internal business courses and technical seminars and supports participation in external education programs, but on-the-job training is still the primary emphasis. For example, Andy Wong, the young engineer who turned the struggling Optical Systems project from a loss generator facing shutdown into a showcase of entrepreneurial success, was carefully prepared for a leadership role over five years. This quiet engineer first caught the eye of Ron Mitsch, a senior R&D executive who was impressed by the young man's tenacious, self-motivated competitiveness—personal qualities that 3M looked for in its frontline entrepreneurs. Wanting to give Wong the opportunity to prove his potential, Mitsch told him about an opportunity to lead a small technical development team in the OS unit. Wong began to expand his knowledge about the unit's optical technologies as he struggled to develop the understanding he needed to focus his team's rather fragmented efforts. After a couple of years in the OS laboratory, Wong was asked to take on the additional responsibility for the unit's inefficient manufacturing operations. Although he had no prior production or logistics experience, he managed to rationalize the complex sourcing arrangements, simplify the manufacturing process, and consolidate production in a single plant—effecting a 50 percent cost reduction and a simultaneous improvement in product quality. These experiences broadened Wong's knowledge of the business and expanded his familiarity with the organization's resources. Through careful career development, in other words, he developed the kind of knowledge and experience he needed to allow him to use his naturally competitive traits as the newly appointed project team leader for optical systems.

While the developmental path for operating-level entrepreneurs focuses on enhancing knowledge and expertise in a particular business, market, or function, the track to the senior level of management usually requires a much richer understanding of the organization and how it operates. Wong's boss, Paul Guehler, also began his 3M career in the R&D laboratory and was also identified as someone who looked beyond the technologies he was developing to the businesses they represented. This budding entrepreneurial attitude led to Guehler's transfer to 3M's New Business Ventures Division, where the company leveraged his natural curiosity and intuitiveness by giving him the task of exploring market opportunities and business applications for high-potential ideas and innovations. After a decade in this division, Guehler was transferred to the Occupational Health and Safety Products Division; here his experience as R&D manager gave him the opportunity to broaden his understanding of mainstream organizational processes and how to manage them. A subsequent move to the Disposable Products Division helped him build on that experience, particularly when he was appointed business director for disposable products in Europe. This responsibility for a highly competitive product in a fast-changing market greatly expanded his experience in assessing the capabilities and limitations of diverse individuals and organizational units and further expanded his understanding of organizational dynamics and strategic tensions. By the time Guehler was appointed general manager and later vice president of the Safety and Security Systems Division of which Wong's Optical Systems unit was a part, he brought not only hardheaded business knowledge but some sensitive organizational insights to his new role. His diagnosis of the OS unit's situation:

> You have to have people in these positions who recognize other people's talents and support their ideals for building a business. My job is to create an environment where people come forward with ideas and are supported to succeed. . . . So while the OS group probably thought I was being too tough, my objective was to get them to recognize their opportunities, to hold them accountable for their actions, to help them build their credibility, and ultimately to support them so they could succeed. . . . One of my most impor-

tant roles is not only to develop business but to develop the people who can develop the business.

At the top level of 3M management, the need for breadth of knowledge and experience was even greater. In 1991, when the company was planning the transition to a new chief executive, board member and ex-CEO Lou Lehr said that the successful candidate was likely to be a career 3M executive five to ten years from retirement, for no other reason than that it usually took thirty to thirty-five years to accumulate the breadth of experience to be effective in the top job in this diversified company.

Desi DeSimone, elected as CEO in 1991, was described in one news account as "a textbook example of the quintessential 3M CEO." Having moved up through technical, engineering, and manufacturing management positions to assume general management roles as managing director of the Brazilian subsidiary and eventually as area vice president of 3M's Latin American operations, he was recognized as a senior manager with top management potential. "There were always people taking an interest in my development," DeSimone recalled; and in classic 3M fashion, he was brought back to corporate headquarters to gain the background and knowledge he would need in top-level positions.

Through the 1980s, he was assigned to head up each of 3M's three business sectors in succession, experiences that broadened his knowledge of markets and technologies while simultaneously allowing him to apply that understanding as he refined his management skills. Having spent most of his career focused on the company's far-flung units in Canada, Australia, and Latin America, DeSimone also needed to get a better sense of the organization's core structures, processes, and culture. By immersing him in corporate-level activities for more than a decade, 3M's top management and the board's appraisal committee wanted to ensure that DeSimone had the requisite organizational understanding to set the behavioral context that was so central in supporting innovation and entrepreneurship. Finally, DeSimone's promotion to the board in 1986 was important not only in bringing his expertise to board-level decisions but in exposing him to the perspectives and experiences of top-level executives from other companies in different industries.

In companies like 3M, where strongly held organizational values and cultural norms are linchpins of competitive advantage, the importance of a career-long development process must not be underestimated. Sometimes, however, a manager's strong links to the company's existing policies and practices can become disadvantageous, particularly when embedded beliefs have deteriorated into reality-defying assumptions or outmoded conventional wisdom. In such cases, bringing in an outsider with the desired personal characteristics can break the pathological cycle of inwardly focused indoctrination. But such a move risks stranding the new leader without the knowledge he or she needs in order to develop the top management skills appropriate for the company. The risks are particularly high where knowledge and experience accumulated in prior work are of limited relevance in the new situation. For example, while Larry Bossidy was able to make a relatively smooth transition from his top management job at GE to the leadership of Allied (another traditionally structured diversified industrial goods company), John Sculley's move from Pepsico to Apple was more problematic because of his lack of computer industry background and his inexperience in managing the more informal network culture of Silicone Valley. Such problems underscore the important linkage between personal traits, acquired knowledge, and the development of the skills and abilities a manager needs to perform a job effectively. In the next section we focus on this final component of the management competencies profile.

Coaching for Skills Mastery

Of all the elements in the competencies profile, the particular skills and abilities an individual possesses (refer to Table 4.2) are probably the best indicators of job success because these are the personal capabilities most directly linked to a position's key roles and tasks. Yet it is difficult to identify those who will succeed in developing these abilities, and even harder to promote such development in individuals. The reason is that most of these skills rely heavily on tacit knowledge and capabilities that often grow out of the interaction between an individual's embedded traits and accumulated experience. So, for example, the critical entrepreneurial ability to recognize potential in people and situations is not an easily trainable skill but one that often develops naturally in individuals who are curious and intuitive by nature and who have developed a richly textured understanding of their particular business and organizational environment.

Thus, while some broader skills can be selected for and other simpler ones can be trained for, most of the critical skills are largely self-developed through on-the-job experience as individuals apply their natural talents and accumulated experience to the particular challenges of the job. In this process, the most effective role management can play is to coach and support those they have selected by providing resources, reinforcement, and guidance.

Goran Lindahl, the ABB executive vice president, clearly articulated the notion that an individual's natural characteristics should be the dominant factor in selection ("I will always pick a person with tenacity over one with just experience," he said); he also spent a substantial amount of his time planning developmental job experiences for the individuals he selected. But he saw his principal and most difficult management role as acting as a teacher and a coach to help people leverage their experiences and fulfill their natural potential. This executive's commitment "to help engineers become managers, and managers grow into leaders" was vital to many managers' development of the skills required for their demanding new roles.

Don Jans was surprised when he was asked to continue to head the relays company that ABB took over as part of the acquired Westinghouse power transmission and distribution business. "The prevailing view was that we had lost the war [and] that the occupying troops would just move in," Jans said. Yet Lindahl and Ulf Gundemark, his worldwide relays business manager, saw that Jans was a very capable individual with long industry experience; and they felt that proper coaching could channel his natural energy, persistence, and competitiveness toward the new skills he would need to manage in a very different way within ABB.

Jans met their expectations and was able to develop a whole range of new abilities that not only helped him turn around his relays company but, on a personal level, made him feel as if he had "rediscovered management." For example, by redefining Jans's company as part of an interdependent global network, ABB's senior management refocused his attention on export markets, thereby helping him reignite his latent ability to identify and exploit opportunities. Through their own highly motivating and inspiring management approach, Barnevik, Lindahl, Gundemark, and others encouraged Jans to tap into his own engaging personality and develop a more motivating approach to drive his people to higher levels of performance. And ABB's cultural norm of high interest and involvement in the operations (what Lindahl called the "fingers in the pie" approach) led Jans to expand on his natural results-oriented competitiveness and develop a skill for creating and sustaining energy around the demanding objectives he set for his organization.

Meanwhile, Lindahl was helping support a very different set of skills in the few operating-level entrepreneurs who had been selected to take on senior-level business or regional responsibilities. One such individual was Ulf Gundemark, the young manager running the Swedish relays company. Lindahl had promoted Gundemark to worldwide relays manager because in addition to having had twelve years' experience in various parts of the organization, Gundemark demonstrated vital personality characteristics; Lindahl described him as "generous, flexible, and statesmanlike." Driven by his boss's urging to become a "giver" rather than a "receiver" of management resources, and constrained by his organizationally designed lack of division-level staff, Gundemark leveraged his naturally supportive disposition into a sophisticated ability to develop his operating-level managers by delegating responsibilities and empowering them to make decisions. Lindahl also encouraged Gundemark to establish formal and informal management forums at all levels of his organization, and by applying his flexibility and his integrative approach to his growing understanding of organizational dynamics, the younger manager gradually became skilled at handling interpersonal relationships and team behavior. Finally, largely by following the example of his boss, Gundemark developed the vital senior management skill of maintaining the pressure for both long- and short-term objectives while helping the organization to deal with the inevitable tensions between them.

At ABB's top levels of management, an even more subtle and sophisticated set of skills and abilities was necessary. More than just driving the company's ongoing operations or developing its resources and capabilities, these individuals had to be able to lead the company to become what Lindahl described as "a self-driven, self-renewing organization." The most fundamental skill was one that CEO Percy Barnevik had encouraged in all members of his top team—the ability to create an exciting and demanding work environment. Harnessing his own innate restlessness, Lindahl focused his naturally striving and questioning personal style on his broad knowledge of the company and its businesses to develop a finely honed ability to challenge managers' assumptions while stretching them to reach for new objectives. At his bimonthly business meetings, Lindahl led his senior managers through scenario exercises that forced them to think beyond straight-line projections and consider how they could respond to new trade barriers, political realignments, or environmental legislation. He also recognized that it was top management's role to develop the organization's values and that one of the most vital values was mutual cooperation and trust. By consistently applying his own natural forthright and open personal approach to a sophisticated understanding of the organization and its processes, he was able to create a belief in the institution and in the fairness of its management processes that undergirded both entrepreneurial risk taking and shared organizational learning. Finally, Lindahl's sharp mind and inspiring personal manner, supported by a broad exposure to ABB's operating context, helped him provide his managers with conceptual insight about the business as well as with concrete motivational challenges. Examples were his far-sighted views about ABB's role in a realigned global economy, and his translation of those insights into challenges to his management to find ways to radically rebalance ABB's own value chain from the developed world to emerging giants such as China, India, and Eastern Europe.

The reason this set of top management skills is so difficult to develop is that it both reflects and reinforces the conflicts, dilemmas, and paradoxes inherent in the posttransformational organization. Unlike the classic top management tasks of managing "alignment" and ensuring "fit," the competencies we have described involve questioning, challenging, and even defying traditional assumptions and embedded practices. Beyond building on the tension between the operating-level ability to drive performance and the senior management skill of conceptualizing long-range goals, top management must be able to maintain a balance between challenging entrenched beliefs and creating a unifying sense of purpose and ambition. Not surprisingly, only a handful of people have the potential to develop these skills. It is perhaps the most critical task of top management to identify these rare individuals and provide them with the necessary development opportunities and the coaching support to allow them to fulfill that potential.

From Organization Man to Individualized Corporation

In earlier decades, when capital was the scarce resource, top management's primary role was to use its control over investments to determine strategy, and to create the structures and systems to shape employees' behavior in ways that would support those capital allocation decisions. This strategy/structure/systems doctrine of management led to the development of the blindly conforming employee that William Whyte termed the "organization man."

As the industrial era evolves into the Information Age, however, knowledge is becoming the scarce resource. The organization's vital knowledge, expertise, and strategic information exist at the operating levels, rather than at the top as scarce capital did. And companies are now recognizing that in this knowledge-based environment, diversity of employee perspectives, experience, and capabilities can be an important asset. This realization is driving a fundamental reconceptualization of management philosophy. The overall objective now is to capture and leverage the knowledge and expertise that each organizational member brings to the company. We describe the new model as the "individualized corporation"—the corporation that capitalizes on the idiosyncrasies and even the eccentricities of exceptional people by recognizing and making the most of their unique capabilities.

This change in organizational philosophy has important implications for management practice. Because the "individualized corporation" has exposed the myth of the generic manager, and the Russian doll model that supported it, organizations must change the multitude of personal practices aimed at recruiting, developing, and promoting people on the basis of a single corporate model. Equally important, employees must understand that their career paths may not lead inexorably up the hierarchy but more likely will take them where they best fit and therefore where they can add the most value for the organization.

[5]

Does It Matter Who Is the Boss?

The Substance and Symbolism of Top Leadership

Jeffrey A. Sonnenfeld

THE WRITINGS in this part of *Navigating Change* are reminders that in this enlightened age of empowered self-directed work teams, the actions of significant individuals still make a difference. Society and the organizations within it are generally changed by the deeds of courageous individuals, and these individuals tend to take on larger-than-life proportions. At the same time, the qualities that help accomplished people to achieve great things can also cause them to stumble. As we close Part I of this volume on top leadership, what can we say about the topic of leadership?

Leadership Prescriptions As the Scout Oath

There are no lack of guidelines on leadership, and yet we hear continued despair over the availability of competent leaders to govern many of our great institutions. In his one hundredth year of life, the late comedian George Burns complained that "It's too bad all the people who know how to run the government right are too busy driving taxis and cutting hair." Leadership scholar and public servant John Gardner has suggested that our childlike and shallow desires for parental figures set us up for endless disappointment (Gardner, 1990).

Many thoughtful writers have offered lists of leadership attributes.

For example, Gardner has offered eight: (1) physical vitality, (2) intelligence, (3) willingness to accept responsibility, (4) task competence, (5) understanding of constituents, (6) skill in dealing with people, (7) need to achieve, and (8) capacity to motivate. A recent book, *How to Think Like a CEO: The 22 Vital Traits You Need to Be the Person at the Top* (Benton, 1996), extends this list to other sensible-sounding truisms, such as "admit mistakes, be gutsy, be humorous, be theatrical, be nice, be acquisitive, be flexible." To many the bible is *The Seven Habits of Highly Effective People* (Covey, 1995). The mere listing of attributes, however, can make the acquisition of the recommended Boy Scout–like qualities appear deceptively simple. As a great management psychologist cautioned long ago, "Such self-perceptions can come to nothing if the individual's talents are negligible" (Zaleznik, 1977, p. 133).

Critiques of best-selling leadership books now often appear in the popular press. A *New York Times* review of popular leadership books titled "Succeed Like Jesus and Attila the Hun" makes the point about what characterizes much leadership writing:

> Struggling to stay atop the highly competitive global marketplace, American business people are turning to some unexpected sources for inspiration: Winnie-the-Pooh, Attila the Hun, and the Little Engine That Could.
>
> Two decades ago, top business books carried weighty titles. . . . now *Business Week*'s best seller list is crammed with M.B.A. Lite like *Make It So: Leadership Lessons from Star Trek, the Next Generation* (Pocket Books) and *Jesus CEO: Using Ancient Wisdom for Visionary Leadership* (Hyperion).
>
> Taking their cue from the multimillion-selling *One-Minute Manager*, books like *Winnie-the-Pooh on Management* (Dutton) and *Leadership Secrets of Attila the Hun* (Warner Books) offer simple solutions for complicated times, promising to transform mere mortals into Masters of the Universe painlessly.
>
> These breezy business books all offer the message that attitude, not information, is the key to success, that expert knowledge earned through serious study is less important than common sense. Cheerleaders rather than economists are the pundits of this new field. Dozens of titles by sports heroes Bill Parcells, Don Shula and Pat Riley peddle muscular motivation while scores of other works tell executives how to become world-beaters by tapping their higher

selves. While millions of people are turning to these books to get ahead, what are they learning?

Plunk down $22 for the *Star Trek* book and be advised, "Deliberation is not delay, but consideration of options" and "To be effective, an officer must have unclouded vision about what is ahead."

Spend $16.95 for *Jesus CEO* and see how He used "focus to turn 12 regular guys into a top-notch team. He could have done literally anything. Yet, he did not build a temple or a synagogue. He did not write or distribute books. He did not even heal all the sick people in the world. He did not go down to the graveyard and raise everyone from the dead. He did not build malls. His mission was specific. Jesus stuck to his mission." (Zane, 1995)

The point of this review is that these books are not earth-shatteringly original. In fact, they are adept repackagings of the oft-repeated aphorisms of age-old self-help literature.

Corporate Heroes or Empty Suits?

The difficulty of saying something original about leadership is heightened further when we try to find something to say about chief executives as leaders. Much of the popular literature and some of the academic literature can be grouped into the historic genre of the "great man" or hero view of leadership. Thus, according to Ralph Waldo Emerson, "An institution is the lengthened show of one man" (Emerson, 1841).

By contrast, economists such as Joseph Schumpeter (1942), John Kenneth Galbraith (1986), and former U.S. Secretary of Labor Robert Reich (1985) argue that strong-willed, colorful, hands-on captains of industry are really faceless oligarchs who administer corporate bureaucracies. Skepticism is also in vogue in management research in the schools of thought known as "population ecology" (e.g., Aldrich, 1979) and "resource dependence" (Pfeffer and Salancik, 1977). According to these theories, firms change over time, but not as the result of heroic management initiative; firms' strategies are seen as consequences of randomly distributed assets or largely as responses to external forces that affect access to supplies, changes in markets, and legal regulation.

Folklorists have always seen heroism as a confluence of societal and personal illusions. The societal illusion is that individuals can provide simplifying road maps to circumvent the barriers that block attainment of collective goals. Heroic leaders, in this vein, are the product of social needs and serve only as long as they satisfy that need. Thomas Jefferson remarked, "When a man assumes a public trust, he should consider himself a public property." The personal illusion is our image of heroes as individuals endowed with near superhuman qualities. We see heroic leaders as people who have arisen from humble origins to achieve greatness, shaping not only their own careers but also those of their constituents.

While scholars continue to debate whether society creates the great leader or whether the great leader stamps his or her visions on society, heroism remains an illusion. Outcomes ranging from societal triumphs to corporate villainy to mere managerial incompetence can be credited to visionary master strategists—or to corrupt and inept top leaders. At the same time, genuine corporate accomplishments can be achieved only by those leaders whose authority is granted to them by constituents.

The Integrated Change Agenda and the Life Cycle of CEOs

The first chapter, "The CEO in the Context of Discontinuous Change" by David Nadler and Jeffrey Heilpern, addresses this interaction between corporate leaders and their constituents. The authors highlight such converging external forces as global competition, new technology and information systems, and public policy in the form of government deregulation and privatization as the drivers of an era of frequent large-scale change. Nadler and Heilpern date the advent of this new era to the mid-1980s. Elsewhere, Dartmouth University scholar Richard D'Aveni has described this new corporate context as one of hypercompetition:

> ...a condition of rapidly escalating competition based on price–quality position, competition to create new knowhow and establish a first-mover advantage, and competition based on deep pockets and the creation of even deeper-pocketed alliances. In hypercompetition, the frequency, boldness, and aggressiveness of dynamic movement by the players accelerates to create a condition of constant disequilibrium and change. (D'Aveni, 1995, p. 46)

D'Aveni argues that the consequences of hypercompetition are reduced market stability, short product design cycles, shortened product life cycles, new technologies, sudden and frequent entry by unexpected outsiders, repositioning by incumbents, and radical redefinitions of market boundaries across industries.

Nadler and Heilpern convincingly argue that such sweeping forces require chief executives to develop an "integrated change agenda" rather than respond in a sequential way with isolated interventions. The core building blocks of this integrated change agenda include such features as purpose, values, strategies, governance, organization, operating environment, operational performance, and talent. While acknowledging that the participation of others beyond senior management is critical to the success of this agenda, Nadler and Heilpern lay the primary responsibility for initiating such institutional change at the foot of the CEO. They contend that the CEO possesses long-validated sources of powers, both formal and informal. Yet they point out that some CEOs have a feeling of powerlessness—which may have to do with CEOs' relationships with various key corporate stakeholders. Nadler and Heilpern divide the world of the CEO into value-chain constituencies with immediate impact upon the core business (the financial community, suppliers, customers); social constituencies with impact upon the societal legitimacy of the enterprise (government regulators, communities, society at large); and "hot-spot" constituencies toward which the CEO should target his or her primary energy in turbulent periods (the share owners and board; the senior management team; and the enterprise as a whole, embodied in its employees).

Nadler and Heilpern's hot-spot thesis contrasts with arguments made in books such as Richard Whiteley and Diane Hessan's *Customer Centered Growth* (1996). Whiteley and Hessan present the active sales roles of charismatic CEOs such as those of Southwest Airlines, USF&G, and Compaq Computer as models of corporate strength. Nadler and Heilpern, however, state that

> the CEO's personal involvement is not a truly essential component of customer transactions. . . . So if, during a period of major change, the CEO decides his/her time can better be spent elsewhere and makes fewer customer visits, it's unlikely that business will suffer.

Nadler and Heilpern name envisioning, energizing, and enabling as roles for effective CEOs. And indeed, Harvard's John Kotter suggests that these qualities are universal to all leaders (Kotter, 1990). Kotter's list of leadership qualities include setting direction, aligning people, and motivating people. In addition to such role requirements, Nadler and Heilpern suggest some stable dispositional traits that are helpful for CEOs to have, such as a particular "towering strength," emotional strength, the ability to convey genuineness, a sense of humor, a capacity for empathy, and a quality of connectedness.

My own research on CEO style, in which I studied the qualities of 400 prominent CEOs of major U.S. firms, revealed four leadership qualities as judged by the CEOs' own top management committees: personal dynamism, recognition and concern, moral integrity, and high expectations. But even these more static leadership qualities are valued quite differently at different times and in different industrial sectors (Agle and Sonnenfeld, 1994). People in the financial services industry, for example, valued moral integrity far more highly in the early 1990s after the exposure of so many financial institutions' ineptitude and corruption in the 1980s.

Turning from static leadership qualities to a more dynamic view of leadership, Nadler and Heilpern discuss the influential work of Donald Hambrick and Gregory Fukutomi of Columbia University on CEO life cycles (Hambrick and Fukutomi, 1991). With a very original synthesis of theory, Nadler and Heilpern suggest that diverse CEO responses to the change imperative—denial, avoidance, bowing out, or succession management—can often be predicted by the CEO's tenure in office. Such an approach sheds a great deal of light on the behaviors of the 150 departing CEOs I studied in *The Hero's Farewell* (1989). I classified departing CEOs either as "monarchs" and "generals" with uncompleted heroic missions or unfulfilled heroic stature needs, who fought changes that threatened their own vision of their legacy, or as "ambassadors" and "governors," who departed with a greater degree of openness to the challenging ideas of their successors.

A Model of CEO Responsiveness to the New Disequilibrium

The Nadler and Heilpern piece has important implications for a CEO's own self-awareness and alertness to personal danger signs, as well as for board governance. How best to meet the challenges of change is the question raised in Chapter 2 by James Houghton, himself a titanic

CEO who recently managed a very dignified "ambassadorial"-type exit from office at Corning Incorporated. Houghton's contribution demonstrates how the CEO defines just such an integrated change agenda as called for in Chapter 1.

Houghton describes the contemporary environment as two paradigm shifts. First, he cites globalization and speaks of the need to see the international contest for superior quality as a journey and not a single destination. Second, he cites the new importance of highly skilled labor. Houghton mentions that at Corning in 1972, "conceptual workers" represented one third of the work force, while two thirds worked with their hands; but by 1996 that ratio was completely reversed. He argues for greater attention to the needs of a more culturally diverse workforce and for employment incentives to attract talented conceptual workers. And he emphasizes the need of firms to "own up to their social obligations and responsibilities to workers," decrying the frequent links between announcements of major layoffs and rises in firms' stock prices.

Houghton's interpretation of major *fin de siècle* industrial changes as entailing obligations for the employer to address (through product quality, training and education, cultural diversity, and social responsibility) stands in stark contrast to the writings of many CEOs of the mid-1980s to the mid-1990s. For example, John Sculley, before being deposed as CEO of Apple Computer, outlined in *Odyssey* how we should approach the twenty-first century (Sculley, 1985). His thoughtful recommendations spoke extensively of the need to prepare for paradigmatic shifts in education and communications—but the onus was on society, not on the private employer, let alone the omniscient CEO. A dramatic example of CEO indifference to "social obligations" is on view in *Mean Business* (1996) by Al Dunlap, former CEO of Scott Paper and now CEO of Sunbeam. Dunlap laid off one third of the workforce and 70 percent of senior management, or 11,000 workers, in one fell swoop in an effort to save Scott Paper—and the eventual sale of the leaner Scott to Kimberly-Clark netted him more than $100 million in compensation for little more than a year in office. Scott's shareholders, too, saw a 225 percent stock price rise. Dunlap attacks the notion of responsibility to stakeholders as an affront to the primacy of a CEO's responsibility to the shareowners, whose own capital is at risk in the business. He has contempt for CEOs who seem to be wasting leadership time and attention on community distractions.

The concept of corporate social responsibility has led to a great deal of debate about a "new social contract." Surveys indicate that Americans clearly want more than the cold "invisible hand" of capitalism; 95 percent of those responding to a recent Harris poll rejected the view that a corporation's only role is to make money. Yet Americans are also leery of regulatory intervention (Hammonds, 1996). Perceptions of injustice are only heightened by the juxtaposition of data such as the Dunlap story, which earned him the moniker "Chainsaw Al," with statistics about stagnating earnings among workers. In fact, during the first five years of the 1990s, hourly wage earners' salaries rose 16 percent, while corporate profits increased 75 percent and CEO salaries were up 96 percent (Byrne, 1996).

Jamie Houghton's model of leadership is a powerful example of how CEOs can lead corporations to do good while also doing well. Houghton has been one who not only espouses values but puts them into action. He has championed arts education and has led business roundtable and federal government efforts on various educational and workforce diversity fronts. For such efforts he won the Lincoln Award for Ethics and Excellence in Business and the Lyndon Baines Johnson Award for Distinguished Service in Building Successful Public/Private Partnerships. Yet none of these efforts distracted Houghton from his corporate roles; they actually enhanced his effectiveness. Upon becoming chief executive in 1983, Houghton defined a strategy of creating a "new balance of corporate perspective and entrepreneurial initiative." Houghton and his senior team focused the company on four discrete business segments and began to energize the culture, emphasizing higher-growth businesses such as telecommunications products (e.g., optical fibers), picture tubes, and medical testing while divesting from slower-growth businesses such as lightbulbs. Thus, despite starting his tenure as CEO in the midst of a recession, Houghton helped revive the company's performance.

Houghton's call for social responsibility, however, may not be one that is echoed by many other CEOs. Al Dunlap is far from alone. My own research suggests that while 84 percent of corporate CEOs nationwide spend at least two hours a week on recreation (48 percent spend more than six hours a week on recreation), only 32 percent spend more than two hours a week participating in civic organizations, and only 4 percent spend two hours or more in political groups (Sonnenfeld, 1996). To be sure, there are some local exceptions; in cities such as

Minneapolis and Atlanta, CEOs are expected to demonstrate a higher level of civic involvement.

Looking Deeper into the Source of the Character of Leaders

Regional variations alone, however, hardly explain the different orientations of CEOs such as Al Dunlap and Jamie Houghton. After leaving the once Philadelphia-based Scott Paper for Florida-based Sunbeam, Dunlap announced plans to sell off or consolidate thirty-nine of Sunbeam's fifty-three facilities and fire 50 percent of its 12,000 employees. And Dunlap's prior leadership roles with Sir James Goldsmith and American Can had also demonstrated his predilection for tough turnaround actions. A psychological perspective might raise the possibility that this leader is the proverbial hammer in search of nails to pound. Dunlap, a son of a Hoboken, New Jersey, boilermaker, may have had less security than Houghton, who comes from patrician New England lineage and was a fifth-generation steward of his Corning, New York, institution. Houghton succeeded his brother Amory, who in turn became a U.S. congressman. Certainly, early life roles matter to the more psychologically oriented leadership scholars, such as Manfred F. R. Kets de Vries. Thus in Chapter 3, Kets de Vries moves from the externally inspired changes highlighted in the two prior pieces to more intrapsychically motivated behavior.

Critical building blocks in Kets de Vries's thesis are not global corporate discontinuities or paradigm shifts but the unfolding of psychic dramas due to determined internal scripts and unconscious wishes and fantasies. This author maintains that intrapsychic and interpersonal processes help determine how all of us, including top leaders, act and make decisions. Kets de Vries expands the classical meaning of *narcissism* beyond customary (derogatory) usage in order to refer to the lingering effects of a stage of psychosocial development. He defines excessive narcissism as a compensatory strategy, a reaction to early disappointments in relationships that leads to the grandiosity, excessive need for praise, paranoia, and so forth of some CEOs.

Kets de Vries also analyzes the dysfunctional "neurotic organization," in which others start to share the delusions of a narcissistic leader. Ultimately, a pathological interaction can begin to take root; at the center is a top executive whose narcissistic style is strongly mirrored in the inappropriate strategies, structures, and organizational culture of his or her firm. Kets de Vries classifies five types of neurotic organizations: dramatic, suspicious, detached, depressive, and compulsive. And he lists several examples of dysfunctional leadership, including Harold Geneen of ITT and Kenneth Olson of Digital Equipment.

Happily, after offering these models, Kets de Vries suggests that such extreme cases are rare. A CEO's capacities for self-reflection and empathy (as described in Chapters 1 and 2) provide some of the remedy here. Kets de Vries then goes on to portray executives whose narcissistic tendencies have taken positive, constructive forms: Richard Branson of Virgin, Jack Welch of General Electric, and Percy Barnevik of Asea Brown Boveri (ABB). Kets de Vries explains that these CEOs have externalized their "inner theater" in effective ways as builders, transformers, and integrators. With vastly different industry, cultural, and corporate situations, and raised in families of varied financial strata, all three of these leaders grew up feeling supported and inspired. Their early childhood experiences fostered in each of them a certain confidence and self-reliance, which in turn helped them deal with power and authority in constructive ways. All three of these leaders have created organizations featuring decentralized structures, delegation, and unification of information systems; and all three minimize bureaucracy. Branson does not have a head office, working out of houseboats and townhouses. Barnevik, too, has an aversion to large head offices, holding the corporate office of the huge ABB to a mere 150 people. Welch's legendary "workout" programs at GE are an example of the many ways he wanted GE's factories not to be chiefly producing internal paper flows. All three CEOs work to build climates for innovation where both commitment and fun are valued. As cultural guardians guided by energizing visions, they foster both trust and contrarian thinking.

In my own work on leadership pathologies, I have found that the self-awareness discussed by Kets de Vries and in the earlier Nadler and Heilpern piece is essential. In fact, it is related to six major ways leaders fail: lacking in self-assessment; not knowing when your mission is failing you; being seduced and abandoned by technology; failing to leave the shop behind; flunking management education; and believing your own press clips (Sonnenfeld, 1997).

The CEO As an Interchangeable Part

Having now moved into the black box of personal character, we should not be surprised to find how transnationally consistent the leadership qualities described by Kets de Vries are. In a recent review of 150 cross-cultural leadership studies from the last two decades, Bernard M. Bass corroborates the universality of James McGregor Burns's (1978) classic paradigm of transactional versus transformational leadership—though Bass points out that cultural contingencies do matter in the way behaviors are manifest (Bass, 1997). This generalizability of top management expertise is the topic of Christopher A. Bartlett and Sumantra Ghoshal's essay, Chapter 4. Bartlett and Ghoshal looked at widely and internationally varied organizations, including AT&T, Komatsu, ABB, Corning, 3M, Royal Dutch Shell, ISS, and Kao and found some surprisingly similar posttransformational leadership and organizational models. All the posttransformational enterprises Bartlett and Ghoshal studied were building from the bottom up on a foundation of small, nimble frontline operating units. In addition, these businesses had instituted cross-unit integrative processes to cut across any vertically oriented relationships that had prevailed before. A shared characteristic was a strong philosophical commitment to genuine empowerment throughout these decentralized organizations.

Bartlett and Ghoshal break out different levels of leadership as their conceptual building blocks; their research suggests that leadership roles vary more by organizational level than by nationality or corporate history. In a sense their model builds upon the three classic levels of subsystems laid out by sociologist Talcott Parsons: (1) the technical interface, which defines the organization's distinctive productive competence; (2) the administrative subsystem, which provides managerial support and coordination; and (3) the institutional interface, which negotiates and maintains the license from society to continue to operate (Parsons, 1960). Bartlett and Ghoshal expand upon these levels and describe concrete leadership tasks in the posttransformational organization, richly illustrating each task with real-life examples. They refer to the first level as the operating-level entrepreneurial role, in which managers pursue business growth opportunities, develop resources, and ensure continuous improvement. At the next level, senior-level managers act as supportive coaches, providing coordination and linkage. Top-level executives are Bartlett and Ghoshal's third tier. These direct their efforts toward providing institutional purpose, norms, and challenges. For each level, Bartlett and Ghoshal go to great lengths to define role-specific management competencies and to debunk the idea that such a thing as a generic "organization man" exists.

Does it matter, then, who is the boss? Clearly, the first four chapters of this book demonstrate that leaders do matter—and testify convincingly to superior forms of leadership in high office. Can the same individual move comfortably across the roles, across the nationalities, and across industries? My own research suggests that one shoe does not always fit all industries (Agle and Sonnenfeld, 1994). While distinct leadership dimensions of CEOs did emerge, the relative priorities of these dimensions varied by industry. The inescapability of the Peter Principle also raises the nagging question of competence ceilings—or, as Bartlett and Ghoshal might put it, the fact that some people are better suited dispositionally to certain work situations than they are to others.

Intel's highly successful CEO Andrew Grove, in *Only the Paranoid Survive* (1996), refers to critical "points of inflection" that a leader must catch. He defines points of inflection as moments when virtually all the fundamentals of a business are about to change. These turning points can occur because of technology changes or competitive changes. They can lead to disaster or to triumph. They exist in all industries. And they require a march through unfamiliar territory, where the CEO and his or her associates have no adequate mental maps. The key to success, Grove states, is the integration of the strategic with the emotional parts of the leader's job. In leadership the substantive and symbolic are inextricably intertwined—as the contributions of the scholars in Part I of this volume have abundantly demonstrated.

References

Agle, Bradley, and Sonnenfeld, Jeffrey. "Defining Charismatic Leadership Style: A Study of US CEOs and Their Impact." *Proceedings of the Academy of Management*. 54th Annual Meeting, Dallas, August 1994.

Aldrich, Howard E. *Organizations and Environments*. Engelwood Cliffs, NJ: Prentice-Hall, 1979.

Bass, Bernard M. "Does the Transactional–Transformational Leadership Paradigm Transcend Organizational and National Boundaries?" *American Psychologist* 52.22 (February 1997): 130–139.

Benton, D. A. *How to Think Like a CEO: The 22 Vital Traits You Need to Be the Person at the Top*. New York: Warner, 1996.

Burns, J. M. *Leadership.* New York: Harper, 1978.

Byrne, John A. "New CEO pay figures make top brass look positively piggy." *Business Week,* March 18, 1996, p. 32.

Covey, Stephen R. *The Seven Habits of Highly Effective People.* New York: Simon & Schuster, 1995.

D'Aveni, Richard A. "Coping with hypercompetition: Utilizing the new 7S's framework." *Academy of Management Executive* 9.3 (1995), 45–60.

Dunlap, Albert J. *Mean Business.* New York: Times Business, 1996.

Emerson, Ralph Waldo. "Self-Reliance." *Essays: First Series.* Boston: James Munroe, 1981, pp. 35–73.

Gardner, John W. *On Leadership.* New York: Free Press, 1990.

Galbraith, John Kenneth. "The Last Tycoon." *The New York Review of Books,* Aug. 14, 1986, p. 3.

Grove, Andrew. *Only the Paranoid Survive: How to Exploit the Crisis Points that Challenge Every Company and Career.* New York: Bantam Doubleday Dell, 1996.

Hambrick, D. C., and Fukutomi, G. D. "The seasons of a CEO's tenure." *Academy of Management Review* 16 (1991): 719–742.

Hammonds, Keith H. "O.K., job security is dead. What happens from here?" *Business Week,* March 11, 1996, p. 60.

Kotter, John P. *A Force for Change: How Leadership Differs from Management.* New York: Free Press, 1990.

Parsons, T. *Structure and Process in Modern Societies.* New York: Free Press, 1960.

Pfeffer, Jeffrey, and Salancik, Gerald. *The External Control of Organizations.* New York: Harper & Row, 1977.

Reich, Robert B. "The Executive's New Clothes." *The New Republic,* May 13, 1985, p. 27.

Schumpeter, Joseph E. *Capitalism, Socialism, and Democracy.* New York: Harper & Brothers, 1942.

Sculley, John. *Odyssey: Pepsi to Apple . . . The Journey of a Marketing Impresario.* New York: Harper & Row, 1985.

Sonnenfeld, Jeffrey. "How Leaders Fail." *Leader to Leader* 3 (Winter 1997), 34–38.

Sonnenfeld, Jeffrey. "Making a Difference: For some corporations, there's a new company line: Doing a good job means more than making a buck." *Atlanta Journal–Constitution,* September 22, 1996.

Sonnenfeld, Jeffrey. *The Hero's Farewell: What Happens When CEOs Retire.* New York: Oxford University Press, 1989.

Whitely, Richard, and Hessan, Diane. *Customer Centered Growth: Five Proven Strategies for Building Competitive Advantage.* New York: Free Press, 1996.

Zaleznik, Abraham. "Managers and Leaders: Are They Different?" *Harvard Business Review* (1997): 126–135.

Zane, Peder J. "Succeed Like Jesus and Attila the Hun." *New York Times,* December 3, 1995, section 4, p. 2.

[11]

Top Management Teams

[6]

Lessons in Teamwork

Paul A. Allaire

I AM BIASED TOWARD TEAMWORK at all levels of the business enterprise. Teamwork is also very much part of my personal orientation, probably because I grew up in a family of six children on a farm. Teamwork was a critical element of both our personal and our economic survival. And at Xerox Corporation, teams are very much a part of the culture. In fact we began calling ourselves "Team Xerox" even before we embarked on our Total Quality Management (TQM) strategy in the early 1980s, and that strategy then reinforced the importance of teamwork.

We implemented our "Leadership Through Quality" program after realizing we might not survive the onslaught of Japanese competition. One of the critical elements of our initiative was to teach more than 100,000 Xerox people how to work effectively in teams, including how to do effective team-based problem solving. Every team in Xerox, starting with the CEO's executive team (of which I was a member at the time), went through the training. Looking back, it's sometimes difficult to recall why something as simple as teamwork wasn't a more obvious part of the strategy for turning the company around.

Over time, we found that teams could be a very valuable management tool. While our original effort was to build operating teams, such as field service representatives or manufacturing teams, we began to realize the value of management teams: Leadership, too, could be enhanced by teamwork. Effective teamwork harnesses creativity and unleashes brain power; it leads to better solutions, better decisions, and improved business results through more effective implementation.

113

But translating the team ethos to the very top level of manage-ment is more frustrating, more difficult, and more complex than at any other level. I have the scars to prove it. If one learns through mis-takes, then I have learned a great deal about teamwork. What I will do here is start by describing the centrality of teamwork at Xerox. Then I'll turn to teamwork at the CEO level—the top management team. I'll conclude with some lessons from experience on what works and what doesn't work.

Teamwork at Xerox

Today teamwork is not only taught but celebrated at Xerox. It has become a highly emphasized concept and practice. Indeed, teamwork has made the ideal of continuous improvement a reality, even as we accept the fact that there is always room for even more improvement.

So far, we've had great success with teams that make use of qual-ity improvement methodologies and tools. Since the mid-1980s we have created literally thousands of quality improvement teams (QITs), which have attacked both problems and quality improvement opportunities throughout the corporation. During the past few years, we've worked to build on our experience with QITs to encourage self-managing and empowered teams to run parts of the operations. We help to develop these teams and qualify them to be designated as what we call "X-Teams." We've built teamwork and self-management into our operating methodology. Teams are used at all levels of the corporation on all types of issues. A good example is a team known as Xerox 2005, made up of selected senior managers, which spent ap-proximately one year analyzing business trends as we sought to un-derstand the nature of our business and where it might be going over the next decade. A few years ago we used a team approach to chart the strategic direction of the corporation. We use teams to design our or-ganization architecture and organization structure. We use teams to design, develop, and improve business processes.

Teamwork is so much a part of our culture that each year we take a day to formally celebrate it. Teamwork Day is the largest gathering of Xerox people each year, with some 5,000 employees attending in person and thousands more watching on television. Some 3,000 cus-tomers and suppliers also join in the celebration.

To be clear, we don't advocate that all work should or must be done in teams. There are many situations where individual performance, individual action, and individual accountability are required. However, we find more and more situations where we gain tremendous benefit by bringing together people who combine their talents, experience, energy, and creativity to work on a common task.

Teamwork and the CEO

Most people would agree that a team is a set of individuals who react with each other, who have a sense of themselves as a unit, who are accountable for their output, and who perform interdependent activities. This definition is quickly illustrated if we look at the difference between a golf foursome and a football team. The golfers are not a team. They do not interact with one another except socially. Their objectives are individual. How one golfer plays has no impact on the play of the others. The football team, on the other hand, is entirely different. Each player has a specific role to play within the team. The players as a group have a shared objective of scoring more points than the other team. And how one person plays affects all the other team members.

I think this analogy has important implications for the CEO's team. If they are golfers—each with his or her own operation to run and with no shared problems or objectives—they in fact are not a team at all. So when we think of teamwork at the CEO level I believe it's important that we stress that:

- Team members work together for the good of the *total* corporation. This means that the team as a whole owns the performance of the corporation as a whole; the team is not just a gathering of individuals, each owning the performance of his or her particular group, operating unit, or function.

- Members of the team are willing and able to make and implement decisions that trade off their individual objectives for the greater good of the total organization.

- Personal relationships among team members are based on trust and cooperation and a realization that the team doesn't win unless all the players come together to beat the competition.

- Team members recognize that their behavior sets a climate for the entire organization. The entire organization watches and takes its cues from the senior team. If top executives can't work effectively as a team, how can we expect others to do so?

The objectives for teamwork at the CEO level should be clear: optimizing corporate results; freely sharing information so that decisions are made with all the available facts on the table; taking full advantage of all the creativity and knowledge of team members; learning from one another; and building trust, which in turn leads to more and better teamwork.

I'm sold on teamwork, but that doesn't mean that everyone is. Clearly, not everyone embraces the teamwork concept, and we all know or know of autocratic CEOs. In the most exaggerated form of this style, the CEO manages by dictate and fear—"My way or the highway." Such CEOs use conflict, competition, and stress to motivate and challenge their subordinates and, in fact, the entire organization.

Another alternative to the team approach is to manage by division. Both the work and the organization are clearly divided. There is no team, no conflict. Everyone does his or her own thing under strict control of the CEO.

Several companies in the defense industry, for example, typify management by division. Not long ago I made a call on a defense customer to talk about Total Quality Management. I was amazed to learn that our meeting was the first time all of this CEO's direct reports had ever been in the same room together. (This extreme degree of division may, of course, be unique to the defense industry; it's an industry in which people tend to work on their own government contracts and may actually be forbidden to share information.)

While the dictate and division approaches may be effective in some industries and in some circumstances, they are not typically suited to the demands of the global marketplace or to the workforce of the twenty-first century. I believe no one in this fast-paced world has enough information and intelligence to manage a large organization in an autocratic manner. In order to succeed you need the brain power of the entire management team.

Some environmental factors should be considered when senior leadership is deciding whether or not to adopt a team approach.

Among them are the CEO's personality and management style. If you have an autocratic leader, you shouldn't pretend otherwise. But there are also factors that have to do with personal style and relationships. If a CEO has created an environment where people feel that they cannot speak up, where people are hesitant to share their perspectives and true feelings with the CEO or with their peers, or where there is low trust, then teamwork is probably doomed to fail.

Corporate cultures and history also come into play. A company, for example, may have had succession fights that destroyed any semblance of teamwork—particularly fights among combatants in senior management. Senior people who have joined from another company—and another culture—can also have an adverse impact on teamwork.

The mission and markets of the business can also be negative factors. The team concept is much less necessary in a conglomerate than in a highly integrated business, for example. There has to be real work that the team can do and that the team needs to do. Teamwork at the top leadership level makes sense when the people on the executive team (and the organizations they lead and represent) have some real and compelling strategic or operational interdependence. When people run very independent and unrelated units, getting them together may be nice; but this is not really a situation where teamwork will lead to significant payoffs.

Finally, the organizational architecture of the company must also foster teamwork. Here I'm referring both to the hardware (the actual organization) and to the software (the business processes, behaviors, and cultural attributes) of the business.

Lessons from Experience

As I have mentioned, I personally have done a lot of work involving the building and managing of teams at the executive level. We've tried numerous different approaches over time. Some of them worked exceedingly well, and some were significant failures. The good news is that I think we've learned some lessons about using teams at the most senior levels of a large enterprise. I want to share some of the key learnings from this experience.

Several things clearly didn't work. So let me share some negative outcomes in the hope that you don't have to repeat them.

- *Self-managed senior teams don't work.* Xerox had experimented with self-managed or autonomous teams in various parts of our company. We had had particular success in the field service area, with teams of people who provided service and preventive maintenance for our machines in customer premises. Based on these experiences, we wondered whether the same approach might work at very senior levels. We tried self-managed teams of very senior people, but found that senior teams need a leader, or at least an agreed-upon leadership process. In one case we formed a self-managed team consisting of sixteen senior people who ran major operations and who needed each other to succeed. You might think this would be an ideal team—but you would be wrong. We kept this group going over an extended period. Sometimes the team had no leader; at other times it appeared there were sixteen leaders; and eventually the team self-destructed.

- *Remotely located teams work less well than teams in physical proximity.* At certain points we had teams including people who were remotely located, in some cases at the other end of the North American continent. We found that it was difficult to build a true sense of team and to create effective teamwork under these conditions. A certain chemistry has to develop among the team members; and that chemistry is best nurtured by lots of informal sharing, drop-in visits, a quick bite to eat together—things that happen only with colocation. The point is that only a small amount of the teamwork actually occurs when everyone is in the room together. Much of the work of the team happens during normal interactions outside of the room. The casual encounter, the social connection, and the informal and unplanned interaction are as important as the formal team activities. Also, when a problem occurs, the ability to bring people together quickly is useful; but this is difficult when there is physical dispersion.

- *Laissez-faire or consensus leadership doesn't work.* Sometimes we mistake a lack of direction for teamwork. We found that a senior team does not work effectively without active leadership. This means that even when an explicit senior team structure and process have been put in place, the CEO must remain the strong leader. This was a big awakening for us. Senior teams still need someone who will step in, end debate, make a decision, and move on. Teamwork does not always equal consensus and democracy. In fact, at Xerox we have probably twisted the dictionary definition of *consensus*. To us it means that everyone gets the opportunity to be heard; that the leader makes the best decision he or she can with the available input; and that the team then accepts the decision, supports it, and implements it.

- *Ill-defined team objectives, processes, and rewards hamper performance.* Sometimes we erroneously believed that if we just got the right people in the room, they would be able to figure out the right work and the right work processes. This turned out not to be true. We learned to beware of poorly defined team objectives, processes, and rewards. Teamwork at the top should be directed at high-leverage, intractable problems, and there should be clear goals and big potential rewards for the entire team. One of the things Xerox has done is design the bonus system so that each individual is rewarded based on how their operation performs, but also on how the corporation performs. We do this by making the corporate matrix a multiplier of the individual matrix. For example, if an individual's operation performs at 120 percent of plan, but the corporation as a whole is at 80 percent of plan, the individual gets 96 percent of his or her bonus. But if both the individual and the corporation perform at 120 percent of plan, the bonus payout will be 144 percent—a big difference.

What are some of the enablers of smooth teamwork at the top? Six factors are vital.

- *Teamwork starts with the CEO.* Not only must the CEO believe in the power of teamwork; he or she must live it with credibility through discipline, consistency, clarity, and trust. It's very tough to be a team player if every day the CEO comes in with a different idea or a different approach; this vacillation causes confusion and is an impediment to working together. The creation of an executive team means that the CEO must be a team player also. While a leadership position provides additional degrees of freedom in action, it does not give the leader freedom to act in ways that would constitute unacceptable behavior in others. The CEO's own personal behavior needs to model the behavior that he/she is looking for in other team members. In addition, the CEO can send signals to members of the executive group about the seriousness of the requirement for teamwork. By rewarding and supporting those who work to the benefit of the team and sanctioning those who undermine the team, the CEO can underscore the seriousness of his/her intent.

- *Total Quality Management tools and processes can enhance teamwork.* We found that the TQM process is a good road map to follow, because it requires management by fact and includes common language, tools, and approaches to issues and capitalizes on interactive people skills. All of these are critical to building teamwork at the top. There are different ways to build discipline, consistency, and a common language within an executive team. We found that having all had the experience of quality training and the use of quality tools, we were able to build effective teamwork much more quickly. It also became evident how important these tools and processes were when new people who did not share our common processes and language joined the team. They found that they had to learn this approach or risk not being able to work effectively within the team.

- *Roles, responsibilities, and expectations must be clarified.* We found that one of the root causes of some problems of senior teams was that people had unclear or conflicting views about the role of the team. They also had widely varying opinions as to what was expected of them and their peers as members of the team. We found that we became more effective when we clarified the role of the team and defined what we called the "value-added work" of the team. We could then figure out what items, problems, or decisions needed to come to us and which ones would not be a good use of our time. Additionally, we clarified what we expected from each member of the team. We identified generic expectations—how every team member was expected to behave—as well as specific expectations of individual team members based on their position, role in the company, or role in the team.

- *An effective governance process must be in place.* The executive team is basically one feature of the governance process of the corporation. This process outlines what responsibilities lie where, and which decisions will be made by specific individuals or teams. If that process is not clear or not effective, then the executive team cannot be effective. When a good, shared, and well-communicated governance process is in place, then everyone understands "how the place is run," what the boundaries are, how decisions are made, and who is responsible for implementation. Under these conditions, effective teamwork is possible.

- *Outside counsel and assistance helps.* The CEO can't run the executive team alone. You need smart, objective, candid, insightful counsel from outside the corporation. The reason is that you, as the CEO, are part of the process; often you can't see the impact that you are having personally on the individuals who work for you and on the team. Given the nature of the CEO role, people may also be hesitant to tell you if your behavior is what's causing a problem for the team. We've also used outside consultants because of their expertise in group process and group dynamics; and they've helped us by assisting us in designing our team processes, by doing real-time facilitation of important work sessions, by conducting periodic team assessments, and by providing feedback and counsel directly to me.

- *Teams need to be explicitly launched and then maintained over time.* Teams, particularly at the CEO level, are complex mechanisms— even, in some ways, complex organisms. You therefore need an effective and rigorous process to get the team started, to define the value-added work, to build the appropriate work processes, to help people define their roles, and to clarify the behavior team members expect of one another. This launch process, by the way, is one of the places where outside help is particularly valuable. At the same time, once a team is built, it is not necessarily a self-correcting perpetual-motion machine. Even the most effective teams need continuing maintenance. Our tradition of "plan, do, check, and act," coming from our quality heritage, pushes us to assess regularly how we're doing and to build, where possible, in-process measures of team performance. We do this in a variety of ways. At least once a year, we spend time in an off-site meeting evaluating how we're doing. We use different survey tools, including 360-degree surveys of individuals, peer ratings within the team, and interviews and/or surveys on team effectiveness. We identify what we're doing well and what we're doing less well, and we then target areas for improvement. I should add that part of this assessment also involves feedback to me, as the team leader, about areas where I might want to change my behavior.

Those are my insights on teams at the senior executive level. I should also point out that there is no free lunch. No matter how deep your commitment, teamwork does have some negative aspects. Teams are time-consuming. You utilize more of the time and energy of top management than if you just dictate a solution or a direction. You also run the risk that a tendency toward groupthink may develop.

I cannot overstate the importance of the CEO's practicing what he or she preaches—of the CEO's walking the talk, as we say at Xerox. We've had thousands of employee problem-solving and quality improvement teams formed by factory workers, managers, sales and services representatives, secretaries, senior staff engineers, administrators, and computer personnel. Continuous improvement means a continuous team approach to solving problems and staying on the right course. Team members need to know how valuable their contribution is. That's why at Xerox we not only teach teamwork, we celebrate it.

[7]

Corporate Coherence and the Top Management Team

Donald C. Hambrick

Today's corporations are under extraordinary pressure, both from their marketplaces and from their investors, to be coherent—to have strategic and organizational unity. Organizations that are loose amalgamations of business units, collections of regional subsidiaries, or portfolios of unrelated activities are at a crippling disadvantage in an era requiring the creation and leveraging of core competences, the exercise of global clout, and the ability to engage periodically in fast, sweeping companywide changes.

Even though most CEOs now recognize the importance of strategic and organizational coherence, far fewer have carried this awareness over to how they design and orchestrate their senior executive groups. In fact, the widely used expression "top management team" is a misnomer for the groups that exist at the apex of many firms. Many such groups are simply constellations of executive talent: individuals who rarely come together (and then usually for perfunctory information exchange), who rarely collaborate, and who focus almost entirely on their own pieces of the enterprise. Senior executives sing the praises of teamwork at lower levels in the organization, espousing reengineering teams, quality teams, multifunctional product launch teams, and so on. But when it comes to their own endeavors, top man-

Syd Finkelstein, Jim Fredrickson, Beta Mannix, Phyllis Seigel, and Ruth Wageman made helpful suggestions on earlier versions of this paper.

agers often exhibit remarkable separateness of effort and parochial perspectives on the firm.

The problem of fragmentation at the top can be traced to a variety of factors, including, in some companies, CEOs who are intently resistant to top-level teamwork, fearing either that it amounts to an abdication of their leadership role or that it runs counter to their company culture of subunit accountability and initiative. What these executives do not understand is that an effective top management team greatly extends and leverages the capabilities of the CEO, rather than diluting or negating them. And a well-functioning top team is also an important complement to, not the antithesis of, business unit drive.[1]

The fragmented senior team has great difficulty creating and systematically exploiting core competences. It has difficulty achieving global strength. And perhaps most importantly, in the face of an environmental shift affecting the whole firm, the fragmented team is slow, acts in a piecemeal fashion, and is often maladaptive.

Corporate coherence, by its very nature, must emanate from the top of the firm. The senior executive group must think and act as a team. The CEO can promote this kind of teamwork through careful and creative attention to group composition; structure; incentives; processes; and, of course, his or her own mode of leading.

The Forces Propelling Corporate Coherence

The forty years following World War II saw the extraordinary ascendance of multibusiness firms and the burgeoning of an attendant wisdom about how such firms should be managed. For more than a generation of senior executives, certain organizational arrangements served as a model: the carving out of discrete strategic business units, each assigned distinct roles (e.g., cash cow, star) within the corporate portfolio; managers pigeonholed to fit the businesses; and a concise set of numbers for monitoring those managers. Even when a firm wasn't a pure conglomerate or holding company, the prevailing philosophy was that the pieces of the firm were highly modular and could be dealt with independently of each other.

Today, however, the achievement of corporate coherence—an integrated logic and basis for action within a company—is an imperative for senior leaders. Companies must now form a concerted whole as they confront competitors who are striving to do the same thing. This widespread quest for coherence is not just a new managerial fad. Rather, there are several fundamental, interconnected forces that give rise to this critical need.

First, companies are under great pressure to create and exploit a limited set of core competences across the full scope of their endeavors. Companies have refocused and now, more than at any time in the past thirty years, have highly related businesses with substantial potential for technology sharing, bundled offerings, umbrella branding, and so on. The word "synergy" may still evoke skepticism in some quarters, but it is precisely the opportunity for synergy that is propelling the refocusing of so many firms. And companies that are able to exploit synergies—such as Intel, Microsoft, CPC International, Xerox, and ARAMARK—achieve remarkable advantages in their cost structures, technology applications, and market power.

Second, the refocusing of companies means that environmental shifts are now likely to have wholesale, across-the-board importance for a company, not just isolated effects on a subset of its businesses. For example, when GTE Corporation was widely diversified, awareness of trends in telecommunications technology was essential for some parts of the company, but only incidental for other parts. Attention to such matters could be compartmentalized. Now that GTE is *only* in telecommunications, developments in this sphere affect the whole company. Today, all of GTE's businesses and executives are directly affected by a greatly overlapping set of forces; and consequently they must be able to think, anticipate, and act concertedly on these important matters.

Third, companies are being pressured toward greater coherence because of the global interdependence of their activities. The worldwide dissemination of information, lowered trade barriers, favorable transportation economics, and a host of other factors are allowing, even requiring, companies to develop highly integrated worldwide strategies. Such global thinking is an obvious must for companies like Honda and Intel; but even packaged goods companies such as Nestlé, CPC International, and Gillette have greatly increased their level of worldwide coordination. Independent regional and local subsidiaries are largely things of the past.

Fourth, and related to the first three reasons for enhanced corporate coherence, companies increasingly meet their competitors in multiple product markets. "Multipoint competition" has become widespread, as many of the world's leading firms strive to exploit their competences across a related set of businesses on a worldwide basis. IBM meets Hitachi on many fronts; CPC meets Nestlé on many fronts; and Pfizer meets Bristol-Myers Squibb over and over again. Such companies must be able to think and act concertedly against their adversaries across numerous arenas.

Fifth, and traceable to all the above, more and more companies are required periodically to transform themselves in their entirety. Shortened product and technology cycles, blurred industry boundaries and heightened competitive intensity, shifting geopolitical and economic conditions, and a continuing flux in employer–employee relations are all among the factors that cause companies to have to re-invent themselves time after time.[2] Piecemeal, isolated changes are no longer sufficient. Accordingly, companies like IBM, Xerox, and Alcoa have undergone major across-the-board changes in the last few years. Even companies that are exceedingly diversified and whose businesses would seem to warrant widely differing paces and directions of change—companies like GE, Corning, Philips, and ABB—have undergone systemic corporatewide changes based upon the vision and energy of their top executives. In these cases the changes have occurred primarily through the adoption, dissemination, and reinforcement of a core set of distinctive values and practices that all parts of the company are expected to follow—intangible factors but, as those who have participated can testify, massive changes nonetheless.

In sum, the forces propelling the need for corporate coherence are multiple, compelling, and unlikely to go away. Companies that achieve unity of perspective and action will prevail. And obviously corporate coherence can occur only when there is coherence among the firm's senior executives.

What Does "Teamwork at the Top" Mean?

Top executives are eager to talk about the importance of teams and teamwork for their subordinates. But when it comes to their own activities, the seniormost managers of many companies exhibit little in the way of true team behavior. A comment by the CEO of a large financial services firm illustrates this gap: "I know teams work. But I still am not convinced it is worth the time and effort to push further in the direction of making our Executive Office into a team."[3] This company—not known for superb performance prior to or since the CEO said that—has fallen into the trap of many firms. Its top executives act as hard-charging individuals, pushing on their own accelerators and often steering in their own directions. Coordination is limited to bilateral exchanges between the CEO and individual executives or between individual staff and line executives. Real collaboration is almost nonexistent. And concerted companywide change is essentially impossible.

But in an era requiring corporate coherence, companies must be able to orchestrate their activities at the highest levels, not just at more operational levels. They must be able to promptly identify and diagnose the need for periodic firmwide changes and be able to execute those changes. Companies can do these things only if their top executive groups have team properties, particularly what I call *behavioral integration.*

The Key: Behavioral Integration

I wish the term were not so cumbersome, but "behavioral integration" is the most apt label for describing the quality so urgently needed in the upper echelons of firms today. Behavioral integration is the degree to which the senior management group engages in mutual and collective interaction. It has three major elements: (1) the quantity and quality (richness, accuracy, timeliness) of information exchange among executives; (2) collaborative behavior; and (3) joint decision making. That is, a behaviorally integrated top management group shares information, shares resources, and shares decisions.[4]

Having a top management group with these properties does not mean management by committee. It does not rule out having a strong CEO, although it does rule out having a CEO who serves as the broker or mediator in all senior executive interchanges or who attempts to formulate firmwide changes singlehandedly. Also, behavioral integration doesn't rule out entrepreneurship by business units, although it does rule out disjointed initiatives or those that are at cross-purposes to the bigger picture. In fact, because many executives seem so skeptical about teamwork at the top, it is useful to specify several things that behavioral integration is not.

It is not like-mindedness. Top executives should have differing experiences and perspectives. Behavioral integration capitalizes on those differences by providing forums and processes of exchange, debate, and ferment.

Behavioral integration is not interpersonal appeal or friendship. Although outright antipathy among executives is almost always harmful, chumminess is exceedingly rare at the senior executive level and is not a necessary ingredient for behavioral integration.[5]

Behavioral integration is not endless meetings. Some amount of face-to-face contact is absolutely necessary for behavioral integration, but extreme amounts are not. Physically convening is not as important as what Karl Weick and Karlene Roberts (1993), in describing the remarkable orchestration of flight-deck crews on aircraft carriers, referred to as "heedful interrelating": thinking incessantly about the implications of one's behaviors for the broader group and enterprise.

Finally, it is not executives trying to run each other's businesses. With behavioral integration, executives collaborate where there are potential points of intersection (which, as I've argued, exist increasingly in firms); they share helpful information and resources; and they deliberate and act collectively on firmwide challenges.

A few years ago Peter Drucker (1992) wrote an insightful article about teams. Drawing parallels to sports, he said, in essence, that "there are teams and then there are *teams*." At one extreme is baseball, he argued, in which the players play *on* the team but don't have much call to play *as* a team; there is extraordinarily little collective behavior on a baseball diamond. In football, players have set positions but there is a great deal of concerted, coordinated activity among the players. At the other extreme is tennis doubles, in which each player has a primary rather than a fixed position, constantly adjusting and covering as needed for his or her teammate.

Most top management groups operate in the baseball mode. And for some companies, that is perhaps appropriate. If a company's businesses have very little in common and only negligible interdependencies exist among them, then the top executives can appropriately be considered a federation of managerial talent. Few things are more unproductive than forcing teamwork when there is nothing to team up for. But, as Wall Street and other financial centers increasingly ask in their own nonverbal but pointed way, "Then why the heck are these businesses all part of the same company? If they don't have much in common, what is the point of having a layer above them to second-guess them and slow them down?" In other words, the absence of a need for teamlike behavior at the top of the firm may be a telling indicator of more fundamental strategic weaknesses.

The increasing requirements for corporate coherence necessitate a shift at least to what Drucker would call the football mode and, in some cases, even to the tennis doubles mode. Behavioral integration is needed at the top of many companies today, and even more will be needed tomorrow.

Two Contrasting Top Management Teams . . . and Their Outcomes

As a way to illustrate the practical dimensions of behavioral integration, I will tell the stories of two widely differing top management teams I have observed in my field research. The top executives of Harsa Industrie AG, a (disguised) European-based medical products company, possessed very little behavioral integration, and the company's performance and adaptiveness were severely impaired as a result. The other group of executives, at a large United States–based media enterprise, MediaTech (again disguised), exhibited substantially more integration and, as a result, were able to make impressive companywide changes in the face of major environmental shifts. These examples will help to illustrate (1) how behavioral integration is gauged, (2) the performance implications of top team integration, and (3) the means CEOs have available to enhance the behavioral integration of their teams.

Harsa Industrie AG had grown rapidly through a series of acquisitions in its three principal groups—surgical, dental, and diagnostic products. These three business areas had much in common: many of the same raw materials, similar manufacturing processes for many products, overlapping distribution channels, numerous common competitors, and common regulatory environments. But the company had a strong culture of decentralization and autonomy; the group presidents (only somewhat jokingly referred to as "barons") had almost no occasion to pool their insights or endeavors, and there was no central staff expertise to aid in resource sharing or pooled support. When all three groups found themselves losing ground to Scandinavian, American, and Japanese producers, the three group presidents came up with separate diagnoses and action plans, even though the root causes for their problems all lay in deteriorating manufacturing capabilities relative to their competitors.

They *could* have pooled some of their purchasing, to great advantage; they *could* have collectively rationalized and modernized their production facilities, in a way that no one of the three groups could afford alone; they *could* have reached a concerted understanding of their common problems and put in place a visible, aggressive companywide campaign for improvement. Instead, they spent two years on piecemeal change efforts, and then the CEO halfheartedly installed a staff manufacturing guru. Corporate performance continued to drop. Ultimately several executives, including the CEO, were forced out.

In the midst of this saga, I had the opportunity to observe and analyze Harsa's top management group. Interviews, extended observation, and surveys made it clear that the group had very little behavioral integration. The survey data were particularly compelling and can be concisely described and portrayed. First, when I asked a series of questions designed to gauge the amount of behavioral integration in the overall group, the aggregate mean score across all executives and all survey items was 2.4 on a 5-point scale—well below the midpoint, and in the bottom quartile of the approximately twenty-five companies where the survey has been used.[6] In Figure 7.1, the short inward-pointing arrow signifies the low aggregate amount of behavioral integration at Harsa; conversely, the large size of the circle indicates the amorphous, detached nature of this management group.[7]

An additional set of survey items identified the amount of integration between every pair of executives in the group.[8] In Figure 7.1, the thickness of the line between each pair signifies their mean ratings of their interactions (rounded off, on a 5-point scale). At Harsa there were several moderate-strength ties between the CEO and the three staff executives (EVP/CFO, VP Administration, and VP/General Counsel); relatively weak links between the staff executives and the three group presidents; and almost no connections among the presidents, or barons, themselves.

The senior executive group at Harsa, not unlike those of many corporations, showed parochial perspectives, separateness of actions, and disjointedness—even though the units of the firm were being buffeted by common forces and had considerable potential for collective adaptation. This indeed is a case of senior group fragmentation as an impediment to corporate coherence. The problems that can result, summarized in Table 7.1, range from tactical losses (such as unrealized economies of scope and uncoordinated actions against

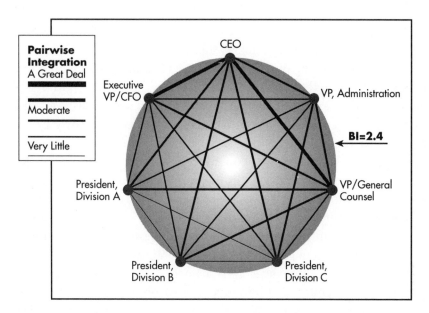

Figure 7.1 Harsa Industrie AG: A fragmented team low in behavioral integration. *On a scale of 1 (very low) to 5 (very high), the overall behavioral integration of this team falls at 2.4, as illustrated here.*

Table 7.1
The Costs of Top Management Team Fragmentation

TACTICAL LOSSES

- *Potential economies of scope* go unrealized.
- *Brands and market positions* are poorly coordinated.
- Business units engage in suboptimal behavior against *multipoint competitors*.
- Business units fail to exchange *key learnings and intelligence*.
- Employees at lower organizational levels become *cynical and skeptical about teamwork*.

STRATEGIC ADAPTATION LOSSES

- The company is slow at *comprehending and interpreting* major environmental shifts.
- The company has difficulty *formulating* companywide strategic changes in response to environmental shifts.
- The company is slow and disjointed in *implementing* agreed-upon strategic changes.
- In sum, company *performance and position deteriorate* substantially following a major environmental shift.

multipoint competitors) to more substantial, survival-threatening losses in adaptive capacity, such as those that devastated Harsa.

Fortunately, companies are not destined to have fragmented top teams, and MediaTech provides a more hopeful example. With businesses in educational publishing, business reference publishing, and industry newsletter publishing, MediaTech's CEO saw early in his tenure that there was great potential for pooled learning, resource sharing, and overall strategic coherence. Particularly because of the rapid growth of new media—on-line services, CD-ROMs, and the Internet—he concluded that the whole company faced a set of interrelated opportunities and threats. Thus, he strived to create a top management team that could capitalize on these pervasive trends, a team that possessed a great deal of behavioral integration.

Even while the three divisions remained under strong pressures for distinct accountability and initiative, the corporate top management team orchestrated, over a three-year period, a major companywide transformation whose goals were substantially greater product innovation, increased revenues from electronic-based distribution, international sales, and cooperative sourcing and production arrangements. As we all know, synergies in the information and media industries are commonly envisioned but rarely obtained. But the top executives of MediaTech made remarkable progress—across the board—in collectively seizing on major shifts in their environment.

This success was made possible in great part by the highly integrated management group at MediaTech. On the same type of survey described earlier, top executives rated their overall behavioral integration at 3.8—well above the midpoint on the 5-point scale and in the top quartile of all companies I have studied. This high degree of integration at MediaTech is diagrammed in Figure 7.2, along with further indication that the interrelationships between all the pairs of individual executives were consistently strong. Not only did the CEO interact extensively with all the executives, and the staff executives with the division presidents, but the division presidents themselves were strongly interconnected.

Importantly, both Harsa and MediaTech had the *potential* for corporate coherence, with highly related lines of business. Of the two, however, only MediaTech was able to achieve full coherence and the accompanying benefits of having multiple units all under the same corporate umbrella. And they did so through their senior team.

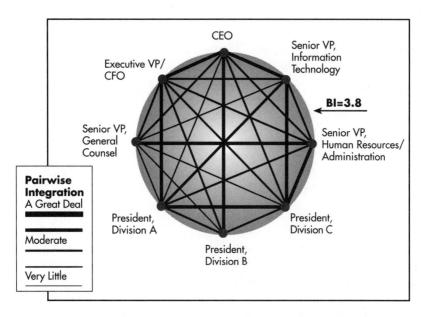

Figure 7.2 MediaTech: A coherent team high in behavioral integration. *On a scale of 1 (very low) to 5 (very high), the overall behavioral integration of this team falls at 3.8, as illustrated here.*

What Can Be Done?

The behavioral integration of a top management team does not just occur by happenstance. After studying numerous senior groups, we have come to understand some of this integration's chief ingredients. Summarized in Table 7.2, the underlying factors range from seemingly minor, but often overlooked, factors (such as giving the group a name) to much deeper and more subtle conditions (such as the degree to which the CEO conveys and reinforces mutual trust within the group).[9] The top groups of Harsa and MediaTech differed widely on almost all the factors that we know to shape a top team's level of integration.

At Harsa, the top executives met only three times a year, each time for a half day, primarily to exchange updates and to hear from the senior staff executives about new corporate administrative policies. The group did not have a name or explicit designation; and in fact the set of executives invited varied a bit from meeting to meeting, which further lessened any sense of group identity. The meetings involved mostly listening, taking notes, and asking clarifying questions. No particular preparation was needed or expected, unless one was making a presentation.

Table 7.2
Behavioral Integration of the Senior Team

TEAM IDENTITY

- Give the group a name and clear identity.

TEAMWORK

- Have the group do "real work" (fact-finding, analysis, and problem solving), not simply exchange updates and review the work of others.

- Convene the group at least several times a year, including at least one in-depth, off-site meeting.

- Establish constructive group norms, especially of openness, informality, and collegiality. Even mundane matters such as attendance, punctuality, and preparation are critically important.

TEAM COMPOSITION AND ROLES

- Give line executives additional responsibilities for companywide endeavors. These "overlay" assignments can be temporary (such as leading a key task force) or more continuous (overseeing a staff or support unit).

- Strive for gradual, staggered turnover within the group. Try to avoid the extremes of uniformly long tenures (which engender too much predictability and staleness) and wholesale turnover (which causes tumult and erratic relations).

- Selectively rotate executives, or at least appoint senior executives with multiunit experience in the company.

TEAM INCENTIVES

- Tie at least one third of every executive's target incentive compensation to overall company performance.

- Pay out at least one third of every executive's incentive reward in restricted stock grants or stock options.

THE CEO'S TEAM LEADERSHIP

- The CEO must personally convey and reinforce openness and constructive candor. There can be no hidden agendas, no off-line deals.

- The CEO must personally convey and reinforce mutual trust. Disagreement and minority views must not be penalized. Debate must stay on business issues, not drift to personal issues.

If an executive raised a question of substantive concern—particularly one that might lead to extended or heated discussion or that might otherwise derail the smooth flow of the meeting—the CEO was likely to propose that the two of them meet later to go over the issue. This CEO greatly preferred to operate through a series of private bilateral exchanges rather than to run the risk that the senior group would "get out of control."

Partly because the top executives at Harsa had all been in their current positions for more than six years, their interactions had become predictable, mechanical, and stale. Also, because they all had risen through the units they now headed, they had no affinity for or comprehension of other parts of the company. Financial incentives for group presidents were based almost entirely on the profits of their own units, reinforcing their parochialism. Small bonuses for the staff executives were determined subjectively by the CEO.

In short, numerous characteristics of Harsa's top group—including its composition, its processes, its incentives, and the CEO's behavior—clearly contributed to the group's entropy and the separateness of its members' perspectives. Given this fragmented leadership, Harsa was unable to mount extensive companywide change when it was needed, and performance deteriorated.

The top group at MediaTech, on the other hand, had many of the characteristics that enhance behavioral integration. Named the Strategy Council, the group met monthly; each year two of their meetings were off-site sessions dedicated to in-depth assessment of emerging issues facing the corporation. One of these off-site sessions, for example, provided the forum for initiating a new companywide thrust into electronic publishing.

Even though the group's meeting agendas sometimes included simple updates and information exchange, the team devoted the vast majority of their time together to analysis and discussion of companywide issues. In fact, it was quite common for the group to subdivide into task forces to explore major opportunities or threats. Most top executives were on one or two of these task forces at a time.

Discussions were typically lively and open. Even though pointed and controversial comments were often made, the meetings were consistently good-natured and constructive. The CEO was very adept at moderating and pacing the discussions, knowing when to wrap up and synthesize the points of view. He also had a talent for soothing the psyches of those executives whose views did not prevail.

The members of MediaTech's executive committee had varying tenures in their positions, ranging from one to eight years; therefore, as a social entity, they had not lapsed into a routine or mechanical pattern in dealing with each other. Several of the executives had served in units other than the ones they now headed, providing breadth of perspective and affiliation. Financial incentives were based on a combination of subunit performance and overall corporate performance, and a large part of the incentive payout was in the form of restricted stock grants, which reinforced a commitment to the entire enterprise.

In short, the senior group at MediaTech had many characteristics that allowed and encouraged members to move out of their parochial bounds, take a companywide perspective, and engage in collaborative behavior. This top team was behaviorally integrated—sharing information, sharing resources, and sharing decisions. And in the face of major environmental shifts, the company as a whole was exceedingly adaptive.

The Senior Team and the Implementation of Change

The highly integrated senior team is central not only to the process of diagnosing the firm's situation and formulating large-scale change but also to *implementing* change. In fact, senior leadership's attitudes and conduct always make the difference between successful and unsuccessful corporate transformation. The top executives obviously have a critical impact on implementation through the substantive actions they take in their respective parts of the firm (say, in setting new patterns of resource allocation and establishing new supporting functional programs). But they also have an essential, and often overlooked, role as the leading advocates for change.

As is well known, organizations are resistant to change. People do not like their vested interests, their influence, their assumptions, or their paradigms to be fooled with. CEOs often step up to this challenge by emphasizing the importance of communication in any change effort. However, they typically dwell on just that—mere communication. Efforts at "telling" employees what's happening, "informing" them of the company's new direction, and keeping people "posted" are directionally smart but woefully insufficient. The CEO who is trying to lead hundreds or thousands of employees to a new competitive readiness must not just communicate but sell—persistently, graphically, and sincerely.

In any large-scale organizational change, employees have four essential questions in their minds. Why do we have to change? Why is this the right change? Why do you think this organization can handle the change? What are you going to do to help me through the change?

Unceasingly conveying answers to these questions is a central leadership task in major change efforts. But the selling effort cannot succeed as a one-person endeavor. This is a job not just for the CEO but for the top team as a whole. Ironically and tragically, however, the greatest obstacles in the internal selling effort are often the CEO's own direct lieutenants—precisely the individuals who are supposed to be leading the change. If any of these key executives drag their feet or emit mixed signals to their subunits, the change effort is doomed.

There certainly is room for debate and disagreement among top executives while the firm's situation is being diagnosed and a new strategic course being set. Once that new direction has been established, however, everyone at the top must be on board. At one company, once a new direction had been endorsed at a meeting of the senior team, the president paused, looked around the room, and said, "Are we sure we're in agreement, then? OK. From here on, there can be no backsliding, backbiting, nail-biting, or nay-saying. We're in this together, and we must present a unified and energetic front to the rest of the organization."

But convincing all the members of the senior team about the need for change is just the basic ante. The CEO must enlist top management to sell others. Corporate transitions can succeed only if the top dozen or so executives all take to the hustings, committing themselves to convincing others of the wisdom and feasibility of the company's new direction.

A little-known aspect of Jack Welch's early days as CEO of GE provides an illustration. Once Welch had assembled a group of senior executives who agreed with several important new themes (such as "We will only be number 1 or number 2, or else we will sell it, fix it, or close it" and "We believe in openness and candor"), the entire senior management group was sent packing to visit all major GE operations around the world and persuasively and energetically spread the message. Each of these executives spent the better part of several months engaged in these visits. It was critically important, of course, that the newly adopted themes were also reinforced by substantive actions: resource allocations, rewards, staffing, and so on. But the role of the entire senior management team in mounting a unified campaign in support of the new direction was probably a key factor in the successful transition that GE experienced.

Since those early days, Welch has further increased his commitment to a team perspective at the top of GE. He created the Corporate Executive Council, which meets quarterly for two intense days to discuss the major issues facing GE. He has moved top executives across business units in order to broaden their perspective on the firm. And the amount of senior executive compensation tied to overall company performance has risen steadily.

Welch is not alone. One of Louis Gerstner's main agenda items at IBM has been to eliminate the attitude among senior executives that they are in charge of very separate fiefdoms. Eager to exploit the breadth of IBM's offerings, Gerstner decided to pursue corporate coherence. Among the tactics he has adopted to enhance the behavioral integration of his senior team are the creation of senior executive task forces, more substantive senior management forums, and incentives tied more closely to overall corporate performance. The same thrusts are under way at distinguished companies as far ranging as Boeing, CPC International, and Xerox.

These companies derive ongoing benefits (such as optimizing their actions against multipoint competitors) because of the high level of collaboration within their senior executive groups. But they derive another important advantage as well: When—not if—a major environmental shift occurs that has companywide implications, these firms will be in the best position to mount responses. Their top teams will be able collectively to comprehend and interpret the shift, formulate a strategic change, and implement it.

The behavioral integration of a senior team is a critically important organizational resource. Like all resources, it requires up-front investment and some time to develop. It cannot be produced on command. As we saw with Harsa AG, a senior group lacking in behavioral integration literally cannot get its act together. In contrast, as we have seen with MediaTech and an increasing array of other companies, the firm with a top team that thinks and acts like a team has vastly superior adaptive prospects.

Notes

1. We know from substantial prior research that differentiation of parts of an organization is *not* the opposite of integration of the parts. Both can occur, and the most challenging business conditions require just that. See Lawrence and Lorsch, 1967; Bartlett and Ghoshal, 1989.
2. Michael Tushman and his colleagues (see Tushman, Anderson, and O'Reilly, in this volume; Tushman and Romanelli, 1985) use the term "reorientation" to describe these wholesale organizational changes. Burgelman and Grove (1996) introduce the concept of the "strategic inflection point"—a major environmental or competitive development that necessitates large-scale transformation.
3. This quote was quoted in Katzenbach and Smith, 1993, p. 212.
4. See Hambrick (1994) for a more complete discussion of behavioral integration.
5. This is why I do not refer to "social integration," a term that researchers of small groups use to indicate how much the members *enjoy* the group.
6. The index of overall behavioral integration is based on seven survey items. For example, executives are asked to indicate their level of agreement with the statement, "Communication among our top executive group is open and fluid." Executives within a company tend to give similar ratings, indicating one important form of survey reliability.
7. The sizes of the circles in Figures 7.1 and 7.2 represent strictly the amount of group interaction, which at the senior management level (at least in my research) is only weakly related to similarity in background characteristics.
8. This index of pairwise interaction consists of five items, such as "[Specific executive, by name] is a frequent source of ideas and helpful information for me." Pair members tend to give similar ratings to the items.
9. For discussion of some of these factors, see Hambrick (1995), Katzenbach and Smith (1993), and Hout and Carter (1995).

References

Bartlett, C. A., and S. Ghoshal. 1989. *Managing across Borders: The Transnational Solution*. Boston: Harvard Business School Press.

Burgelman, R. A., and A. S. Grove. 1996. Strategic dissonance. *California Management Review, 38* (Winter): 8–28.

Drucker, P. F. 1992. There's more than one kind of team. *Wall Street Journal*, February 11, 1992.

Hambrick, D. C. 1994. Top management groups. A conceptual integration and reconsideration of the "team" label. In B. M. Staw and L. L. Cummings (eds.), *Research in Organizational Behavior, 16:* 171–214.

Hambrick, D. C. 1995. Fragmentation and the other problems CEOs have with their top management teams. *California Management Review, 37* (Spring): 110–127.

Hout, T. M., and J. C. Carter. 1995. Getting it done: New roles for senior executives. *Harvard Business Review*, November–December 1995.

Katzenbach, J. R., and D. K. Smith. 1993. *The Wisdom of Teams.* Boston: Harvard Business School Press.

Lawrence, P. R., and J. W. Lorsch. 1967. *Organization and Environment: Managing Differentiation and Integration.* Boston: Division of Research, Harvard Business School.

Tushman, M. L., and E. Romanelli. 1985. Organizational evolution: A metamorphosis model of convergence and reorientation. In L. L. Cummings and B. M. Staw (eds.), *Research in Organizational Behavior,* 7: 171–222. Greenwich, CT: JAI Press.

Weick, K. E., and K. H. Roberts. 1993. Collective mind in organizations: Heedful interrelating on flight decks. *Administrative Science Quarterly, 38:* 357–377.

[8]

Conflict and Strategic Choice

How Top Management Teams Disagree

Kathleen M. Eisenhardt, Jean L. Kahwajy,
and L. J. Bourgeois III

S ENIOR EXECUTIVES within corporations are visionaries for the future, spokespersons to external constituencies, role models and coaches for employees, and cheerleaders for corporate accomplishments. Senior executives also guide corporate destiny in their own particular areas of functional, geographic, or product responsibility. Yet while all of these activities are critical, the role of senior executives as members of the top management team is perhaps their most central task.

Senior executives form the inner cadre or circle of people who collectively formulate, articulate, and execute the strategic and tactical moves of the corporation. Whether their focus is on dramatic corporate transformation or simply on the relentless day-after-day demands of competition in high-velocity global industries, the ability of senior executives to work together as a cohesive and effective team is critical to the success of the firm.

Top management teams typically face situations with high ambiguity, high stakes, and extreme uncertainty. Discord, contention, debate,

We appreciate the very helpful advice of Max Bazerman, Greg Dess, Kim Elsbach, Jim Frederickson, Etty Jehn, Laura Kopczak, Rod Kramer, Arie Lewin, Jim March, Keith Murnighan, Judy Park, Lisa Pelled, Richard Priem, Susan Schneider, Bob Sutton, Behnam Tabrizi, and Anne Tsui. We also appreciate the very generous support of Stanford Computer Industry Project and the Alfred P. Sloan Foundation.

disagreement—in short, conflict—are natural in such situations. Why? Reasonable people are likely to perceive an ambiguous and uncertain world in different ways, to make differing assessments about what might happen in the future, and so to prefer different alternatives. In addition, given the high stakes facing senior executives, these particular people are likely to be passionate and vocal about their beliefs. The likelihood of conflict is further exacerbated by the fact that senior executives usually lead their own large and important sectors of the corporation. So they receive information and pressure from their own unique constituencies and develop perspectives that reflect their differing responsibilities.

Conflict within top management teams is not only likely, it is usually valuable. Conflict at senior levels surrounding appropriate paths of action—what may be termed "substantive," "cognitive," or "issue-oriented" conflict—is essential for effective strategic choice.[1] For example, in a series of carefully conducted academic studies, Schweiger, Amason, and colleagues found that high conflict led to the consideration of more alternatives; better understanding of the possible choices; and, overall, significantly more effective decision making. Similar work by Tjosvold also revealed that high substantive conflict was related to superior performance. Perhaps most striking is Janis's classic work on a series of high-profile public decisions by top management groups, including the formulation of the post–World War II Marshall Plan, John Kennedy's handling of the Bay of Pigs invasion and the Cuban missile crisis, and the U.S. involvement in Vietnam in the 1960s. Janis observed that vigilant, conflict-oriented group interactions within the top management cadre played a vital role in the successful decisions (e.g., Cuban missile crisis, creation of the Marshall Plan). In contrast, Janis found that a lack of conflict—what he termed "groupthink"—was a primary causal factor in major debacles (e.g., Bay of Pigs invasion, Vietnam involvement). The overall argument is that conflict is critical in liberating relevant information and shaping effective courses of action.

Given the likelihood of conflict in the kinds of situations that top management teams face and the importance of conflict to successful performance, it is surprising that conflict is often minimal within top management teams. The work by Janis mentioned above, gives many examples in the public domain where senior executives engaged in strikingly conflict-free group interactions, despite vast uncertainty and high stakes. Academic studies by Hickson and colleagues, as well as our own work, also indicate that conflict is much less widespread among top management teams than one would anticipate.[2] Agreement, or at least apparent agreement, is startlingly common.

Yet the evidence is also overwhelming that low conflict levels are associated with poor decision making. A classic example is the so-called "Abilene paradox." This proverbial story begins with family members sitting on their front porch on a very hot Texas summer afternoon. One person suggests a trip to Abilene, many miles away. No one wants to go, but everyone thinks that the others do and so acquiesces. The subsequent trip to Abilene is hot, dusty, and thoroughly unpleasant. It is only afterwards that the family members realize that none of them really wanted to go! The moral of the story? Too little conflict can be disastrous.

The Abilene paradox, obviously, describes a low-stakes situation. Unfortunately, however, similar failures—such as the Vietnam escalation, the abortive rescue of the Iranian hostages in the Carter administration, and the Challenger disaster—are also linked to too little conflict. This linkage is further corroborated by numerous research studies. Without conflict, groups lose their effectiveness. In the case of top management teams, members often become apathetic, disengaged, and only superficially harmonious. They fail to offer significantly different alternatives. They miss the opportunity to question falsely limiting assumptions. And such teams ultimately achieve, on average, lower performance.

Why does conflict fail to occur in top management teams? In some cases powerful CEOs crush dissension, as apparently happened under Iacocca's rule of Chrysler in the 1980s. In other cases "groupthink" takes hold: Executives come to value the camaraderie of the team to the point where they suppress their own conflicting viewpoints, engaging in self-censorship to maintain the veneer of harmony. In such settings lack of conviction about one's own perspective and ignorance of other points of view, coupled with the implicit assumption that everyone agrees, limit conflict. Some executives, too, find conflict unpleasant; they fear that conflict may spiral downward into interpersonal animosity, which will harm working relationships. They also eschew conflict to avoid appearing uncooperative, offensive, or even foolish. Finally, some top management teams may avoid conflict simply because of fear that endless debate will lead to slow decision making and divert attention from critical issues. Overall, constructive conflict can be stymied by a whole range of cognitive, emotional, and power barriers. How can these be overcome?

This chapter describes the *management of conflict* in the senior echelons of corporations. We highlight the differences between the two extremes of high- and low-conflict teams and suggest tangible mechanisms to build productive conflict. Our particular focus is on the nurturing of "substantive" conflict—that is, conflict centered on alternative courses of action and interpretation of facts, not conflict centered on interpersonal friction and dislike. We explain how some top management teams overcome the barriers to substantive conflict and gain the rich fruits of fully debated courses of action—and why some do not.

We begin by briefly sketching our research base. We then describe four crucial levers for creating conflict within top management teams: team heterogeneity, frequent interaction, distinct roles, and multiple-lens heuristics. We observe that a low level of conflict tends to be a signal of apathy, distraction, and disengagement from the executive team. High levels of conflict, on the other hand, involve intense interaction among key decision makers. We conclude with managerial lessons about how to nurture and sustain conflict.

Research Base

We developed our ideas about conflict from an in-depth study of twelve top management teams. We supplemented our study data with insights from our consulting experiences and other research. In the focal study, we interviewed five to nine senior executives at each firm, all of whom directed major sectors of their corporations. We explicitly measured conflict surrounding goals, key decision areas, and preferences for action, using both questionnaires and open-ended interview questions. We also observed strategic interactions firsthand and tracked the making of one or two specific strategic decisions. The result was an in-depth understanding of conflict processes within these teams.

We conducted our work in technology-based firms in Silicon Valley. Such firms typically compete in high-velocity environments of enormous technical and competitive change, which create natural hotbeds of conflict. Yet there are also pressures to decrease conflict: Conflict is seen by many executives as slowing business pace, a particularly problematic effect in this setting where speed is essential. Also, the enormous competitive pressures may bond executives so that they favor mutual support and friendship over substantive conflict in these difficult surroundings. This tension between forces that both stimulate and repress conflict provides a compelling setting in which to analyze the management of conflict.

Of the twelve teams we analyzed, four exhibited *very high* levels of conflict surrounding organizational goals, key decision areas, and specific decisions. One executive described the conflict at her firm: "We air opinions, and they're often heated. . . . We argue about most things." A senior executive at another firm summarized, "We yell a lot . . . we get it out on the table and argue about it."

Another four top management groups had *very low* conflict. They had little disagreement about goals, key decision areas, or specific decisions. Typical was the following comment: "There isn't much dissension." Another senior executive said of his team that "There is a very cooperative attitude—not like other companies where there is tension and conflict." A third exclaimed, "Disagreement! It's certainly not the norm." Table 8.1 summarizes our data on the four high-conflict and the four low-conflict firms in our study.

Why do some top management teams have very high substantive conflict? Although these high-conflict teams are led by CEOs with different personalities, are competing in different markets, and are managing in the context of unique corporate cultures, there are also striking similarities among them regarding conflict. That is, there are apparently conflict generation tactics that cut across managerial styles and firms. Four effective levers of conflict management—heterogeneous teams, frequent interaction, distinct roles, and multiple-lens heuristics—appear to be universal mechanisms for creating conflict within top management teams. High-conflict top management teams pull these levers, while low-conflict teams do not. Table 8.2 summarizes these levers and their implications; we'll now look more closely at each one in turn.

Heterogeneous Teams

One path to creating high-conflict top management teams is simply to build heterogeneous teams. Teams that have members who differ across demographic characteristics such as education, gender, functional background, ethnicity, and socioeconomic origin are more likely to have conflict (Table 8.3). Particularly powerful are age differences. High-

Table 8.1
Substantive Conflict

Firm "Name"	Goal Conflict[a]	Policy Conflict[b]	Interpersonal Disagreement (0 to 10)		Conflict Rank	Decision Interaction[c]	Examples
			Given	Received			
Star	2.13	2.58	3.8	3.6	1	Mixed	"We yell a lot . . . we get it out on the table and argue about it" (VP, engineering). "It's open, forthright; it isn't placid" (VP, sales).
Cowboy	2.05	2.39	3.7	3.4	2	Agreement	"Enlightened opposition to make decisions honest" (dir., marketing).
Mercury	2.01	1.78	4.1	4.1	3	Disagreement	"There is debate and disagreement" (VP, sales). "They're a dedicated group that feels free to disagree" (president).
Premier	1.83	2.06	3.3	3.4	4	Mixed	"We argue about most things" (VP, sales). "There is some open disagreement. . . . We don't gloss over the issues, we hit them straight on" (VP, finance).

Table 8.1 (con't)
Substantive Conflict

Firm "Name"	Goal Conflict[a]	Policy Conflict[b]	Interpersonal Disagreement (0 to 10) Given	Received	Conflict Rank	Decision Interaction[c]	Examples
Zeus	1.36	2.14	3.3	3.0	5	Agreement	"There is a very cooperative attitude—not like other companies where there is tension and conflict. The tone of the meetings is relaxed" (VP, manufacturing).
Omega	1.84	1.58	3.2	3.0	6	Mixed[d]	"There was not enough disagreement" (VP, field engineering).
						Mixed[d]	"Consensus was very important" (VP, sales).
Presidential	1.46	1.75	3.2	2.3	7	Agreement	"I'm basically in agreement with most people . . . the tone is cordial" (VP, sales).
Mob	1.71	1.29	2.4	2.6	8	Agreement	"The tone is pleasant—a high level of agreement" (dir, marketing). "[It's] mostly harmonious" (VP, manufacturing).

[a] Mean of within-team variance on importance of each of 10 corporate goals.
[b] Mean of variances on importance of key decision areas.
[c] Disagreement = final decision opposed by entire team. Mixed = final decision opposed by some on team. Agreement = final decision agreed to by entire team.
[d] Two decisions were studied at Omega.

Table 8.2
Conflictual versus Nonconflictual Top Management Teams

Conflictual	Implications	Nonconflictual	Implications
Assemble heterogeneous teams, including varying ages, genders, and functional backgrounds	Adds multiple perspectives	Create homogeneous teams, emphasizing similarities and common culture	Loses multiple perspectives
	Heightens awareness of potential conflict		Lessens awareness of potential conflict
Frequently and intensely interact	Builds a team of "friends" who feel confident to express dissension	Rarely interact	Builds a group of "strangers" who lack familiarity
	Sharpens understanding of issues and preferences		Keeps preferences and issues unclear
Cultivate a symphony of distinct roles	Adds new perspectives, especially around fundamental tensions such as short- versus long-term and status quo versus change	Default to obvious roles such as functional, divisional, or geographic ones	Encourages parochial debates around familiar tensions
Rely on multiple-lens heuristics	Motivates multiple and unique vantage points	Avoid conflict-inducing tactics	Settles for obvious perspectives and first solutions

Table 8.3
Top Management Team Heterogeneity

Firm	Age Range	Number of Decades Represented	Number of Technical PhDs	Number of Women	Previous Joint Experience	Functional Background					
						R&D	Engineering	Manufacturing	Finance	Marketing	Sales
Star	28–55	4	1	1/7	0/7	X	X	X	X	X	X
Cowboy	38–57	3	0	0/7	5/7		X	X	X	X	X
Mercury	32–56	3	0	1/6	2/6		X	X	X	X	X
Premier	28–48	3	1	0/7	3/7	X	X	X	X	X	X
Zeus	35–45	2	0	0/6	0/6		X	X	X		X
Omega	32–46	2	0	0/9	2/9		X	X	X		X
Presidential	35–51	3	0	0/5	2/5	X	X				
Mob	34–46	2	0	1/6	2/6		X	X	X		

conflict top management teams often include executives with age spreads of twenty or more years.

A good example of a heterogeneous team reigns at a company that we call Premier. The CEO is in his mid-forties and has spent his entire career in sales at a major electronics corporation. Also on the team is the VP of R&D, who is a late-twenties computer prodigy; this executive has primarily an academic background. A third executive had worked at a variety of other firms before arriving at Premier. This industry veteran is in his fifties. Several other VPs, who are about forty, round out the team.

A company that we call Star also has a heterogeneous team. Here the age range is again late twenties to mid-fifties. The team includes several Europeans and a woman. Two of the senior executives are PhDs who were trained in electrical engineering and computer science, respectively. The president is an MBA. The VP of engineering came from another top company, while the senior sales executive is a well-traveled industry pro. All of these executives bring different corporate backgrounds to the executive suite.

The executives at Star and Premier, as well as at the other two high-conflict teams (which we call Cowboy and Mercury), claim that they argue most of the time about almost everything. At Star, the VP of finance emphasized "different opinions" among the group; another executive noted that "The group is very vocal, they all bring their own ideas." In these companies every decision that we studied entailed significant conflict. Typically, the older executives relied on expertise drawn from many years in the industry and often from many companies. Younger executives brought fresh ideas about new ways to compete. The distinctive corporate backgrounds meant that perspectives based on different corporate experiences came to the table. This conflict typically had positive results: These executives made better, more informed, and often more innovative choices. As one executive related, "We scream a lot, then laugh, and then resolve the issues."

In contrast, many low-conflict teams have little diversity on the senior team. Senior executives are often similar along key demographic dimensions like age, gender, and ethnicity. Not surprisingly, they are prone to thinking alike. A good example is a company that we call Mob. Here the entire senior team consists of people in their early forties. Most members of the team also went to the same major West Coast university, and several were students together in the same department. Moreover, these executives enhance their collective similarity by a very careful selection process within the corporation. They deliberately select people who share what they term "midwest" values—but who also lack variety in perspective. The feeling among senior executives is comfortable and cohesive. As one described it, "We agree most of the time." But the team is missing the energy of the high-conflict teams.

In another company the entire senior team is composed of people with engineering and science degrees. Here, too, there is little conflict. Although these executives handle issues involving marketing and finance, all of the senior team came up through engineering and thus lack true functional diversity. There is also no gender diversity, no ethnic diversity, and little age difference (all are Asian Americans in their late thirties and early forties). Their cultural backgrounds further restrict the degree to which these executives are comfortable with expressing conflict. Overall, while these executives have a good sense of some issues, they lack differing viewpoints on many key issues that face the firm.

Why does demographic heterogeneity in the executive suite create conflict? The obvious reason is that such diversity is usually associated with different life experiences and so with diverse perspectives. For example, executives who have grown up in sales and marketing typically see opportunities and issues from vantage points different from those of executives who have had primarily engineering experience. Seasoned executives who have spent decades in an industry will bring different ideas to the table than will executives who are either from outside the industry or much younger. Women, minorities, and international executives bring yet other sets of perspectives.

But demographic heterogeneity has a more subtle impact: While the worldviews of demographically dissimilar people are likely to diverge, their diversity also cues an *expectation* of conflict within the top management team. When decision makers look across the table and see visibly different people, they expect and come to listen for contrasting viewpoints. So a diverse team is much more attuned to picking up on disagreement. In contrast, when executives gaze around the group and see people similar to themselves, they are likely to assume agreement and so to be less cued into the possibility of conflict.

Finally, what about teams where diversity is hard to achieve? Some firms are in geographic locations or industries where heterogeneity is unlikely. Especially in many large corporations, executives are promoted to the senior ranks only after extensive experience, often within the firm. In these situations, how can a heterogeneous top management team be created in a manner that is also fair to rising executives and realistic regarding needed skills? Consultants and board members can make a difference. For example, the inclusion of diverse board members or the hiring of appropriate consultants can increase the range of viewpoints within the executive suite without actually changing the composition of the top team. Bringing junior-level employees into discussions can also provide alternative perspectives. Although these tactics are probably less effective for stimulating conflict than true top management team heterogeneity, they can help create debate when a diverse senior team is just not feasible.

Frequent Interactions

Some top management teams fail to have conflict because their members have not sharply defined their own opinions or clearly understood those of their colleagues. This is understandable in contemporary business; information is vast, and it is simply extraordinarily difficult for senior executives to engage in the full spectrum of issues that face them, especially when these executives also carry extensive responsibility for managing major sectors of the corporation. Rapid change increases the challenge. Yet conflict is ineffective and even nonexistent when executives have a poor grasp of their own or others' points of view. What we found is that interaction (see Table 8.4) is critical to one's understanding of one's own position and those of others. That is, preferences emerge and are shaped through discussion. Such well-articulated preferences are crucial to effective conflict. In contrast, top management teams that interact less frequently, or only in pairs, often never really engage in the discussion of critical issues. As a result, their understanding of their own and others' positions on these key issues is impaired. The result is often apathy and only the appearance of agreement. Indeed, we found that the opposite of conflict is usually not agreement but apathy and disengagement.

A telling example is a company that we call Mercury. Mercury executives are constantly talking with one another. The president said, "I talk with everyone daily—we talk about everything and nothing. We discuss pricing, personnel, and so on. With Lance, it's marketing, new

Table 8.4
Interaction Intensity

Firm	Mean Frequency of Interaction (0 to 10)	Number of Scheduled Meeting Hours Weekly[a]	Percentage of Strong Dyadic Interaction Ties[c]	Decision Interaction[d]	Examples
Star	7.00	3	50	Entire team	"The whole staff is really involved" (VP, marketing).
Cowboy	7.70	4	58	Entire team	"Daily [contact], with all" (VP, marketing).
Mercury	6.60	4	57	Small group	"I talk with everyone daily" (president).
Premier	6.90	2	50	Entire team	"Lots of interaction" (VP, sales).
Zeus	6.20	2	29	Small group	"Should talk more" (VP, finance).
Omega	6.10	2	27	Small group	"A lot was getting done among Ron, Bill, and Ed over weekends that ended up impacting others" (VP, sales).
Presidential	6.10	0[b]	36	Small group	"People build a lot of walls" (EVP).
Mob	6.50	0[b]	29	CEO	"Not much work-related interaction" (VP, finance).

[a]These are meetings of the entire team.
[b]Presidential and Mob were just beginning weekly team meetings.
[c]Percentage of dyads whose mean interaction score was greater than 7 (0 to 10 scale).
[d]Entire team = all highly involved in the decision interaction. Small group = a small group of executives highly involved in the decision interaction. CEO = CEO alone highly involved in the decision.

products, and advertising; with Matt, it's operations issues and any little thing; and with Mitch [VP for finance], it's finance and personnel issues." The VPs also described lots of interaction with one another and with the president. In addition, Mercury executives spend significant time in meetings together. Monday is a no-travel day that is dedicated to staff meetings, and several subgroups within the senior team get together at scheduled times during the week. Overall, there is a dense web of communication among the executive team members.

Not surprisingly, conflict at Mercury is substantial. There is disagreement about goals and key decision areas as well as in the strategic decision making that we studied extensively. According to one executive, "Meetings are a free discussion with much debate and disagreement. This is a dedicated group that feels free to disagree."

Extensive interaction also describes the communication pattern among Star executives. The CEO claimed to interact with three of his VPs "always" and to talk "all day via e-mail" with his VP of engineering, who was located in a separate building. A VP described his communication with the CEO and the other senior executives as "daily." Other senior executives also reported meeting often together. And the range of subjects discussed was extensive. One executive discussed customers and the organization with the others; hot prospects, salespeople, and the market were typical topics for a second executive; and competition and the stock market were on the agenda with the VP of finance. The CEO also kept up with "what's happening in the company" with several VPs and mapped out public relations tactics with the head of R&D. As one executive summarized, "The whole staff is really involved." Star executives also have a high level of conflict surrounding, for example, key decision areas and the alliancing decision that we studied in depth.

In contrast, low-conflict top management teams had strikingly less interaction. Executives claimed to be too busy to interact. They did not schedule common meeting times or communicate effectively through aids such as e-mail. Most of the interaction that did occur was in pairs, between the CEO and a focal executive, rather than among the full team. Surprising to us was the revelation that some of these executives did not know each other very well.

A good illustration is Zeus. Zeus executives reported low overall interaction. The VP of finance observed that his job consists of being an "intelligent observer" and maintaining a "detached view-point." While this VP meets frequently with the CEO, he sees the other top executives "rarely." He blamed travel schedules for this lack of contact. Although he expressed regret over the limited communication, he had no plans to change. Several executives told us that they did not even know each other very well.

When asked about conflict, Zeus executives claimed that the atmosphere feels "relaxed." As one senior executive described conflict, "[It's] very seldom. Occasionally. It's certainly not the norm." Another senior executive claimed that he is "basically in agreement with most people." A third executive observed that discussions among senior executives are usually "light . . . with little disagreement."

Interaction is modest at Mob as well. To some extent this pattern reflects the style of the CEO, who "sits at home over the weekend, sorts things out, and announces his decision on Monday." Also, there is a preference among Mob senior executives for resolving issues in pairs to avoid "wasting other people's time." Staff meetings are much less frequent at Mob than at the firms with high-conflict senior teams. When they do occur, they are described as "a series of one-on-one interactions" rather than true group interactions. While a few pairs of executives communicate frequently, low interaction is more typical. For example, one executive described his communication with the others as "not much." The VP of engineering confers often with the CEO, but not with others. And several senior executives are seen as loners who concentrate on their own parts of the business. One does not see others because he is often too "buried in detail," while another admits to "hiding a lot." Here too conflict is limited and some executives feel that they simply lack the knowledge of both the issues and each other to effectively offer dissenting opinions.

Why does interaction among senior executives trigger conflict? Obviously, more interaction increases opportunities for conflict. That is, more issues arise over which executives could experience conflict because they talk with each other often. And there is simply more time in which conflict can occur.

More importantly, interaction sharpens preferences. People tend to formulate opinions about issues, especially complex topics, in debate and discussion with others. Such contact forces executives to develop and articulate arguments more effectively and clearly so as to convey them to others. In turn, executives not only learn and shape their own views but come to learn those of others. They also become more confident in expressing their own views. In this way interaction creates a process of social discovery in which continued communication builds an increasingly complex and realistic understanding of key information and preferences.[3] This paves the way for productive conflict.

Finally, interaction helps senior executives to get to know each other. Paradoxically, familiarity and even friendship lead people to feel less constrained by politeness and therefore more confident and willing to argue for conflicting views. There is a sense of security in familiarity that permits the expression of antithetical viewpoints.[4] In contrast, lack of interaction leads to situations in which executives do not know each other well. As virtual strangers, they often avoid the expression of disagreement for fear of antagonizing or offending others.

Distinct Roles

A third tactic for creating conflict is cultivation of a symphony of distinct roles. In high-conflict senior teams executives usually have clear roles, even taking on almost caricature positions. Often these roles are organized around poles of conflict that are natural within a business. In particular, five distinct roles are apparent in most of the high-conflict teams: Ms. Action, Mr. Steady, Futurist, Counselor, and Devil's Advocate (Table 8.5).

Ms. Action is described in terms such as "a doer," "a go-getter," "real-time oriented," "what's happening now," and "impatient." The Ms. Action role involves behaviors that are seen as pushing for quick action, particularly in response to immediate concerns and opportunities. As one Ms. Action said, "Don't slow me up. I like to make things happen."

Ms. Action creates conflict by constantly bringing up opportunities and reminding the group to act. For example, Premier's Ms. Action executive initiated consideration of a strategic decision by pointing out a new product move by one of the company's leading competitors. She then kept the issue alive by pushing the others for immediate action. In ensuing meetings, this executive advocated the most immediate alternative, a quick response through the rapid introduction of a new product. Others favored either inaction, a different product, or future introduction of a more advanced product. As

Table 8.5
Symphony of Roles

Firm	Ms. Action	Mr. Steady	Futurist	Counselor	Devil's Advocate
Star	VP, sales	VP, finance	VP, R&D VP, technology (part of Star line)	VP, sales VP, engineering (part of Star line)	VP, manufacturing
Cowboy	VP, finance	VP, manufacturing			VP, human resources
Mercury	VP, finance	President	CEO		VP, finance
Premier	VP, sales	VP, manufacturing VP, marketing	VP, R&D	VP, sales	
Zeus					
Omega		VP, manufacturing	CEO	VP, corporate development	VP, finance
Presidential			VP, R&D		
Mob			CEO		

is typical of the Action role, this executive was less concerned with long-term strategic impact than her colleagues were, and more concerned with making something happen.

Mr. Steady is often characterized in words such as "Pop," "Rock of Gibraltar," "moderating influence," or "solid." Executives who play this role are the advocates for caution and the status quo. For example, Mercury's president was described as a "great moderator." He characterized himself as "the leveling influence" and as tempering enthusiasm within the team. He frequently brings up details to ensure that nothing is overlooked. Another Steady executive said, "I'm a check on runaway enthusiasm. I slow down marketing and speed up R&D and still make the best possible product."

Mr. Steady is usually the advocate for structure and planning. For instance, one Mr. Steady claimed, "Very little gets written down around here. . . . I encourage everyone to write things down. . . . We need more structure." Another Steady executive complained, "I'd do more planning. We're working too fast and lean now. You need time for planning (short-, mid-, and long-range). . . . We must spend more time planning." In the strategic decision that we studied, this executive pushed for more planning, especially regarding the market positioning of new products. In this role he acted as a counterpoint or balance to his team's Ms. Action.

Another common rule is the *Futurist*. Futurists are often regarded as "visionaries," "gurus," or "rocket scientists." They focus on the marketplace three to five or even ten or more years out. Star's Futurist, concerned with setting the strategic direction of the firm, saw his primary job as creating new standards for the industry and "doing things that others will be using in the future." Another Futurist executive, seen as "very strategy-oriented" and as having "great insight into the industry," kept abreast of the latest technical and market developments by speaking frequently both to customers and analysts. Futurists, typically uninterested in day-to-day management, often have difficulty thinking in the short run. One described being so bored by staff meetings that he read the *Wall Street Journal*. Often viewed as "ineffectual" managers who have difficulty actually "getting things done," these guru-type executives nonetheless exhibit a visionary grasp of long-term fundamentals within their industry.

Counselors play yet another role. These executives tend to be older members of the top management team. The CEO and sometimes other executives often rely on Counselors to be sounding boards and personal advisors. Counselors frequently help other managers at the early stages of deliberation by providing private advice and feedback for early-stage problems. Given their years of experience, they also provide savvy and street smarts to the group. These executives typically view themselves as off the fast track, having accomplished what they set out to do in their careers. Because of this, their advice is regarded as particularly wise and candid rather than as self-serving or politically motivated.

Finally, *Devil's Advocates* are often described as challengers or dissenting voices. They are seen as frequently offering objections and alternative points of view. Fellow executives portrayed the Devil's Advocate at Cowboy as a person who "listens and, if it doesn't sound right, will challenge [us] to explain. He puts his finger on things that don't sound right." These executives are often junior members of the top management team who may well lack the confidence to present their own points of view, but do feel comfortable with offering objections and alternatives.

High-conflict senior teams typically have executives filling most or all of these roles. For example, at one firm, the VP of sales was Ms. Action, the senior finance executive played Mr. Steady, two R&D-focused VPs were the Futurists, executives from engineering and sales were the Counselors, and the VP of manufacturing was the Devil's Advocate. The CEO orchestrated the players to create a very high-conflict team.

In contrast to the highly elaborated role structure of high-conflict teams, extremely low-conflict teams lack many or even all of these roles. At best, these teams have one or two roles filled. For example, a firm that we call Presidential has only the Futurist role filled. Moreover, often when roles are filled on these teams, one role occupant is often the CEO. For example, at Omega and Mob, the CEO is the Futurist. While this is probably better than having no one in the role, the CEO is usually less effective than other executives at taking a distinct role because he or she is also responsible for orchestrating the entire group. Sometimes, as well, the executives who fill these roles are not well suited to the task. At Omega, for example, the Counselor is a very young person (in his early thirties) whose experience is solely in manufacturing. While this executive is very bright, he lacks the wisdom and experience of the more effective Counselors in the high-conflict teams. Overall, low-conflict teams tend to have simple role structures consisting primarily of advocacy for the role occupants' obvious product, geographic, or functional responsibilities.

How can senior teams create the needed spectrum of roles? One critical factor is the CEO. Effective CEOs cultivate distinct roles by encouraging other executives to take them on and develop them. Much like a symphony conductor, these CEOs recognize the particular strengths of individual executives and map those strengths onto the needs of the team.

The other critical factor is the senior executives themselves. We found that executives often self-organize into roles via a process of self-designation. That is, these executives recognize that a particular point of view is absent and so voluntarily take on a role that relates to the missing perspective. This process is particularly aided by frequent group interaction, because such interaction clarifies for the team members which perspectives are filled and which are not. Executives then step in to take on roles that are often somewhat more extreme versions of their own actual positions on issues. In turn, playing a role stimulates others to take on roles.[5] For example, one Ms. Action claimed, "I depend on him [Mr. Steady] to watch out for tomorrow—I look out for today."

Finally, why do distinct roles promote conflict? Perhaps most importantly, these roles highlight fundamental tensions in competitive, high-velocity industries—for example, tensions between short-run and long-run thinking, between status quo and change, between structure and flexibility. These tensions force teams to confront important yet competing considerations, so senior executives gain a deeper grasp of their business and a sharper understanding of their preferences and those of others, from which conflict can emerge.

Most obvious is the interplay between roles triggered by the Action executive, who creates a constant welling up of new issues, and the Devil's Advocate, who indicates flaws in others' thinking. At Premier, for example, Mr. Steady continually advocates more structure and planning, while Ms. Action fervently believes that structure just hampers flexibility and that continual reaction to changing circumstances is key. In a decision regarding a new product challenge by a competitor, the Action executive kept pushing the team to react to the competition, while Mr. Steady kept bringing up the details and loose ends that made immediate action problematic. Together, the occupants of the two roles embodied the fundamental tension between stability and change within the business.

Similarly, the interplay between the Futurist and Ms. Action provides complementary time perspectives. Futurists prefer a long-term and well-considered strategic view of the business. In one firm the Futurist complained that the rest of the team was "driven by customers . . . our actions are always crisis-oriented." He preferred to think in terms of long-term competitive issues as opposed to the more immediate press of quarterly sales. In contrast, Ms. Action sees just doing something as pivotal. As Mercury's Action executive explained, "You need to commit and act." Another Ms. Action defended her short-term, flexible orientation by asserting, "You have ten things to do, but you can only work on one thing, so your priorities are constantly shifting." This executive further lamented that her firm's Futurist "lacked an interest in more tactical things."

In sum, the distinct and elaborate role structures of high-conflict top management teams highlight the fundamental tensions of managing. In a sense, these roles routinize the thorough consideration of the competing factors that underlie these tensions.

A second reason that distinct roles generate conflict is that being in a role gives executives the confidence to adopt dissenting viewpoints. This is particularly important for lower-status executives within the senior management team. These executives are likely to self-censor conflicting viewpoints, because they are especially unwilling to annoy or even alienate others on the team. But roles provide a familiar, legitimated platform from which executives can convey their views. In a process that psychologists term "minority influence," role occupants can be very persuasive advocates. That is, since role occupants push a persistent and focused point of view, they can create a very sharp image of their perspective rather than present a diffuse viewpoint that may be difficult to follow and thus ineffective.[6]

Multiple-Lens Heuristics

A final key to creating conflict is the use of multiple-lens heuristics: heuristics (problem-solving or discovery techniques) that focus on the creation of multiple lenses or perspectives for examining the critical strategic issues that face top management teams. Four heuristics are particularly effective: multiple alternatives, multiple scenarios, competitor role playing, and overlapping subgroups. The procedures are relatively simple to execute, and synergistic with fast decisions and cohesive teamwork. Three of these tactics are useful when particular issues arise, while the fourth may be utilized on an ongoing basis. As shown in Table 8.6, high-conflict senior teams use many or all of these heuristics, while low-conflict teams use few if any tactics to develop multiple perspectives. Sometimes low-conflict teams even openly suppress disparate points of view.

Multiple alternatives involves the explicit creation of at least three, and often four or five, options for addressing strategic issues. In high-conflict teams, when a strategic issue arises, executives almost immediately begin to develop alternative paths. It is considered entirely appropriate to suggest options that, while plausible, are not favored even by their proponent. Rather the idea is to put multiple alternatives on the table as rapidly as possible. When stuck with only one or two alternatives, high-conflict teams typically engage in nonjudgmental brainstorming sessions to generate additional alternatives. Thus, multiple alternatives force executives to go beyond the obvious solutions that first come to mind and into more creative ones; this effort may spur a fruitful reconceptualization of the issue.

At Cowboy, for example, a major new product choice involved strategic issues of hardware, software, and distribution. Senior executives at

Table 8.6
Multiple-Lens Heuristics

Firm	Multiple Alternatives[a,b]	Multiple Scenarios[a]	Competitor Role Playing[a]	Number of Overlapping Subgroups
Star	Yes, 4	Yes	Yes	3
Cowboy	Yes, 8	Yes	Yes	4
Mercury	No, 2	Yes	No	2
Premier	Yes, 3	Yes	No	2
Zeus	No, 2	No	No	0
Omega	No, 2 & 2	No	No	0
Presidential	No, 2	No	No	0
Mob	No, 1	No	No	0

[a]Composite assessment of use in strategic decision making, from interview data.
[b]Number of alternatives considered in the strategic decision(s) studied.

the firm actively created multiple alternatives involving various options for microprocessor technology (current versus next-generation), major operating systems, and distribution channels. The idea was to generate many potential paths and only then to narrow the range. As one executive claimed, "There should be three or four solutions to everything." The result was a substantially more innovative product than these executives had initially conceived. At another firm, senior executives generated multiple alternatives for obtaining a critical technology, including in-house development, licensing, and alliancing with several different partners. Here too executives promoted alternatives that they themselves did not favor simply to ensure a broad range of options.

In the *multiple scenarios* heuristic, teams systematically consider strategic decisions in light of several possible future states of demand and competition. In contrast to multiple alternatives, which are options within a single scenario, multiple scenarios describe a variety of background conditions that could conceivably occur in the future. For example, in the computer industry, possible scenarios include the continued dominance of Microsoft and the explosion of diverse competition because of the Internet. Scenario thinking, then, means either thinking about how today's choices would play out in each scenario or thinking about what events could lead to the occurrence of each scenario. Scenario thinking, in effect, compels executives to reverse their normal patterns of thought. Most people think linearly and forward in time, from today to tomorrow. In contrast, scenario thinking forces executives to start with the future and think backwards to the present. This reversal of normal linear thinking provides an alternative lens and yields an unusual and unexpected perspective on strategic issues.

For example, executives in one high-conflict team had to make several strategic decisions about financing and product innovation alternatives. These executives developed several scenarios for how their industry might unfold over the next five to ten years. They then considered how each of their options would be affected by each scenario. This is the usual method of using multiple scenarios. In addition, this team also used their scenarios in what is known as "backcasting" to further extend their thinking. Specifically, they envisioned their preferred future (i.e., one in which their firm dominated the market), then thought backwards as to how this ideal future might occur. They then compared the options at hand with the actions needed to create their preferred scenario. Overall, the backwards and convoluted thinking process precipitated by multiple scenarios created a richer understanding of the decision environment—and more conflict.

A third multiple-lens tactic is *competitor role playing*, in which one or more members of the top management team take on the task of identifying the perspective of key competitors (or of other relevant organizations) and then acting out that perspective. Like the other tactics, this one changes the frame on strategic problems from the familiar and obvious (e.g., the perspective of the team's firm) to less obvious, but nonetheless important, alternative frames (e.g., the perspectives of key competitors, customers, or buyers). New angles on old problems become apparent as the preferences and likely actions of others become easier to envision. The result is another distinctive lens through which to view critical strategic issues.

The above three tactics help foster conflict in particular situations. The final tactic, *overlapping subgroups*, is a heuristic to ensure ongoing conflict within the top management team. To create overlapping subgroups, the team subdivides into smaller groups that are usually focused on particular issues, such as strategic direction, alliance relationships, or R&D planning. These groups typically include just three to five people, which allows members to gain greater familiarity with one another and the issues at hand and to get more air time in discussions.

High-conflict teams are typically organized into multiple overlapping subgroups that supplement teamwide interactions. At Star, for example, one subgroup that includes the president plus three VPs focuses on strategic direction. As one executive observed, "Basically, we prioritize on what we should be doing." This subgroup complements two other subgroups within the top management team. One centers attention on corporate interfacing between engineering and manufacturing, and the other on technology thrusts. These subgroups' membership overlaps to some degree but not completely.

Frequently, overlapping subgroups are organized around classic functional interface issues. For instance, at Premier, a Markets and Products subgroup includes VPs of engineering, marketing, and sales. Their task in their weekly meetings is to hammer out product planning issues. One of the executives characterized the clashes in this group: "When an engineer says we can do something, he means get one working. Sales hears 'Now we can sell that.'" At other companies these subgroups are organized around product divisions that have overlapping customers and/or technology. Finally, subgroups can be focused on specific problems (e.g., cash flow or quality).

Why are multiple-lens heuristics associated with conflict? The obvious reason is that multiple-lens heuristics bring new perspectives to the executive suite. Much like team heterogeneity and differentiated roles, multiple-lens heuristics keep top managers from settling too soon on the predictable approach. In turn, this sets the stage for conflict. Moreover, multiple-lens heuristics are a salient cue that it is acceptable and even desirable to have debate and disagreement. For example, multiple scenarios signal overt encouragement of conflict.

The less obvious reason is that multiple-lens heuristics are motivating. Entertaining multiple simultaneous alternatives and multiple scenarios actively compels senior executives to explore and manipulate ideas. Such mental gymnastics are inherently interesting and engaging. These tactics also involve mental variety, which again triggers interest and engagement.[7] And they give executives the opportunity to improve their understanding of critical business issues, which most executives see as important to their personal advancement.

In contrast, low-conflict top management teams rarely use multiple-lens heuristics. They examine few alternatives, rarely employ scenario or competitor role-play thinking, and usually have few subgroups. As a result, they have a somewhat limited range of perspectives. They tend to jump on obvious first options and can become predictable to wise competitors.

Managerial Implications

The levers that we have described create conflict in top management teams by forcing executives to recognize more perspectives; team diversity, elaborate roles, and multiple-lens heuristics all expand the range of viewpoints on the executive team. At the same time, frequent interaction creates familiarity among senior executives so that they can be more relaxed and confident about offering dissenting points of view; roles smooth social interactions by providing comfortable and familiar platforms from which to engage in debate; and multiple-lens heuristics clearly signal that conflict is appropriate and even expected. Taken together, these tactics lower the cognitive, emotional, and political barriers to conflict.

Is conflict associated with high performance? We found that, indeed, conflict is essential for effective top management teams. The highest-conflict teams led the highest-performing firms.[8] In contrast, firms with lower-conflict executive teams did less well. Among the firms we observed, low-conflict teams tended to forget to consider key issues or were simply unaware of important aspects of their strategic situation. It also appeared that their actions were easy for competitors to anticipate. Simply put, these low-conflict teams made poor strategic choices. Ironically, they often realized that they were ineffective. For example, after Omega executives misjudged the implications of a key technological change for competitive conditions, one executive said, "We didn't think through what would happen in the marketplace." In the wake of a poor strategic decision, an executive at Mob commented that "Inexperience and naïveté went a long way here." But what these executives failed to see was the connection to conflict.

The most telling case was the turnaround of Omega. After several years of disappointing performance (and just as our study was ending), Omega hired a new CEO. Subsequently, we learned that this executive explicitly increased the level of conflict, using many of the tactics described here. The firm has since turned around, and members of the top management team attribute some of their gains to greater conflict within the team. As one executive says, "There is not any table pounding, but we are getting closer. There is more contention. It's part of the new CEO's style."

Why are conflict and performance linked? High-conflict top management teams are forums for more numerous points of view; these, in turn, lead to more thorough and creative discussions and the avoidance of premature closure. Executives gain a richer understanding of strategic issues and develop more cognitively complex perspectives. Strategic choices reflect more and better use of information. Implementation is enhanced, because senior executives who have engaged in conflict are more likely to understand and support the strategic choice. In low-conflict teams, the understanding of strategic issues is often superficial or one-sided, and executives often miss or forget important considerations.

How do managers actually create high-conflict teams? The four key levers of conflict identified in this chapter involve simple behaviors that top management teams in a variety of settings can use. To summarize:

1. Begin by assembling a diverse team. If everyone in your executive meetings looks alike and sounds alike, the chances are excellent that they think alike to a great extent.

2. Make it a practice to meet together as a team regularly *and* often. Team members who don't know one another very well can't argue very well with one another either.

3. Encourage team members to assume roles beyond their obvious product, geographic, or functional responsibilities. Work to ensure that the two sides of fundamental tensions (e.g., short versus long run and status quo versus change) are well represented.

4. When particular strategic issues arise, use multiple-lens heuristics. They create fresh perspectives as well as engage and motivate interest in problem solving.

5. Overall, think in terms of managing conflict. Don't let your team acquiesce too soon or too easily. Identify team apathy early. And don't confuse a lack of conflict with agreement. Too often, what passes for agreement is really apathy and disengagement.

Conclusion

Previous scholarly research has often taken a static view of conflict. It has assumed that managers have fixed views reflecting some form of static self-interest related to their job responsibilities or personal ambitions. Conflict, in this view, entails no emotional attachment to a position, no fear of offending colleagues, no reluctance to engage in what is for many an unpleasant and time-consuming activity. It is conflict without soul. Moreover, conflict is often mistakenly seen as necessarily slowing pace and creating divisive politics.[9]

Our perspective is that conflict is *dynamic*, in that it unfolds as executives gain a deeper grasp of their business and their preferences for action through constant immersion in alternative viewpoints.

Conflict reflects not a set of fixed self-interests among senior executives but a continuously evolving understanding of the world gained through interaction with others. Moreover, conflict is highly *emotional*, in that it requires both the confidence and the motivation to engage in a process that many executives dislike and avoid. And high-conflict teams can be *fast* and *cohesive*.

To sum up, in exploring the possibility of leveraging control over conflict, we are suggesting a new area for executives to develop skills that improve leadership team effectiveness. The best top management teams focus on what they can control, and they develop skills toward that end. A crucial lever of control is the management of conflict. That is, the ability to manage conflict can distinguish world-class executive teams from all the rest. Teams that adopt the tactics described in this chapter will most likely—by managing conflict—harness their energy, experience, and creativity more effectively.

Notes

1. A. Amason, "Distinguishing the Effects of Functional and Dysfunctional Conflict on Strategic Decision Making: Resolving a Paradox for Top Management Teams," *Academy of Management Journal* (1996). D. Schweiger et al., "Group Approaches for Improving Strategic Decision Making: A Comparative Analysis of Dialectical Inquiry, Devil's Advocacy, and Consensus," *Academy of Management Journal* (1986). R. Priem, "Top Management Team Group Factors, Consensus, and Firm Performance," *Strategic Management Journal* (1990). D. Tjosvold, *The Positive Conflict Organization* (Reading, Mass.: Addison-Wesley, 1991). I. Janis, *Groupthink: Psychological Studies of Policy Decisions and Fiascos* (Boston: Houghton Mifflin, 1982). K. Jehn, "A Multimethod Examination of the Benefits and Detriments of Intragroup Conflict," *Administrative Science Quarterly* (1995). L. Pelled, "Demographic Diversity, Conflict, and Work Group Outcomes: An Intervening Process Theory," *Organization Science* (1996).

2. D. Hickson et al., *Top Decisions: Strategic Decision Making in Organizations* (San Francisco: Jossey-Bass, 1986). K. Eisenhardt & L. J. Bourgeois III, "Politics of Strategic Decision Making in High Velocity Environments: Toward a Mid-Range Theory," *Academy of Management Journal* (1988). K. Eisenhardt & M. Zbaracki, "Strategic Decision Making," *Strategic Management Journal* (1992).

3. P. Anderson, "Decision Making by Objective and the Cuban Missile Crisis," *Administrative Science Quarterly* (1983).

4. K. Back, "Influence through Social Communication," *Journal of Abnormal and Social Psychology* (1951). D. Pruitt & J. Rubin, *Social Conflict: Escalation, Stalemate, and Settlement* (New York: Random House, 1986).

5. H. Guetzkow, "Differentiation of Roles in Task-Oriented Groups" in D. Cartwright & A. Zander (Eds.), *Group Dynamics: Research and Theory* (New York: Harper & Row Publishers, 1968).

6. L. Van Dyne & R. Saaverda, "A Test of the Minority Influence Paradigm in Work Groups" (unpublished manuscript).

7. H. Harlow et al., "Learning Motivated by a Manipulation Drive," *Journal of Experimental Psychology* (1950). J. R. Hackman & G. Oldham, *Work Redesign* (Reading, Mass.: Addison-Wesley, 1980). R. White, "Motivation Reconsidered: The Concept of Competence," *Psychological Review* (1959).

8. In two companion papers ("Taming Interpersonal Conflict in Strategic Choice: How Top Management Teams Argue, but Still Get Along" and "How Teams Have a Good Fight," in V. Papadakis and P. Barwise [Eds.], *Strategic Decisions: Context, Process and Outcomes* [*Harvard Business Review*, 1997]), we further examine the performance implications of conflict by focusing on the management of interpersonal conflict. We find that the very highest-performing firms limit this kind of affective (emotional) conflict, while fostering the substantive conflict that we describe here.

9. Eisenhardt & Zbaracki, op cit.

[9]

Confronting Senior Team Conflict
CEO Choices

Charles S. Raben and Janet L. Spencer

T HERE'S A CERTAIN IRONY in the growing attention being showered on CEOs. That attention, and the near celebrity status it sometimes brings, typically focuses upon the CEO's most public roles—the CEO as corporate icon, the CEO as charismatic leader, the CEO as master strategist, the CEO as turnaround artist. But the same shock waves of change that have turned so many CEOs into public figures have simultaneously created an unprecedented need for chief executives to become more effective leaders in ways most people never see. The press, the public, and the financial community rush to judge CEOs' grand maneuvers in the public arena. But much of the real drama is played out backstage, in the private setting where the CEO's ability to lead a small but powerful senior team can make the crucial difference between success and failure for the organization.

The dynamics of organizational change fundamentally expand the complexity of the CEO's role. Discontinuous change, in particular, requires the CEO to perform a variety of functions that no one else can. Clearly, the CEO must act as both visionary and strategist, articulating a clear and compelling notion of where the organization is headed. Only the CEO can personally embody the organization's values and ideals. Only the CEO can function in an array of public settings as the undisputed spokesperson for the institution, communicating both a substantive message and a subtextual tone. Only the CEO can spark the energy, rally the commitment, and inspire the shared sense of purpose so crucial to an organization caught up in the angst and instability of radical change. And, much of the time, these demands play directly to the strengths of the CEO. The abilities to formulate strategy, articulate a vision, and motivate the masses are likely to be the same talents and personal imperatives that propelled the CEO to the top job in the first place.

Yet in times of major change, those skills are important but insufficient. In today's complex organization, no CEO can single-handedly bring about significant, long-lasting change. True change requires execution and implementation, involving the collaborative efforts of the entire senior team. The job of reshaping the strategy, structure, performance, and culture of an enterprise demands the wholehearted commitment and unified action of the senior team, which must act in concert as the collective extension of the CEO's leadership.

Consequently, the CEO's effectiveness as a leader of change is inextricably tied to his or her effectiveness as a builder and leader of the senior team. Our experience and observation make it abundantly clear that success in leading senior teams depends, to a great extent, on the CEO's capacity to recognize, confront, and constructively manage the range of conflict that is inherent—and often necessary—within these groups of powerful individuals. Moreover, the demands of change require that CEOs reach beyond their tried-and-true repertoire and master new techniques for effectively managing conflict with and among their direct reports.

Sources of Senior Team Conflict

In relatively stable times, the challenge of managing conflict within the senior team is difficult enough. But periods of significant change escalate the opportunities for conflict to entirely new levels. Ambiguity and instability abound. Executives worry about their jobs, their futures, and their power and prestige. Beyond personal concerns, they generally harbor profound beliefs about how the company should be run, how it should compete, what kind of people it should employ—and all those issues are suddenly open to debate.

To begin with, the formulation of new strategies—an activity senior teams are called upon to perform with increasing frequency—is a process rife with opportunities for conflict. As discussed in Chapter 1, new technology, powerful social forces, and rapidly changing public policy reshape the nature of competition in one business sector after another, requiring companies constantly to reexamine their basic strategies. Ideally, the process of developing a new strategy—sometimes referred to as "strategic choice"—is a collaborative activity involving the full engagement of the senior team. If this group of experienced, knowledgeable, and strong-willed individuals are open and honest about their perceptions of the changing environment, some disagreement is inevitable. Moreover, strategic choice involves fundamental decisions about what kind of organization the enterprise should become, an issue that typically surfaces widely differing—and deeply held—personal models of how organizations should be designed and managed.

Frequently, new strategies dictate a need for radically new organizational designs. And the very shape of today's emerging forms of organizational architecture lays the groundwork for conflict at the top of the enterprise. In the traditional, vertical organization, executives were clearly responsible for operations within rigidly defined functional boundaries. But the clear trend today is toward "customer-facing" designs with an external, market focus. As the emphasis moves from internal operations to external opportunities and demands, the old architectures based on functional structures are giving way to new designs formed around customer-driven processes. The resulting horizontal designs, while offering the potential of greater responsiveness to the marketplace, also demand an unprecedented degree of cooperation and collaboration. As lines of responsibility become blurred, opportunities for conflict expand.

Similarly, the implementation of a new strategy and a new organizational design raises a host of difficult issues at the operational level, each providing the potential for additional conflict. Customer-focused processes require the seamless integration of a variety of activities that cross traditional organizational boundaries. Additionally, the more complex the organization, the more crucial the need for internal congruence, or fit, among the components of the organizational architecture—the strategy, the formal structures and processes, the actual work to be performed, the people within the organization, and the informal operating environment (Nadler and Tushman, 1987; Nadler and Tushman, in press). The proper alignment of people, processes, structures, and systems requires an endless series of delicate balancing acts, each involving a range of hard choices, trade-offs, and readjustments.

Strategic choice, strategic design, and strategic implementation all demand successful teamwork at the top of the organization. In reality, however, cohesive team performance rarely comes easily. In most organizations, conflict remains a constant threat to effective collaboration in the executive offices.

That threat grows as the CEO attempts to build and shape a senior team over time. As noted by Hambrick and Fukutomi (Hambrick and Fukutomi, 1991), CEOs' skills, interests, and areas of strength change over the course of their tenure. As time goes on—and particularly in the face of an impending period of major change—CEOs should think about how well their senior teams supplement and complement their own evolving strengths and weaknesses, and should make the necessary adjustments.

As the builder of the senior team, the CEO must also be sensitive to the issue of diversity, in its broadest sense. The CEO—and, for that matter, the entire organization—is likely to benefit from a heterogeneous senior team that brings diverse strategic perspectives and management styles to the top leadership. But there's a trade-off: The more diverse the group, the greater the likelihood for conflict and the greater the challenge to the CEO's skills as a team leader.

A final source of potential conflict lies in the very uniqueness of the senior team. Nearly every executive who has reached the position of CEO has had some experience in leading teams. But the senior team is different from other teams in important ways, creating different management challenges for the CEO whose job it is to lead it.

In most cases, for example, executives have ascended to the senior team by virtue of their achievement, ambition, and political acumen. Their corporate positions are inherently powerful, political, and subject to intense pressure from a variety of internal and external forces—the board, competitors, customers, shareholders, employees. Their tasks are complex; their decisions involve substantial risk; and numerous different audiences are watching their every move. Every one of their actions, and the resulting consequences, has intensely political overtones.

No element of the senior team environment is more politically charged than the "horse-race" phenomenon of executive succession. Competition for advancement within the senior team is essentially a zero-sum game played for enormous stakes. Consequently, even minor interactions take on major political implications. The opportuni-

ties for conflict are endless, and the CEO plays a pivotal role in resolving—or exacerbating—them. Often there is real and palpable
conflict between the leading horses in the race. Sometimes this conflict is played out through allies, supporters, and proxies, because the
actual candidates perceive they would hurt themselves in the eyes of
the CEO if they were seen to be battling in public.

Considering the numerous possibilities for dissension, disagreement, and dysfunctional competition within the senior team, conflict
presents one of the most critical threats to the effective management
of organizational change. In that context, the CEO's role as builder
and leader of the senior team takes on exceptional importance.

The CEO As Team Leader

Why is the senior team's performance so central to the success of
change management? The answer lies in the crucial nature of the strategic and operational issues that fall within the purview of this group.

It is the senior team, along with the CEO, that shoulders the responsibility for making the fundamental strategic decisions that will
define the organization's role in the marketplace. It is the senior
team, working with the CEO, that must select an organizational architecture that will capitalize upon the company's special capacities to
achieve competitive advantage. It is the explicit responsibility of the
senior team to execute the strategy, converting strategic objectives
into effective operational plans. And it is the senior team's job to
achieve and maintain the smooth integration of performance
throughout the organization.

Just as the senior team is unique among teams, the CEO's role is
similarly unique among team leaders. At the most basic level, the
CEO plays an unparalleled role as the arbiter of conflict within the
team because there is no recourse beyond his/her decisions; there is
no appeal to a higher court. If there are performance or relationship
problems within the team, there is nowhere to take them except to
the CEO. The CEO plays the ultimate role in determining both rewards and punishment. And, of particular importance to the senior
team, the CEO usually plays the primary role in handing out the
grandest prize of all—the keys to his/her own office.

Additionally, the CEO's role differs from that of other team leaders by virtue of tenure. Generally speaking, the CEO's tenure is longer

and more explicitly defined than that of leaders at lower levels. That means CEOs usually have sufficient time to put their personal stamp on both the composition and the operating style of their senior teams.

Forms of Senior Team Conflict

Central to the CEO's role in leading the senior team is the ability to recognize the various forms of conflict that arise at that level. Much scholarly work has been devoted to distinguishing among the many nuances of conflict. For our purposes here, it is sufficient to differentiate between overt and unsurfaced conflict within the team.

Overt Conflict

In any typical team, there's plenty of overt conflict to go around, even in normal times. Inevitably, given a group of strong-willed, ambitious, and powerful individuals, there will be personality differences that lead to occasional clashes. Differing operating styles will occasionally lead to open disputes. At times, one of the CEO's direct reports will underperform in such obvious ways that some form of confrontation becomes unavoidable. Other times, an insubordinate direct report who is strongly opposed to an executive decision will subtly go about sabotaging it; conflict, though deferred, is practically guaranteed.

The range of issues inherent in hammering out a new strategy and organizational architecture often leads to philosophic divisions and outright conflict within the senior team. That's not necessarily a bad thing. Profound differences of opinion nearly always exist, and it is best to have those conflicts surfaced and resolved, one way or another, early in the process. Left to fester, they generally manifest themselves down the road as roadblocks to implementation. Consequently, a well-managed strategic choice process will almost inevitably induce senior team members to get their differing perspectives out on the table.

Unsurfaced Conflict

More problematic for the CEO and the senior team are the various forms of conflict that remain below the surface. Unsurfaced conflict frequently develops when two or more contenders are vying to become the next CEO but are clever enough to keep their conflict from erupting in front of the boss. These battles, waged outside the CEO's normal range of vision, can critically disrupt essential operations.

But succession doesn't have to be the issue. Members of the senior team rarely want to violate traditional business etiquette by pursuing an open conflict. They may fear that their perceived inability to get along with colleagues could hurt in very tangible ways: poor performance reviews, disappointing financial consequences, and curtailed career advancement. Instead, team members may be in conflict at a level invisible to the CEO—but destructive nonetheless. These conflicts become seriously dysfunctional when warring executives play out their personal differences indirectly through the way they manage their respective segments of the enterprise. If left unresolved, such differences ultimately disrupt the orderly flow of processes across organizational boundaries, and can seriously damage overall performance.

Another common source of unsurfaced conflict involves situations in which a senior team member isn't performing well, and everyone seems to know it except the CEO. Through their own personal information networks, other team members learn that one of their colleagues—someone with an impressive demeanor in senior settings and a solid record of short-term results—is actually doing a poor job of leading his/her own team. The individual may be too controlling, unappreciative of talent, unsupportive—there may be any of a number of problems. But in most organizations, it's considered extremely bad form to be seen as interfering with the internal operations of a colleague's organization. As long as other senior team members remain reluctant to surface the issue, this kind of conflict is likely to brew for a considerable period of time before coming to the CEO's attention.

Finally, newly formed senior teams present a special case. Precisely at the time when underlying conflicts ought to be surfaced and resolved, the team is decidedly unlikely to engage in open dissension. Because all members were handpicked by the CEO, none wants to be perceived as disrupting or disagreeing with the new team. It's also likely that the same events that led to the naming of a new team— events such as the appointment of a new CEO or a major housecleaning in the context of a radical organizational change—will have swamped the team with pressing, critical business that easily masks the real but unarticulated internal conflicts.

Approaches to Conflict Resolution

Clearly, senior team conflict comes in all shapes and sizes. Yet over time, in practice, many CEOs grow comfortable with only one or two techniques for handling it—a kind of one-size-fits-all approach to conflict resolution. We would argue that the distinctive characteristics of various forms of senior team conflict require the CEO to select markedly differing approaches to handling specific conflicts situations.

Which approach is most appropriate in a given situation? That choice will be shaped by a wide range of variables:

- How severe is the conflict and how closely is it linked to the strategic success of the enterprise? In other words, how much longer can the conflict be allowed to continue?

- What is the history of the conflict? How long has it existed, who has been involved, and how public has it become?

- Is the conflict primarily related to a particular person—an individual's personality, management style, value system, skill set, or other factor(s)?

- What is the length of the CEO's tenure, and how might that relate to the senior team's operating style? Are there behavior patterns that are holdovers from a previous regime? And if so, how long have they been allowed to continue?

- What are the company's accepted norms for resolving conflict? What kinds of war stories are told about previous conflicts and how they were resolved—and which resolutions are perceived as successes or failures?

- How much publicity, both within the organization and in the general public, is the CEO willing to accept in resolving the problem?

- To what extent is the conflict part of an ongoing issue, rather than a discrete event? If there is an ongoing issue, how important is it that the players involved learn to resolve what are likely to be continuing conflicts inherent in their particular situation?

- Can the conflict be resolved in a way that becomes a developmental experience for the team? Can it be used as an opportunity for helping team members learn how to deal with conflict and resolve it on their own?

There's a final element to be considered: What, if any, are the constructive elements of the conflict? What trade-offs would be involved in allowing it to go on? Without question, there is a potentially healthy aspect to some conflict; disagreement can be a source of energy, it can stimulate productive debate, it can reinforce an open and free exchange of information, and it can free team members from the grip of groupthink.

The Seven Options

Depending on the unique characteristics of each conflict, the CEO must carefully select the most suitable role to play so as to achieve the most appropriate solution. Each CEO, based on his or her own personality and experience, will favor a predominant style for dealing with conflict. But the challenge to the CEO, in the role of team leader, is to go beyond tried and true techniques and draw upon an expanded array of alternatives. We believe there are at least seven distinct roles CEOs can play in order to resolve senior team conflict.

1. THE OPTIMIST

The Optimist operates on the assumption that the senior team consists of mature, experienced people who are capable of recognizing and resolving their own conflicts without the CEO's intervention. This role is particularly characteristic of CEOs who enjoy long, well-established relationships with their senior team, and it is so common that we sometimes refer to it as the "default position" for many CEOs in dealing with conflict.

The Optimist's thinking typically goes like this: "These are my people. I chose them. I trust them. They owe their jobs and their loyalty to me. At the end of the day, I know I can count on them to do the right thing to support both me and the company." This approach rests largely on the perception of mutual loyalty and trust. Just as the CEO expects the team to support him, he appears to reciprocate by vowing to "let them run their own show."

Unfortunately, this view is sometimes nothing more than a rationalization for not dealing with conflict. The fact is that while the senior team's members may sincerely want to do what's right for the company and for the CEO, the source of conflict may be too deeply rooted to melt away on its own. This is particularly true when the basis for conflict lies in an individual's firm beliefs about the company's organization and strategy. When the CEO and a team member develop starkly different ideas about what constitutes success, the conflict can't simply be papered over or left to work itself out.

That said, it's also clear that one reason the Optimist role is so common is that it's also so appropriate in many situations. For example, we referred earlier to conflict arising from differences in operating style among members of the senior team, in terms of the way they manage their own units. CEOs may not get involved simply because unless they hear differently, they assume their direct reports are managing effectively. Once made aware of the brewing conflict, however, the CEO may deliberately adopt a hands-off approach to encourage diverse management styles within the organization. As long as a particular style works effectively within its respective unit, the CEO is not inclined to intervene and enforce a uniform management style throughout the organization.

2. THE TERMINATOR

Another common role is that of the Terminator. This is the role sometimes adopted by CEOs who choose to resolve a conflict by taking decisive action to remove its immediate source. Sometimes that means removing one or more of the key players in the conflict. In other situations, it involves structural changes.

This approach tends to be used when one or more of the following factors are present. First, the CEO may be convinced that the conflict is so destructive that there's just no time to patiently work through it. Second, the CEO may be fed up with a recurring conflict that just won't seem to go away with more delicate handling. Third, the conflict may be inherent in the current cast of characters or structural environment, and no resolution may be possible without fundamental change in one or more of those elements. Finally, the Terminator role may play strongly to a personal management style that features a directive, authoritarian approach characterized by personal intervention and swift action.

As an example, this approach is often used when two highly visible and critical members of the senior team repeatedly demonstrate their inability to resolve differences and work together effectively. In these situations, the CEO is likely to remove one or both of the direct reports, or to reassign one or both to new positions in which their need for them to interact and collaborate is substantially diminished.

CEOs frequently take this approach when the persistent conflict is obviously hurting the organization's performance, and when its continuation could have serious ramifications. The CEO may also be convinced that the senior-level conflict is sending divisive messages throughout the organization.

The key issue for a CEO inclined to assume the Terminator role is to first distinguish the symptoms from the cause. Removing the key players won't end the conflict if the source of their antagonism is rooted in inherent conflicts in their respective assignments. If two units are pursuing strategic objectives that are plainly at odds with one another, replacing the unit heads won't solve the problem; more often than not, the same conflict will recur with a different set of antagonists.

The judicious use of the Terminator approach requires a keen sensitivity to the nature of conflict. While this approach is sometimes essential and unavoidable, it can also be extreme and unnecessary— and counterproductive, in terms of helping the senior team learn how to work though and resolve its conflicts. The Terminator role should be viewed only as a final recourse.

3. THE DELEGATOR

A third role frequently adopted by CEOs is that of the Delegator. Typically, a Delegator becomes aware of a problem, communicates clear expectations that it must be resolved, and then instructs either those involved or a third party—outside consultants or, more frequently, the human resources director—to handle it.

This approach communicates a clear message that the CEO is aware of the problem, concerned about it, and absolutely determined that it will not continue. On the other hand, it requires that the CEO somehow establish that the conflict has been resolved, but without knowing the details of *how* it was resolved. To that extent, the Delegator approach limits the CEO's full understanding of the nuances that lie at the heart of the conflict.

The Delegator role is quite common in situations in which one of the CEO's direct reports is doing a poor job of leading his/her own team. For example, a Delegator who learns that a certain unit head is too authoritarian and is stifling the talent of his/her own direct reports is strongly disinclined to become personally involved in problems within the unit. That kind of intervention, the CEO fears, could easily undercut the unit executive's standing within his/her own team. So the CEO expresses a personal expectation about getting the problem solved and then assigns the HR director to work closely with the executive in question to resolve the issue.

This approach can be effective if it sends the message that the CEO is using an adult model of conflict resolution—"I know you're capable of working this out; you don't need me to do it for you." And the final outcome can be a good one if the parties involved can in fact get to the root of the problem and produce a substantial and lasting improvement.

However, there are some serious potential pitfalls. Too often, the Delegator role is used by CEOs who simply want to avoid involvement in important but highly unpleasant conflict situations. While allowing direct reports to work out their problems without having the CEO constantly looking over their shoulder, this approach also distances the CEO from personally observing how senior team members actually deal with conflict resolution. All the CEO sees is the final result. Furthermore, there is a danger that the conflict resolution may be delegated to the wrong person (as in "It's a people problem, so HR should handle it"). Over time, if the CEO uses this approach too often, there will be a perception that the CEO is abdicating responsibility and ducking the tough chores.

4. THE TIEBREAKER

In the Tiebreaker approach, the CEO resolves conflict by assigning the involved direct reports to present alternative solutions to the problem, then casting the deciding vote.

Consider this example: A relatively new CEO is confronted with a conflict involving two direct reports. One has a functional role and the other has line responsibility. They disagree over recruitment and staffing policies that resulted from recent organizational changes. These policies leave some room for interpretation regarding who has responsibility for these tasks at senior levels. In other words, do the new policies mean that the process will be centralized or decentralized?

Upon being approached by the two executives, the CEO tells them: "I want you both to prepare your cases, then come back and give me two alternatives. If, in the process, the two of you can't reach some agreement, then I'll choose one alternative or the other."

The Tiebreaker role offers some distinct benefits. First, it allows the CEO to become actively involved in resolving an issue while remaining distanced from the actual conflict. Second, it effectively minimizes the CEO's investment of time in matters that are less than crucial. Third, it forces the players to think through their positions thoroughly as they prepare their cases for presentation to the CEO. That thought process sometimes has the unintended but happy consequence that the antagonists hit upon some common ground that enables them to resolve their problem without taking it back to the CEO.

The downside of this approach is that it casts the CEO in the role of the heavy who must select a winner and a loser. The implications of that choice may extend far beyond the issue at hand, reshaping the CEO's relationship—or perceived relationship—with each of the players. The "loser" may feel a deep-seated resentment that surfaces in other, unrelated situations. The "winner" may be seen as the CEO's favorite in terms disproportionate to the relatively minor victory in question.

On another level, the Tiebreaker tactic diminishes senior team members' responsibility for figuring out how to resolve conflict among themselves. It also requires deliberate follow-up on the part of the CEO to ensure that the conflict has indeed been resolved. If the CEO's tie-breaking decision merely resolved a surface issue without addressing an underlying conflict, then it's important that the CEO understand that the dispute was superficial and the resolution inconclusive.

In short, this approach is most effective when the CEO structures the situation in a way that encourages the direct reports to work through the problem together and adopts the Tiebreaker role only as a last resort.

5. The Coach

In situations where a direct report is clearly having trouble meeting performance requirements, the most appropriate approach may be for the CEO to take on the role of the Coach. Before assuming this role, the CEO must first have thoroughly diagnosed the conflict and determined that the source of the difficulty does, in fact, revolve around one individual's performance.

CEOs tend to take on the Coach role when they perceive that improving the direct report's performance—and resolving the associated conflict—will have a direct impact on the organization's strategic success. In such critical situations, the CEO may decide, quite correctly, that the problem is simply too important to delegate to someone else.

For many CEOs, this is a difficult role. It requires, first of all, that the CEO communicate his or her concerns to the direct report in an unambiguous, completely straightforward manner. It takes considerable skill to deliver this kind of serious message without leaving the person involved feeling under attack. With a combination of firmness and empathy—and in absolute privacy—the CEO must successfully communicate that his/her goal is to coach the direct report toward improved performance.

It then becomes incumbent upon the CEO to follow through— to work closely with the direct report on improving performance and monitoring progress. And if the performance objectives are not met in a reasonable period of time, then it's the CEO's responsibility to either reassign or remove the individual.

To a great extent, the effectiveness of the Coach role is largely dependent on two factors: first, the CEO's interpersonal skills; and second, the CEO's credibility with the direct report. If successful, the approach has obvious benefits. It strengthens the relationship between the CEO and the direct report, improves the performance of a key player, and ultimately helps the organization meet its strategic objectives.

There are also plenty of ways in which this approach can fail. Through denial or defensiveness, the direct report may refuse to acknowledge the link between his/her own behavior and the unsatisfactory performance outcomes. The direct report may strongly disagree with the CEO's diagnosis of what has to change. Once the coaching has begun, the direct report may refuse or in some other way fail to implement the CEO's suggestions; after that happens a few times, the coaching relationship evolves into a more directive and disciplinary role, with the CEO specifically ordering the direct report how to change.

CEOs also need to be aware that the positive relationship they develop with the individual they're coaching can easily sow the seeds of new conflict and dissension among other direct reports, who may believe their colleague is benefiting from favoritism. Indeed, if the CEO has been successful in keeping the nature of the relationship totally confidential, other direct reports can easily mistake coaching for grooming.

6. THE SYNTHESIZER

An even more complex role for the CEO to play is that of the Synthesizer. At the same time, this role can be one of the most productive, both in terms of resolving specific conflicts and in building the team's ability to deal with conflict on an ongoing basis.

Again, let's consider a specific example. A recent structural change within an organization has created considerable ambiguity and confusion about roles and responsibilities within the senior team. Two team members who respectively head two of the units have failed to work out their differences; now, they're playing out their conflict in the way they manage their units. The result: a serious lack of alignment within the organization that is disrupting cross-unit processes and hurting overall performance.

The stakes of the conflict are high. The problem can't be allowed to continue much longer. Yet the situation is too complex for the CEO simply to play a Tiebreaker role. Instead, the CEO has to bring the parties together and act as a mediator, placing the onus on the direct reports to deal with each other through negotiation, cooperation, and conciliation. The CEO is far from a disinterested party to the proceedings, however, in that he or she is the architect of the structural changes that sparked the conflict in the first place. The process, ideally, becomes one of working out solutions, rather than of arguing a case and waiting for a ruling from on high. For that to happen, the CEO must resist the inevitable urge to dictate a solution until it becomes clear that the parties have no chance of reaching agreement within a suitable length of time.

There's no doubt that the Synthesizer role is time-consuming for the CEO. We would suggest, however, that in general this is time well invested. A Synthesizer builds the team's ability to work through and resolve the kinds of conflict they're likely to encounter on a fairly regular basis.

7. THE CONDUCTOR

The most difficult—and, in the long run, the most valuable—role for the CEO to play is that of the Conductor. This approach requires the full engagement of the CEO in orchestrating an environment that enables the team to surface and deal with conflict in an open and direct manner. The CEO acts as a facilitator, directly intervening to help build the team's collective ability to recognize, confront, and resolve the range of conflicts that may exist, both among team members and between team members and the CEO.

Consider the senior team's process for developing and selecting new strategic objectives. If the process is characterized, as it should be, by openness and intellectual honesty, then sharply opposing ideas will usually emerge. This kind of conflict, and the manner in which it is handled, presents some inherent dangers. Clearly, this is not the sort of conflict that the CEO can delegate to someone else. Nor is it a situation where the CEO should be issuing unilateral rulings. The goal is for the team to surface the conflict, examine it, give full expression to all views, honestly consider all options, and then make the appropriate decisions.

The cost of unsurfaced conflict on strategic issues can be enormous. First, the best strategic decisions always emerge from a vigorous, candid consideration of the widest possible range of plausible alternatives. And that simply won't happen if the team's working environment discourages the expression of minority views.

Second, senior team members who are compelled to accept a strategic decision that was made over their heads will inevitably harbor a sense of resentment. They're unlikely to support the new strategy with wholehearted fervor; and in some cases, whether consciously or not, they may take formal actions and/or engage in informal behaviors that actually subvert the new strategy.

Third, the airing of all possible alternatives—and the full discussion of them by members of the team—creates a collective memory of how and why particular strategic decisions were made. With the passage of time, as team members encounter difficult situations in which they must decide how to apply the strategy, that collective memory acts as a guide, reminding individuals of the underlying reasons for the strategy and why it was selected over competing alternatives.

Finally, the process of open debate in itself holds inherent value for the senior team. The fact that the process has been encouraged and guided by the CEO builds a shared understanding that conflict, in certain situations, is not only acceptable but valuable, and that surfacing and resolving conflict is an important skill that each team member should master.

The Conductor role requires CEOs to see themselves as team builders—as people who can genuinely help resolve complex and sensitive conflicts among others, and between themselves and others. This role requires sophisticated facilitation skills. It demands that the CEO create an environment in which team members are assured of continued support when they raise issues involving conflict, and in which team members know they'll be expected to work together to resolve conflict. It means that the CEO must actively assist the team in establishing norms for acceptable behavior in dealing with conflict. In short, the Conductor CEO must develop a team setting that not only accepts but encourages and rewards the expression of conflicting views and the raising of unpleasant, uncomfortable, even traditionally undiscussable issues.

This role requires enormous personal commitment, a thick skin, sensitivity toward others, and the resolve to invest a tremendous amount of time. The Conductor role, if it is to be effective, cannot be limited to a single event. It requires constant nurturing, continual monitoring, and the creation of special mechanisms by which the CEO can assess whether conflict is in fact being handled constructively by senior team members, both within the team and at lower organizational levels.

Of all the roles, that of the Conductor offers the potential for both the highest risk and greatest reward. There's a reason people tend to avoid open conflict: In its raw, unmanaged form, it can be ugly and ultimately destructive. The customs and conventions of business etiquette have evolved over time for the express purpose of shielding individuals from potential embarrassment. Open conflict brushes aside those customs and conventions and lays bare a battleground where there are clear winners and losers, with enormous consequences for both.

And yet, when handled well by a skillful CEO, this role can be an essential tool for building a creative and productive senior team, one with the confidence and ability to embrace and resolve its own conflicts.

The Required Competencies

Under any circumstances, some of the roles we've just presented require fairly sophisticated team-leading skills. As was probably apparent, the roles became increasingly complex as the list progressed, culminating in the highly demanding Synthesizer and Conductor roles. But—and this fact ought to be of particular concern to CEOs—the competencies required of effective team leaders are often absent from, and sometimes clearly at odds with, the managerial repertoire of many CEOs.

Many of the abilities and personality traits that make a person an attractive CEO candidate—strategic thinking, the ability to mobilize quick turnarounds, a talent for communicating a compelling message to large audiences, mastery of finance or some technology at the core of the business—have little to do with the skills of a team leader. Indeed, the required patience, empathy, and ability to deal comfortably with personal conflict may be totally alien to many CEOs' background and temperament.

Some of the required competencies were described in Chapter 1, in Nadler and Heilpern's discussion of the traits required of CEOs during periods of significant change. Briefly, these included the ability to empathize with employees during times of stress; the emotional strength and perspective to deal with widespread turbulence and adversity; the capacity to "open up" and convey a sense of sincerity and candor; and a sense of humor, to help maintain perspective and soften tense situations.

Beyond that list, we would suggest that the role of team leader requires CEOs to develop an additional set of competencies. Depending upon the individual, some of these some competencies may come easily and naturally; others may require that the CEO make a substantial effort to improve personal skills. In the end, each is important.

The first required competency can be termed *peripheral organization vision*. This involves the CEO's ability to think like a chess player—to focus on a particular point of attack while maintaining a clear overall vision of the entire board. Peripheral organization vision demands a full grasp of the dynamic relationships that exist at any given time among all of the various elements of the organization, and the capacity to anticipate the ripple effect of any single decision on the entire set of relationships. In terms of conflict resolution, it means thinking through in advance how each alternative solution will affect peripheral players and issues.

The second competency is skill at *diagnosis:* the ability to assess a complex situation quickly and accurately. This involves sifting through the surface clutter to determine the root causes of the problem at hand, as well as identifying both the core players and the related stakeholders who are likely to be affected by the outcome of the conflict. Diagnostic skill also implies the capacity to give full consideration to a wide range of options for resolving the problem. A crucial aspect of this competency is the ability to step back and objectively examine all sides to an issue before settling upon an appropriate course of action.

A related competency is *situational outlook.* This requires the CEO to understand each conflict as a unique combination of problems and players, and to apply an appropriate resolution rather than a generic response based largely on past experience. In particular, a situational outlook includes an appreciation that at the behavioral level, a solution that has worked in the past may not work with the particular individuals in the conflict at hand.

Clearly, the CEO must develop competency in the area of *coaching and facilitation.* This requires a strong set of interpersonal skills far removed from the "corporate icon" role so often associated with the position of CEO. Coaching and facilitation include the ability to seek clarification of surface conflict through probing questions. They include the capacity to interpret what people are really saying—rather than what they appear to be saying in the messages they deliberately convey—and to identify and synthesize related issues. Through these skills a CEO must also be able to help people separate their emotional concerns from the true content of their messages so they can find common ground for conciliation and negotiation and go on to deal with the genuine issues.

Effective coaching and facilitation, of course, demand a willingness and ability to become actively and personally involved in the conflict resolution process. This can be extremely difficult for CEOs who have habitually attempted to remain above the fray by delegating conflict resolution to others. This competency entails an unusual tolerance for ambiguity and an enormous capacity to remain cool under pressure—to refrain from personal attacks and to confront and deal with anger and aggression without losing perspective and retaliating.

To be truly effective in coaching and facilitation, the CEO must open up and express emotions that are typically considered inappropriate for the CEO to acknowledge. Direct reports can't be expected to drop their defenses and bare their souls if they believe they're the only ones who are about to become vulnerable. Because this role succeeds only if the CEO and direct reports deal with each other with absolute candor, it requires considerable self-confidence on the part of the CEO; it's likely that difficult, typically unspoken issues are about to land squarely on the table. This competency is attainable only if the CEO has already earned the genuine respect of the senior team.

Finally, in order to be a successful coach and facilitator, a CEO must be motivated by a genuine desire to help others become more adept at resolving conflicts. A CEO whose overarching concern is resolving the conflict at hand and getting everyone back to business as usual will lack the patience and commitment to see the process through to a successful conclusion. CEOs are, by nature, impatient and action-oriented; they see a problem, they want it solved. To develop competency as a coach/facilitator, then, often requires the CEO to develop new skills and adopt a new perspective; but effective coaching and facilitation hold the potential for enormous benefits to the senior team and the organization as a whole in the long run.

Mediation is a closely related competency that requires many of the same skills as coaching and facilitation. Mediation, however, demands special emphasis on the characteristics of objectivity and self-restraint. Like coaching and facilitation, it requires the CEO to become deeply involved in the process, and to be committed to helping the participants work through their problem to achieve a long-term solution. But mediation involves the capacity to remain a dispassionate noncombatant, to help guide the discourse without becoming an active participant in it.

Finally, and perhaps most crucially, CEOs cannot hope to resolve conflict effectively without the skills of *clarity and candor*. Perhaps that seems self-evident. And yet, given the performance of so many CEOs, it's important to emphasize how critical it is for the CEO to be able to deliver clear, unambiguous messages in pressured situations. One of the most common internal drivers of CEO success is an inordinate desire to be revered, admired, and in some cases even beloved by nearly everyone who falls within the CEO's personal sphere of influence. If understood and kept in perspective, that desire is not necessarily unhealthy—it's part of what compels certain people to aspire to difficult, all-consuming jobs. But that need for approval also makes it unusually difficult for CEOs to deliver bad news, face to face, to individuals with whom they work on a regular basis. It's a major reason why CEOs so often delegate unpleasant personnel chores to the COO or HR director.

But in conflict situations—particularly in the context of major organizational change—what people want and need to hear is what the CEO is thinking. It is essential that CEOs first be clear, in their own minds, on their precise position, then communicate their perspective in specific, unambiguous terms that leave no room for misinterpretation. There can be no qualifiers, no caveats, no conditions—just a straightforward and honest statement of the CEO's position.

Summary

In summary, then, conflicts—both actual and potential—are a fact of life within the senior teams that play such a crucial role in managing organizations. The sources of conflict that are always present within these unique collections of senior managers are magnified by the turbulence and uncertainty that inevitably accompany major organizational change. And because the pressure for change is accelerating in almost every industry and business sector, the ability to resolve conflict within the senior team effectively will assume even greater importance in the years ahead.

Over time, each CEO tends to rely increasingly on the method or methods of conflict resolution that worked best in the past. That's understandable—but not good enough. In truth, there are a wide variety of roles the CEO can play. The real challenge is to assess thoughtfully the nature of the conflict at hand and then select the appropriate strategy for resolving it. The solution should both enhance performance and enable the team to acquire the skills they need to resolve their own conflicts in the future.

In order to perform a variety of roles and execute them proficiently, most CEOs will have to enlarge some of their existing skills and acquire still others. But considering the enormous risks inherent in conflict at the senior team level, that's a small price for any CEO to pay.

References

Hambrick, D. C., and Fukutomi, G. D. The seasons of a CEO's tenure. *Academy of Management Review,* 16:719–742, 1991.

Nadler, D. A., and Tushman, M. L. *Competing by Design: A Blueprint for Organizational Architectures.* (In press.)

Nadler, D. A., and Tushman, M. L. *Strategic Organization Design: Concepts, Tools and Processes.* New York: HarperCollins, 1987.

[10]

Teams at the Top
Managing the Madness

Deborah Ancona

NIETZCHE TELLS US that madness is the exception in individuals but the rule in groups, and so one might conclude after reading Part II's chapters on top management teams. There seems to be something inherently difficult about managing this entity we call a team. Add to the basic built-in complexity of a team the issues of politics and succession, a tendency toward autocratic leadership, a changing business environment, the unique role of the CEO as team leader, and the attitude that "teams are good for everyone else in the organization, but not us," and it's a wonder that teams at the top work at all. Luckily, the contributors to this book provide some direction as to how to harness this top team madness. Assistance comes in the form of ideas about design and process. I will try to summarize some of the questions asked and the suggestions made in both these areas, then I will add some of my own ideas to the model.

Team Design

Is a Team Warranted?

The first question that any CEO has to ask is, Why create a top team in the first place? Several factors intensify the need for a team at the top—and unless these conditions are present, it may not be worth the effort. One factor working in favor of a top management team is what Don

Hambrick (Chapter 7) refers to as the need for corporate coherence. Coherence requires that diverse parts of the organization work together from an integrated logic to present a consistent view of the organization to outsiders, to meet competitive challenges across product lines and markets, and to create product families that share common features. An organization needs coherence to leverage core competencies across diverse business units and to react as a whole to environmental jolts. If corporate coherence is a strategic objective, then coordination across the firm is important, and consequently there is a need for a top management team.

A second factor creating the need for a top team is the rapidity of technological, market, social, and therefore organizational change in an industry. All of the CEOs at the April 1996 conference at Columbia (see Preface) spoke of the need to engage the top management team in the implementation of major organizational changes. It was only through intensive "organizational campaigns," in which the top team traveled throughout the firm explaining, motivating, and structuring change, that the rest of the organization could quickly follow the vision and strategy laid out at the top. Several CEOs mentioned that companies' competitive advantage will be determined increasingly by the speed at which they implement change.

A third factor motivating the need for an executive team is the sheer variety of demands on the CEO. Increasing global competition, technology-based change, federal regulation, shareholder and community demands, and turbulence in financial markets create a more complex task for the CEO and require that she or he spend more time dealing with external stakeholders. As a consequence, CEOs are looking for strategic and operational help.

Finally, the makeup of the top team and the personality of the CEO are key parameters in the decision as to whether or not to create a top management team. Significant questions include: Do top team members have the necessary skills? Can the CEO delegate decision-making authority? Do political and succession issues prevent the team from working together? Thus, the need for coherence, organizational change, the nature of the demands on the CEO, and the makeup of the team are key determinants of the need for an executive team.

Composition and Setup

The second basic question is whether we want to put a team together with the people that we have or with other people. Several of the CEOs at the conference spoke of the mistake of trying to build a top team with the wrong people. Hoping that people will change or struggling to build a team with one group while wanting to work with a different set of people creates tension and wastes time. Central issues are team members' expertise, willingness to change directions, complementarity with the CEO, and degree of diversity. The key lesson learned was, Don't set up a team until the appropriate people are present.

Conference participants made several suggestions about how to get a newly formed team off to a smooth start. First, the CEO has to serve as a role model. If the leader says that teams are important, he or she has to live that message in day-to-day interactions. This means that meetings with team members should appear on the CEO's calendar, decisions should be made both by the CEO and by the team, and rewards and promotions should be based on both team and individual performance. Second, the team structure needs to be put in place. Team members need to be colocated, or at least able to meet often enough to work together. The team should be given a name and should appear on the organizational chart. The identity and function of the team should be communicated throughout the firm. Through these steps the team acquires legitimacy in the corporation.

These design decisions having been made, how should team members interact with one another?

Basic Team Processes

At the April 1996 conference, much of the time allocated to the topic of executive teams focused on how teams need to operate to be successful. Participants identified four modes of operating: maintaining frequent interactions, taking on a corporate mindset, creating conflict, and managing conflict.

Frequent Interactions

In most of the papers and presentations at this conference, a common theme was the need for team members to meet often and intensively.

Team members are meeting not merely to report on their quarterly results or to deliver slide shows of their latest products; they are also meeting to work. They are meeting to confront, discuss, plan, strategize, share information, develop coherence, build scenarios, and make decisions. At a more basic level, they are meeting to learn about the views and opinions of their colleagues and to sharpen their own positions on critical issues (Eisenhardt, Kahwajy, & Bourgeois, Chapter 8). And in the process they are developing trust in one another. Thus, members are engaging in "real work" and confronting current issues within the firm.

All of the authors in this book share a model of the top team as a set of people who are tightly linked to one another. This does not mean that team members are necessarily always convening in formal meetings, although some amount of joint meeting time is mandatory. They may be meeting in smaller groups of two or three, or having regular e-mail correspondence. As Hambrick points out, "Physically convening is not as important as what Karl Weick and Karlene Roberts (1993) . . . referred to as 'heedful interrelating.'" Thus, as members make decisions in their own sphere of influence, they think about the implications of their decisions on others. When collective decisions about the firms are made, they are made with a full understanding of everyone's views and after large amounts of debate and disagreement.

Taking on a Corporate Mindset

One of the most important and difficult tasks for members of the top team is the need to take a corporate perspective. As each executive may be in charge of a set of business units or regions or customers or functions, there is a tendency to want to take an advocacy position for that part of the business. Similarly, as team members may be competing for the position of CEO of the future, there are many personal agendas. But executive teams need to consider the broader good of the firm. In the words of Paul Allaire of Xerox, "This requires that people shed a portion of who they are." The top team needs to move beyond serving solely as an arena for individual agendas, for this lessens the possibility for joint optimization.

Corporations are experimenting with a wide variety of mechanisms to motivate top executives to take this broader organizational perspective. Meeting off-site is one way to take people away from the local pressures and reminders of their day-to-day concerns. New reward structures, in which executive incentives are tied increasingly to corporate profits and to the output of their peers, are replacing bonuses based solely on individual performance. Finally, new organizational designs in which executives are given responsibility for multiple portions of the firm (e.g., both several business units and a particular geographic area) are pushing top managers to think about juggling differing local demands.

Creating Conflict

While many teams try to avoid conflict, Kathleen Eisenhardt, Jean Kahwajy, and L. J. Bourgeois (Chapter 8) view some conflict as useful and productive. The type of conflict that they are talking about is "substantive" or issue-oriented conflict as opposed to "affective" or personal conflict. The former arises from the clash of varied opinions, perspectives, and priorities, whereas the latter focuses on interpersonal friction. Issue-oriented conflict can help teams examine a greater range of information and more alternatives, achieve a deeper understanding of key issues, and generate better solutions.

According to Eisenhardt, Kahwajy, and Bourgeois, top management teams can foster productive conflict by building heterogeneous membership, meeting frequently, creating distinct roles (Ms. Action, Mr. Steady, Futurist, Counselor, and Devil's Advocate), and utilizing multiple-lens heuristics (multiple alternatives, multiple scenarios, competitor role playing, and overlapping subgroups). The key motivation behind these tactics is to bring divergent perspectives into the team. The team can then debate and balance short versus long run, stability versus change, multiple options, optimistic versus pessimistic views of the future, customer versus competitor focus, and so on. Eisenhardt and her colleagues, working from the hypothesis that conflict and high performance are related, argue that the techniques they propose can enhance both.

Managing Conflict

While issue-oriented conflict may be beneficial for a leadership team, other forms of conflict can be detrimental. As Charles Raben and Janet Spencer (Chapter 9) point out, personality clashes, the effects of many strong-willed individuals interacting, competition for succession, and differences in performance across members of the top team can all create conflict that is often just below the surface. Under these conditions it is often the CEO who must manage the conflict and ensure that effective and timely decision making takes place. Corresponding to the need for productive differences of opinion, then, is the need for top management to come together as a team and to show a united front. A team may go through several cycles of highlighting differences and then converging on a unified view.

Raben and Spencer lay out seven options for the CEO as conflict manager—the roles of Optimist, Terminator, Delegator, Tiebreaker, Coach, Synthesizer, and Conductor. Each role has a number of pros and cons associated with it. Discussions at the conference made it clear that, in fact, the CEO needs to take on many different roles. When decisions must be made in a timely manner and consensus is not working, the CEO may simply have to decide. When a new organization structure is set up in which authority is pushed down into entrepreneurial units, then the role of coach may be more dominant. While strategic direction is being decided, the CEO may invite the airing of differences of opinion; during strategy implementation, however, the top team may need to stand firmly behind the agreed direction.

Jamie Houghton pointed out at the conference that the most important thing for the CEO is to be clear about what role he or she is taking on at the moment. "You've got to let them know if you've got on your cowboy hat or your bowler hat." He argued that senior team members can deal with many CEO roles, but they do not want to spend time providing input only to find that the CEO has already made a decision. Thus, clarifying the parameters of decision making at a given point in time is key. This is quite consistent with research indicating that a leader should clarify whether the top management team is operating as a democracy, or the team is functioning as a set of consultants to the leader, or the leader is making the decision alone (Vroom & Jago, 1975). This need for the CEO to engage in multiple roles underlines the importance of flexibility in the management of executive teams.

Managing and Adapting to the External Environment

The conference discussions and the papers incorporated in this book do an excellent job of articulating the internal behaviors that help create an effective team. To meet intensively, create divergent perspectives and conflict, then pull together and take a firmwide perspective are all critical. What I would like to contribute here is what has been termed the "external perspective" (Ancona & Caldwell, 1992). This perspective argues that the key to understanding teams, including teams at the top, is to focus not only on what goes on inside the team's boundaries but also on what goes on between the team and the wider external environment. According to this external perspective, three processes are essential. The first is creating a corporate context that shapes team member behavior in appropriate directions. Second is engaging in active management of the external environment, and third is mapping team activity to the speed and timing of external cycles.

Creating a Supportive Corporate Context

The corporate context can strongly help or hinder team functioning. The context consists of the organizational culture, the reward system, and task design. Team success is amplified to the extent that the norms of the organization include teamwork, the reward structure supports team as well as individual achievement, and task completion is designed to require interdependence. Team members need to know how to work in teams, to know that they will not be penalized for working in teams, and to have tasks that demand that they work together. It is these background conditions in the environment that set the stage for effective team functioning.

External Activities

Another tenet of the external perspective is that top team members should scan, interpret, focus attention on, react to, and mold the broader external environment and then guide the organization. They should interact with customers, competitors, financial markets, the board of directors, shareholders, and other parts of the organization. Understanding and managing this external environment is a central and critical task of the team. Furthermore, external relationships play a large role in determining the internal behaviors that are, and that should be, taken on.

The CEO and the top management team must act as ambassadors to the external world. Ambassadorial activity includes representing the interests of the firm to outsiders, locating external resources and contacts, interpreting the political environment, and negotiating differences with outsiders. It is the top team that will shape the way Wall Street reacts to lower-than-expected earnings, delays in new product development, and management shakeups. The top team decides on major strategic alliances and joint ventures and on which technologies to adopt or reject. It sets the tone of relationships with customers and competitors, and it decides how to lobby the government in relation to legislation and regulatory change. It determines how the organization will react to significant external events and what strategies are most important.

This external activity requires that top team members spend large amounts of time outside of the corporation and the corporate offices. To obtain information and to interpret, influence, and understand the numerous external groups requires a large network and a dense set of interactions. Corporate leaders must also have detailed knowledge of current issues and positions within the firm in order to couple internal competencies and understanding with the changing external landscape.

Ideally, executive team members want to meld internal and external activity. A team with a thorough understanding of trends and changes in the external environment is better able to determine strategy and provide a rationale for its implementation. A team that is able to interact successfully with the media, customers, government, community, competition, and so on is more likely to develop trust and cohesion within its boundaries and to gain support from within the firm (Ancona, 1992). Team structures and processes may shift depending upon environmental conditions. For example, a new competitive challenge may require intensive meeting time with all team members as a new strategic direction is chosen. Conversely, team members may meet solely in subgroups or not very much at all when the focus shifts to improving internal efficiencies. Thus, the external perspective complements the focus on how team members interact with one another.

Speed and Timing

Another important facet of aligning the organization and the environment has to do with speed and timing. The top management team needs to synchronize or mesh its actions with the external environment. For example, as the speed of technical, market, and social change quickens, so too must the decision making of the leadership team. Eisenhardt (1989) illustrates how teams of executives who worked in "high-velocity environments" performed better when they were able to make decisions quickly so as to match the accelerated pace of change. These teams did not sacrifice thoroughness or the number of alternatives considered; yet through frequent meetings, up-to-date operational data, mechanisms for conflict management, and simultaneous consideration of multiple alternatives they could accelerate the decision-making process.

The timing of top team activity is also critical. If the team is going to come up with a new strategy, it has to do so when the market is ready. If the company is going to engage in large-scale organizational change, it is best to do so at a time when the environment is undergoing major environmental shifts or jolts (Tushman & Romanelli, 1985). Changing at a later point in time, or changing more frequently than the environment does, will not achieve the same result. Environmental jolts may emanate from changes in government regulation, alterations in a firm's competitive positioning, or new technologies that replace older ones. For example, Digital Equipment Corporation did extremely well when it reorganized around the Vax system and rode the wave of the minicomputer boom. Digital failed, however, to move quickly enough when the PC and Unix were introduced, and it suffered the consequences.

Unfortunately, matching the speed and rhythm of the external environment can be very difficult for the top team. The CEO and team may well be working on their own cycles—cycles related more to age, experience, accomplishments, and career aspirations than to changes in the environment. Also, top team members may fail to see changes in the environment, because over time they may engage in less and less environmental scanning. Teams and organizations may also fall prey to habits and routines; they may be able to change only when their own planning and budgeting cycles provide a window of opportunity to do so. These difficulties emphasize the need for top team members to remain both vigilant in their interaction with the external environment and capable of planning and implementing change quickly.

Conclusion

Given the great complexity of the top management team task, and the difficult set of internal and external activities required for team effectiveness, it is not hard to understand why many leadership teams fail.

Part II of this book has made it clear that if we are to harness the "madness" that plagues teams, we need to pay a lot more attention to team design, team processes, and the nature of the relationship between teams and the external environment. Flexibility in structure and mode of operating, creating and managing conflict, and succession planning are all key to managing the madness.

References

Ancona, D. G. (1993). The classics and the contemporary: A new blend of small group theory. In J. Keith Murnighan (Ed.), *Social psychology in organizations: Advances in theory and research* (Ch. 11, pp. 225–243). Englewood Cliffs, NJ: Prentice-Hall.

Ancona, D. G., & Caldwell, D. F. (1992). Bridging the boundary: External activity and performance in organizational teams. *Administrative Science Quarterly,* 37 634–665.

Eisenhardt, K. M. (1989). Making fast strategic decisions in high-velocity environments. *Academy of Management Journal,* 32, 543–576.

Tushman, M. L., & Romanelli, E. (1985). Organizational evolution: a metamorphosis model of convergence and reorientation. In L. L. Cummings & B. M. Staw (Eds.), *Research in organizational behavior* (Vol. 7, pp. 171–222). Greenwich CT: JAI Press.

Vroom, V. H., & Jago, A. G. (1988). *The new leadership: Managing participation in organizations.* Englewood Cliffs, NJ: Prentice-Hall.

Weick, K. E., & Roberts, K. H. (1993). Collective mind in organizations: Heedful interrelating on flight decks. *Administrative Science Quarterly,* 38, 357–377.

[III]

Boards of Directors

[11]

The Need to Improve the Board's Role in Corporate Governance

John L. Vogelstein

N O PRODUCT, group of products, or service is so extraordinary that its maker can prosper over the long run without excellent management. In the same vein, management excellence cannot be achieved without a truly superior CEO. On the other hand, I have observed that the worst of all possible worlds can occur when a company is headed by a CEO who is highly intelligent, a charismatic leader, a dynamic personality, and a great communicator—and yet somehow has it wrong. The damage that such an individual can do is incalculable. And the role of the board of directors is the key to preventing such damage.

Starting with this last observation, I will first explore the relationship between the board and the underperforming CEO; then I will discuss some ideas I have for improving the way boards of directors function generally.

First let me introduce myself. In my capacity as president of E. M. Warburg, Pincus & Co., I have observed and interfaced with a great many CEOs in a great many structures over extended periods of time; and I have participated in and watched the interaction between many CEOs and their boards of directors. The investment firm of Warburg Pincus manages money conventionally, which is to say we invest in stocks and bonds on behalf of individuals, institutions, and a group of

---

This material, originally delivered as a speech, has been edited for the purpose of inclusion in this book.

mutual funds that carry our name. Combined, this is a $20 billion business. We also manage money somewhat unconventionally, as "venture bankers." In our venture business we act as principals, investing in situations in which we can play a significant role at the policy-setting level. We started this activity in a formal way in 1971 and currently have about one hundred companies worth more than $7 billion in our portfolios and more than $1 billion of uninvested cash. The companies that we invest in range from start-ups to New York Stock Exchange–listed, multibillion-dollar enterprises. These companies' activities cover most industries and can be United States–based or foreign. Our investments, although broadly diversified by business, have several things in common: All of them are long term—we take a five- to seven-year view, and it is not unusual for a holding to go ten years or more. Each of our investments has a unique characteristic that brings us in, such as undervaluation, financial need, superior management, technological or socioeconomic dynamics, or deal structure. And in almost all cases, we are represented on the boards of directors of the companies in our portfolios by one or more Warburg Pincus senior executives. Over the years I have served on the boards of seventeen companies; I am often called upon to serve as a director of our larger investments, and I also tend to get involved in those companies that develop problems.

The Problem of the Underperforming CEO

Boards of directors of publicly traded United States corporations continually fail to face up to the issue of an underperforming chief executive officer. Examples of this failing have been celebrated in the popular and business press again and again. Companies in which such failure has been extremely visible include, among many others, General Motors, Eastman Kodak, American Express, K-Mart, Westinghouse, Woolworth, and Morrison Knudsen.

Obviously, there is a problem: Boards don't like to face up to the necessity of removing CEOs. Why is this so? Does the board function differently if major (20 percent or more) ownership is represented on the board? Are there changes in the American system of corporate governance that could be instituted to alleviate the problem?

I believe that the first issue that must be addressed is the combination of human nature and politics. Boards of directors usually consist of friends and acquaintances of the CEO of the company in question. The typical board structure of an American company is such that all board members are equal, which means that leadership within a board doesn't take place easily and that when leadership does emerge, it results more from personality characteristics than from any formalized structure. Also, most human beings resist the kind of confrontation that is involved in the removal from office of a chief executive officer. This tendency to draw back from painful confrontation is exacerbated by the difficulty of politically corralling other board members to an adversarial point of view. Adversarial mobilization is difficult because too many independent directors just don't care enough; they have no financial incentive driving them, so they see no urgent need to rock the boat.

Additionally, too many independent board members don't do enough homework to understand in depth the business of the companies on whose boards they sit. Therefore, they have trouble judging whether their managements are doing well or poorly. All too often, a rising stock price will be the test of doing well, whereas declining earnings will be the test of doing poorly. But how many times have we seen a combination of clever public relations, clever accounting, and short-term expediency—cutting research and development, for example—produce a rising stock price while a company was deteriorating internally? And conversely, how many times have we seen management excoriated for poor performance because it put long-term strategy ahead of immediate profits?

It should be noted that in a great many cases where top management is finally forced out, including most of the highly publicized cases I listed earlier, it is the behavior of the stock market and the outraged cries of investors that finally galvanize the directors to take action they should have taken years before.

The standpoint of an owner–director (the role I usually find myself in) is somewhat different from that of an independent director. Because vast sums of Warburg Pincus capital are at risk, our representatives on companies' boards of directors really do care; they really do their homework, and they really try to understand the business. This tends to pull the nonowner directors along to produce a better, more activist board. In turn, this usually enables our companies' boards to force the issue with an underperforming chief executive far more easily than can a purely independent board of directors.

I must admit, however, that even an organization such as ours, driven by exposure to underperformance of its own capital, often does not face the issue of CEO underperformance as promptly as it should. In fact, we have a saying at Warburg Pincus: "We have never fired a bad CEO too soon." On the other hand, although we haven't been perfect, we don't have any General Motors examples in our history.

Having defined what I view to be the principal problem of corporate governance in the United States, I would like to explore two possible structural changes that might improve the functioning of the American board of directors.

The British System

First, we could adopt the British system. In the United Kingdom it is typical for a company to be governed by two people: a nonexecutive chairman, who is paid well and is expected to devote considerable time to the affairs of the company, and a chief executive officer. The chairman deals primarily with board matters, stockholder issues, public policy matters, and the relationship between the board and the CEO. The day-to-day management of the company is in the hands of the CEO and subordinate officers. The advantage here is that the chairman is expected to be fully knowledgeable about the affairs of the company and carries a great deal of responsibility to the stockholders and the public for the company's performance. The chairman also is able to make a considerable impact on such key matters as CEO compensation. The chairman is the leader of the board and sets its tone.

I believe that a nonexecutive chairman, as the leader of the board, can be highly effective in mobilizing a board to remove, relatively promptly, an underperforming chief executive officer.

I am a director of a U.K. company that functions in this manner. In this particular case, my relationship, for historical reasons, is with the chairman, and although Warburg Pincus owns 30 percent of the company's shares, I usually make our point of view known through him. In this company it has been necessary to go through two CEO changes, and the changes were accomplished effectively by close cooperation between my firm and the chairman. (Of course, it was helpful that the company kept running out of money and we were the only source of additional capital.)

Until 1996 I was also a director of a U.S. corporation that operated with the same structure—a nonexecutive chairman who was paid and who worked, and a CEO who managed the business. In this case Warburg Pincus owned close to 40 percent of the company's shares, and my relationship was primarily with the CEO. This situation worked well and the investment was very successful; but I should point out that the CEO was, by birth and by business background, well attuned to the British system.

Unfortunately, I think that there are real barriers to the widespread importation of the British system. In the United States there is neither a history nor a culture of this kind of corporate governance; and without a cultural history to define the relationship, the risk of strife between an independent chairman and a chief executive is substantial. I do not believe that American CEOs will be prepared to accept this form of governance, which significantly reduces their "imperial power," for a great many years, if ever.

The "Lead Director" Concept

A possible variation on the British approach, which is beginning to be adopted in a few publicly owned U.S. companies, is to create the role of "lead director" or to establish a "committee on corporate governance" with a chairman. The lead director concept has real merit, and I urge that some way be found to have it broadly adopted. It clearly designates the person responsible for evaluating in depth the CEO's performance, and it obviates the need for extensive politicking if the CEO is found wanting. In fact, in those public companies where Warburg Pincus has large interests and is represented on the board, our firm's representative invariably serves as lead director (usually without a title). And, generally speaking, this works well.

The Activist Board

Let me move from the preceding two ideas, which would involve a fundamental change in how U.S. boards of directors operate, to several less traumatic changes that I believe also have the likelihood of improving the functioning of U.S. boards.

I have observed that directors who own meaningful (to them) amounts of stock pay more attention to the stockholders' interests and generally do a better job. Consequently, I would increase and formalize the ownership requirements for board representation.

There are far too many 100-share directors engaged in determining the fate of multibillion-dollar corporations.

I would pay all directors' fees 50 percent in cash and 50 percent in stock, with the requirement that the director continue to hold the stock so long as he or she remains on the board. But stock acquired in this manner would not substitute for the ownership requirements I mentioned above; a director has to have some personal net worth on the line.

I would require a reasonable participation, even a majority, of business and financial persons on a board. Academicians, scientists, lawyers, consultants, and so on bring interesting and diverse views, but they usually don't have a deep understanding of the practical aspects of business, commerce, and finance.

I would do away with annual retainers—a director who misses a meeting shouldn't get paid—and I would significantly increase attendance fees.

I would also require that any director who missed more than 50 percent of a company's board meetings for two years in a row resign from the board.

I would elevate the board's audit committee in importance, perhaps by paying double fees. I would require that every audit committee member be sufficiently versed in finance to comprehend fully the group's discussions of financial statements. Audit committees are often boring—thus my proposal for hardship pay; but I have seen more problems uncovered in audit committee work than anywhere else.

I would take steps to ensure that the compensation committee be entirely independent in its relationship with the CEO. There should be no interlocking directorates or other "friendly" relationships.

If there is a lead director, as I think there should be, that person should also be chairman of both the audit committee and the compensation committee.

Some of the foregoing ideas will be simple to put into effect. Some will be more challenging. Perhaps the most difficult is the ownership test, partly because what is a significant investment to one individual may well be small change to another. But the fact that something is difficult doesn't mean we should abandon it. And the ownership test is immensely important in terms of its potential to modify behavior. If we want directors to represent the best interests of owners and the long-run interests of the company, they must think like owners; and there is only one way to see that they do.

The changes I have described would, I believe, get rid of the "professional director" who sits on a dozen boards and collects a half a million dollars annually for doing very little other than not rocking the CEO's boat.

I would like also to see directors better protected against "strike suits." The fear of legal attack often freezes intelligent board action. It makes directors think about history and precedents, rather than about the future and new and better ways to do things. I also believe that the implementation of some or all of my suggestions would be sufficient to justify demands to curb, legislatively, the strike suit bar; and indeed, there already seems to be a sentiment moving in this direction.

Conclusion

Although I perceive that the boards of U.S. corporations need change, I would not want change to promote greater democracy in business governance or to empower stockholders further. I don't believe that democracy is an appropriate way to manage a business. I am strongly opposed to measures that would enlarge corporate bureaucracy, which is already tremendously burdensome; and increased bureaucracy would be the inevitable result of an increase in shareholders' rights to participate. We should bear in mind the ageless truism: "When the devil decided that nothing was to be done, he formed the first committee."

I think it is very important that people such as those who have contributed to this book try to push U.S. corporate governance in a direction that will avert future repetitions of what I call the General Motors problem: decline in one of the United States' largest companies that continued for more than a decade before the board acted. I fear that if changes in corporate governance are not made voluntarily, they will be imposed upon U.S. business by a combination of institutional stockholder pressure and regulatory or legislative action—just as perceived abuse of top executive compensation was attacked through the adoption of tax penalties. I have already observed increased stockholder activism (much of it poorly thought out) on the part of certain pension funds. Obviously, it would be better for business to find its own solution than to have the solution created and imposed by Washington.

[12]

The Board As Agent of Change

Jay W. Lorsch

T HE IMPORTANCE of companies' ability to adapt to changing circumstances has become a well-accepted truism. Organizations that
learn and managers who are creative and innovative are the stuff of
courses in MBA programs and executive education and management
training courses by the score. The rapid rate of technological change, the
globalization of consumer markets, and the rapid economic emergence
of Asia and Latin America have combined to create a pace of change that
may be unprecedented in modern history. Adaptive companies must have
the capacity to innovate strategically and organizationally: to develop
new products and markets, to improve manufacturing and service, to
boost productivity and quality, all toward the end of assuring profitable
long-term growth and improving financial returns to shareholders.

Conventional wisdom and the business literature have promulgated
the notion that a company's chief executive officer, all powerful and all
knowing, is somehow solely responsible for his or her company's success.
If the company is adapting well and growing profitably, the CEO gets
paid well and gains the kudos. Business leaders like Barnevik at ABB,
Iacocca at Chrysler, Eisner at Disney, Welch at GE, and Gates at Microsoft are often cited as examples in support of this view. Similarly, when a
company's performance lags and it fails to adapt to new circumstances,
the CEO is sacked like the manager of a losing baseball team. Stemple
at General Motors, Olson at Digital, Robinson at American Express,
Lego at Westinghouse, and Akers at IBM exemplify this pattern.

But this view of the sole responsibility of the CEO for corporate
success or failure ignores the credit or blame subordinate levels of

management should be given for either successful or failed adaptation. The strategic and organizational changes necessary for successful adaptation require the efforts of many individuals at all organizational levels. Failures to make needed adaptations may be attributable as much to lower-level managerial failures, organizational rigidities, and/or cultural resistance as to ineffective leadership by the CEO. In reality few CEOs are as knowledgeable, wise, and far-reaching in their influence as the popular view might suggest. Thus, the practical danger inherent in the image of the omnipotent CEO is that this image can foster a mistaken belief that bringing in a new CEO will by itself quickly solve preexisting problems.

On the contrary, anyone who has observed a new CEO trying to transform an organization that previously has not adapted successfully will recognize how difficult and complex the process is. Executives have to be changed. New strategies have to be developed and new organizational forms created. The multiple strategic and personnel changes and organizational moves taken since Jack Smith became CEO of General Motors in November 1992 provide a well-publicized example of this complexity, and of the time required for change. This observation is supported by academic research; for example, Gabarro suggests that it takes an effective new general manager of a division eighteen months to understand and lead his/her business.[1]

Even more significantly, the idea of the all-powerful and all-knowing CEO is inconsistent with the increasingly activist role directors are taking to create more adaptive companies. This new activism among directors has led to a broader definition of the board's responsibilities and to the need for organizations to rethink and alter the relationship between the board, especially nonmanagement (independent) directors, and the CEO. In this chapter I shall examine the board's new role as agents of change, the factors limiting the board's ability to perform in this regard, suggestions for ameliorating these hindrances, and important aspects of the relationship between outside directors and the CEO.

The Emergence of the Board As Change Agent

In all the previously mentioned examples of CEOs being removed, it was the board—or at least a few directors—who initiated the change. Directors in the companies in question became agents of change because they felt pressure from external sources to act. In some cases, such as Westinghouse and General Motors, there had been various public and private messages of disapproval about company performance from institutional investors (like Calpers and the New York State Employees Pension Fund), which collectively own more than half of such companies' shares.

In some companies, too, directors were concerned about the company's long-term financial health if they did not act. For example, at General Motors the outside directors stepped up their plans to investigate their company's problems and removed Robert Stempel when they became aware that credit rating agencies were about to downgrade the company's debt. Of course, many directors are also concerned about the impact on their personal reputations if they do not act and their company continues to go downhill. Finally, there has certainly been a snowball effect: After a few boards removed their CEOs (especially the CEOs of prominent corporations like General Motors and IBM), it became easier, perhaps even fashionable, for other boards to follow suit if their companies' performance was lagging.

In the language of the literature about organizational change, these CEO firings "unfroze" the situation across many corporations.[2] Old assumptions and beliefs were cast aside and the need for change was accepted, first by the board, then by senior management.

The next step for the board of a company needing transformation had to be to find a new corporate leader who could take the organization in the new directions required. While I am sure most directors did not think in these terms, implicitly they were looking for a leader who would continue the unfreezing process in the wider company, define new directions, and create a new equilibrium, presumably one that would allow for continuing adaptability going forward.

The board's emerging role as an agent of change was quickly noted by several experienced practitioners in corporate governance. John Smale, former CEO and chairman of Procter and Gamble and, at the time, chairman of the board of General Motors, said: "I believe the board of directors bears a unique responsibility and must play a unique role in trying to ensure that the company's management and its culture are able to anticipate and adapt to change. The board's role is to act as an independent auditor of management's progress, asking the tough questions that management might not ask itself—particularly when the company is doing well and is a recognized company leader."[3]

Speaking from a European perspective, Ellen Schneider-Lenne, herself on the management board of Deutsche Bank and on the supervisory board of several German companies, made a similar point. "In my eyes the main reason for corporate failure is the inability of management to adjust to changing market conditions and to implement the necessary changes. We have seen many companies which were driven out of business by a structural decline in their business area. Good companies, however, adjust in time; they cut costs, develop new products, and enter new markets. In this sense, good business means mastering the 'management of change.' Corporate governance should assist the process."[4]

Perhaps most significant of all, Chancellor William Allen of the Delaware Court, which has oversight over so many of America's large public companies, called for outside directors to become ongoing "monitors." "Outside directors should function as active monitors of corporate management, not just in crisis, but continually; they should have an active role in the formulation of the long-term strategic, financial, and organizational goals of the corporation and should approve plans to achieve the goals. They should as well engage in the ongoing review of short- and long-term performance according to plan and be prepared to press for corrections when in their judgment there is need."[5] While Chancellor Allen was speaking to an audience at a university and not ruling from the bench, this statement from such an important and widely respected jurist clearly provided legitimacy for directors' close oversight of their company and its managers. The obvious message is that directors should be on the lookout for the need for change and be ready to stimulate management to bring it about, precisely the same conclusions drawn by Smale and Schneider-Lenne.

None of these three calls for more vigilant corporate boards was specific about how directors might perform their responsibilities as monitors and agents of change. But if we review the recent examples of troubled corporations, we can see that the overriding problem in almost all cases was that the board was unable to recognize that they and management were failing to adapt to change in time to prevent the company from experiencing a substantial decline in competitive position and financial performance. As a consequence, the directors seemed to see only one solution to their problems—removal and replacement of the CEO. Clearly, waiting so long and taking such extreme steps are not the most desirable courses of action. In fact, the drama of CEO sacking resulted from the failure of all these boards to monitor company performance closely; to reach consensus about the need for change; and, working with the incumbent CEO, to achieve change in a timely fashion. In my judgment, these are the responsibilities boards must undertake in the future, if their companies are to be adaptive to change and to be spared the trauma of serious decline and CEO firings.

Factors Limiting Board Action

Understanding why boards have had difficulty acting promptly in the past will help define what we can realistically expect them to do in the future—and what needs to change within the boardroom for this to happen.

As I have pointed out elsewhere, a primary cause of boards' failure to act in the past has been the nature of the relationship between the outside directors and the CEO.[6] The directors lacked both the means (in terms of their power vis-à-vis that of the CEO) and the will (in terms of their relationship to him—and all of these CEOs were male). Why this was so has been explained in detail elsewhere,[7] so I shall only summarize here the factors that led to this state of affairs:

1. Most of the outside directors had been selected by the CEO and felt beholden to him.

2. Many of these directors (about two thirds) were CEOs of their own companies and felt empathy, if not sympathy, for their CEO.

3. This meant that most of the directors in the boardroom, especially those who were most respected and influential, were also busy running their own companies and may not have had adequate time to understand the problems in the company upon whose board they served.

4. In 85 percent of all U.S. companies, the chairman and CEO were the same individual. This meant that in the vast majority of boardrooms, the independent directors had no legitimate leader other than the CEO. Not only did this impede independent dialogue; it meant that the source of the board's informa-

tion, the setter of the agenda, and the leader of all deliberations was the person who should also be accountable to the board for company performance.

5. Finally, there had evolved in these boards a set of norms that affected the members' conduct with each other and their CEO. Most significant were the beliefs that it was improper to criticize the CEO in a board meeting and improper for directors to speak together without the CEO present.

It should be apparent that these circumstances alone made it very difficult for any board to reach a judgment about its company's situation that was contrary to the opinions of the CEO. But there are two other endemic problems.

First, the problem of information and knowledge. Even directors who are willing to take on their formal leader do not feel comfortable acting without thorough knowledge of their company's situation. But directors' primary, if not only, normal source of such data is the CEO (or other members of the top management team). Thus, at the time when the General Motors board acted to remove Robert Stempel, John Smale had already been asked by a few of his colleagues to interview GM's other top managers to gain insight into the company's problems, unfettered by Roger Smith, who was still on the board, or by Stempel himself.

A second problem is the matter of time. Typical boards meet four to six times a year for a day or less at each meeting. Even if we assume directors use another day to prepare for each meeting, this is very limited time in which to understand a complicated global company and its problems. Ask any of the directors who have taken leadership in the types of situations we are contemplating how much of their time it took, and the answers will be daunting—days and days at a stretch. Therefore, it is not surprising that the leaders of the change efforts of boards in the past have usually been retired CEOs, such as Smale at GM, Jim Burke at IBM, and Don Perkins at Kmart. These individuals had not only experience, knowledge, and credibility but the flexibility in their schedules to devote the needed time. The problem is that most directors do not have such time to understand their company's decline.

Given all these constraints, it may seem almost miraculous that so many boards have actually acted to bring about change. Looking to the future, in light of these difficulties, is it plausible to think the boards can play the roles of monitor and change agent that so many experts want them to adopt? I do believe that boards can and must be successful in these roles. Progress in dealing with the hindrances I have mentioned is already evident in many boardrooms. With more attention to board processes and to the new relationship needed between CEOs and directors, I believe even more progress is likely in a widening array of companies.

Progress to Date

The evidence about what changes have been occurring in boardroom practices is mostly anecdotal; it is not possible to document precisely how much change has taken place in how many boardrooms. Yet I believe that since the mid-1980s there has been a significant shift in the way directors of large publicly traded companies think about their roles. The performance problems of the companies mentioned above and the downfall of so many once respected CEOs have caught the attention of directors of other companies. The widespread interest focused on the role of boards by these events and by the ongoing pressure from institutional investors has also caused directors to take their jobs more and more seriously. Also contributing to this new sense of responsibility have been the fuss over CEO compensation and the SEC's new rules for reporting to shareholders about it.

One concrete piece of evidence about the change in directors' attitudes has been the spate of "corporate governance principles" being promulgated by many boards. The instigator of this trend was probably the General Motors board with its Board Guidelines. Like the other statements that have followed, the GM board's guidelines outlined how they intended to manage their activities going forward. These principles cover such topics as board leadership, the board's responsibility to meet without management, the composition and selection of the board, the board's evaluation of the CEO, the board's self-evaluation, directors' right to information and contact with managers, and so on. Without reviewing such statements in detail or trying to account for differences in emphasis from one company to another, I can say that the broad intent of all such guidelines I have seen is to give the outside directors more control of the board's affairs.

What is even more important is that these statements of governance principles reflect a major departure from attitudes and norms that existed in many boardrooms several years ago. Many directors now believe that they have the right and obligation to meet without management, and in fact do so periodically. They also no longer feel that it is inappropriate to interact freely among themselves outside of board meetings and/or without the CEO's presence. Further, such contacts have become so common on many boards that neither the directors nor the CEO seems to feel it necessary for the directors to keep the CEO apprised about them.

These changes clearly indicate a new relationship between the CEOs and the directors involved. While on most boards the CEO is still board chair and therefore the board's leader, the directors on these boards are finding ways to balance their power with that of the CEO. This newly complicated relationship between CEOs and directors will need to be clarified if boards are to be effective monitors and change agents. I shall turn to this shortly.

The fact that within a decade or so there has been such movement in boardroom norms and director behavior may seem surprising; such cultural aspects of group behavior are often very difficult and slow to modify. I believe one reason there has been so much change so quickly is that boards are not especially cohesive groups and therefore such norms are loosely held. If one or two directors on a board begin to call for change or actually behave differently, other directors quickly embrace the new way of doing things. I am sure, too, that movement is supported by pressures for change from outside the boardroom, which legitimate these new ways of acting. Finally, there are also instances of CEOs, especially new younger ones, calling for these new director behaviors, because they believe the new kind of board–CEO relationship will be in their and the company's best interests.

I am very optimistic that in boardrooms where the new norms are taking hold, boards will be able to take on the roles of monitor and strategic change agent. To do so, however, directors must not only clarify their relationship with their CEO but consider how to deal with the barriers of time and information mentioned above.

These barriers have not changed in recent years as much as boardroom norms have. True, there are more boards holding an annual two-day retreat at which they review the company's strategy with management. In crisis circumstances, too, directors have been spending more time together on board affairs. Yet the frequency and length of regular board meetings has not changed.

A related matter is, of course, just how directors use their limited time together. While I sense that in many boardrooms directors are attempting to use the time more productively, in general boards still have to deal with a great many specific issues, from committee reports to routine decisions, which make it difficult for them to dedicate adequate time to monitoring corporate performance. Like any deliberative group, boards are likely to prolong discussion on the early agenda items and to find themselves running out of time for broader issues left to the end of the session. And there are always specific legal and business details to address; so when strategic discussions are left to the end of the meeting, boards are even more likely to run out of time for careful and thoughtful consideration of them.

Yet time together is of little value if directors do not have the information and knowledge to hold intelligent discussions and reach consensus. Today, if the information directors receive is not adequate to their requirements, it is not because management is deliberately withholding it. Every director with whom I have spoken is quite clear that she or he can get any information they request. Rather, the difficulties have to do with the complexity of information directors require to understand company performance, with the challenge of interpreting the data, and with inadequate attention on management's part as to how best to present and communicate data to directors. The severity of these difficulties varies from company to company depending on organizations' size and scope. For example, directors trying to understand a multiproduct global company such as Hewlett-Packard or Johnson & Johnson have a much more complicated problem than do their peers on the board of an equally large single-service or single-product company such as Delta Airlines or Levi Strauss. The board members of the former companies need to get a view of how their company is doing not only in various parts of the world, but also in at least its major business segments. Those in the less diversified companies have only one business to understand, even though it may be operating in many different locales.

In order to monitor performance in any company, the monitors need not only financial information but data about product market performance, customer reactions, competitor results, and so forth. In many companies, however, there is still too much reliance on financial information and not enough on such product market data. While management can usually provide directors with information on these matters, these more complicated data are often difficult and time-consuming for directors to absorb and understand. In too many companies, too little attention is being paid to how such information can be organized and communicated efficiently to directors.

It is also true that formal reports, no matter how well presented, are only one ingredient in the information directors should have. Monitoring performance, it seems to me, also requires a broader sense of what the data mean and how to interpret them. Why are we losing share of market? Why do customers prefer competitors' products? Why is one of our new products doing well and another not? Answers to such questions, in most boardrooms, have traditionally been provided by the CEO. The problem is that if the CEO is wrong in his/her assessments, as CEOs must have been for many years at companies like GM or IBM, the board is also going to be tardy and ineffective in its change agent role.

Needed Improvements in Board Practices

If directors are going to be effective in monitoring company performance and in stimulating needed strategic change, therefore, I believe that U.S. corporate boards must make several improvements in how they conduct their affairs.

First, outside directors must continue to strengthen the present trend toward open communication among themselves, with and without the CEO present.

Boards must also pay explicit attention to how they can more effectively have time together. One obvious possibility is to hold more meetings each year, although these would likely be a burden on the already too busy individuals who serve as directors. Another, and I believe more feasible, possibility is to lengthen each existing board meeting. Most board meetings in reality do not last a full day, even including committee meetings, so this simple step would give directors a few more hours together at each meeting. Even a few more hours at each meeting could actually mean about 30 percent more time spent together. Lengthening existing meetings would mean that on large national and global company boards, out-of-town directors would not be asked to make extra trips.

Equally important is how directors actually spend the time they do have together. A board's time allocation is at least initially controlled by the agenda, which in turn is usually established by the board chairman (who is usually also the CEO). Meeting agendas must provide the board with time to review and discuss strategic plans and progress. How detailed these discussions should be will vary from company to company depending upon each firm's complexity. In all cases, however, an agenda should be structured and sequenced to ensure that the time for reviewing strategic progress is protected. Beyond the agenda, the board chair must manage the board's actual discussions, keeping directors focused on major strategic issues and not allowing them to spend inordinate amounts of time on minutiae.

It is also important that outside directors meet periodically without management or inside directors. Again, how frequently these meetings should be held will vary from company to company. The important point is that such meetings allow directors to share their thoughts on the company's strategic progress and to develop understanding and consensus about how well it is doing financially and competitively. Especially important, at at least one such meeting annually, the outside directors should discuss and reach consensus about their assessment of their CEO's performance. Such executive sessions should be scheduled not because of any mistrust of the CEO, but rather in recognition of the fact that directors feel more comfortable expressing their opinions, especially those that may be seen as critical, if the CEO is not present. Such sessions are vital for any CEO who wants the highest-quality advice and feedback from the board.

Board meetings will be of the most value if the directors are operating with the best possible information and knowledge. This means directors must receive more than just financial data. They need information that will help them understand the company's competitive situation, the way it is seen by customers and by financial markets, and the attitudes of employees. Even for a relatively uncomplicated company, such data can present directors with a formidable problem of synthesis and comprehension unless it is well organized and presented. Present computer technology, along with more sophisticated ways to measure and conceptualize such issues, should make it possible for managers responsible for disseminating information to the board to deliver it in a timely and organized fashion to each director in advance of board meetings. If directors understand these data before board meetings begin, there will be more time for discussion in meetings.

The information discussed so far, of course, will be supplied by management, in most instances with the explicit direction of the CEO. This is natural and desirable, since the CEO is probably the person best positioned to judge what data directors need to see. But because CEOs have biases and blind spots, directors also need other sources of information. One source is other senior managers in the company, to whom directors should have access if they feel the need for another perspective or more in-depth understanding of an issue. Such contact, however, should be made with the knowledge of the CEO and with the understanding that directors will discuss with the CEO any new information or ideas they receive. Beyond this, directors should be given pertinent information from any outside sources—trade journals, security analysts' reports, and so on.

Finally, I recommend that each board adopt five steps to ensure that it is effectively monitoring its company's performance:

1. The board must agree with management on a strategic plan for one year and a longer period (e.g., three to five years). The specifics of what such plans cover will vary among companies but should always include financial and competitive goals.

2. At each board meeting there should be a review of how well the annual plan is being executed and of the results achieved.

3. Once each year the board should review company performance against both the annual and the longer-term plans to see how well the plans are being executed. Is the actual strategy being used consistent with the plans? Where there are deviations, are they occurring because of changes in the business environment, failures in execution, or flaws in the original plan?

4. This strategic review should be a central input to the board's annual performance review of their CEO.

5. Based on this annual review, the board should discuss, revise if necessary, and approve management's strategic plan for subsequent years with special attention to the match between this plan and any changes in the company's environment.

The Board's Choice: New CEO or Not?

If boards adopt the above five steps and the other improvements I have discussed, I am confident that they will be able to act as monitors of company and management performance and to identify the moments when strategic change should be contemplated. At such moments the directors will have two choices. One is to persuade the existing CEO of the need for such change so that he or she can lead the transformation effort. The other is to replace the incumbent (as we have seen so many boards do in recent years) because he or she is either unwilling or unable to make the necessary alterations in strategic direction.

Changing the company's leader is a very dramatic and traumatic event for the directors, the CEO, and the entire organization. Why, despite this fact, have so many boards chosen this course of action? One obvious answer is that directors believed in the concept of the omnipotent CEO; in light of this belief, replacing the incumbent seemed the simple solution. A second answer, which is not inconsistent with the first, is that the directors, for all the reasons cited above, had waited so long to act that they had no other realistic course of action. By the time they realized the severity of their company's problems, the incumbent CEO was so much a part of the persistent inability of the company to adapt to changing conditions that the leader's departure was a necessary preliminary to any effort to establish new direction.

At the root of all of this was the relationship that existed between the CEO and the outside directors. In 1989[8] I described that relationship in power terms: The board had too little real power compared to the CEO to effect timely change. While this is still one valid way to describe directors' past difficulties in stimulating change, power is only one dimension of the relationship that has existed between the CEO and the board. Other dimensions include information symmetry and goal congruence and openness of communication and affect.[9] There is no systematic data on these aspects of the relationships that existed between the CEOs and the boards in the troubled companies we have been considering, but it is not hard to imagine how these relationships deteriorated as the companies' performance declined and why this deterioration led to the boards' decisions to remove their CEOs.

Clearly, in the past, asymmetry of information typically prevailed between the CEO and the outside directors: The CEO had more data than the directors. Many of the recommendations I have already made to improve board practices are aimed at creating a better balance of information between the two parties.

Apropos of the congruence of their goals, at one level most CEOs and outside directors have shared the goals of improving shareholder wealth and of ensuring the long-term health of the corporation. Even though they may have disagreed about which goal to emphasize at a given time, there seems to have been general agreement that both were important. But there is a third goal, the CEO's personal objective of prolonging his or her career, in which directors may gradually lose interest if a company's performance declines. When their company seems healthy, the directors and the CEO agree that the CEO's having tenure to normal retirement is desirable. As the directors develop the perception that their company is in difficulty, however, they are likely to abandon this goal, while most CEOs do not. This said, it is also worth noting that even when goals become incongruent, boards are very careful to put the best possible face on a CEO's departure, wanting to protect not only their own image of sagacity but their departing leader's reputation and ego.

In the past, as I have indicated, lack of openness of communication between the CEO and the board was another serious problem. There were few opportunities for directors to communicate openly with their CEO in board meetings. When the CEO and a director talked privately, the great respect and empathy directors generally felt for their leader dampened clear communication of the director's message of concern about performance. Also, the desire to stay in office was, consciously or unconsciously, an increasingly strong inhibitor on the CEO's openness about problems and ability to hear negative feedback.

Over time, as a company's problems continue, directors become more suspicious about the inconsistency between information on declining performance and the CEO's optimistic communication that progress is just around the corner. The result of this dissonance and the lack of open communication with the CEO leads to a growing mistrust, and this sense of mistrust erodes the positive feelings that the directors previously held for their leader. In place of respect— even reverence—for the CEO, directors begin to feel doubt about the CEO's abilities and sympathy for his or her plight. Having lost confidence in their leader, they begin talking to one another about what should be done. In the troubled companies I have mentioned, this process of deterioration in the board–CEO relationship seems to have lasted for a year or longer—with the result that by the time the board had developed a consensus to act, its mistrust and lack of confidence in the CEO had reached the point that the only viable option seemed to directors to be the CEO's removal.

Board–CEO Relationships of the Future

This portrait of the declining relationship between the CEO and outside directors suggests another significant but less tangible change that must occur in the future if boards are to be effective monitors and stimulators of strategic change: Directors and their CEOs must develop a new and more complex kind of relationship than has existed in the past.

Whereas in the past the CEO has clearly been the more powerful party, in the future he or she will have to share influence over board-related matters with the directors. As the earlier discussion of progress to date indicates, directors are already gaining more control of their own activities. Increasingly, directors will also be explicitly approving corporate strategy and reviewing the performance of the company and the CEO. In a sense, the CEO and the directors will be acting as peers, with the CEO being primarily concerned with the leadership of the company and the directors with their oversight functions. Even though in most companies the CEO will probably retain the title of chairman of the board, there seems little doubt that her or his impact on board activities will be more limited than it has been in the past.

Directors will also be better informed, which will have the effect of diminishing this source of the CEO's past power. This greater symmetry of information should also make communications between CEO and directors more open, a direction that changing boardroom norms support. A part of this openness will have to be more willingness on the part of CEOs to express their doubts and concerns to the directors and to involve the board in discussing uncertainties and problems. Directors, too, will have to be more open in articulating their concerns—not only about company direction but about the way the board itself is carrying out its duties.

In sum, shared power, more symmetrical information, and more open communication will be the characteristics of these new board–CEO relationships. But while necessary and desirable, these characteristics will also heighten the possibility of misunderstanding and conflict between the parties. It is going to take careful communication between the CEO and the directors to define each party's responsibilities and to correct any misunderstandings. If this communication is done well, and assuming (as I do) that the parties continue to share the goals of shareholder wealth and corporate health, I believe this new type of relationship between management and directors will be based on trust and mutual respect. In the final analysis, it is trust and respect that will enable directors to monitor company performance in a timely manner and to prevent the major company declines and the CEO firings we have seen in past years.

Notes

1. John J. Gabarro, *The Dynamics of Taking Charge* (Boston: Harvard Business School Press, 1987).
2. Kurt Lewin, "Quasi-Stationary Social Equilibrium and the Program of Permanent Change." In *The Planning of Change*, Eds. Warren Bennis, Kenneth Benn, and Robert Chin (New York: Holt, Rinehart and Winston, 1961).
3. John Smale, "Why Do Great Companies Lose Their Leadership?" (speech to the Commonwealth and Commercial Club of Cincinnati, Ohio, 21 October 1993).
4. Ellen Schneider-Lenne, "The Governance of Good Business" (lecture presented as part of the Stockton Lectures, London Business School, 26 November 1992).
5. William Allen, "Redefining the Role of Outside Directors in an Age of Global Competition," Ed. Ray Garrett Jr. (speech to Corporate Securities Law Institute, Northwestern University, Chicago, 30 April 1992).
6. Jay W. Lorsch and Elizabeth MacIver, *Pawns or Potentates: The Reality of America's Corporate Boards* (Boston: Harvard Business School Press, 1989); Lorsh, "Empowering the Board," *Harvard Business Review* 73 (January–February 1995).
7. Lorsch and MacIver, *Pawns or Potentates*.
8. Ibid.
9. Chris Argyris, "Teaching Smart People How to Learn," *Harvard Business Review*, May–June 1991.

[13]

Control and Creativity
in the Boardroom

Andrew Pettigrew and Terry McNulty

T HE THEME OF THIS CHAPTER is the balance between control and
creativity in the contributions of part-time board members.
Drawing on data from chairmen and nonexecutive directors of major UK public limited companies (PLCs), we report on the perceived influence of part-time board members in a range of board
and company activities. Many of these activities focus on control,
notably in governance mechanisms and policy and in the selection,
succession, and compensation of directors. But there can also be a
creative role for part-time board members; for example, in strategic
decision making; in contributions of ideas, experience, and knowledge to governance arrangements and key personnel decisions; and
in the fashioning of the processes through which strategies evolve.

The control activities of part-time board members also demand
creativity in the use of political power. Micropolitics differ not only
from board to board but also, over time, within the same board. The
shaping of the appropriate mixture of political will and skill to realize
control ambitions is one of the tasks part-time board members find
particularly challenging. In the final section of this chapter, we use two
illustrative examples of the dismissals of two full-time company chairmen by their boards to illustrate some of the emotional, analytical, in-

The authors wish to acknowledge the financial support of the Economic Social Research Council (grant number R000236109).

226

terpersonal, and political demands made on part-time board members. This ultimate expression of control requires considerable creativity.

Board Structure and Conduct in the UK

The corporate governance arrangements in Germany, Japan, France, the United States, and the United Kingdom have been shaped by features of the political, economic, social, and legal contexts of these societies (Charkham, 1994). In the UK the conduct of many institutions reflects a preference for the adversarial approach—as any observer of Parliament will attest. The more destructive features of collective bargaining and customer–supplier relationships also bear witness to antagonistic structures and behavior. In the UK it is also curious that accountability has played a less obvious role in the economic than in the political sphere. There remains a constant preference in the UK for institutions to be self-regulated, and in the sphere of corporate governance even the law takes second place to codes of best practice.

The legal framework that shapes board structures and conduct in the UK offers a light touch. Charkham's lucid 1994 account points to several critical features relevant to the themes of this chapter. The legal structure in the UK rests on the simple principle that the owners (shareholders) appoint agents (directors) to run the business, and the directors report annually on their stewardship. In practice, in public limited companies (of which there are around 2,000 in the UK), there is a two-link chain of accountability—management is accountable to directors, and directors are accountable to shareholders. PLCs registered after 1 November 1929 are legally required to have at least two directors. There is no distinction between classes of directors: for instance, between executive (inside or full-time) directors and nonexecutive (outside and part-time) directors. The law refers only obscurely to chairmen and barely mentions boards. This legal minimalism leads Charkham (1994, p. 262) to conclude that "the superstructure as we know it: boards, board committees, chairmen, nonexecutive directors—are pragmatic adaptations. In law none is essential; to this day ICI could legally be run by two directors, like the consulate of the Roman Republic."

Because there is no requirement in UK law to have a board, there can be no requirement to have a chairman; but in fact directors tend to meet in committee, and they choose a chairman to lead them. (There are no female chairpersons in the top 350 PLCs in the UK.)

Most large UK boards now divide the chairman and CEO roles, and the position of chairman is often part time. Most chairmen have had successful careers as CEOs or as executive directors of major PLCs, but some have political or civil service backgrounds. Chairmen have major responsibilities in determining the size, balance, composition, and agenda of the board. They can also play a significant part in handling external relationships with key stakeholders such as government, institutional investors, regulators, and banks. Chairmen are normally appointed by nonexecutive directors, sometimes after a consultation process involving the outgoing chairman and the current CEO.

Nonexecutive directors now play an increasingly important role in UK PLCs. They can be current or retired CEOs or executive directors of PLCs, and some may also have political, military, or civil service backgrounds. In the UK there are very few academics on the boards of major PLCs. The nonexecutive role is also a part-time one.

The aphorism "The chairman runs the board and the CEO runs the company" captures aspects of the reality of UK board functioning. Despite the reality of chairman power, CEOs are themselves very influential and, with their executive director team, play a fundamental part in shaping the board process and company strategy. In practice all directors are appointed by the board and elected by the shareholders.

Beyond these various roles, the key individuals may belong to a series of board committees. The most important of these are the audit, remuneration, and nominating committees. Normally populated by the part-time members of the board, these committees represent opportunities for the chairman and nonexecutive directors to caucus and legitimately intervene on crucial matters of financial reporting and control and on executive remuneration and succession. The CEO chairs an executive team that develops and tests ideas before final decision at the board.

Just as features of macrocontext shape the broad framework of UK governance structures and processes, an equally crucial set of local microcontextual features mold a given board's particular arrangements. These features include the history and performance of sector and firm; custom and practice in board structure and culture; the experience and expectations of individual chairmen and chief executives; the caliber of the executive and nonexecutive directors; and the board members' skill and will in intervening in and outside the boardroom. From this mixture emerges the unique constellation of structures, interactions, and sentiments felt by every board member. One of the most constant refrains we hear in our interviews with part-time board members is, "Well, of course, every board is different."

Differences there may be, but there are also patterns and themes to be observed (Lorsch and MacIver, 1989; Mace, 1971; Pettigrew and McNulty, 1995). A major preoccupation of board researchers and commentators is the issue of control. Finkelstein and Hambrick (1996) give great emphasis to board vigilance and the extent to which boards effectively monitor and discipline senior executives. This view is mirrored in "agency theory": Fama and Jensen (1983) and others portray shareholders as principals and executives as agents. According to this view, the major corporate agency problem is the potential self-interested behavior of the agents, and the board must serve as a monitoring device that governs executive decisions and assesses their impact on shareholder wealth. Beyond the boardroom, institutional investors (Useem, 1993) and hostile takeovers (Morck et al., 1989) may also function as corrective mechanisms to remove unresponsive managers in poorly performing firms.

A further major tradition of debate and analysis rises out of the Berle and Means (1932) thesis that although shareholders have legal ownership of large corporations, they no longer effectively control them. Although this area of research has been bedeviled by conceptual disagreements about the term *control* (see Herman, 1981; Mizruchi, 1983) there is now a body of analytical work in this tradition. In an oft-quoted study, Mace (1971) concludes that the powers of control rest with the president, not the board. Herman (1981) argues that management (the CEO and executive directors) control the firm, but always in the context of the varying sets of constraints and latent powers of stakeholders such as outside directors; shareholders; and, at certain moments, creditors. Studies using what Kosnik (1987) describes as the "managerial hegemony theory" offer different analyses of management's control over the board. Factors often cited include the management's control over the selection of part-time board members and the consequent co-optation of those members; the limited time outside directors have to devote to their duties; the superior expertise, information, and advice available to management; and norms of board conduct that restrict the outsiders' ability to function as independent dissenting voices (Herman, 1981; Lorsch and MacIver, 1989; Mace, 1971).

Lorsch and MacIver (1989) confirm the stream of work in the managerial hegemony tradition in saying that real power lies with the governed—that is, with the top management team—and that the success or failure of individual companies normally rests with them. The problem for the nonexecutive directors on the board, then, is to translate their legal mandate into effective power over the top managers, especially the CEO. The Lorsch case studies illustrate that this translation can be achievable in crisis situations (e.g., takeover attempts; the death or incapacity or succession of CEOs; or legal, environmental, or performance threats); but control relations are quite different in normal times. Lorsch and MacIver argue that gradual declines are tremendous challenges to directors.

Policy debates about board governance and control in the UK have been dominated by the Cadbury Report (1992). Set up in May 1991, the Cadbury Committee probed deeply into (among other topics) boards, nonexecutive directors, and executive directors. The Cadbury code of best practice advocates the retention of the single board of executive and nonexecutive directors. It also recommends that power be evenly distributed among board members—who are, after all, equally liable for their collective actions. The code also emphasizes principles of "openness, integrity, and accountability."

Nevertheless, the issue of control is focal to the Cadbury recommendations. The report gives due emphasis to the chairman's role and powers and to the monitoring and independent stance of the nonexecutive directors. Although the report does not rule out CEO duality (that is, the CEO's also serving as board chairman), it suggests that the power of the nonexecutives is bolstered by their election of a leader of their own. The report also recommends the setting up of audit, remuneration, and nominating committees, all led by nonexecutives or by the chairman and composed largely of part-time board members. And indeed, the UK's top 350 PLCs have now implemented most of these structural mechanisms.

But is the part-time director on the board just to monitor, control, and confront? PRO-NED (pro-nonexecutive director) (1987) advocates an advisory and supportive role for nonexecutive directors. Fundamental to this ideal scenario is the requirement that nonexecutives maintain good working relationships and remain independent and free to challenge executive opinions and decision making.

In a 1992 review of these various theories and recommendations, Matthew Pettigrew (1992) asks for a more effective synthesis of the literature on part-time board members. He argues that it is unsatisfactory to pose the contradictions and dilemmas in the outside director's role merely as a choice among control, confrontation, complementarity, and support. In this chapter we take up this challenge to explore the contribution and style of part-time board members. We begin by reporting changes in the structure and composition of the UK's top 350 PLCs in the 1990s—changes that demonstrate the impact of the Cadbury Report in shaping the boardroom context. Next we move from structure to process; we return to our theme of control and creativity in the boardroom and compare and contrast the perceived contribution and influence of our sample of chairmen and nonexecutive directors. In the third section we pick up one of the central influence areas of part-time board members—their contribution in dismissing their chairman and/ or chief executive. Two illustrative case studies indicate how and why this exercise of control is dependent on creativity, ability, and agility in the use of power. In the concluding section we summarize our argument and outline some of the challenges part-time board members face in exercising control and creativity in the boardroom.

The Cadbury Influence in the Boardroom

The Cadbury Report (1992) and its accompanying code of best practice have been used to justify numerous attempts to reform corporate governance. Research studies (Bostock, 1995; Conyon, 1994, 1995) have reported on the extent of company compliance with the code of best practice, and in 1995 the Cadbury Committee published its own report on compliance (CADS, 1995). Between them these studies demonstrate some remarkable changes in the composition and structure of UK boards since the late 1980s. What these studies cannot establish, however, is the extent to which the changes have occurred in response to the Cadbury Report and the code rather than to recent high-profile attention focused on corporate governance matters in the UK.

Conyon (1995), using data supplied by the Hemmington Scott Corporate Information Database on the *Financial Times* (FT–SE) top 100, mid 250, and top 350 quoted UK companies, reveals a clear pattern of company adherence to the Cadbury recommendations. (Conyon notes that there is no statutory requirement for a company to reveal its board committee structure, so the failure of a company to reveal the existence of a committee does not necessarily mean it does not exist; since Cadbury, however, it is in companies' interests to be as transparent as possible in reporting noncontroversial matters about board structures.) Tables 13.1, 13.2, and 13.3 summarize the main patterns in the data from the Conyon study.

The noteworthy conclusions are:

1. The overall average board size for the FT–SE 350 companies is 9.87. The ratio of nonexecutive directors for large UK companies is approximately equal. The average of 5.02 nonexecutive directors per company considerably exceeds the Cadbury minimum recommendation of three and more than meets the PRO-NED target of a third.

Table 13.1

Boardroom Size and Structure in UK Companies, 1994

	Average Size of Board	*Average Number of Nonexecutive Directors*	*Average Number of Executive Directors*
FT–SE top 100 companies	12.3	6.15	6.16
FT–SE mid 250 companies	8.89	4.57	4.32
FT–SE top 350 companies	9.87	5.02	4.85

Source: Conyon (1995).

Table 13.2

Remuneration Committee Structures in UK Companies, 1994

	Number of Companies with Remuneration Committee	*Average Size of Remuneration Committee*	*Average Number of Nonexecutive Directors on Remuneration Committee*	*Number of Nonexecutive-only Remuneration Committees*
FT–SE top 100 companies	100	4.61	4.28	73
FT–SE mid 250 companies	233	4.07	3.63	161
FT–SE top 350 companies	333	4.23	3.82	234

Source: Conyon (1995).

Table 13.3
Audit Committee Structures in UK Companies, 1994

	Number of Companies with Audit Committee	Average Size of Audit Committee	Average Number of Nonexecutive Directors on Audit Committee	Number of Nonexecutive-only Audit Committees
FT–SE top 100 companies	100	4.24	4.05	92
FT–SE mid 250 companies	246	3.94	3.59	208
FT–SE top 350 companies	346	4.03	3.73	300

Source: Conyon (1995).

In a 1993 postal survey of 400 of the *Times* 1,000 top UK companies between 1988 and 1993, Conyon (1994) found the average proportion of nonexecutives on the main board in 1993 to be 44 percent, up from 38 percent in 1988. There is clearly a rising trend in the use of nonexecutive directors in large UK PLCs.

2. Table 13.2 indicates close adherence to the Cadbury and institutional shareholders' committee recommendations on the creation and composition of remuneration committees. Almost all the FT–SE 350 companies have remuneration committees that set top pay. Table 13.2 also shows the minimal presence of executive directors on such committees. Even so, among the 1994 FT–SE 100 companies, there were still thirty-three executive directors who sat on their company's remuneration committee.

   According to Conyon's 1993 study, in contrast, only 54 percent of companies sampled had had remuneration committees in 1988.

3. The Cadbury Report states that "all listed companies should establish an audit committee" (1992, 4.35, p. 28) in order to help safeguard shareholder interests. Table 13.3 shows that by 1994 98.9 percent of the FT–SE 350 companies had audit committees and that nonexecutive directors were a dominant feature of the audit committee.

This high disclosure of the existence of audit committees
again shows considerable change from the disclosure rate in
1988, when a Bank of England (1988) company survey found
that only 56 percent of the *Times* 1,000 top 250 companies reported the existence of audit committees.

The picture that emerges from the Conyon studies (1994, 1995) is
one of substantial change in the prevalence of remuneration and audit committees between 1988 and 1994. Bostock (1995), however, has
shown a lesser rate of adoption of board nominating committees.
Nominating committees, when available, may be able to bring a more
objective approach to the selection of executive and nonexecutive
board members. But, again using publicly available data disclosed in
company annual reports, Bostock (1995) showed that 53 percent of
the top 100 UK companies by market capitalization did not have a
nominating committee. Conyon (1994), too, found that although the
incidence of nominating committees had trebled between 1988 and
1993, still only approximately 40 percent of UK quoted companies
had them in 1993, despite the Cadbury code of practice.

The Cadbury code of practice doesn't require companies to split
the roles of chairman and chief executive, although it does recommend that where the roles are not split, there should be a strong independent element, with a recognized senior member, on the board.
The Cadbury Committee's own research on compliance (CADS,
1995) shows that by 1994 the roles of chairman and chief executive
were split in 82 percent of UK firms in the top 500 by market capitalization. Conyon's (1994) postal survey of 400 firms in the *Times*
1,000 found that in 1993 77 percent of quoted companies had split
the two roles, compared with 57 percent in 1988.

We must qualify the above very clear trends of structural compliance with Cadbury in light of several considerations. First, apparent
compliance with the Cadbury recommendations may also be a product of the wider UK debate on governance matters. Second, compliance does not necessarily prove universal acceptance of the Cadbury
message. Notable high-profile skeptics such as Sir Owen Green
(1994) and Sir Christopher Hogg (1994) argue for some reform but
also bridle against overemphasis on the monitoring and independent
roles of nonexecutive directors. In the context of the UK unitary
board, Hogg (1994) argues for power equivalence and a climate of

quality thinking and debate between nonexecutives and executives. Third, however, the real limitation of the trend data is their distance from the behavioral dynamics of the boardroom itself. We need to know much more than we do about the processes, procedures, actions, and outcomes of boards and their committees. How are committee agendas set, how is committee membership decided, and what kind of formal and informal information and advice shapes committee policy and outcomes? It is ironic that just at the point when 95 percent of FT–SE 350 companies have remuneration committees and when we have maximal structural compliance with Cadbury, there is also maximal public and political furor about the decisions emanating from these committees and structures (Conyon and Singh, 1995). The question can legitimately be asked, What are these part-time board members *doing* on all these remuneration committees?

Board Processes and Dynamics

In a review of the published literature on managerial elites, A. M. Pettigrew (1992) has argued for much more serious attention to be given to behavioral dynamics in and around the boardroom—the crucial processes that shape the impact and effectiveness of directors and boards. How do chairmen and nonexecutive directors create a role and power base for themselves? What kind of contribution do directors make in and outside the boardroom, and how is that contribution shaped by experience and skills they bring to the boardroom and by their ability to mobilize and use a variety of power sources and influence methods? How are powerful part-time board members bolstered by linkages outside the firm—and checked by executive management inside the firm? Is it easier for part-time board members to exercise influence in times of corporate crisis? Under certain conditions, do part-time board members succeed in blocking executive initiatives but fail to originate other approaches themselves? Are some kinds of board contributions easier than others for part-time board members to make? How does the relationship between chairman and CEO affect the scope for nonexecutive director influence? What circumstances enable part-time board members both to exercise control and to perform a creative role in the board? These are some of the central behavioral questions informing our current work, the Warwick Business School study of boards and directors.

The Warwick study has the following aims:

1. To examine the backgrounds and careers of 80 part-time board members from the UK's top 200 industrial and commercial companies and top 50 financial institutions.

2. To study the contributions, power, and influence of part-time chairmen and nonexecutive directors within and across the firms they serve as part-time board members.

The sample of part-time board members (either chairmen or nonexecutive directors) for the study is drawn from the top 200 UK industrial and commercial firms by turnover listed in the *Times* 1,000 for 1992–93. We added the top 50 financial institutions on the basis adopted by Scott and Griff (1984). The list of directors for these 250 firms was compiled from the official *Stock Market Yearbook* for 1992–93 by Professor John Scott and Nurmal Puwar of Essex University as part of their plans for a different but complementary study of political and economic elites in the UK. We have updated the list using the Arthur Andersen Corporate Register for March 1994, and have identified the distribution of multiple-board directors across the total population of directors.

We intend to interview 160 board members from the 250 firms. Eighty of the interviews will be with part-time board members; the other eighty interviews will be full-time board members (CEOs and executive directors) and company secretaries. As these full-time board members are in a position to observe part-time board members in action and to evaluate their contributions and influence, we believe this second set of interviews will enhance the reliability of the data gathered from the self-reports of the part-time chairmen and nonexecutive directors.

We have carried out a pilot study of twenty interviews, on the basis of which we have already published two papers (McNulty and Pettigrew, 1996; Pettigrew and McNulty, 1995). A key feature of each interview is the "critical incident" question. We ask part-time board members to describe in some detail instances where, either as a chairman or as a nonexecutive director, they have succeeded or failed to influence board behavior on matters of substance. These critical incidents allow us to examine the way features of the context, process, and content of an issue interact. In this way we are able to disentangle why and how part-time board members are able to exert leverage in different content areas of the board process and agenda. An early content analysis of these critical incidents (McNulty and Pettigrew, 1996) reveals the range of contributions claimed by part-time chairmen and nonexecutive directors. It also begins to highlight their different power sources and influence methods. Part-time chairmen influence most by assertiveness, building on the authority that comes with leading the board. Nonexecutive directors without the same positional power lean more heavily on their personal experience and expertise, their skill in forming relationships and coalitions inside and outside the boardroom, and their skill and will in persuasion.

The Warwick study continues, but this chapter (written in 1996) draws only on a limited analysis of our first 36 interviews. These 36 part-time board members include 23 people who hold one or more chairmanships (several of whom hold multiple nonexecutive directorships). This group is entirely male. The other 13 hold multiple nonexecutive directorships, and 5 of this group are female. Looking across the subsample of 36, 27 have industrial and commercial backgrounds; 3 are former senior civil servants; 2 are former politicians; and the remaining 4 have backgrounds either as part-time public servants or, in one case, as an academic. This chapter's appendix lists the individuals interviewed.

Board Functions and Part-Time Board Member Contributions

There is now an established literature on the functions performed by boards; it ranges from well-informed prescription (e.g., Cadbury, 1990; Charkham, 1986) to research data from interviews and questionnaires (e.g., Demb and Neubauer, 1992; Lorsch and MacIver, 1989). Lorsch and MacIver (1989) argue that the major duties of boards are: selecting, assessing, rewarding, and if necessary replacing the CEO; determining strategic direction; and ensuring legal and ethical conduct. Demb and Neubauer (1992) concur with Lorsch and MacIver on the personnel and strategy duties but also give emphasis to the controlling, monitoring, and supervisory aspects of board functioning and the need for boards to address issues of resource acquisition and external relationships. In the UK, the Institute of Directors (1995) has argued that the four main tasks of the board are: establishing vision, mission, and values; determining strategy and structure; delegating to management; and exercising responsibility to shareholders and other parties.

Unfortunately, such prescriptive lists of duties can tell us little about the actual contributions made by part-time board members. There is a need for basic descriptive evidence to identify whether and how part-time chairmen and nonexecutive directors contribute to board processes and outcomes. For example, are part-time board members more involved in setting strategic direction than in hiring and firing members of top management? If part-time directors are involved in the strategy development process, at what stage in the process does their involvement peak? Are there significant differences in the relative influence of chairmen and nonexecutive directors across the range of board tasks? And if contributions are being claimed or made by part-time board members, what is the role of power mobilization and use in the contribution process? We now turn to illustrative data to answer some of these questions.

From our pilot study and from responses to the "critical incident" questions, we have compiled a list of influence processes covering the activities of chairmen and nonexecutive directors. We are now using this list as an instrument to assess the perceived influence of these part-time board members. We ask the following standard trigger question:

> Across your experiences as a nonexecutive director [or chairman], how much influence do you feel you have on the following issues?

Following the question is a list of 36 items for nonexecutive directors, or 34 for chairmen; see Tables 13.4 and 13.5. We instruct each interviewee to score his or her degree of influence on a scale of 1 to 5, where 5 is "very influential."

Table 13.4

Items Ranked by Amount of Influence Reported by *Part-time Chairmen*

Rank (1=top)	Item	Mean Influence Score	Median Influence Score
1	Appointment of the chief executive officer	4.96	5.0
1	Replacement of the chief executive officer	4.96	5.0
3	The process and conduct of board meetings	4.91	5.0
3	Annual general meeting of shareholders	4.91	5.0
5	Selection of nonexecutive directors	4.87	5.0

Table 13.4 (con't)

Items Ranked by Amount of Influence Reported by *Part-time Chairmen*

Rank (1=top)	Item	Mean Influence Score	Median Influence Score
6	Creation of board subcommittees (e.g., audit, nominating, remuneration)	4.69	5.0
6	Response to a takeover bid	4.69	5.0
8	Compensation of full-time executive directors	4.61	5.0
9	Appointment of executives to the main board	4.43	5.0
10	Decisions about acquiring other firms	4.39	5.0
11	Decisions about merging business	4.35	5.0
11	Ethical conduct of the firm	4.35	4.0
13	Relations with government	4.26	4.0
14	Replacement of executive board members (other than the chief executive)	4.22	4.0
15	How the firm develops strategy	4.13	4.0
15	Policy making in board subcommittees (e.g., audit, nominations, remuneration)	4.13	4.0
17	Issuing of dividends	4.09	4.0
17	Social responsibility of the firm	4.09	4.0
17	Management succession planning within the firm	4.09	4.0
20	Decisions about disposing of business operations	3.91	4.0
21	Decisions about joint ventures	3.87	4.0
21	Relations with institutional shareholders	3.87	4.0
23	Appointment of senior executives to the company	3.83	4.0
24	Structure of the firm's business activities	3.65	4.0
25	Relations with noninstitutional shareholders	3.63	4.0
26	Exit from markets	3.61	4.0
27	Management structure within the firm	3.56	4.0
28	Raising finance	3.52	4.0
29	Relations with industry regulators	3.48	3.0
30	Management culture within the firm	3.45	4.0
31	Financial planning and control in the firm	3.43	3.0
32	Entry into new markets	3.3	3.0
33	Marketing behavior of the firm	2.87	3.0
34	Use of information technology	2.35	2.0

Table 13.5

Items Ranked by Amount of Influence Reported by *Nonexecutive Directors*

Rank (1=top)	Item	Mean Influence Score	Median Influence Score
1	Replacement of chairman	4.53	5.0
2	Appointment of the chairman	4.5	5.0
3	Appointment of the chief executive officer	4.15	4.0
4	Replacement of the chief executive officer	4.12	4.0
5	Compensation of full-time executive board members	4.03	4.0
5	Response to a takeover bid	4.03	4.0
7	Policy making in board subcommittees (e.g., audit, nominating, remuneration)	3.88	4.0
8	Decisions about acquiring other firms	3.82	4.0
9	Creation of board subcommittees (e.g., audit, nominating, remuneration)	3.68	4.0
10	Selection of nonexecutive directors	3.62	4.0
11	Decisions about merging businesses	3.59	4.0
12	How the firm develops strategy	3.56	3.0
13	Issuing of dividends	3.50	4.0
14	Ethical conduct of the firm	3.44	3.5
15	Appointment of executives to the main board	3.38	4.0
16	Social responsibility of the firm	3.15	3.0
17	Decisions about disposing of business operations	3.12	3.0
18	Decisions about joint ventures	3.09	3.0
19	Replacement of executive board members (other than the chief executive)	3.09	3.0
20	Management succession planning within the firm	3.03	3.0
21	Annual general meeting of shareholders	3.0	3.0
22	Entry into new markets	2.91	3.0
22	The process and conduct of board meetings	2.91	3.0
24	Financial planning and control in the firm	2.85	3.0
25	Raising finance	2.68	3.0
25	Relations with government	2.68	3.0
27	Exit from markets	2.65	2.5

Table 13.5 (con't)
Items Ranked by Amount of Influence Reported by *Nonexecutive Directors*

Rank (1=top)	Item	Mean Influence Score	Median Influence Score
28	Structure of the firm's business activities	2.62	3.0
29	Appointment of senior executives to the company	2.44	3.0
30	Management structure within the firm	2.32	2.0
30	Management culture within the firm	2.32	2.0
30	Relations with institutional shareholders	2.32	2.0
33	Marketing behavior of the firm	2.15	2.0
34	Relations with industry regulators	1.94	2.0
35	Use of information technology	1.85	2.0
36	Relations with noninstitutional shareholders	1.79	2.0

There are, of course, well-acknowledged limitations to using self-reports to study power and influence in organizational settings (Finkelstein, 1992). Actual firsthand observation of board influence processes has been attempted (see Ferlie et al., 1996), but this approach was not possible in the Warwick study. In sum, there is no ideal way to study the contributions and influence of board members; but we feel that detailed analysis of a wide range of critical incidents, together with the use of the instrument to measure perceived influence, will add to the little field-based knowledge available.

Shown in Tables 13.4 and 13.5 are the results from interviews with 36 respondents, of whom 23 hold both chairman and nonexecutive director positions and 13 hold multiple nonexecutive directorships. From the two groups we have 23 usable chairman responses and 34 usable nonexecutive director responses. Because of the relatively small size of the sample at this stage (and the absence of any executive interview data as a cross-check on these part-time board members' self-perceptions), these results are indicative rather than definitive. Nevertheless, as this chapter's appendix suggests, our 36 interviews have already generated findings never before achieved in a UK field study of boards and directors. And Tables 13.4 and 13.5 demonstrate a range of contributions from part-time board members not identified in previous empirical research on boards—even including limited influence in operational matters.

Table 13.4 indicates that our sample of chairmen consider themselves very influential across most of the contribution areas. The mean and median influence scores are very high at the top of the rank order; only in items 33 and 34, which relate to the operational areas of marketing behavior and use of information technology, do the chairmen consider themselves relatively uninfluential. It is notable that 5 of the first 10 items in the rank order, including 3 of the first 5, relate to personnel matters. Our chairmen feel themselves very influential indeed in decisions to replace or appoint a CEO, and in decisions to appoint executive and nonexecutive directors to the board. It is evident that most chairmen and nonexecutive directors consider the hiring, firing, and remuneration of their fellow board members to be a critical feature of their responsibilities.

Chairmen also feel themselves to be very influential in determining the processes and conduct of the board and in governance matters. The presence of "Response to a takeover bid" and "Decisions about acquiring other firms" in the 10 top-ranked items points to the chairman's defensive role in takeover threats and to his role as an initiator and negotiator in acquisition decisions. The ranking of "How the firm develops strategy" at 15 indicates that the chairman's role in strategy also incorporates process considerations.

At the other end of the spectrum, chairmen perhaps understandably feel themselves much less influential in a range of operational matters. Five of the 10 bottom-ranked items relate to operational contributions in areas such as IT, marketing, financial planning, and the culture and structure of firms.

Table 13.5 indicates that nonexecutive directors see themselves as noticeably less influential in board matters than their chairmen. These results are quite understandable, given the range of power sources potentially available to chairmen compared with those available to nonexecutive directors. In the UK the chairman's role is pivotal across a wide range of responsibilities. Among these responsibilities are constructing the size, balance, composition, and climate in the board; monitoring and testing company strategy; acting as a confidant and/or possibly as terminator to the CEO; and handling relationships with important external stakeholders. The chairman thus has not only positional power but access to critical people and information, the prestige of the office, the capacity to shape the context and climate of the board's deliberations, and the ability to stop most board appointments and/or to remove key people who seem to be underperforming. For all these reasons, in the UK the chairman role is critical in terms of both prestige and power—and many of the CEOs we have interviewed feel they will not have made it until their name plate moves from the CEO's to the chairman's door.

As Table 13.5 shows, nonexecutive directors share with chairmen the perception that their greatest influence is in the personnel area. Six of their 10 top-ranked influence areas and all of their top 5 relate to the firing, hiring, and compensation of board colleagues. Topmost of all are the replacement and appointment of the chairman. Two areas of governance appear in the top 10, along with the same two strategy areas mentioned by the chairmen: responses to takeover bids and acquisition decisions.

Why do nonexecutive directors feel they are so particularly influential on personnel matters? There are clearly a combination of factors. First, they have the sole legitimate stewardship right to hire and fire the chairman. Also, our interview data suggest that outside directors can and do intervene more in the personnel sphere because no direct technical expertise needs to be deployed. One interviewee commented that "you do not need a very profound database to take a judgment of people, whereas in financial or technical matters you may require skills and a depth of knowledge that nonexecutives do not have." Outside directors also argue that in standing back from detailed involvement in the daily struggles of the firm, they can exercise a perspective and judgment that the firm's executives may find more difficult to achieve.

When we look at the low end of the nonexecutive director influence areas in Table 13.5, it is clear that nonexecutives have a wider range of low-influence areas than do chairmen. Taking a mean influence score of 3.0 as the cutoff point between the two groups, only 2 contribution areas lie below 3 in the chairman list, whereas 15 appear in the nonexecutive list. Of the 10 bottom-ranked influence areas for nonexecutives, 5 are operational matters and 3 relate to external relations—matters often dealt with by the chairman or by the chairman and the CEO together.

These perceptual data strongly reaffirm the control aspects of the part-time board member role, and nowhere more than in contributions in the personnel realm. With or without the availability of nominating committees, our sample of chairmen and nonexecutive directors appears to have the legitimacy and the necessary power to intervene in hiring and firing their board colleagues. But even in this most manifestly control-related contribution, there are creative elements. Some of these are strictly judgmental issues: fitting the right person to a changing executive role in a changing top team that is facing a new business context and strategy. As we shall shortly discuss, however, part-time board members also need considerable skill and will to affect that ultimate expression of control, the removal of the company chairman.

As for other influence areas, Finkelstein and Hambrick (1996) assessed the research literature on the impact of boards on strategy formation; they confirmed that while board involvement is shaped by contextual conditions and by the power of the board itself, strategy formation is not the primary job of today's typical board. Our study concurs with the Hoskisson and Hitt (1994) findings about board involvement in acquisition decisions, but also points to relatively high part-time board member influence in responses to takeover bids and in decisions about merging and disposing of businesses. These areas of strategic decision making, and the perceived influence of chairmen and nonexecutive directors on how firms develop strategy, also represent potential creative contributions for part-time board members.

Finally, the interview data charted in Tables 13.4 and 13.5 also confirm the post-Cadbury UK interest in the governance arrangements of firms. The perceived influence of part-time board members in the creation of, and policy making in, board committees shows the monitoring and control recommendations of the Cadbury code of practice in action.

Wherever there are control aspirations, there is a need for strong-willed and skillful action (Pettigrew and McNulty, 1995). In the boardrooms of the largest and most prestigious companies in the UK, personalities are large; in fact, individuals are often recruited specifically for their personal qualities and the prestige they bring. Individuals differ in their personal needs for power; in their experience of and perspective on power relationships in firms; in their ability to make sense of the experience they have; and in their skill in matching awareness and style to the requirements of different boardroom encounters in and between companies they serve. These conceptual, interpersonal, and political skills are an expression of the process of creativity so crucial to making control aspirations happen. But the skills must be accompanied by the political will to make something happen. Nowhere is this more evident than in the process of dismissing a chairman.

Dismissing the Chairman As an Expression of Control and Creativity

The involuntary departure of CEOs and other visible power figures in organizations has attracted considerable research interest. Excellent reviews of the executive turnover and succession literature by Ward and his colleagues (1995) and Finkelstein and Hambrick (1996) point to a cluster of related factors that seem to explain senior executive dismissal. These include decline in company performance and loss of power by the CEO relative to other key figures on and below the board. Poor performance is generally assumed to be a necessary, if not a sufficient, condition for CEO dismissal. The sufficient conditions include various personal characteristics of the dismissed executive and agency conditions in and around the boardroom, such as the presence of a vigilant board and high ratio of nonexecutive to executive directors. Finkelstein and Hambrick (1996) also examine a set of organizational characteristics, such as company size and industry type, that may put some firms at greater risk of CEO dismissal than others.

As with many other areas of board conduct, we know remarkably little of the processes and patterns inside the organizations that choose the extreme and often highly public step of removing the person at the top. Vancil's (1987) account of "passing the baton" is a rare analysis of such succession processes. In this section of the chapter we draw on interview-based accounts of the enforced departure of two executive chairmen of UK PLCs to reveal aspects of the processes relevant to our theme of control and creativity in the boardroom. We will call the two PLCs Firm A and Firm B and their respective chairmen Chairman A and Chairman B. Both chairmen were in full-time executive positions. Chairman A was both the chairman and CEO; Chairman B worked alongside the company CEO.

There are certain similarities in the precipitating conditions that built up to endanger the positions of Chairmen A and B. Chairman A inherited a board culture that was highly formal and procedural; there were little open debate and few opportunities for the nonexecutive directors to do anything other than endorse Chairman A's powerful and highly successful predecessor. Before Chairman A took over, there were already murmurings outside the boardroom by the nonexecutives (who were in a solid majority on the board) about how late they were informed about, never mind involved in, major strategic decisions. Any involvement by nonexecutives had to occur outside the boardroom rather than in it, in a series of one-on-ones with the old executive chairman. But in the relatively successful business era of the old chairman, there was no public and very little private challenge to this closed board culture.

The personal style of Chairman A, however, quickly mixed with the nonexecutives' slowly building resentment and began to cause tension in and outside the boardroom. The new chairman came across to most of the board as full of "reforming zeal"; "he wanted to change everything!" A nonexecutive director commented:

> He is very arrogant. He thought he should force through his changes almost regardless of the board, and it was that which caused some of us at quite an early stage to question whether or not he should remain as chairman. He looked upon the board as his tool, and he used to talk about "my board." We were not his board. He was our chairman, and that is a very different conception. . . . What I am saying is, the way the board operated was further highlighted by [Chairman A's] own modus operandi.

At this early stage Chairman A was quietly and privately counseled by a few of the nonexecutive directors:

> We tried to persuade [Chairman A] that strategic decisions, major structural changes should be brought to the board to discuss when they were in an embryonic stage. He never succeeded in achieving that. . . . A lot of us made the point in our separate ways. [Chairman A] was a friend of mine and he used me as a confidante. But he refused to recognize the warning lights.

In Company B, too, the new chairman's behavior fed smoldering embers of discontent; but this time the process took longer because of some critical power conditions in and around the boardroom.

The old Company B chairman was described as autocratic. He had led the company through a period of successful business change but had personalized this into a patriarchal aura (Vancil, 1987) and had had to be pressured by the board into thinking seriously about his own succession and about the need, as part of the succession process, to appoint a CEO. Preoccupied with the CEO appointment, the nonexecutive directors failed to give due consideration to the personal characteristics of the incoming Chairman B. He was a close personal friend of the outgoing chairman and had been promised the executive chairman role without the opportunity for full board debate. Chairman B quickly and quietly removed all except one of the old nonexecutive directors and brought in his friends, one as deputy chairman and others to head key board committees. The sole remaining nonexecutive from the previous regime tried but failed to have a nominating committee set up. The new chairman had apparently effortlessly consolidated his power base; but resentment began to build up, both on the part of the doubting nonexecutive and because of increasingly obvious stylistic and business differences between Chairman B and his CEO.

In both these cases there was a crucial prehistory that was ignited by the personal characteristics of the new chairman. However, the further necessary condition of performance weaknesses also played its part in the accelerating loss of confidence in Chairmen A and B. One respondent in Company A commented:

> Our debt was growing, our capital expenditure was growing, and we had a negative cash flow. There were some hideous indicators coming out about performance. . . . [Chairman A's] reaction to these indicators was "It's all going to get right. We have to get through the bad patch before we reach gold."

We asked whether Chairman A could have survived had it not been for this atmosphere of developing crisis. The response:

> It would have been very difficult to get rid of him if he had been the architect of a highly successful strategy which was transforming the financial fortunes of the company.

In Company B the performance weaknesses were not quite so visible as in Company A. What was visible in Company B was the conflict between the chairman and the CEO and the exiting of a series of able senior managers who became frustrated by the tensions and inconsistencies at the top. Eventually, in the context of now visible performance weaknesses and institutional shareholder concern about top management arrangements (but little action to do anything about that concern), increasing media criticism of the company helped prepare the ground for the coup against Chairman B.

Agency conditions and therefore power relations at the top of both organizations affected the speed of the process and certainly the precise timing of the nonexecutive directors' moves against both chairmen. In Company A the growth of personal doubt and the subsequent corrective action by the nonexecutives took about twelve months. The process was hastened by several agency and performance factors. In Company A the nonexecutives were in a clear majority and were steeled in their negative sentiments by the increasing number of complaints about Chairman A from senior executives below the board. This draining of power from the chairman/CEO, combined with the ready availability of a very credible successor, facilitated the mobilization of individual nonexecutive doubts into collective action. Eventually one of the nonexecutives closest to Chairman A took him aside.

> [I said,] "The tide is running out. You have got to split your job and make a go of being chairman with Bob as chief executive, or either he or you will have to go." His answer to that was, "Bob will have to go." It was afterwards that Fred and I realized we had to do something about it. Fred spoke to one or two others [nonexecutives]. Then we met two or three times. The decision was taken. It was then just a question of how best to do it.

In Company B the agency conditions were more favorable to the chairman: He brought his own group of nonexecutive directors onto the board, plus a deputy chairman who was a close family friend. The conflict between Chairman B and the CEO weakened them both, but the CEO's team was fragmented by turnover and differences of views about strategy. It was only the widening internal and external awareness of a leadership vacuum at the top, and the increasingly critical interest of a major institutional shareholder, that provided the pretext for the sole nonexecutive from the previous regime to begin to question whether a succession crisis should be precipitated.

Leadership struggles, then, breed in receptive contexts and are nourished by the personal characteristics of the threatened leader and the changing balance of power at the top. However, decisive action against the regime also requires leadership and organization; and here we see some of the central issues and dilemmas. There are always questions of judgment: Is the case to overthrow actually there? When is the appropriate time to act? There are confused feelings about loyalty to the company and disloyalty to the leader, whose appointment you may have applauded or even encouraged. There may be huge personal risks to the director who steps forward to think the unthinkable and say the unsayable—and then finds the caucus of supporters edging into the background when the existing regime fights back. There is the slow buildup of steely commitment within the coup leader—when shall I, or should I, begin to share my doubts with potential allies? Will I and the others have the political will, ability, and agility to see this process through?

In Company A the leadership of the coup was made easier by the firm's manifest performance weaknesses, the nonexecutives' majority on the board, the chairman's loss of power vis-à-vis his top managers, his refusal to heed warnings, and the availability of a successor. And it was clear who would lead the coup: the designated leader of the nonexecutive directors.

In Company B, however, the business case for the coup was less clear-cut, the context and power dynamics less auspicious for the coup, the leadership of the coup more precarious, the struggle more protracted and more publicly visible, and the eventual result more contestable. For all these reasons, the mobilization of will and skill by those who wished to challenge Chairman B was a much riskier process and required a degree of persistence and creativity not demanded in Company A.

The leader of the coup in Company B was the sole surviving nonexecutive director from the previous leadership era. This person described the required mixture of will and persistence this way:

> There was a point in the late summer, early autumn when I knew that stamina and persistence on my part were vital. When one thinks about persistence with nonexecutive directors, it is first of all sort of corralling people, if you like; getting them to proceed on a roughly similar course, particularly when nearly everybody has got complicated and distracting affairs of their own. . . . You have to keep ringing them up and be there when they ring you up, and

chasing them and getting them to chase you, and chasing each other and making sure that everybody is absolutely in the picture all the time. That is when you really have to be persistent.

But it is important to do what has to be done, because there is case after case in the *Financial Times* of nonexecutive directors not doing their job. I have always wondered and thought, "Why did they not stand up to him earlier? After all these are big strong chaps." I now know more of the answer—which is loyalty, friendship, don't like to, feels uncomfortable, horrible actually, but somebody has got to.

The Company B coup leader brought the situation to a head over the issue of Chairman B's contract with the company. The leader had persisted for some time and had formed a concerned caucus about the chairman. A dinner was arranged with all nonexecutive directors present; and twenty-four hours before the dinner was to take place, the nonexecutives invited the deputy chairman (and friend of Chairman B) to come to the dinner. He arrived expecting the subject of discussion to be the CEO, but found to his horror that it was a soirée to discuss the fate of his friend.

Dismissing the chairman is the ultimate act of nonexecutive power, the clearest symbol of vigilance and control. It is not a process to embark on without a rationale or without considerable political will and skill. Forty years ago C. Wright Mills, in a cryptic discussion of organizational life, noted the unfortunate necessity for agility to be combined with ability. This deliberately obscure phrase conceals the wide set of emotional, analytical, interpersonal, and political skills board members need if they are to succeed in exerting control at the top of the firm under the kind of pressure evident in a dismissal process. The weaving together of these skills around the multiple issues that intrude in a dismissal process is certainly one possible expression of creativity in and around the boardroom—an aspect of creativity rarely appreciated or discussed.

Conclusion

The closer one gets to board process and dynamics, the more real becomes the generalization that all boards are different. But there are still patterns to be observed in board structure, composition, and behavior; and it has been the purpose of our work to begin to reveal some of those patterns. Without doubt the Cadbury Report has had a considerable impact in shaping the composition and structure of UK boards. However, boardroom arrangements and their impact on executive and nonexecutive behavior are also influenced by various features of microcontext in each firm. In an earlier paper (1995) we argued that the history of company and board culture, the ebb and flow of company performance, the expectations of key power figures, the qualities of the board members themselves, and the changing balance of issues and power in and around the board can all help to mold board behavior.

A key pattern identified in the Warwick study is the range of perceived contributions made by part-time board members—part-time chairmen and nonexecutive directors. These areas of contribution include critical personnel decisions, governance matters, strategy development, the handling of key external relationships, and even some operational matters. When we have completed the executive director part of our study, we will be in a position to see whether the executives recognize the same areas and relative degrees of influence claimed by their part-time board colleagues.

Our data on chairmen and nonexecutive directors of major PLCs confirm the significance of the monitoring and controlling features of board conduct. The three predominant areas of perceived contribution and influence—personnel, governance, and features of strategic decision making—can all be seen as manifestations of board vigilance. Our early findings also point, however, to a creative role for part-time board members that needs to be acknowledged alongside the monitoring and control functions.

Paradoxically, nonexecutive directors' attempts to control the top executives may require considerable political will and skill, which themselves demand a measure of creativity. Such political processes have remained relatively unstudied and unreported; and removing the chairman, in particular, is a process for which there can be no recipe, only a set of behaviors that have to be adroitly customized case by case. Even from the limited description and analysis in our two illustrative cases, it is evident how much judgment, risk taking, persistence, political and personal sensitivity, and interpersonal skill come into play.

But creativity in and around the boardroom has many facets, of which some are idea- and task-related and others more obviously process-related. For nonexecutive directors who enter a minimalist board where there are low legitimacy and low expectations of the part-time director (Pettigrew and McNulty, 1995), the first task may be to create a legitimate role for themselves. Such a process may require the exiting of the incumbent CEO and/or chairman as a necessary preliminary step and can also require long-term processes of experimentation and coalition formation with established and new entrants to the board. Among our highly prestigious sample of part-time directors, most would claim they try to select out boards that are known to be minimalist in character. Even on boards that give legitimate roles to part-time directors, however, directors must achieve some reasonable level of personal credibility in order to be influential; even the most prestigious part-time board member with some knowledge of the sector and the firm will have to go through a learning curve. This will involve firm- and sector-specific knowledge, of course; but also crucial are appreciation of the political and cultural context and the ability to handle the mixture of personalities and interests around the boardroom table and in the executive dining room. Here again, creativity in the spheres of both ideas and processes can be vital in building the personal credibility of each board member.

Legitimacy of role and personal credibility are necessary but rarely sufficient ingredients for a nonexecutive board member's power base and platform for influence. The influential nonexecutive has always to make keen judgments not only about how to intervene but about which political issues are worthy of intervention; effective political action demands the careful building of political capital, which can all too easily drain away on lost causes. The quantity, quality, and timeliness of formal and informal information available to part-time board members are likely to condition such judgments. But obtaining good information often requires a liberty to roam beyond the boardroom that may not be available either to the nonexecutive director on the minimalist board or to the part-time board member with a demanding set of competing commitments across several firms.

Another aspect of judgment that may call for creativity is the question of how to behave after a public demonstration of the part-time board members' power vis-à-vis the executives. The unitary board in the UK espouses a collaborative style of operation: Our interviewees express a clear preference for power equalization and a smooth problem-solving process between the executive and nonexecutive directors. For the most part the predominant pattern of actual boardroom behavior fits this espoused board culture; but when the executives appear overpowerful or the nonexecutives act more like lions than mice, there is a major dissonance to be resolved.

The chairmen and nonexecutive directors we have interviewed perceive that they have influence in areas of strategic decision making and in fashioning the process through which strategy is developed. The strategy area is clearly another domain where creativity in both ideas and processes is claimed to be desirable and feasible, and we will explore this aspect of potential part-time board member creativity as our project develops.

Board chairmen are normally expected to work hard to get the size, balance, and composition of a board right. But two boards with seemingly identical composition and structure may behave quite differently. As we investigate such behavioral differences, one of the central questions is how a board simultaneously handles the dual challenges of control and creativity.

Appendix to Chapter 13

Preliminary Interview Sample

Sir Michael Angus	Lady Elspeth Howe
Lord Armstrong	Pru Leith
Mary Baker	Sir Richard Lloyd
Lady Balfour	Robert Malpas
Sir John Banham	Sir Peter Middleton
Sir Derek Birkin	Sir John Milne
Roger Boissier	Lord Nickson
Sir Peter Carey	Sir Edwin Nixon
Sir Peter Cazalet	Joe Palmer
Neil Clarke	Sir Brian Pearse
Sir Alan Cockshaw	Lord Prior
Sir Colin Corness	Sir Alick Rankin
Lady Eccles	Hubert Reid
Richard Giordano	Sir Ralph Robins
Sir Christopher Harding	Sir David Simon
Sir Ronald Hampel	Anthony Stenham
Sir Timothy Harford	Anthony Stoughton-Harris
Sir Denys Henderson	Lord Walker

References

Bank of England (1988), The Composition of Company Boards, *Bank of England Quarterly Bulletin*, May, 242–245.

Berle, A. A., and Means, G. C. (1932), *The Modern Corporation and Private Property*, New York: Macmillan.

Bostock, R. (1995), Company Responses to Cadbury, *Corporate Governance: An International Review*, 3, 2, April, 72–77.

Cadbury, A. (1990), *The Company Chairman*, Cambridge, England: FitzWilliam Publishing.

Cadbury Report (1992), *Committee on the Financial Aspects of Corporate Governance*, London: Moorgate.

CADS (1995), *The Financial Aspects of Corporate Governance: Compliance with the Code of Best Practice*, May, London: Stock Exchange.

Charkham, J. P. (1986), *Effective Boards*, London: Chartac.

Charkham, J. P. (1994), *Keeping Good Company: A Study of Corporate Governance in Five Countries*, Oxford: Oxford University Press.

Conyon, M. J. (1994), Corporate Governance Changes in UK Companies between 1988 and 1993, *Corporate Governance: An International Review*, 2, 2, 97–109.

Conyon, M. J. (1995), Cadbury in the Boardroom, in *Arthur Anderson Corporate Register*, London: Hemmington Scott.

Conyon, M. J., and Singh, R. (1995), *Taking Care of Business: The Politics of Executive Pay in the UK*, Trinity College, Dublin, mimeograph.

Demb, A., and Neubauer, F. (1992), *The Corporate Board*, New York: Oxford University Press.

Fama, E. F., and Jenson, M. (1983), Separation of Ownership and Control, *Journal of Law and Economics*, 26, 3127–3349.

Ferlie, E., Ashburner, L., FitzGerald, L., and Pettigrew, A. M. (1996), *The New Public Management in Action*, Oxford: Oxford University Press.

Finkelstein, S. (1992), Power in Top Management Teams: Dimensions Measurement and Validation, *Academy of Management Journal*, 35, 505–538.

Finkelstein, S., and Hambrick, D. C. (1996), *Strategic Leadership: Top Executives and Their Effects on Organizations*, Minneapolis: West Publishing.

Green, Sir Owen (1994), "Corporate Governance—Great Expectations," Pall Mall Lecture, Institute of Directors, London, 24 February.

Herman, E. (1981), *Corporate Control, Corporate Power*, New York: Cambridge University Press.

Hogg, S. C. (1994). Who Governs? Unpublished paper, London, Reuters, 25 March.

Hoskisson, R. E., and Hitt, M. A. (1994), *Downscoping: How to Tame the Diversified Firm*, New York: Oxford University Press.

Institute of Directors (1995), *Good Practice for Directors: Standards for the Board*, London: Institute of Directors.

Kosnik, R. D. (1987), Greenmail: A Study of Board Performance in Corporate Governance, *Administrative Science Quarterly*, 32, 163–185.

Lorsch, J. W., and MacIver, E. (1989), *Pawns and Potentates: The Reality of America's Corporate Boards*, Boston: Harvard Business School Press.

Mace, M. (1971), *Directors: Myth and Reality*, Cambridge, Mass.: Harvard University Press.

McNulty, T., and Pettigrew, A. M. (1996), The Contribution, Power and Influence of Part-Time Board Members, *Corporate Governance: An International Review*, 4, 2, July.

Mizruchi, M. S. (1983), Who Controls Whom?, *Academy of Management Review*, 8, 426–435.

Morck, R., Shleifer, A., and Vishny, R. (1989), Alternative Mechanisms for Corporate Control, *American Economic Review*, 79, 842–852.

Pettigrew, A. M. (1992), On Studying Managerial Elites, *Strategic Management Journal*, 13, Winter Special Edition, 163–182.

Pettigrew, A. M., and McNulty, T. (1995), Power and Influence in and around the Boardroom, *Human Relations*, 48, 8, 845–873.

Pettigrew, Matthew A. (1992), *Boards of Directors: A Review of Recent Literature*, unpublished paper, CCSC, Warwick Business School, University of Warwick, July.

PRO-NED (1987), *A Practical Guide for Non-Executive Directors*, London: PRO-NED.

Scott, J., and Griff, C. (1984), *Directors of Industry*, Cambridge, England: Polity Press.

Useem, M. (1993), *Executive Defense: Shareholder Power and Corporate Reorganisation*, Cambridge, Mass.: Harvard University Press.

Vancil, R. F. (1987), *Passing the Baton*, Boston: Harvard Business School Press.

Ward, A., Sonnenfeld, J. A., and Kimberly, J. R. (1995), In Search of a Kingdom: Determinants of Subsequent Career Outcomes for Chief Executives Who Are Fired, *Human Resource Management*, 34, 1, 117–139.

[14]

Toward a Behavioral Theory of the CEO–Board Relationship

How Research Can Enhance Our Understanding of Corporate Governance Practices

Edward J. Zajac and James D. Westphal

THE MASSIVE AMOUNTS of business and scholarly research and writing devoted to the CEO–board relationship have actually led to fragmentation of ideas rather than to any growing consensus. In this chapter we intend to provide a framework for a systematic redirection of thinking about CEO–board relations, in the hope that such a framework can spur new insights and promote greater consensus. We also hope to show how alternative research traditions affect the way we think about CEO–board interactions.

Specifically, we propose that current debates regarding the CEO–board relationship are, to their detriment, often couched primarily in the language and intellectual traditions of economic and/or legal perspectives. As we'll discuss, such perspectives typically emphasize the formal legal ("textbook") roles and responsibilities of the actors in the relationship and/or the various formal incentive and control mechanisms that exist to ensure a presumably well-functioning relationship. While not dismissing such perspectives, we argue that a too heavy reliance on these approaches neglects the strong possibility that the

---

Both authors contributed equally to this chapter.

CEO–board relationship is shaped significantly by behavioral factors. Our alternative perspective draws upon behavioral science research and considers sociological, sociopolitical, and social–psychological elements in social exchange relationships. We will seek to show that corporate phenomena such as CEO succession, CEO compensation, new director selection, and other CEO–board processes can be better understood when informed by a behavioral theory of the CEO–board relationship. We begin by briefly addressing the dominant economic perspectives on CEO–board relations; then we'll outline our behavioral theory.

Economic Perspectives on the CEO–Board Relationship

Perhaps the most influential economic perspective on CEO–board relationships is derived from agency theory.[1] This theory examines the problems—and partial contractual solutions—that exist as firms grow and move away from having owner/entrepreneurs running the organization, while making greater use of professional managers who exercise considerable control over corporate decision making without facing the risks of ownership.

Some economists contend that "incentives are the essence of economics," so it is not surprising that a substantial literature drawing from agency theory focuses on top management incentives and the monitoring function of boards of directors.[2] One stream of agency research is interested in formal modeling of the optimal principal–agent contract, while another more empirical stream seeks to explain the observed existence of certain contractual structures and governance arrangements.

Interestingly, recent empirical work on the relationship between CEO compensation and organizational performance in large corporations is similar to earlier work that was spurred by the growth of managerialist theory in the 1960s. Like agency theory, managerialist theory addresses conflict between owners and managers, but without the agency researchers' typical explicit emphasis on contract solutions.[3] Thus, much of the empirical agency-based literature on executive compensation resembles that of the traditional managerialist school. In fact, Jensen and Murphy's widely cited study[4] can be viewed as yet another descriptive managerialist study that searches—with little success—for evidence of a strong CEO-pay-for-firm-performance relationship in large corporations. This unsuccessful search often leads to calls for greater regulation or reform of executive compensation practices, invariably with an implicit or explicit recommendation for an increase in the pay-for-performance component of compensation contracts.

Beatty and Zajac suggest, however, that agency studies neglect potentially important organizational factors that might explain the variations in compensation contracts.[5] Specifically, they note that while some agency researchers highlight the value of tying managerial wealth more closely to firm performance, other agency researchers stress the potential *disadvantages* of forcing managers to bear "excessive" compensation risk.[6]

Thus, while theorists originally defined the agency problem in terms of the degree of separation between owner and manager interests, subsequent work suggests that linking a manager's compensation too closely to firm performance may lead to risk-avoiding behavior on the part of the agent. (The point where linkage becomes "too close" remains unclear, however.) As Myron Scholes commented in a roundtable debate[7] on the pay-for-performance contingency for top management,

> Managers are more likely to attach significantly more value to a given level of cash than to the same expected level in stock or options because they can use that cash to buy a diversified portfolio of common stocks, bonds, or whatever. But, as you force managers to reduce their cash compensation while making a larger investment in their own firm, you're asking them to bear more risk—risk that cannot be diversified away by holding other stocks and bonds. And because that risk cannot be diversified, companies will be forced to pay their executives disproportionately more in total compensation to compensate them for bearing this nondiversifiable risk.

Interestingly, while a substantial body of economic research seeks to find strong correlations between managerial compensation and firm performance, there is little corresponding empirical research on managerial incentives and risk aversion.[8]

Recently, however, Beatty and Zajac have examined the question of risk aversion in a large study of firms undertaking an initial public offering.[9] They suggest that there is a need to (1) recognize explicitly the potential *costs*, rather than just the benefits, of using incentives, and (2) start to identify the organizational and individual contingencies that could affect the consideration of the incentive cost–benefit trade-off. They focus on one such organizational contingency, firm risk, that may make managers particularly reluctant to accept incentive compensation contracts. They find evidence that more risky firms face greater difficulties (and thus greater costs) when using incentive compensation contracts, given the risk aversion of top managers, and that as a result these firms are less likely to emphasize incentive compensation. They also find that these same firms structure their boards of directors to provide greater levels of monitoring. Beatty and Zajac's findings suggest that incentives, monitoring, and risk bearing are important factors shaping the structure of firms' executive compensation contracts, ownership, and boards of directors.

Zajac and Westphal find similar results using longitudinal data over five years from a sample of more than 400 of the largest U.S. corporations.[10] They develop and test a contingency cost–benefit perspective on governance decisions as resource allocation decisions, proposing how and why the observed levels of managerial incentives and monitoring may vary across organizations and across time. Increases in incentive compensation may have diminishing "behavioral returns."

In summary, agency theory and the literature that has developed from it have brought at least two significant issues to the study of CEO–board relations: the need to acknowledge managerial risk aversion when designing optimal incentive arrangements, and the need to improve the managerial pay-for-performance relationship, perhaps by substituting board control for some incentive compensation.

The Role of Power in CEO–Board Relationships

The central focus of behavioral research on CEO–board relationships has been the role of power. Ironically, agency theory has provided a theoretical basis for political perspectives on CEO–board relationships.[11] Agency theory assumes that corporate directors represent shareholder interests, rather than the interests of top management, thus providing a basis for political behavior. That is, growing empirical evidence indicates that board decisions about incentive contracts and other matters frequently do *not* fully reflect shareholder interests, and this finding has spurred behavioral researchers to consider the political dimension of CEO–board relationships.[12]

More specifically, a growing stream of empirical research has explored how structural and demographic sources of relative power in CEO–board relationships can impact corporate policy outcomes. Perhaps the most studied source of CEO power is formal board structure. For instance, does a high ratio of inside to outside directors diminish a board's effectiveness in protecting shareholder interests? Given that insiders are beholden to CEOs for their jobs, will they defer to CEO preferences?[13] The overall evidence is mixed. Several studies have found a weak or insignificant relationship between board composition and various indicators of board effectiveness, including firm performance, the adoption of poison pills, the commission of illegal acts, and the level of corporate diversification.[14]

One explanation for a weak relationship between formal board structure and CEO compensation is that additional, more informal political processes tend to compromise the nominal independence of outside directors. In this regard researchers have focused primarily upon the role of board co-optation. Given that top managers usually identify new director candidates and that control over appointments and promotions provides an important source of power, it is argued that CEOs co-opt the board by appointing sympathetic new directors during their tenure.[15] Consistent with this argument, Finkelstein and Hambrick found a relationship between the CEO's tenure and the level of CEO compensation.[16] And other research has shown that the correlation between CEO pay and firm performance declined with increases in CEO tenure; it seems that the incentive effect of CEO compensation declines as CEOs co-opt the board.[17]

While these findings are consistent with the co-optation hypothesis, however, they are also consistent with a human capital perspective—the idea that long-tenured CEOs are rewarded for their accumulated firm-specific knowledge and expertise. Moreover, researchers have suggested that the effect of CEO tenure may also derive from distinct political processes, such as the emergence of a personal mystique or patriarchy[18] over time, or from the creation of image dependencies as CEOs link their personas with their companies in the eyes of the stockholders. And, using a measure of co-optation introduced by Wade, O'Reilly, and Chandratat in their study of golden parachute adoption, Westphal and Zajac found (after controlling for CEO tenure) that the greater the proportion of out-side directors appointed after the CEO, the less the use of perfor-mance-contingent CEO compensation.[19]

Although this research provides the starting point for a behav-ioral model of CEO–board relations, its theoretical and empirical domain is rather limited, focusing on how board structure and demo-graphics affect certain specific aspects of board decision making. We turn now to the question of how existing perspectives on CEO–board relations might be incorporated within a broader theoretical frame-work that embraces both micro-level psychological factors and macro-level sociological factors.

Microsocial Forces and CEO–Board Relationships

Researchers have typically not considered how social psychological processes could mediate the effects of economic and political factors on CEO–board relationships; research has implicitly assumed that CEO–board power and economic incentives influence decision mak-ing in economically rational ways. For instance, theorists have as-sumed that greater board power over management increases the likelihood of decisions that promote shareholder interests. But O'Reilly, Main, and Crystal cast doubt on this assumption; they showed that "social comparison" processes (people's tendency to evaluate what they do, are, or have by comparing themselves with others), rather than—or in addition to—more economically rational factors, may influence the determination of CEO compensation.[20] In other words, psychological processes could affect CEO–board deci-sions, with implications for shareholder interests. For example, O'Reilly and colleagues' social comparison perspective suggests that board power over the CEO may lower CEO compensation because directors are motivated to keep their own compensation (as CEOs in their own firms) higher than that of the CEO, not necessarily because the directors have the shareholder's best interests in mind.

Research on CEO selection has also provided evidence of other psychological factors that may cause boards to influence decision mak-ing in ways that deviate from shareholder interests.[21] In keeping with social identity theory, Zajac and Westphal hypothesized that both CEOs and board members would favor demographically similar CEO successors, and that relative power in CEO–board relationships would determine whose preferences for similarity were satisfied. Research findings confirmed that while CEO power was positively related to similarity between old and new CEOs, board power was associated with change in CEO characteristics toward the characteristics of board members. Moreover, more strategically rational determinants (e.g., diversification and environmental instability) had comparatively weak effects, suggesting that social psychological factors (i.e., in-group bias) might actually be primary determinants of CEO selection.

Interestingly, a concurrent study found little evidence that industry conditions explained variations in CEO characteristics, although high-performing companies appeared to have better alignment between the two than did lower-performing companies.[22] Social psychological factors may help explain why environmental and strategic imperatives are not necessarily reflected in leader characteristics, and why greater board power over management does not necessarily increase this alignment. (Traditional economic and political perspectives, of course, would suggest that greater board power should encourage the selection of CEOs who can better promote performance for shareholders.)

Walsh and Seward have also theorized that social psychological factors can diminish the effectiveness of governance structures, including boards of directors.[23] They discuss how attribution biases (errors in assessments of why things happen) can distort board evaluation of CEO performance. The well-documented "fundamental attribution error," for example, can lead directors to overattribute firm performance to the CEO's leadership rather than to relatively uncontrollable environmental factors. And greater board involvement in strategic decision making can exacerbate biases, as directors become psychologically committed to the policies they have helped to shape. Thus, from a social cognitive perspective, boards are beset by biases that can seriously compromise their ability to monitor management decision making, even in the absence of political activity in the CEO–board relationship.

And political behavior can reinforce these biases in powerful ways. CEOs can use various "entrenchment tactics" to enhance directors' attributions of their performance. As noted previously, CEOs often use the director selection process to perpetuate their control over boards of directors. Although the evidence is somewhat mixed, several studies have found indirect evidence that the greater the proportion of the board appointed after the CEO, the less the board's vigilance in monitoring management.[24] But exactly why do outsiders appointed after the CEO act more like insiders than like truly independent board members? The governance literature has been largely ambiguous about the mechanism(s) driving co-optation.

As an initial step toward pinpointing these mechanisms, we examined whether preferences for demographic similarity can provide a basis for co-optation.[25] We predicted that in-group bias and related social psychological factors would lead CEOs to favor demographically similar new directors and that over time the resulting increases in similarity between the CEO and the board would influence board monitoring of CEO performance. And indeed, initial results showed that CEO characteristics such as professional background, age, and educational background were typically related to the characteristics of new directors. As these relationships became stronger, the CEO's structural power over the board (as measured by board leadership structure and other indicators) increased. Further, greater demographic similarity between the CEO and the board was positively related to subsequent rises in CEO compensation, and negatively related to the use of performance-contingent CEO compensation. Main, O'Reilly, and Wade have also found some evidence that greater CEO–board similarity is associated with higher CEO compensation.[26]

Thus, it appears that board monitoring and evaluation of CEO performance is compromised by CEO–board demographic similarity. Overall, these findings may have important implications for those who are endeavoring to prescribe new norms for corporate boards. If social psychological factors impede effective board monitoring, simply prescribing greater board involvement in monitoring and evaluating management will not necessarily lead to better management decision making. At a minimum, it may also be necessary to increase board diversity across multiple characteristics, including professional background, age, education, ethnic background, and gender.

Social psychological research on CEO–board relationships also illustrates the potential benefit of linking insights from top management team literature with perspectives on power and control from governance literature. Research on top management teams has explored how the combination of personal backgrounds and experience can influence top managers' decision making, while the governance literature has considered how political factors can influence who the decision makers are.[27] We argue that more powerful models can be developed if we integrate these perspectives.

A potentially important but underdeveloped area of research on CEO–board relationships involves the interaction of economic and social factors. Social psychologists have examined how performance attributions and other judgments are affected by "outcome dependency"—the extent to which one's outcomes (e.g., financial rewards) are contingent on the behavior of others.[28] In general, this research suggests that outcome dependency reduces the impact of cognitive biases (such as attribution errors) on people's judgments. Accordingly, incentives that increase the outcome dependency of board members (e.g., director stock options) may improve the board's chances of making sound evaluations and selection decisions.

Macrosocial Forces and CEO–Board Relationships

While political perspectives and, more recently, social psychological perspectives have provided an important foundation for behavioral research on CEO–board relationships, political and psychological factors are typically assumed to operate in isolation from broad social forces and societal trends. But macrosocial factors do play a role in CEO–board relations; two examples are the cases of interlocking directorates and symbolic management.

Interlocking Directorates

Studies on interlocking directorates have examined the impact of directors' ties to other firms on their decisions about strategy, structure, and policy (such as the adoption of takeover defenses or multidivisional structures) and have shown how corporate boards can serve as a conduit for the diffusion of information across firms.[29] But the contribution of this research to the topic of CEO–board relationships is limited in several respects. First, these studies tend to treat corporate leaders as a unitary "inner circle" of elites and to assume that most boards and CEOs are highly cohesive and share very similar interests.[30] As a result this literature generally ignores variations in relationships between managers and board members. Second, although research on interlocking directorates commonly invokes social theories to explain interlock effects, the effects can be explained without reference to social processes. For instance, the spread of an innovation through director ties can simply result from individuals' behaviors, as directors become aware of specific policies, structures, and so on through their experience on one board, then promote those changes on other boards. A third limitation of the interlocks literature is that it does not address macrosocial forces beyond the world of corporate boards, such as changing expectations among broader groups of corporate stakeholders.

We have attempted to address some of these limitations by developing a social exchange perspective on how interlocking directorates affect CEO–board relationships.[31] Our study indicates that while boards are increasingly under pressure from institutional investors and other stakeholders to increase their control over management, the structure of interlocking directorates can help perpetuate board passivity and CEO power. How does this work? Social exchange theory suggests that CEOs enjoying board support at their home companies should feel a generalized social obligation to support the power of CEOs at companies where they serve as outside directors. At the same time, however, CEOs serving as directors who have experienced increased board control at their home companies should feel less obligation to support fellow CEOs. Therefore, while the presence of CEO/directors on a board may typically help sustain CEO power, the presence of directors who have experienced increased board control at their home companies should increase the likelihood of greater board control at the focal firm. We found support for this prediction in a longitudinal sample of 422 large U.S. corporations. Moreover, separate results indicated that CEOs' experiences as directors on other boards (i.e., other than at their home company) were generally *not* predictive of increased board control at the focal firm. This finding seems to invalidate traditional perspectives on interlock diffusion and validate the proposed social exchange perspective.

We suggest that the interlock network, and the network of CEO/directors in particular, can be seen as a positive social exchange network, in which "exchange" (or the use of power) in one relation (the focal CEO–board relationship) is contingent upon exchange in other relations (changes in CEO–board relationships at other organizations). Thus, social processes originating outside the focal organization can impact the CEO–board relationship.

Social exchange theory also links macrosocial processes with political factors, by addressing how changing social obligations among corporate leaders can affect the relative control of top managers and board members over decision making. We have studied how power in CEO–board relationships can affect the structure of interlocking directorates through the director selection process.[32] We proposed, for instance, that powerful CEOs seek to maintain their power by proposing and supporting directors with experience on relatively passive boards and by excluding directors with experience on more active boards. Conversely, we predicted that powerful boards seek to maintain control by favoring directors with a reputation for more actively monitoring management while avoiding directors associated with board passivity elsewhere. Results confirmed that directors' experience with increased board control resulted in more subsequent appointments to boards with high control over management and fewer subsequent appointments to passive boards, and vice versa.

In an earlier study, Davis predicted that directors with experience in adopting takeover defenses would be more attractive as board candidates, increasing their subsequent appointments.[33] Although we found some tantalizing evidence to support this hypothesis, overall the results were somewhat mixed; we found stronger evidence when we included political factors in CEO–board relationships in the analysis. That is, it appears that relative power in CEO–board relationships affects the structure of interlocking directorates by reducing ties between active and passive boards while maintaining ties between boards with similar power structures. The effect is a segmented interlock network. Powerful individuals tend to circumscribe the diffusion process by cutting off ties to boards that have changed their orientation toward the CEO, while adding ties to boards with similar CEO–board relationships.

An agency perspective would suggest that directors of high-performing companies should enjoy reputational benefits in director "labor markets," while directors at low-performing companies should be less attractive to other firms. Davis found, however, that the performance of companies where individuals served as directors did not significantly predict subsequent board appointments.[34] While we also found that directors of high-performing companies did not gain more appointments to relatively passive boards, directors did gain more appointments to relatively powerful boards. With respect to director selection, therefore, the applicability of the agency perspective is strongly contingent on political factors in CEO–board relationships.

Symbolic Management

Although these studies begin to address the reciprocal influence of social factors on CEO–board relationships, they do not address the role of larger, environmental macrosocial influences. In an important paper Davis and Thompson adopted a "social movement perspective" to explain the increased activism and apparent influence of institutional investors over corporate governance in the early 1990s.[35] They document how institutional investors successfully championed proxy reform as a means of restraining CEO compensation. Useem, too (although he characterizes investors as separate entities and not as a broad-based movement), provides some evidence—mostly anecdotal—that institutional investors have been successful in their efforts to affect corporate governance structures, executive succession, and CEO compensation.[36] Still, several recent large-scale empirical studies have found that institutional investors' activism is not necessarily associated with changes in governance. For example, greater institutional investor ownership does not boost the likelihood of changes that increase the board's independence from management[37] or of CEO replacement,[38] even where company performance is poor.

How have managers successfully defended themselves against shareholder power? The answer has to do with "symbolic management"—the use of symbolic actions to respond to societal norms and values. Managers of large companies must consider their reputation among government officials, labor, and the general public. Taking a defensive posture against powerful investors does not convey the best impression to other stakeholders; and confrontational strategies may actually be less effective than strategies that give the appearance of conciliation. As a result, corporate executives may turn to symbolic action.

For example, in the case of CEO compensation (often cited as a visible indicator of the need for governance reform), top managers may institute CEO long-term incentive plans (LTIPs) to symbolically demonstrate commitment to shareholder interests.[39] LTIPs have been widely advocated by economists and corporate governance experts as a means of aligning managerial interests with the interests of shareholders. Such plans enable companies to grant CEOs stock or cash incentives, which then become vested over time to the extent that the company meets specific performance goals over a three- to five-year period. Presenting an LTIP to shareholders for their approval gives management an opportunity to cast CEO compensation in a new light: as an invaluable mechanism for ameliorating agency problems in the management–shareholder relationship rather than as a symbol of managerial excess. LTIPs also provide an apparent indication of board control over management, thus potentially reducing the perceived need for investor interference in governance. As a result, LTIP adoption may generate significant symbolic benefits for top management.

As we noted earlier, however, risk-averse CEOs seek to avoid compensation risk in their pay packages.[40] Thus in our work on symbolic management, we hypothesized that powerful CEOs would favor the adoption of LTIPs while minimizing their use in actual compensation packages. This apparent contradiction is possible because newly adopted LTIPs do not require a particular amount of incentive compensation; a board can announce a new LTIP and then subsequently not make any grants under the plan. Consequently, the creation of an LTIP can be a symbolic action in which formal policies are decoupled from actual compensation arrangements. And in fact, we found that a significant portion of adopting firms did not subsequently make grants under their LTIPs—and that the more power a given CEO possessed, the greater the likelihood of such decoupling.

We also looked at the consequences of symbolic incentive alignment. Studies in the financial economics literature demonstrate a favorable stock market reaction to the announced adoption of executive incentive plans.[41] We replicated this finding, but we also showed that favorable shareowner reactions occur in response to symbolic, as well as to substantive, LTIP adoption.[42] Moreover, reactions are more positive when LTIPs are presented to shareholders with an "agency explanation" emphasizing how LTIPs align management and shareholder interests, whether or not the plans are implemented. Thus, it appears that stockholder perceptions can be influenced by symbolic management.

We suspected that symbolic LTIP adoption might ultimately help perpetuate managerial power. We hypothesized that symbolic action would decrease the likelihood of specific changes in board structure and composition that could enhance board independence and control over management, and that this "symbolic substitution effect" would be greatest where ownership by institutional investors was high. Our research findings supported these hypotheses: It seems that company executives can use symbolic management to defend themselves from changes in CEO–board relationships advocated by institutional investors. (This dovetails with our finding that increases in board control, when they occur, may result primarily from social exchange dynamics among corporate leaders rather than from external pressure on the part of institutional investors.)

CEOs can use symbolic action not only to manage shareowners but to manage other stakeholders, including labor and public opinion. Often described as a critical aspect of leadership, symbolic management may be more fundamentally important as a means of legitimizing leadership and the existing distribution of power and status within and across organizations.[43] For instance, the ceremonial adoption of LTIPs in response to shareholder pressures sends two signals to other stakeholders. First, it creates the impression that top managers experience pressures similar to those faced by lower-level employees; this impression tends to minimize perceived status differentials within the organization (while also making such pressures appear normative and acceptable). Second, LTIP adoption creates the impression of conflict, or at least checks and balances, within the corporate elite, while also validating shareholder interests (as opposed to the interests of other stakeholders) as the primary, legitimate determinant of managerial behavior.

In effect, the sequence of events from shareholder pressure to LTIP adoption is a drama that reinforces rationalistic conceptions of corporate governance—conceptions featuring boards of directors and CEO compensation as mechanisms of control, and CEOs as agents of the organization rather than as dominant elites. This drama legitimizes the actors and their positions in the larger status structure. Board explanations for new LTIPs use agency theory notions in an explicit way, thus showing—ironically—how rationalistic theories can help to reproduce and perpetuate existing power structures.[44]

In sum, CEO–board relationships, as well as other visible aspects of governance structure, can play considerable symbolic roles. Of course, board control over CEOs can also be substantive, as suggested by recent firings of CEOs at large companies. Even firings, however, have symbolic dimensions, notably for purposes of scapegoating.[45] Fired CEOs may serve not only as scapegoats for the organization's performance problems (symbolizing a commitment to change) but as scapegoats for the benefit of the existing governance structure: They demonstrate the board's ability to exercise control over management. CEO dismissals are vivid and interesting to report and consequently have been widely discussed in the media. This publicity appears to have contributed to a general belief that boards commonly exercise control over management. In this way, individual cases may acquire symbolic content through a social construction process. We can liken CEO dismissals to ritualistic sacrifices that help rationalize and perpetuate the larger social structure.

Future Directions

A promising direction for future research and thinking on CEO–board relations could involve the links among microsocial and macrosocial forces. For instance, research investigating the relationships among CEO power, board power, and the structure of interlocking directorates illustrates how individual action can influence social structures, and vice versa. Our approach also raises questions such as: How does the potential for symbolic board control or scapegoating affect the dynamics of CEO–board interaction? CEOs may have difficulty trusting outside directors if they fear the possibility of being sacrificed as scapegoats for short-term performance declines, and this mistrust could lower the quality of CEO–board interaction on important strategic matters.[46]

Issues relating to compensation policy can also be conceptualized in a new way if we link micro- and macro-level thinking. For example, strategic management scholars have long presumed that incentive compensation facilitates strategy implementation simply by affecting individual employees' reward expectancies, thus shifting individual motivation and effort in the desired direction. But this view may seriously understate incentives' potential to facilitate organizational change. Incentives can provide a vehicle for articulating to employees the organization's goal and priorities. Accordingly, incentives can have symbolic value independent of their effect on effort–reward expectancies. Indeed, the mere introduction of performance-contingent compensation can send a powerful signal to employees.[47]

Similarly, conventional economic and psychological perspectives on incentive compensation cannot fully explain the motivational effects of "group incentives." Group reward schemes serve as a concrete symbol of an organization's new emphasis on teamwork, thus reinforcing a more team-oriented employee culture even without affecting individuals' financial motivation. So while group incentive plans can symbolize commitment to shareholder values, as discussed above, they can also constitute a vehicle for importing normative values into the organization.

Finally, by accepting greater compensation risk in their pay packages, top executives can signal a willingness to "share the pain" during periods of downsizing or cost cutting, thus enhancing their attractiveness and credibility as transformational leaders. Such a gesture may be especially important where organizational cynicism is high; in such cases, concrete evidence of top management's personal dedication may help shore up the commitment of employees.

Our approach also suggests fruitful areas for research on other governance issues, such as how governance structures, including the board, affect managerial perceptions about strategic imperatives. Boards of directors are boundary spanners in close proximity to top management; so they could play an important role in setting premises about, for example, trends in the business environment and how to respond to them strategically.[48] Greater board diversity might lead to greater "integrative complexity" in CEO perceptions of the external environment and in strategic responses to environmental threats.[49] Research is needed that examines how managerial perceptions about environmental threats and opportunities are socially constructed through interactions with the board. In other words, how might the composition of a board, and the interactions of the CEO with that board, affect a CEO's worldview?

Conversely, research could also usefully examine how and when outside directors are influenced by the strategic decisions of CEOs and how such perceptions diffuse to other organizations. Such research could shed light on the process of interlock diffusion. For instance, greater board involvement in strategic decision making could affect diffusion in two ways: (1) by increasing the likelihood that directors (especially CEO/directors) will influence the perceptions of CEOs, and (2) by increasing the likelihood that directors themselves will also be influenced by their involvement. In general, we need to know more about how behavioral aspects of CEO–board relationships influence diffusion processes and, more generally, about how CEO behaviors may affect a board member's approach to governance.

Implications and Conclusions

The various perspectives on CEO–board relationships outlined in this chapter are summarized in Figure 14.1. As shown in the figure, each perspective offers its own insight about changes in CEO–board relationships that can increase board effectiveness. The managerial literature on boards has focused primarily on economic and legal factors, and consequently prescriptions for board reform have emphasized changes in formal structures—in incentive and monitoring structures or in the board's legal responsibilities. Several of these measures, including changes in board structure and composition aimed at increasing the board's control over management, are also emphasized by the power perspectives that fall under the "Behavioral" heading in the figure.

But the "Networks," "Social Psychology," and "Symbolic Management" cells have been largely ignored in managerial discourse. For instance, research on interlocking director networks has very important but largely neglected implications for CEO–board relationships, as

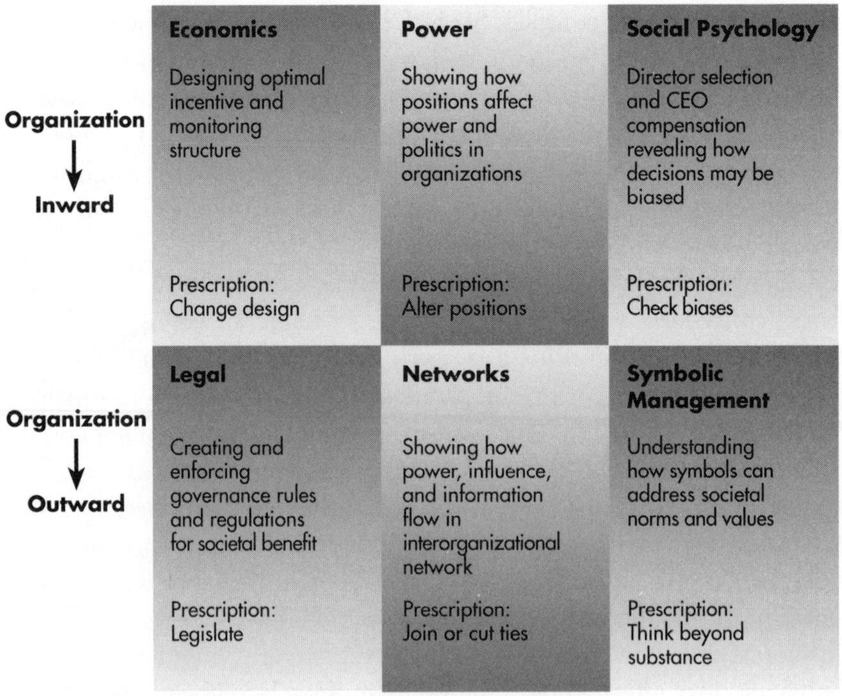

	Economics	Power	Social Psychology
Organization ↓ **Inward**	Designing optimal incentive and monitoring structure	Showing how positions affect power and politics in organizations	Director selection and CEO compensation revealing how decisions may be biased
	Prescription: Change design	Prescription: Alter positions	Prescription: Check biases
	Legal	**Networks**	**Symbolic Management**
Organization ↓ **Outward**	Creating and enforcing governance rules and regulations for societal benefit	Showing how power, influence, and information flow in interorganizational network	Understanding how symbols can address societal norms and values
	Prescription: Legislate	Prescription: Join or cut ties	Prescription: Think beyond substance

Figure 14.1 Perspectives on CEO–Board Relationships

discussed earlier. Thus, boards can build their capacity for monitoring and control by selecting directors who have experience on relatively active boards. Similarly, while a director candidate's general expertise and prestige still represent important criteria, the individual's expertise and experience *as a director* are also key qualifications. Individuals who serve on active boards will not only be skilled in performing board functions; they will also be useful conduits of information about the activities of other firms, because they are more involved in those activities. Accordingly, firms seeking to increase board involvement in organizational decision making should consider increasing their ties to active boards and cutting off ties to passive boards.

Social psychological perspectives on boards also appear to have important implications for practitioners. For instance, our research has provided strong evidence that new directors and new CEOs tend to closely resemble existing powerful actors in the CEO–board relationship across many demographic characteristics. Firms must find ways to reverse this natural tendency toward homogenization. One partial solution is simply to pay more explicit attention to how new board members compare with existing directors across multiple attributes, including background, skills, age, and so forth. One problem with this approach is that many important attributes (e.g., behavioral style) are difficult to objectify and compare. Another approach is to increase the involvement of outside parties. Some firms use search consultants to help generate a pool of qualified candidates, but CEOs and/or directors exert strong influence over the criteria used to generate that pool, and they make the final decisions. Thus, firms should consider how to give consultants or other outside parties a greater role in CEO succession and director selection decisions.

The observed potential for biases may also have implications for executive pay practices. The strong potential for in-group biases to influence the size and composition of CEO pay suggests that more objective performance criteria could yield a stronger relationship between executive performance and pay.

Finally, CEOs must recognize the symbolic roles of corporate boards. Boards are highly visible in their position between top management and shareholders. Boards can magnify negative images of managerial entrenchment, aristocratic privilege, and indifference to shareholders; or they can symbolize management subordination, shareholder control, and the presence of checks and balances within the corporate elite. Thus, board structure and processes should be designed not only to increase board effectiveness internally but to capitalize on the board's symbolic assets and minimize its symbolic liabilities.

CEOs and directors who stubbornly refuse to separate the CEO and board chair functions, for example, are forgetting the symbolic importance of boards. Even if changes in board leadership have little substantive effect on board effectiveness, they can have an enormous symbolic effect. Separation of the CEO and board chair positions has become a rallying cry for board reform among institutional investors, labor leaders, politicians, and the media. As a result, separation is a potent symbolic act that evokes positive images of the board as a control mechanism for stakeholders and downplays images of the board as a bastion for managerial dominance and elite privilege. By failing to make the most of the board's symbolic value, top managers as a group may ultimately risk losing their leadership autonomy.

Clearly, this chapter is intended as a point of departure, not an ending point, in the continuing discussion around the CEO–board relationship. We have sought to use recent streams of governance research to suggest systematic and productive new channels for study and debate. The importance of the topic demands that we move beyond oversimplified claims and anecdotal evidence. A more cohesive body of theory and rigorous empirical findings will add to our understanding of governance practices; and we hope our attempt to outline the foundations of a behavioral theory of the CEO–board relationship will serve as a useful step in that direction.

Notes

1. M. C. Jensen and K. J. Murphy, "Performance pay and top-management incentives," *Journal of Political Economy*, 98 (1990): 225–263.
2. E. P. Lazear, "Incentive contracts," in J. Eatwell, M. Milgate, and P. Newman, eds., *The New Palgrave: A Dictionary of Economics*, vol. 2 (London: The Macmillan Press, 1987).
3. R. T. Masson, "Executive motivations, earnings, and consequent equity performance," *Journal of Political Economy*, 79 (1971): 1278–1292; W. G. Lewellen and B. Huntsman, "Managerial pay and corporate performance," *American Economic Review*, 6 (1970): 710–720.
4. Jensen and Murphy, op. cit.
5. R. P. Beatty and E. J. Zajac, "Top management incentives, monitoring, and risk sharing: A study of executive compensation, ownership, and board structure in

initial public offerings," *Administrative Science Quarterly*, 39 (1994): 313–336; R. P. Beatty and E. J. Zajac, "Managerial incentives, monitoring, and risk-bearing in initial public offering firms," *Journal of Applied Corporate Finance*, 8 (1995): 87–96.

6. Beatty and Zajac (1994), op. cit.

7. Beatty and Zajac (1994), op. cit.

8. The lack of debate on this issue is somewhat surprising, given that the organizational behavior literature on compensation has historically recognized that different forms of compensation, such as pay-for-performance, vary in their attractiveness to individuals and, therefore, vary in their appropriateness as incentive/motivational tools.

9. Beatty and Zajac (1994), op. cit.

10. E. J. Zajac and J. D. Westphal, "The costs and benefits of incentives and monitoring in the largest U. S. corporations: When is more not better?" *Strategic Management Journal*, 15 (1994): 121–142.

11. E. J. Zajac and J. D. Westphal, "Managerial incentives in organizations: Economic, political, and symbolic perspectives," in Z. Shapira, ed., *Organizational Decision Making* (Cambridge: Cambridge University Press, 1996).

12. Political models contrast with economic perspectives, which presume a unitary set of organizational interests. Of course, political perspectives may be entirely consistent with microeconomic models of managerial behavior, wherein top managers utilize political influence tactics to promote their own welfare.

13. J. W. Frederickson, D. C. Hambrick, and S. Baumrin, "A model of CEO dismissal," *Academy of Management Review*, 13 (1988): 255–270.

14. See G. F. Davis, "Agents without principles? The spread of the poison pill through the intercorporate network," *Administrative Science Quarterly*, 36 (1991): 583–613; B. E. Hermalin and M. S. Weisbach, "The determinants of board composition," *Rand Journal of Economics*, 19 (1991): 589–606; R. E. Hoskisson, R. A. Johnson, D. D. Moesel, "Corporate divestiture intensity in restructuring firms: Effects of governance, strategy, and performance," *Academy of Management Journal*, 37 (1994): 1207–1252; I. F. Kesner, B. Victor, and B. T. Lamont, "Board composition and the commission of illegal acts: An investigation of Fortune 500 companies," *Academy of Management Journal*, 29 (1986): 789–799.

15. M. L. Mace, *Directors: Myth and Reality* (Boston: Harvard Business School Press, 1971); J. Pfeffer, *Power in Organizations* (Cambridge: Harper and Row, 1981).

16. S. Finkelstein and D. C. Hambrick, "Chief executive compensation: A study of the intersection of markets and political processes," *Strategic Management Journal*, 10 (1989): 121–134.

17. C. W. Hill and P. Phan, "CEO tenure as a determinant of CEO pay," *Academy of Management Journal*, 34 (1991): 707–717.

18. Finkelstein and Hambrick, op. cit.; J. P. Walsh and J. K. Seward, "On the efficiency of internal and external corporate control mechanisms," *Academy of Management Review*, 15 (1990): 124; 421–458.

19. J. B. Wade, C. A. O'Reilly III, and I. Chandratat, "Golden parachutes: CEOs and the exercise of social influence," *Administrative Science Quarterly*, 35 (1990): 587–603; J. D. Westphal and E. J. Zajac, "Substance and symbolism in CEOs' long-term incentive plans," *Administrative Science Quarterly*, 39 (1994): 367–390.

20. C. A. O'Reilly III, B. G. Main, and G. Crystal, "Compensation as tournament and social comparison: A tale of two theories," *Administrative Science Quarterly*, 33 (1988): 257–274.

21. E. J. Zajac and J. D. Westphal, "Who shall succeed? How CEO board preferences and power affect the choice of new CEOs," *Academy of Management Journal*, 39 (1996): 64–90.

22. N. Rajagopalan and D. K. Datta, "CEO characteristics: Does industry matter?" *Academy of Management Journal*, 39 (1996): 197–215.

23. Walsh and Seward, op. cit.

24. See W. Boeker, "Power and managerial dismissal: Scapegoating at the top," *Administrative Science Quarterly*, 37 (1992): 400–421; Wade et al., op. cit.; Westphal and Zajac, "Substance and symbolism" (1994).

25. J. D. Westphal and E. J. Zajac, "Defections from the inner circle: Social exchange, reciprocity, and the diffusion of board independence in U. S. corporations," *Administrative Science Quarterly* (forthcoming).

26. B. G. Main, C. A. O'Reilly III, and J. Wade, "The CEO, the board of directors and executive compensation: Economic and psychological perspectives," *Industrial and Corporate Change*, 4 (1995): 293–332.

27. D. C. Hambrick and P. Mason, "Upper echelons: The organization as a reflection of its top manager," *Academy of Management Review*, 2 (1984): 193–206.

28. H. H. Kelley and J. W. Thibaut, *Interpersonal Relations: A Theory of Interdependence* (New York: Wiley-Interscience, 1978); S. T. Fiske and S. E. Taylor, *Social Cognition* (New York: McGraw-Hill, 1991).

29. See Davis, op. cit.; P. R. Haunschild, "Interorganizational imitation: The impact of interlocks on corporate acquisition activity," *Administrative Science Quarterly*, 38 (1993): 564–592; D. A. Palmer, P. D. Jennings, and X. Zhou, "Late adoption of the multidivisional form by large U. S. corporations: Institutional, political, and economic accounts," *Administrative Science Quarterly*, 38 (1993): 100–131.

30. M. Useem, "Classwide rationality in the politics of managers and directors of large corporations in the United States and Great Britain," *Administrative Science Quarterly*, 27 (1982): 199–226.

31. J. D. Westphal and E. J. Zajac, "The symbolic management of stockholders: Corporate governance reforms and shareholder reactions," *Administrative Science Quarterly*, (forthcoming).

32. E. J. Zajac and J. D. Westphal, "Director reputation, CEO board power and the dynamics of board interlocks," *Administrative Science Quarterly*, 41 (1996): 507–529.

33. G. F. Davis, "Who gets ahead in the market for corporate directors: The political economy of multiple board memberships," *Academy of Management Best Papers Proceedings* (1993).

34. Ibid.
35. G. F. Davis and T. A. Thompson, "A social movement perspective on corporate control," *Administrative Science Quarterly*, 39 (1994): 141–173.
36. M. Useem, *Executive Defense: Shareholder Power and Corporate Reorganization* (Cambridge: Harvard University Press, 1993).
37. J. R. Harrison, D. Biswas, R. Dey, and D. McNulty, *Keeping Score on the Institutional Investor Movement*, paper presented at the Academy of Management meeting, Dallas; Westphal and Zajac (1994), op. cit.
38. H. Kim and W. Ocasio, "Investor exit, investor voice: Institutional investors, performance monitoring, and CEO succession," working paper, MIT.
39. Westphal and Zajac (1994), op. cit.; Westphal and Zajac (forthcoming); E. J. Zajac and J. D. Westphal, "Accounting for the explanations of CEO compensation: Substance and symbolism," *Administrative Science Quarterly*, 40 (1995): 283–308.
40. D. F. Larcker, "The association between performance plan adoption and corporate capital investment," *Journal of Accounting and Economics*, 5 (1983): 3–30; H. L. Tosi and L. R. Gomez-Mejia, "The decoupling of CEO pay and performance: An agency theory perspective," *Administrative Science Quarterly*, 34 (1989): 169–189.
41. R. Kumar and P. R. Sopariwala, "The effect of adoption of long-term performance plans on stock prices and accounting number," *Journal of Finance*, 67 (1992): 561–573.
42. Westphal and Zajac (forthcoming).
43. R. Bendix, *Work and Authority in Industry* (New York: John Wiley, 1956).
44. Bendix, op. cit.; M. Horkheimer, *Eclipse of Reason* (New York: Seabury Press, 1974).
45. W. Gamson and N. Scotch, "Scapegoating in baseball," *American Journal of Sociology*, 70 (1964): 69–72.
46. J. D. Westphal, "Cooptation or collaboration? Behavioral and performance consequences of social ties in the CEO/board relationship," working paper, University of Texas at Austin (1997).
47. Zajac and Westphal (1996), op. cit.
48. K. E. Weick and L. D. Browning, "Argument and narration in organizational communication," *Journal of Management*, 12 (1986): 243–259.
49. P. E. Tetlock and P. Suedfeld, "Integrative complexity coding of political explanations," in C. Antaki, ed., *Lay Explanation* (Beverly Hills: Sage, 1988), pp. 116–134.

[15]

Corporate Boards in Times of Turbulent Change

Gerald F. Davis

THE ENVIRONMENT facing boards of directors of major U.S. corporations has undergone dramatic change since 1980. In the early 1980s, according to the standard accounts,[1] a director joining a board would have had reason to expect the position to be a sinecure. Boardroom behavior was guided by a protocol of gentility and deference toward the chairman of the board, who was generally also the chief executive officer. Directors were not expected or encouraged to have detailed knowledge of the business, board meetings were short and well structured, and decision making was largely ceremonial. Short of an attempted takeover or an unanticipated departure of the CEO—infrequent events at that time—boards were rarely called on to be proactive and directors could expect a relatively secure tenure until their retirement.

The takeover wave of the 1980s, activism by the institutional investors that own an ever increasing share of corporate equity, and greater scrutiny by both the judiciary and the business press have changed the rules for corporate boards. More than one quarter of the largest U.S. corporations were subject to takeover bids during the 1980s; and regardless of the outcome of the bid, subsequent lawsuits against the board were common. Moreover, the courts have held directors to more exacting legal standards—most famously in the 1985 *Smith v. Van Gorkom* case, in which the directors of Trans Union Corporation were held personally liable in the amount of $23.5 million for accepting too low a bid for the company. The demands of investors, particularly of activist pension funds, have increased substantially and have progressed from bread-and-butter issues, such as rescinding unwanted takeover defenses, to boardroom practices per se.[2]

Perhaps most surprisingly, boards of directors have achieved substantial notoriety in the business and popular press. While the shake-ups at General Motors, American Express, and Westinghouse are often cited, more recent cases such as the departures of CEOs at Morrison Knudsen and W. R. Grace also held these boards up to extensive public scrutiny. The "business judgment rule" may protect boards from second-guessing by the courts, but public infamy is another matter—as the directors of Morrison Knudsen found out from the flood of press coverage that accompanied that firm's rapid financial downfall. Investors and other critics wondered how a board loaded with luminaries such as Zbigniew Brzezinski, Peter Lynch, and Peter Uebberoth could be seemingly so out of touch with the company's condition. Individual directors as well as boards are now singled out for censure by the press (*Business Week* published a list of the ten directors associated with the most corporate disasters, complete with pictures, in late 1995) and by activist investors (the Teamsters developed and publicized a list of "Corporate America's Least Valuable Directors" in early 1996). Whereas board membership was once considered a largely honorific but relatively anonymous post— as Jay Lorsch put it, directors were "ornaments on the corporate Christmas tree"—boards are now subjected to a level of scrutiny unheard of only a decade ago.

The expectations of investors and the public are challenging boards to assume a more engaged role and a greater degree of accountability. Yet there is substantial question as to whether boards as they have traditionally been constituted are up to the task; and if the traditional architecture is inadequate, what structures and processes can be put in place to bring about change? This is an area where research can inform the change process. First, systematic research can move beyond the highly publicized anecdotes mentioned above to map out the terrain of corporate governance and identify common pathologies as well as best practices. Second, in light of these findings and work in adjacent areas, such as small groups research, one can identify changes in board structure and process that are likely to overcome old difficulties while not making things worse.

The chapters in Part III of this book contribute to this enterprise in substantial and complementary ways: They contemplate how to understand and improve boards' functioning through a mosaic of firsthand experience, extensive interviews, large-scale quantitative research, and informed theorizing. Drawing on his experiences as a director of several corporations and as president of Warburg Pincus, John Vogelstein argues that the central problem facing boards is their frequent incapacity to oust CEOs quickly enough when the time has come. This incapacity stems from the fact that boards are often composed of friends and acquaintances of the CEO with little financial stake in the firm: Such individuals are hesitant to confront a faltering CEO, and in any case they often have not educated themselves enough about the business to judge management's performance. One way to fix this would be to have an individual who was not an operating executive of the firm run the affairs of the board, either by holding the formal position of chairman of the board (as in the UK), or, less formally, as "lead director" (as proposed by Jay Lorsch and Martin Lipton). A more direct but less radical approach is to give directors incentives to think and act like owners, by requiring directors to own a meaningful stake in the firm and by structuring their fees both to reflect their level of participation and to increase their ownership. Another way to increase the board's competence is by making practical business and finance experience a criterion for directorship. The goal is not to have the board be a second management team; Jamie Houghton noted at the April 1996 conference that directors are sometimes "management wannabes," and both Houghton and Vogelstein emphasized that it is not the board's job to run the company. Rather, boards are most useful as sounding boards for management and as monitors to keep things from going too far off course.

It is traditional to describe the dynamics of boards in public corporations in terms of the separation of ownership and control and to focus on the "agency problems" created when nonowning managers and directors—agents—have control over the assets of dispersed shareholder/principals. Top managers may use the firm's cash flow to pursue misguided or self-interested policies, such as buying an unnecessary fleet of corporate jets, and directors with little ownership stake may have little incentive to stop them. The straightforward cure for this problem is to align the incentives of directors and managers with the interests of shareholders. But while the traditional analysis in law and economics often divides the primary constituencies of corporate governance into managers and shareholders, with boards falling into either one camp or the other, Edward Zajac and James Westphal argue that nonexecutive directors may have interests that are distinct from those of both managers and shareholders. As their research, reported in Chapter 14, indicates, the dynamics of CEO–board relations are influenced by political and other social processes not reducible to the types of incentives contemplated in the "shareholder interests/managerial interests" dichotomy. Thus, increasing the power of the board vis-à-vis the CEO will not necessarily result in a "better" board from the shareholders' perspective, but simply one driven by a different agenda.

There is some evidence that the prior norm of an omnipotent CEO complemented by a deferential board has been giving way to a new arrangement in which the power of the CEO is balanced by more genuinely independent outside directors. While the numerous CEO ousters of the past few years provide the most vivid evidence, Jay Lorsch catalogues some of the more subtle but ultimately more consequential changes in boardroom protocol that have occurred since he and Elizabeth MacIver surveyed the practices of American boards for their book *Pawns or Potentates* in the 1980s. Lorsch (Chapter 12) finds that directors no longer feel constrained to meet only in the presence of the CEO, and that information about the company's operations and performance is accessible to outside directors on their request. More formal changes that would structure meetings more effectively, improve communication among outside directors, and give them more useful information would be relatively easy to implement. These changes could move boards toward a regime in which boards and CEOs would have a more balanced power relationship, and in which minor interventions early on by a proactive board could forestall the need for shake-ups at the top and the organizational instability they introduce.

Formal structures and processes are undoubtedly important in shaping boardroom dynamics, yet it is remarkable how much is determined by more amorphous factors less susceptible to direct intervention, such as an individual director's ability to persuade or form coalitions. In Chapter 13 Andrew Pettigrew and Terry McNulty survey the evidence on formal changes in boards in the United Kingdom since the Cadbury Report outlined a set of best practices in 1992, and they find substantial structural change. Their interviews with outside directors reveal that hiring, firing, and compensating management and the chairman of the board—the traditional functions staked out for the board—are still the greatest source of directors' influence. The norm for UK corporations is to have a nonexecutive chairman separate from the CEO, each with distinct responsibilities: The chairman runs the board and the CEO runs the company. An examination of the processes required to oust chairmen at two companies shows just how much individual entrepreneurship is required to pull off such actions. In light of the wide range of performance possible within the same structure, Pettigrew and McNulty conclude that "The closer one gets to board process and dynamics, the more real becomes the generalization that all boards are different."

Several themes worth highlighting emerge across the four chapters in this part of *Navigating Change*. Perhaps the most prominent is the nature of the CEO–board relationship and how it has been—and should be—renegotiated. Vogelstein argues that getting boards to change CEOs when the current one is moving in the wrong direction is the most pressing problem in corporate governance; yet boards are often stacked with the CEO's friends and acquaintances, and the impulse to "dance with the one who brought you" often overwhelms the incentives for vigilance. Recent research by Elizabeth MacIver Neiva indicates that boards in general have become more independent of CEOs. Recruiting new directors is no longer considered the sole prerogative of CEOs, and the heightened scrutiny has been felt acutely within boards; as one prominent director Neiva interviewed put it, "If you kill one wildebeest, then all the other wildebeests will start running a little faster."[3]

The demands being placed on boards have clearly had an influence on how they operate, and the effects on power dynamics within the boardroom are being played out in a variety of forms. These include the formal changes described by Pettigrew and McNulty—such as the almost universal establishment of compensation and audit committees in the wake of the Cadbury Report—and the changes in norms catalogued by Lorsch, which give outside directors independent power resources. Yet transitions in the balance of power between boards and CEOs have been uneven: Over the past decade there has been no perceptible change in the tendency of boards to combine the positions of CEO and chairman, and some top managers have been particularly successful at resisting outside pressures to cede control. CEOs who came up under the old rules are not anxious to abandon those rules—and they often have sufficient resources to maintain them. Thus, changes in CEO–board relations are often the result of generational shifts and turnover in membership on the board, as Zajac and Westphal describe.

The roles of ownership and pecuniary incentives in shaping the board's performance are subtler than prior analyses credit, according to the writers of these four chapters. The problem created by the separation of ownership and control in the public corporation was recognized by Adam Smith and articulated most forcefully by Adolph Berle and Gardiner Means in their famous 1932 book *The Modern Corporation and Private Property*. Dispersed owners have little control over the management of the firm, while professional managers have control but little ownership. This parsing of the issue yields the traditional solution—align management's interests with those of shareholders through compensation tied to corporate performance. Yet surprisingly, the evidence on incentive alignment is not as simple as this straightforward analysis might suggest. Increased ownership by management may increase incentives to act like owners; but it also increases the risk exposure of managers, as Zajac and Westphal point out, as well as the power and "entrenchment" of management—it's harder to throw out an incompetent CEO who owns 10 percent of the company than one who owns little. Along these lines, evidence from the past few years indicates that the relationship between managerial ownership and stock market performance is quite complex: Stock prices seem to increase at low levels of managerial ownership, then decrease at moderate levels (the so-called entrenchment effect), and finally increase again with higher ownership.[4] This implies that at some points increasing management's ownership position may actually harm stock performance rather than enhance it. In short, the mapping of action onto incentives is not as transparent as it seems.

On a related note, while there is some evidence that boards with greater ownership stakes are more vigilant, it is considerably less clear that an organization can transform its nonowning board to an owning board without introducing other, possibly worse, difficulties. To use an extreme analogy, women have longer life expectancies than men, yet this is probably not sufficient reason for most men to undergo sex-change procedures. The most desirable outside directors are successful top managers of other firms who have hands-on experience and credibility; yet such individuals already have great demands on their time and are increasingly reluctant to join new boards, given that the financial rewards are (for them) relatively slight and the potential exposure to legal liability and public notoriety far from trivial. (Peter Lynch, for instance, received $31,500 for serving on the Morrison Knudsen board in 1994.) These exceptionally able individuals join boards out of a sense of obligation, for the intellectual challenge, and in order to see how other CEOs do it; pecuniary incentives, although not irrelevant, are low on the list of reasons such persons join boards. Thus, any initiative that makes it more costly to join boards will undoubtedly scare off even more of the most desirable directors.[5]

While incentives may be less important in motivating directors' behavior than we thought, norms and culture are even more important than we guessed. This conclusion is highlighted by the differences between British and American boards of directors. Among advanced industrial economies, boards in the UK bear the closest resemblance to those of North American firms—the two communities of boards are often referred to collectively as the "Anglo-American system of corporate governance"—yet the differences are striking. On average, fewer than one quarter of the directors of a U.S. corporate board are executives of the firm (insiders), while in the vast majority of U.S. firms the chairman of the board and the CEO are the same person. In the UK, in contrast, according to Pettigrew and McNulty, half the directors of the typical firm are insiders, while more than four out of five boards have a full-time nonexecutive chairman of the board who is independent of the CEO. Even between maximally similar systems, as Vogelstein notes, reforms such as separating the positions of CEO and chair are not readily transferable, because of differences in culture and history.

More generally, the corporate board is a social institution as much as an economic one, and thus boards are steeped in norms and webs of mutual obligation that often blunt the impact of economic incentives.[6] At the 1996 conference Ralph Biggadike asked whether it was appropriate to think of boards as teams, and Lorsch noted that they were not particularly cohesive as groups. A more appropriate analogy for the traditional board might be the club, in which the formal purpose of the assemblage is overlaid with social ties among the members. For instance, several Morrison Knudsen directors and their spouses also served on the board of a charitable organization run by the wife of Morrison's CEO, and the meetings of the two boards were often arranged to coincide. This overlay of social ties undoubtedly helped make it difficult for directors to raise uncomfortable issues until it was too late. Even highly competent directors with the right incentives to think like owners may find it difficult to act accordingly. The beleaguered Peter Lynch served on the board of W. R. Grace at a point when he was vice-chairman of Fidelity, a fund management firm owning more than 11 percent of Grace's shares. Yet the Grace board enraged investors by first firing J. P. Bolduc, who had helped turn the company around but had fallen into a personal dispute with Chairman J. Peter Grace, and then awarding Bolduc a $20 million severance package. As it happened, Lynch and several other Grace directors had long-standing social ties with Peter Grace, which again may have swayed their judgments. As this example illustrates, because boards are social institutions, board effectiveness does not necessarily follow even if directors are accomplished individuals and have interests aligned with those of shareholders. Rather, as the chapters by Zajac and Westphal and Pettigrew and McNulty show, power politics, obligations, and norms of "appropriate" behavior often shape what goes on in the boardroom as well as limiting the prospects for reform.

Finally, the significance of boards, and the prospects for change in their practices, must be put in context. Corporate governance implicates a configuration of institutions involving boards of directors, managerial labor markets, compensation systems, capital markets, the takeover market, securities regulations and (in the United States) state corporate laws, as well as more diffuse cultural elements. The board of directors is only one part of this system; and while boards are currently subject to immense public scrutiny, their significance should not be overstated. Comparisons between the systems of corporate governance in the United States, Germany, and Japan highlight the fact that alternative configurations are compatible with economic success. Boards look vastly different in Japan—Toyota's board has fifty-four members, representing a variety of interests, compared to GM's fourteen; but it would make little sense to try to import Japanese board practices without taking into account the broader institutional context. Manfred Kets de Vries noted at the conference that the Continental model of governance provided an illuminating comparison, yet it is clear that Germany's two-board system, like the system in Japan, is alien to American corporate governance. And, as Vogelstein notes, even practices that are widespread in the UK, such as having a nonexecutive chairman, are not readily grafted onto the American system, regardless of their manifest merits.

Paul Allaire asked in the discussion what is to be done in situations where both the CEO and the board perform poorly for an extended period (as occurred at General Motors). When governance is considered as a web of institutions, the traditional answer would be that such a firm's share price would reflect its poor performance and thus that it would likely be taken over (admittedly an unlikely scenario for GM). The hope articulated by Lorsch and Vogelstein, however, is that with the reforms that have been proposed, a proactive board would prevent things from slipping that far.

Corporate boards are in some sense the soft underbelly of the system of governance in the United States. Boards are more immediately susceptible to pressures than are other institutions (with the possible exception of state corporate law), and the various reforms proposed would not generally be costly or time-consuming to implement. But there are limits to what even the best board can do; even a good board probably can't save an asbestos company. Once again, it is not the board's job to run the company. In the United States the board's mandate is to hire, monitor, compensate, and if necessary fire management. The board has to fulfill this mandate within a set of constraints imposed by the other elements of the system of governance. (For example, executives of competitor firms cannot legally serve on the board, even though such individuals would undoubtedly have the most pertinent strategic insights; directors cannot vote themselves tenure, even though this might facilitate their taking a long-term perspective.) On the other hand, the open-ended nature of U.S. and UK corporate law allows boards to be exquisitely customized to their particular situations. Thus, there is a danger that one-size-fits-all reforms will be imposed indiscriminately on boards that are already well adapted to their situation, as Houghton pointed out. According to Neiva's interviews, when the activist California Public Employees Retirement System circulated to the boards of roughly 200 of its largest holdings a set of suggested governance guidelines (based on the changes GM had implemented in the wake of its record-breaking losses), directors reacted with almost universal scorn.

Nevertheless, the preceding four chapters contribute to a growing literature on corporate governance that can inform efforts at reform. Recent evidence indicates that boards are endeavoring to meet the demands of their environment on many fronts: Recruitment of new directors is increasingly independent of the CEO, compensation is increasingly tied to share price performance (e.g., through compensation paid in equity), outside directors are increasingly free to meet independent of the CEO, formal means of encouraging the retirement of ineffective directors are spreading, and director turnover is increasingly tied to poor corporate performance and not simply the director's age.[7] All these changes indicate that boards are responding to the pressures for accountability I mentioned at the start of this chapter. Because formal changes will be channeled through the culture of the boardroom, however, their ultimate impact on corporate performance remains to be seen.

Notes

1. The classic reference is Myles Mace, *Directors: Myth and Reality* (Boston: Harvard Business School Press, 1971). See also Jay W. Lorsch and Elizabeth MacIver, *Pawns or Potentates: The Reality of America's Corporate Boards* (Boston: Harvard Business School Press, 1989).

2. For an excellent overview of these developments, see Michael Useem, *Investor Capitalism: How Money Managers Are Changing the Face of Corporate America* (New York: Basic Books, 1996).

3. Elizabeth MacIver Neiva, "The current state of American corporate governance" (unpublished paper, Institutional Investor Project, Columbia University Law School, New York).

4. Randall Morck, Andrei Shleifer, and Robert W. Vishny, "Management ownership and market valuation," *Journal of Financial Economics* 20:293–315.

5. An alternative to the current regime of director recruitment, described by Ronald Gilson and Reinier Kraakman in their 1991 *Stanford Law Review* article "Reinventing the outside director: An agenda for institutional investors," would have a cadre of professional directors vetted by, and responsible to, a consortium of institutional investors. While they would not themselves be owners, these directors would be more directly answerable to owners.

6. See Gerald F. Davis, "The significance of board interlocks for corporate governance," *Corporate Governance* 4: 154–159.

7. See Neiva, op. cit.; Gerald F. Davis and Gregory E. Robbins, "Changes in the market for outside corporate directors, 1986–1994" (paper presented at the Academy of Management Annual Meetings, Cincinnati, Ohio, August 1996).

[IV]

Senior Leadership and Discontinuous Change

[16]

Leading Discontinuous Change
Ten Lessons from the Battlefront

David M. Lawrence

Few sectors of our economy have undergone the kind of profound, discontinuous change that has radically reshaped the health care system in the 1990s. Telecommunications and financial services may be the only other industries to have experienced upheaval on a similar scale. Both in those fields and in health care, decades of gradual evolution, marked only by tranquil periods of "business as usual," have been shattered by startling advances in technology, major shifts in public policy, and wholesale change in the competitive landscape.

For better or for worse, my five years as chairman and CEO of Kaiser Permanente—the United States' biggest health maintenance organization, as well as the country's largest not-for-profit organization—have provided me with some firsthand insights into the challenges awaiting others who may someday lead an organization through discontinuous change. We have made some significant progress at Kaiser Permanente, and along the way we have also made our share of mistakes. I would not presume to claim that we have mastered the art of managing change—I do not know that anyone ever truly perfects that complex process—but I do think we have been at it long enough for me to reflect upon our experience and share some of what we have learned.

Obviously, each change scenario involves different elements. Changes in health care literally can have life-and-death consequences; and they affect the well-being of every American family, influence the

291

bottom line of every American business, and raise serious public policy issues at many levels of government. Kaiser Permanente, as I will explain shortly, occupies a unique position within the health care sector. We are a not-for-profit, nationwide confederation of health care providers and medical facilities driven by a social mission that historically has placed a premium on improving health care for members and their communities, rather than on providing a healthy return to investors and shareholders. That combination of circumstances— the unique nature of our organization coupled with the complexity of the health care environment in which we operate—has led more than one management specialist to observe that our change process is perhaps the most difficult they ever have observed.

Nevertheless, some aspects of human nature and, by extension, of the organizations human beings design and populate, are fairly common and reasonably predictable. At the end of the day, changing an organization really means changing people—their values, beliefs, attitudes, behavior, and relationships. And the general processes required to bring about those changes are universal, regardless of the specific organization or industry under the microscope at any particular moment. Consequently, despite Kaiser Permanente's institutional idiosyncrasies, there are aspects of our experience with organizational change that could be useful to leaders in practically any field.

Let me begin, then, with a brief background on our organization and the radical change that engulfed us in the early 1990s—a transformation, I might add, for which we were woefully ill prepared.

Discontinuous Change: Health Care in the 1990s

First, some basic facts about Kaiser Permanente. From the beginning, we have been a loosely governed collection of autonomous local health plans allied with local medical groups. I report to a single board that oversees both the Kaiser Foundation Health Plan and Kaiser Foundation Hospitals. While we at the national level have general oversight responsibilities, the directors and managers of our seven divisions across the United States have traditionally enjoyed substantial independence. We also have a parallel structure of twelve Permanente Medical Groups, the physicians' groups with whom we contract to provide health care to our members in each division. Though the relationship between Health Plan/Hospitals and the

Permanente Medical Groups has been a long and close one, it is a contractual, rather than a reporting, relationship. Each medical group has its own board, which appoints its own managers.

Together, we are a $13 billion organization with 90,000 employees and more than 10,000 physicians serving 8.6 million members. We are headquartered in California, where about 70 percent of our members reside. We own and operate twenty-eight hospitals and about 250 ambulatory care centers in sixteen states and Washington, D.C. This is a massive operation; we deliver 95,000 babies and process 40 million outpatient visits each year. We are also involved heavily in medical research, particularly in studying the outcomes of treatment among large populations.

We actually began in the 1930s as a revolutionary company health plan for Henry Kaiser's industrial empire. We opened our membership to the public in 1945, when we began operating as a not-for-profit organization with a clear social mission: to deliver high-quality, affordable health care to our members and our communities through innovative delivery systems. Not surprisingly, ideology became an important force within the organization. Although we have incorporated a set of accepted business principles since 1945, our values have been driven by our mission, and our emphasis has been on providing social value. Our highly politicized management culture has been driven by our confederation structure, with decision making rooted in consensus rather than in control. Consequently, our decisions historically have represented an attempt to balance ideological concerns with business considerations. Complicating the situation even further is the fact that we have forty-two labor contracts with fifteen different unions, making Kaiser Permanente one of the most highly unionized organizations in the country.

For three decades, through the 1980s, we were firmly entrenched in the oligopoly that dominated health care throughout the United States. In the decades following World War II, the health care industry was reasonably stable, characterized by steady growth and orderly, incremental change punctuated by the occasional major event—the advent of Medicare, for example. Kaiser Permanente fit right in; we evolved with a mission, culture, structure, and set of practices well attuned to that minimally competitive era of slow, relatively predictable change.

Then, in 1990 and 1991, two major forces combined to topple the structural underpinnings of the health care business and funda-

mentally to reshape its basic economics. First, squeezed by both recession and intensified across-the-board competition, big business
led the charge to combat annual double-digit increases in health care
costs. Spiraling upward year after year, health care costs constituted
a major hit on employers' bottom lines—at a time when businesses
were looking for every possible way to cut expenses.

Second, years of expansion by providers—ourselves included—
had created an extraordinary level of excess capacity in health care
services and facilities. Oversupply, in turn, spurred the emergence of
managed care organizations: aggressive, well-financed companies
that acted, in effect, as brokers of health care on the spot market.
They bought health care services at well below historic market prices,
bundled and rearranged them in attractive packages, and resold them
at a very healthy profit.

Together, these two developments radically revamped the economics of health care, rearranged traditional power relationships between providers and customers, and profoundly altered the entire
basis of competition.

Kaiser Permanente was unprepared to confront these forces. We
did not have a decision-making structure capable of responding
quickly and decisively to new threats and opportunities. In truth, we
simply did not understand the full depth and scope of the change that
was taking place all around us—in large part because we had developed such a strong inward focus. Our managers had become concerned more with internal power issues than with addressing the
needs of customers. Finally, even if we had understood how drastically the marketplace was changing, our culture was not sufficiently
innovative or risk-oriented to fuel the creative responses called for.

Fairly late in the game, we found ourselves facing the painful but
inescapable need for radical change. Merely doing a better job of the
same things we had been doing for forty-five years wasn't going to
help us survive in the new marketplace. We suddenly were sur-
rounded by swarms of new competitors playing a new game with new
rules. We were losing our edge in cost, quality, and customer satisfaction. The situation was critical.

We began nibbling around the edges of the problem in 1992–93,
but our full-scale change effort did not engage in high gear until early
1995. By then we were finally seeing substantial and encouraging
signs of progress. After some early missteps, I think we now are mov-

ing down the right path. Although our effort is far from over, I think we have accumulated sufficient experience for me to share some of our "ten lessons from the battlefront."

Lesson 1: Do not expect people to embrace easily the need for change.

It is your job to create a sense of readiness. You have no chance of getting people to accept, let alone embrace, the need for radical change until you have successfully created widespread dissatisfaction with the current state of affairs. It is simply a matter of human nature: We prefer the present we know—no matter how undesirable it may be—to the future we do not know at all. People are not going to buy into change until they have become thoroughly convinced that standing pat is not an acceptable option. They may smell smoke, but they are not going to leap from the burning house until the flames are licking at their heels.

In our case, conveying that sense of dire need for change was unusually difficult. Our competitors, for example, are profit-driven; in their case, the need for change was clearly signaled by quantifiable financial performance indicators. But Kaiser Permanente is driven by its mission, culture, ideology, and social goals. There is no single indicator of success or failure. Nor do we have any dramatic standard of measurement, such as stock price, to sound the alarm.

As a result, we had no common language or perception about what was going on around us. Neither our managers nor our frontline employees really understood the changes that were taking place among our markets, competitors, and customers. They had no sense of how quickly our traditional advantages in quality and cost were being eroded. They saw nothing to shake their fundamental belief that Kaiser Permanente had an inviolable, God-given right to exist in perpetuity, floating in serene isolation high above the tawdry forces in the marketplace.

Consequently, few of our people perceived any desperate need for change. Without that understanding, it was unreasonable to expect any widespread readiness to do things differently—a particularly critical problem for a service organization, in which interactions between frontline employees and customers are so crucial. It finally became clear that if we were to create a critical mass of support for change, we would have to take some aggressive steps to build a sense of readiness. Beyond that, given the essentially local nature of our organization and of health care in general, it was obvious that a top-down change process would not work. The desire for change, and the plans for accomplishing it, would have to come from the people in each of our markets.

We finally embarked upon an extensive, market-by-market process, plowing the ground and coming up with data to enable the people in each of our divisions and markets to see how they were doing in comparison with their competitors, as well as how they were perceived by present and former customers. We had outside consultants work with our local people in each market to analyze the data. Then it was up to the local leaders to disseminate the information, define their own specific problems, and develop their own approaches to dealing with them. The goal, in short, was to create a widespread sense of readiness by helping people recognize, accept, and own the problems and solutions in their local markets.

The lesson we learned was that real change cannot possibly begin until the organization as a whole has developed a readiness to move forward and a common understanding of what kinds of changes are required. That readiness comes through a process of education; people have to be guided to their own conclusion that change is essential. You cannot dictate readiness from the executive offices.

Lesson 2: Sometimes it is better to experiment than to plan.

Traditionally, Kaiser Permanente has been an organization with a high aversion to risk. Our culture did not place a particularly high value on experimentation that might fail. But we had to shatter that pattern if we were to transform ourselves into a new organization. For too long, the requirements for excruciating planning and guaranteed results were used as a crutch for not trying anything new. We had to take that crutch away from people. So we began encouraging innovation at every turn.

Here is how I would describe the results: At this moment, if you were to compare our organization to a house, that house would look as if it had been designed by a committee. That is because we have been trying—and sometimes failing—new tactics, new approaches, and new processes. If they did not work, we tried something else.

For example, we experimented with more innovative approaches to providing payors with new insurance products, and with new ways to charge for those products. Because of our social mission, we wanted to find new ways to offer comprehensive coverage for vulnerable groups, such as older people who are not yet eligible for Medicare. Another group of particular concern was small-business employees. That group normally was charged on the basis of narrowly defined year-to-year experience-based ratings that were subject to wild fluctuations. If your group included only a dozen covered employees and one individual developed a serious illness requiring expensive treatment, everyone's premiums would skyrocket. So we began experimenting with new ways to cross-subsidize certain populations we wanted to protect, spreading the costs of health care across our customer base at large.

We also have experimented on the delivery side—with networks of physicians, with different models for delivering primary care, with providing clinical advice on a call-in basis, with handling customer service requests through member services. Time after time, we found ways to take away the "crutches" and tell our people, "Yes, you are free to experiment. You can try that. Figure out how to do it."

Some people adapted to the new approach better than others. Some felt liberated by it and seized the opportunity to experiment. Others were uneasy and confused. Obviously, my sympathies were with people who wanted to take chances. Discontinuous change demands that we become more willing to try, to fail, and to learn from our mistakes. We continue to figure out both how to learn more quickly and how to transfer that learning from one part of the organization to another. And there is no doubt our risk profile is higher than ever before. But the long-term risks of failing to adopt a culture of experimentation far outweigh the short-term instability.

Lesson 3: Pay close attention to the timing of change.

In hindsight, there were times when we moved hastily and situations when we responded with lethargy. For example, even back in the 1980s we knew that we had to offer a point-of-service option—but it took us five years to do it. Why? Because, given the political nature of decision making in our organization, we had to go through a prolonged internal struggle in order to get everyone comfortable with the idea. Similarly, when it came to setting up our own insurance company, it took us a year longer than it should have because of internal control issues. We also should have dealt more quickly with a range of service issues involving customers who employ people in more than one of our markets.

On the other hand, there were times when we should have been more deliberate. We moved too quickly when it came to investing in infrastructure. We should have looked for other options before building more hospitals. As a result, we now are grappling with a problem of excess supply and overcapacity.

Likewise, some of our organizational changes were made too hastily, resulting in serious confusion. I was extremely impatient. Seeing the competitive threats mounting all around us, I felt we had to move rapidly. I was frustrated that our organization was not prepared to move more swiftly and decisively. But we were dealing with very difficult issues, both internally and externally; and the unavoidable fact is that in health care it takes a long time to figure out what to do and how to do it well. In any event, the mission, strategies, and approaches we adopted took several years to mature.

What has become increasingly apparent to me is that the timing of change is critical. I have become convinced that the real art of leadership lies in careful pacing. *Pacing* means moving simultaneously in a variety of areas and keeping each area progressing so that the combined cadence does not tear the organization apart. I'm positive that nobody gets timing 100 percent right. But the winners do it less wrong.

Lesson 4: When the need to remove people becomes clear, do not put off the inevitable.

For CEOs this may be the most difficult lesson of all. In separate discussions, I asked both Jack Welch of General Electric and Paul Allaire of Xerox what they would do differently if they had the chance to launch their organizational changes all over again. Interestingly, both said exactly the same thing: They would have removed certain people sooner, because their own procrastination merely forced them to play the opening rounds with a weakened hand. My personal experience was much the same.

It is inevitable in most change situations that some people are just not going to make it. Perhaps it is not in their nature to handle change well. Or perhaps, because of their background, attitudes, ideology, or style, they are not going to be a good match with the new structures, processes, or culture. There are lots of reasons why smart, able, well-meaning people may not be able to succeed in their old job in a new era. And it is up to the CEO to figure that out and act accordingly. The sooner you remove or reassign the necessary people, the better for everyone involved.

But that is easier said than done. For one thing, it is not always immediately clear which players are going to succeed and which are destined for failure. In many cases you must assess how people actually operate under fire before you can make informed judgments. Beyond that, particularly if you are a CEO who, like me, was a product of the organization rather than an outsider, it is difficult suddenly to begin treating people in ways that run counter to the culture that shaped and nurtured you.

The Kaiser Permanente culture involved two particularly relevant themes. First, because of who we are, we operate from the medical premise that with the proper treatment, people can get better. There is an inherent belief in the potential for improvement and recovery. So when we encounter someone who is not doing well professionally, we bend over backwards to help that person improve his or her performance and behavior. The second theme involves fairness. We are deeply committed to the concepts of equity and fairness in the processes we use for dealing with performance problems, and we go to great lengths to pursue a series of progressive steps before entertaining any thought of the unthinkable—outright dismissal.

As intellectually and emotionally appealing as the healing approach and fairness may be, they also can be wrong. I have come to believe there is a certain arrogance in the attitude that "I know that if I work closely with people, I can turn them into the managers they ought to be." Why would I think that? It's taken ten, fifteen, maybe twenty years for them to become the kind of managers they are today. What would make me think that I, alone, possess the talent and influence to suddenly transform a person into someone else?

Moreover, in our efforts to be compassionate and fair, I think we have actually demeaned some of our employees by failing to be honest and direct with them—by not dealing with them candidly when they obviously are not a good match for the changed organization.

The CEO has to come to grips with the fact that putting off these tough decisions usually has more to do with avoidance than with sensitivity and fair play. In the process, everyone gets hurt. For the employee, who sees the writing on the wall but cannot make the required change, it means waiting that much longer for some final resolution to an agonizing situation. For the CEO it means waiting that much longer to mold an effective, focused senior team. For the organization it means a delay in the pursuit of the change agenda.

If I had to do it over again, I would follow the example Lou Gerstner set at IBM: Create an artificial deadline, draw a line in the sand, and publicly commit to making the key personnel changes by a certain date. I finally did that in late 1995, when I gave myself a December 31 deadline for deciding on the makeup of our senior team and a January deadline for announcing the changes. By imposing that deadline, I forced myself to make the unpleasant but inevitable decisions I had been avoiding.

Lesson 5: You cannot succeed without a senior team that thinks and acts as a team.

When it comes to creating a senior team, I sometimes feel as if I have made practically every mistake a CEO can possibly make. The most grievous of my errors surfaced in 1995, when I realized I had created a team that was too big and filled with the wrong people.

These mistakes demonstrate yet again how strongly my management style had been shaped by the Kaiser Permanente culture. We tend to be highly inclusive. We would rather have too many people involved than too few. Moreover, I had developed a high degree of tolerance for our decision-making processes, which allowed people to move gradually toward consensus and eventually, it was hoped, toward resolution.

I had named a senior team of eight people, including myself. It did not work. These were very smart, capable, experienced people—but that did not mean they could function as a team. Some of them had a hard time assuming the role of "team member" and placing the team's priorities ahead of their own—a particularly dangerous problem in a governance situation such as ours, where fuzziness around boundaries presents constant hazards. Unfortunately, this team included several people who were not committed to our basic ideas of change but instead had their own priorities and agendas.

And the problems went beyond the specific players. I soon realized that our internal processes were not working harmoniously either. I had not fully appreciated the limitations of our old pattern of debate and consensus building or the urgency of our present need to reach decisions and move on. My high tolerance for disagreement was misplaced; the constant dissension began to sap our energy, our focus, and our will to move forward.

We were spending one day each week working through strategies, and that was not the best use of everyone's time. Some of the team members needed time to focus on issues they were uniquely positioned to address, such as urgent operational matters. Consequently, for several reasons, I decided to reduce the team from eight members to four. I realized I needed a center, an absolute core to this effort, in the form of a team I could depend on without reservation. I needed a team who would fight the battles even when I was not there, or when we were not all together. I had to know what stands they would take, what language they would use, what changes they would support.

As a result, the four of us meet for a full day each week, and we spend time making decisions about the organization, about strategy, about communication. We also have divided the work in ways that give each of my three direct reports fairly large realms of responsibility, particularly in the operational areas.

I also came to understand that in order to be a truly effective CEO, I needed to focus my energies on the things that only the CEO can do—strategy, change, external relations. That meant delegating some operational issues that were taking up too much of my time and energy. Once I had the new team in place—one in which I had absolute confidence and with which I enjoyed a functional working relationship—I finally was able to divide up the work in ways that made sense.

Lesson 6: Enlist your board of directors as active partners in change.

Traditionally, our board was the last to hear about any major changes in the organization. But in the early 1990s, as the pace of change quickened, they grew increasingly irritated about continually finding themselves at the tail end of the communication chain. As a result, they initiated a change in our relationship—a change that has been enormously beneficial.

Turnover in board membership gave me the opportunity to reshape the board. Over time, I was able to create a more vital group by appointing new people with diverse opinions and backgrounds. Some of the new appointees brought years of experience in specific content areas that were important to us—public and environmental health, for instance. These changes improved the overall chemistry of the board, and we were better able to tap the capabilities of all of our directors.

At the same time, we provided the board with systematic exposure to the major issues, developments, and trends within our organization, and in the health care field in general. We shifted the board's focus from operational details to strategic issues. We increased the number of board meetings and added an annual board retreat with senior management. We restructured the board to create a more active committee structure, with the committee chairs playing a key role in working with me and preparing for full meetings of the board.

As a result, the board is now more aggressive and involved in sharing responsibility for the changes we are experiencing. They have become not only my sounding board but a crucial source of support on difficult decisions.

As board members have become more involved and more knowledgeable, their demands on me have grown tougher. The level of information and accountability they are demanding from me is much higher than it was three or four years ago. This change represents a major step forward for everyone: The directors are helping me do a better job, and they have become a much more effective force in their own right. I have come to believe that in a situation such as ours, an informed, activist, and supportive board is absolutely essential.

Lesson 7: Give coherence to the change process by clearly articulating a central mission and a consistent set of themes.

Sometimes it seemed as though every time I turned around someone was lecturing me about the power of vision and strategic coherence. I have to admit I dismissed much of what I heard as consultants' hype. Now, with the benefit of experience, I am convinced that the ability to articulate and convey a focused sense of purpose, a clear statement of values, and a consistent set of themes is crucial to successful change.

Particularly in an organization such as ours, where each locality and each constituency has traditionally set its own agenda, pursued its own set of interests, and developed its own themes, communicating a common vision was vital. It was not just that the national program, the regional management, and the medical groups each had its own perspective. If you had visited one of our larger regions and interviewed seven managers from different operations within that region, you would have heard seven different views on what ought to be changed and how. And indeed, the challenges we faced varied dramatically from one market to another.

What we had to do was provide some coherence to the broad range of change activities: to place them within an understandable framework and to communicate them in language that would become universal throughout the organization. I sometimes picture our change process as a duck on a pond. From a distance the duck seems to be floating effortlessly. But if you get under the surface, you see the duck's legs and webbed feet paddling furiously. During periods of change, people keep looking at the legs; they get so close to some detailed aspect of change that all they see is furious churning. A clearly articulated vision helps people to get their head above water, take in the entire scene, and understand that there is a purpose to all the motion.

Our basic aspiration was, and is, to be the world leader in providing integrated, affordable, quality health care for our members and the communities we serve. But the articulation of themes quickly got bogged down in politics. We had trouble fleshing out the central themes of quality and performance, because the medical groups and some of our regional managers viewed any discussion of quality on the part of national leadership as an unacceptable encroachment on local turf. Many of them resisted the very notion of national standards as a violation of our historic relationships.

Eventually, we did communicate a set of themes. They were synthesized from interaction with many people: the board, the senior team, managers, and physicians at the local level. In the end, however, I realized that the only way we would have a coherent vision and set of values would be for me to impose them unilaterally—which is what I did. I could not have made that decision if I had not first restructured the senior team to create a cadre of capable, committed people who I knew would support the themes and speak the language. Nor could I have succeeded without the involvement of the board of directors, who served as advisors and allies.

Lesson 8: Even though the content of change may be radical, the building process has to be methodical.

You have to cement each building block of change in place before moving on to the next. It took us time to learn this lesson. Initially we set out to do everything at once, and to do all of it well. As it turned out, we did very little of it well—in part because there was so much confusion, but more importantly because we had not understood the importance of deliberately assessing our organizational capacities from the outset of our change effort. We were telling the baby to sprint before learning whether it could crawl.

In my opinion, some theories of change do not place enough emphasis on the initial analysis of the organization's capacities. Where is your organization in relation to where it has got to go? Which capacities must be added or enhanced before you can get there? There is no way around it: You must drive the basics into the organization before you are ready to move on.

Secondarily, you need to formulate a plan for putting the building blocks in place and in proper sequence. Planning is a rational process of deciding how you are going to progress from point A to point B in order to move to point C. In retrospect, although we certainly gave this issue a good deal of thought, our process was still more random than it should have been.

Early on I became concerned that as a not-for-profit organization, we had evolved without any real commitment to performance as a quantifiable value. Instead, there was a fairly ethereal value, based on our social mission, of trying to do the right thing. But "doing the right thing" was not linked in any way to measurable outcomes. During our decades as a virtual monopoly in many regions, and as one of only two competitors in others, we had evolved without any thought of measuring our own performance—let alone of comparing our performance to that of others. There was little connection between performance and compensation. Local operations simply had financial targets. Period. They also had growth targets, but those were merely for planning purposes. Our whole cost structure had gone haywire, but there were no performance goals related to controlling costs.

And yet here we were, constantly pounding away at the need to become more competitive. How could we talk about competitive strategies without the most rudimentary understanding of basic performance? Without performance standards and goals—and accountability for achieving them—how could we even talk about outperforming our competitors? Clearly, we were missing one of the most basic building blocks; and we had to get it in place before we could hope to move on.

We went back to square one, instituting performance goals tied to specific outcomes. We created detailed objectives linked to growth, costs, quality, and customer satisfaction. For the first time, we linked compensation to performance at both the local and national levels.

Another of our basic building blocks involved outstanding leadership. No matter how clear your vision or how sound your strategies, you cannot implement your design without top-notch leaders. We looked around and realized that at the senior levels, our bench strength was pretty thin. So we began aggressively promoting capable people to leadership positions. A little later we also began recruiting talent from the outside to complement the people we already had. We not only went outside the organization, we went outside the healthcare field to find people with the kinds of talent and expertise we needed. Leadership was a keystone in our building-block approach.

Lesson 9: Think of change as a campaign that must be waged simultaneously on a variety of fronts.

Some of the things you read about discontinuous change suggest that it is a clean, linear, and somewhat mechanistic process. That may be true if you are working with an organization that is very cohesive from top to bottom, inside and out, and if everyone agrees on where the organization ought to be headed and how to get there. It certainly was not true for us.

Successful change—and this includes the process of stacking your building blocks—really means altering the way people think and act. In my experience, managers tend to underestimate how difficult it is to win the hearts and minds of their people, to build a support base, and to overcome resistance. That is why I think of change in terms of a campaign. It is not only the content and planning that are important; it also is how you go about winning people over. You have to use a range of tactics, all aimed at winning broad support for a common vision. I would like to see more work done on how to think about managing change in terms of a long, arduous political campaign.

We made numerous errors because we failed to invest heavily enough in planning the campaign aspects of our change. We started out with the assumption that once we had the mission, values, strategies, and some tactics, our work was done; all we would have to do was implement. We were wrong.

We failed to think through a process for winning support and for dealing with the whole spectrum of different responses to change. Some people will gladly rally to the banner. Others, given time, can be persuaded, cajoled, or enticed. But in other situations, you must capture positions from people who are staunchly opposed to what you are doing. You must plan for dealing with pockets of organized resistance. If I had it to do again, I do not think I would be as gentle or as patient. I was engulfed in the culture of consensus building, and so failed to appreciate the strength of my own position. If I were to launch a campaign again, I would act faster and I would be a bit tougher than I was. There are some people who are so recalcitrant, who feel they have so much to lose, that no matter what you do you will never win them over. You have to deal with them decisively. Otherwise, they simply will hold you hostage to their never ending demands.

The reality is that there are two distinct elements of the campaign. To be sure, you are waging a campaign for people's hearts and minds. But you also are trying to win for the enterprise as a whole. Within the context of your own values and beliefs about how people should be treated, you must be willing to do what it takes to win.

Lesson 10: This race may not have any finish line, so keep looking for reasons to stop and celebrate along the way.

This final lesson really involves two closely related issues involving the CEO and the organization as a whole.

From a very personal standpoint, I have to admit that I was not prepared for how isolating, enervating, and de-energizing the task of leading discontinuous change would be. Without question, it has also been an exciting and stimulating experience; but the fact is that if you're engaged in real change, rather than organizational cosmetics, it is inevitable that there will be more than a few people resisting you at more than a few turns. There will be individuals who have much at stake and who will perceive you as trying to take it away from them.

You will be creating confusion, instability, sometimes even chaos, and people will not thank you for that. It also is intensely frustrating—sometimes to the point of being painful—to watch energy, commitment, thought, and planning being poured into various initiatives yet producing results that often seem too small and too slow.

The change process is difficult for the rest of the organization as well. It can be a grueling environment. I constantly hear people say, "My God, this stuff is hard." They are right. Not only is it hard—there is no clear end in sight. People tend to become frustrated and depressed; often, they lack any sense that we are making progress. It is not surprising. As a society, we like to keep score, declare winners, move on to the next game. But with organizational change, you could watch a long time without seeing any game-winning grand slams. The change process is more like a soccer match; you have to appreciate the seemingly endless positioning that precedes the sporadic scoring.

Our organization has an additional problem. Just as we lack the dramatic external signals—such as stock price—that alert publicly traded companies to deepening problems, the absence of those clear indicators also makes it harder for us to measure our success in the marketplace. Without them, it is as hard to declare victory as it is to persuade people of an impending crisis.

Instead, for us as for many organizations, the progress resulting from discontinuous change is actually the sum of dozens, even hundreds, of difficult and unheralded events that together keep the battleship turning in the right direction. These accomplishments rarely match the drama of a big day on Wall Street. But it is the CEO's job to aggressively seek out the small victories and subtle successes, draw attention to the people responsible, and celebrate their efforts. It is up to the CEO to select milestones, trumpet progress, and reassure people that their contributions are recognized and appreciated.

I have not done this part of the job nearly as well as I would have liked. In focusing on distant goals, I often have failed to step back and recognize the successes of today. Not only have I often failed to re-energize the people in my organization; I have also failed to use these opportunities to rejuvenate myself. It is an aspect of the CEO's job to which I hope to devote more work.

Conclusion

Taken together, these ten lessons—and the experiences underlying them—seem to bear out Paul Allaire's oft-repeated belief that "the soft stuff is really the hard stuff." If leading change were nothing more than an intellectual exercise in rearranging structures and redesigning processes, our lives would be a lot simpler.

But the CEO's job is to *lead* change, not just manage it. Leading people in a new direction means reshaping their view of the world. It means shattering their sense of stability, tossing out their old standards of success, and prying them loose from the status quo. And then it means replacing what you've wiped out with a new, coherent, and energizing vision of what you believe the future can and should be.

That is a tall order—and one that no CEO can achieve without support from above and below. The board and the senior team are the crucial supporting players in this drama; without their enthusiastic involvement, the CEO stands alone on a stage, delivering an unsettling soliloquy to a skeptical audience.

I do not know that anyone every truly masters the art of leading change. How do you declare victory in a battle that never really ends? But I am more convinced than ever that the surest road to success lies in thinking about change in terms of building and channeling support for a shared vision. You cannot do that by ordering people to come back tomorrow with new attitudes and beliefs. It will not happen. Nor can you do it by gently urging people to change at a pace they find comfortable; the enterprise cannot afford to wait forever, which is how long most people will take if left to their own devices.

Instead, you do it by truly leading change—by sharing your vision, building support, making hard decisions when you have to, and recognizing the efforts of those who have thrown themselves into the fight on your behalf. It is hard work. It is, alternately, the most energizing and the most draining challenge you will face as a CEO.

And never doubt that each day you will come to work and be faced with fresh lessons.

[17]

Five Requisites
for Implementing Change

Robert P. Bauman

T HE ASPIRATION to be "the best in the field" is what I believe drives many organizations to try to implement radical, transformative change. This aspiration is vital: Without it, why go through something as difficult as discontinuous change? Yet even with the loftiest intentions on the part of company leadership, many organizations experience difficulty in implementing change. It is estimated that of all change initiatives started, more than half fail. I believe this happens because while the concepts of how to change are well described and well known, it is getting the change *done* that is tough—challenging and frustrating. In this chapter I will focus on the issue of how to implement desired behavioral change in an organization. I will base my discussion on my experience as former CEO of SmithKline Beecham (SB), and I'll use examples from the SB change effort to illustrate what I see as the five key requisites for implementing and sustaining a culture of change.

Let me begin by saying that successful large-scale change needs to be implemented according to a holistic master plan that addresses change in several distinct but related areas: strategy, leadership, the

---

This material, originally delivered as a speech, has been edited for the purpose of inclusion in this book. Another version of this chapter appeared in *Promise to Performance: A Journey of Transformation at SmithKline Beecham* by Robert P. Bauman, Peter Jackson, and Joanne T. Lawrence (Boston: Harvard Business School Press, 1997).

top team, culture, organizational behavior, and other components that are part of making an organization successful. If you are going to be the best, you need to identify all of these important components in order to determine how you should move forward on them. (This critical implementation issue is related to the notion of the "integrated change agenda" explained by David Nadler and Jeffrey Heilpern in Chapter 1.) The problem is that you cannot move forward all at once; you must plan phases of implementation that take into account the organization's ability to understand the needed changes and its ability to execute them. There were four distinct phases in SB's transformation: establishing our *strategy*; putting in place a new *structure*; creating a *culture* of continuous change; and, finally, designing an entire *management system* to sustain that new culture.

In 1986 the Beecham Group, a British pharmaceuticals firm, was number twenty-three in the very fragmented $130 billion worldwide pharmaceuticals industry—an industry in which even the largest company had only a 4 percent market share. It was clear at that time, from growing government concern over health care costs and from the rising costs of research and development, that there would have to be consolidation if companies were going to achieve the scale that would allow them to compete effectively. So strategy was the first phase of our work: Beecham needed to increase the scale of its R&D and marketing and to broaden its global scope, especially in the United States Our response was a "merger of equals" with United States–based SmithKline Beecham. Once the transatlantic merger was approved, we moved quickly to phase two, which was to integrate the two companies immediately into one, structuring the new SmithKline Beecham to realize its full potential in sales and cost savings. Having defined the strategy and established the structure, we turned next to the issue of culture. How could we create a single organizational culture that would mesh with our strategy? That is, what behavior would enable us to become the best marketer, the best at R & D, and ultimately a leader in our industry? The process through which we created that culture needed to reflect and be consistent with the kind of company we desired to be in the end. For that reason, it was important that the whole organization participate in defining the process of change. This inclusive approach meant that our cultural phase took two to three years to complete, but it was worth it, because we wanted to create an involved, accountable, and committed organization. Finally, our fourth phase consisted of designing the management systems that would (1) fully and consistently implement change throughout the organization, and (2) systematize a culture of continuous change. Today SB's new chief executive is building on what occurred during each of these phases and going forward with further changes. And I suspect that at SmithKline Beecham, as at other organizations, the phases will repeat themselves; because if you're really going to be the best, you never stop changing. It's a continuous activity.

One of the most difficult things in implementing a change effort is understanding how these phases fit together, as well as how fast or how slow to move through them. It's not always evident how or where to begin your efforts. For example, we tried to undertake behavioral change at Beecham back before the merger was even contemplated—but got absolutely nowhere. At that stage some top managers had recognized the need for change, but we had failed to make our case clear or to instill a sense of urgency among the wider group of managers, the ones who would have to make change happen. It was the most frustrating experience I ever had: We could not make progress in changing the culture of the organization until we were, in fact, in a kind of crisis—which was how I would characterize the feeling of both uncertainty and opportunity created by the merger. And indeed, in many cases a crisis is the only thing that precipitates serious change. Ideally, however, change should grow naturally out of an ongoing companywide aspiration to become and to remain "the best." Requisite number 1 addresses this "winning attitude."

To recap, the first step in implementing change is to view the organization holistically and to recognize that the ultimate goal is to have strategy and behavior work hand in hand toward a clearly defined purpose. The master plan requires understanding all the components of the organization, identifying those that need to be changed, determining and appropriately sequencing the phases of change, and implementing the planned changes. The following sections describe what I view as the five fundamental requisites for the implementation effort.

Requisite 1: Cultivate a Winning Attitude

Most people want to be winners, not losers. More important, if your organization is going to be the best, people need to feel that they are winners. And it is well proven that an organization with a purpose to

311

which individuals can feel aligned is going to give people more of a sense of success than one that doesn't. But the implementation challenge here is not simply to define the company's purpose in terms of a mission; the challenge is to translate that mission into something that is meaningful to everyone in the organization. If you translate the mission into an aspiration and four, five, or six core values that people can relate to—such as customer focus or integrity—you can then operationalize those values and give individuals ways both to understand them and to contribute to their realization. To be sure, many organizations express values such as integrity and customer focus. But I believe that *how* employees practice these values can become the distinguishing characteristic that sets one company apart from another, and can become a company's true source of competitive advantage. SmithKline Beecham had five values that seemed to take hold. The challenge was to translate those values, along with the basic aspiration to win, into something everyone in the organization could feel they were part of.

We began developing this winning attitude at Beecham in the first phase of our work on strategy. This was the point at which we decided that we wanted to become a new and better, more competitive health care company. This goal basically set the winning tone for everyone and became the shared vision that drove the merger with SmithKline Beckman. In the second phase of our work we focused on integrating the company immediately. The value we established here was integration. The theme "Now We Are One" focused our efforts to organize both structurally and mentally into a new company—one that would be better than our competitors—in six months. The "Now We Are One" concept drove the integration process and governed all our decisions. It enabled those involved to reach beyond their personal agendas to create an organization that was truly different from and better than either of its two predecessors, and to begin to set the new company apart from the competition. We worked hard at defining the integration process to involve all of our people. That is, all the activities that 3,000 people engaged in were directed toward goals they set for themselves which in turn were aligned to one ultimate companywide aspiration. The completion of the integration was a milestone, an event by which employees could measure their success and feel proud of it.

It is important to set a winning goal that is broad, yet finite enough for the people in the organization to see their role and feel it is attainable. This balance is difficult but not impossible to attain. Translating a broad-gauge goal into milestones and measurements that people can understand and toward which they can direct their personal efforts helps employees see how their success drives the organization's success. Once successful, people want to keep on winning; and at that point the organization has developed a winning mentality that will guarantee its continued success.

Requisite 2: Make the Organization the Hero

Making the organization the hero requires senior managers to play a different role than they may have played previously: They must create an environment in which others can succeed, rather than taking upon themselves all responsibility for the organization's success. In fact I do not think you can become the best or consistently hold that position if the people in your organization do not feel they have played an important role in making that success a reality. Employees need to be able to say, "Look at what has been accomplished—we did that. We had a significant part in making all those changes. And it worked."

But how do you engage people to this degree in implementing change? If widespread employee involvement is a critical, essential aspect of any successful change effort, it is also one of the most difficult aspects to realize. Note that I am not speaking of employees' just doing what others have decided needs to be done. I am talking about employees' having a role in determining what needs to be changed, designing how those changes should be implemented, and then assuming responsibility for doing them. Cultivating this level of involvement takes time. Many a manager has opted to limit involvement in a change effort to just a few individuals at the beginning, hoping to achieve efficiency by executing the changes among the many later on.

When we speak about change, however, what we are really talking about is changing the way work is done. And changing the way work is done usually means identifying existing problems and possibilities for improvement, then designing new procedures that will ensure the desired outcome. Consistent achievement of desired outcomes requires the procedures to be systematic and reliable. Creating disciplined procedures can sometimes be viewed as contrary to the concept of empowerment and ownership—as antithetical to the notion of people in the organization feeling free to do their own thing, which is what many believe leads to employee feelings of "I really did this; I own it." What should be controlled and standardized, and what should be left up to individuals?

For me, the foundation of an appropriate "balance of empowerment" is for top leadership to establish what it is that they're trying to achieve as a complete organization. They design the overall process, including how employees in their local operations are to become involved. This approach helps to align individuals' efforts with the companywide purpose, yet allows those frontline people who pinpoint needed procedural changes to decide what they should be and how they should be executed. While this balance can be very challenging to accomplish, getting the whole organization to feel it is the hero in making change happen is vital. It takes a long time and hard work to involve everyone along the way, but with each step you are building a critical mass of committed people. Implementing the change will go far quicker and require less rework, because those who need to change will know what must be done and, most importantly, why.

Requisite 3: Establish Cumulative Learning

Establishing cumulative learning is not about skills training; it is about building an organization's broad knowledge bank over time. Skills training plays an important role in change efforts, but I don't believe it is pivotal in enabling an organization to become "the best." Establishing cumulative learning means educating people in ways that are in line with what an organization believes to be the best and designing the tools and techniques that are, in the end, going to bring about the desired changes within the organization. The organizational transformations I have been associated with have fundamentally changed the way people have been working for years. In changing to new ways—such as focusing more on processes than on individuals tasks, and working more in teams across functions rather than down them—people need a tremendous amount of help. Providing that help is not easy in any circumstances, let alone in situations that may involve thousands of people working in complex businesses at hundreds of locations all around the world. The methodology for fostering learning should be designed to help people make the transition from one way of thinking about their work to another—and to let them apply the new principles as quickly and as successfully as possible. Employees must see the learning as instrumental to winning. Learning and winning must constitute a virtuous circle, consistently reinforcing each other.

We didn't do it very well, at first, at SmithKline Beecham. When we first set out to integrate the company, we organized what we thought were going to be 200 teams (it turned out later to be more than 300 teams) involving more than 3,000 people. On the one hand that was wonderful; because, consistent with the "organization as hero" requisite, all these people eventually owned the plans for integrating the new company and as a result felt accountable and responsible for all the changes that were made and the targets that were set. On the other hand, however, we in management did a terrible job of preparing people to take on the team member role. Before employees could make any recommendations, they first struggled with how to work together. This cost us a lot of time. When we went forward with defining the culture and trying to change the method of work, we finally recognized that we had to stop and put a lot more effort into providing employees not just with methods and tools to aid problem solving and process improvement but, equally important, with the learning that was fundamental to successful teamwork.

The kind of training I am talking about here focuses on building a common approach or attitude toward work that reflects the company's desired values and helps employees put them into practice. Ideally this training should be done not by consultants but by people in the operations. I believe it is necessary to free up some employees from some of their day-to-day work and train them as facilitators so *they* can lead the teaching of methods and tools—and ultimately lead the process of change. Using the employees themselves builds the internal competence of the organization and adds to the effect of cumulative learning. Each learning builds on what has come before, allowing the organization to adopt, adapt, or augment the learning to make it uniquely its own.

Requisite 4: Promote Strategic Communication

Strategic communication is a requisite that many people may not have high on their list as integral to change, but one that I see as absolutely critical when we are talking about long-term, major alterations in behavior. Strategic communication is part education, part marketing. It is taking the change effort and considering it as you would a new product: How would you convince customers that they need it? How do you build trust and loyalty to the product? Strategic communication requires actually looking at what it is you want employees to do, then convincing them why it is in their best interest to change what they have been doing—maybe for years. It is all about merchandising your concepts in a way that makes the desired changes relevant and appealing to those who must carry them out.

In the case of SmithKline Beecham, each phase of our change effort had a major marketing campaign that built on what had come before. In each campaign an expression captured the goal of the phase. When we went through the merger, the *"new and better health care company"* theme helped the merged organization distinguish itself from what each company had been before. The phrase established a higher goal to measure ourselves against. When we entered the integration phase, we had the slogan *"Now We Are One,"* and all the related strategic communication aimed at explaining how we were going to attain oneness in spirit as well as in structure. We then wanted to introduce a culture of values designed to make us *"Simply Better"*—a slogan that played on the initials SB, for SmithKline Beecham. *"Simply Better"* became the "brand name" for the essence of constant striving that lay at the heart of our desired new culture. All our communications addressed and reinforced that concept and reflected our values, especially integrity, in practice. *"Simply Better"* helped to capture employees' imaginations and helped to link hearts and minds. When we reached phase four, the process of creating a systematic, sustainable approach to change, the brand became "the *Simply Better* Way." The idea was that the way we would become *"Simply Better"* was to have our own common way of working companywide. All the training and all the educational programs were branded "the *Simply Better* Way."

In each phase, communications ranged from simple information to education and from one-way to two-way. For example, we didn't stop with sending out newsletters; we supported face-to-face dialogue that included feedback. The campaigns for all four phases were linked, each one showing how what was being proposed was a step toward the achievement of what had become the company's definition of winning—toward our becoming *the* better health care company as defined by our core values.

Requisite 5: Align Strategy and Behavior

Aligning strategy and behavior means reinforcing each of the "soft," fuzzy company values and concepts of behavioral change through management processes and systems that can measure and promote the desired change. For example, if teamwork is the desired behavior, then part of an individual's performance appraisal should measure and reward that person's work as a team member. If process reengineering is desired, then a strategic planning system should identify which activities are critical to the attainment of specified goals and should ensure that reengineering efforts focus on those activities by measuring their results against those goals. In short, business activities and values-driven behavioral change are not discrete activities but must be seen holistically. In a successful management system, they are integrated into a cohesive whole, with measurement being the hardwiring that links the two together.

Concluding Thoughts

I will close by emphasizing that successful implementation of major change starts with a clear purpose, supported by a well-defined strategy and the appropriate behavior required to realize that strategy. Successful change is promoted by a carefully designed and articulated plan outlined by senior management. Management must communicate the plan strategically to help employees understand their role, get excited about the opportunities presented by change, and take ownership of its implementation. Ultimately, the goal is for the employees as a group to become the heroes of the organization's success.

All of this takes time, hard work, and perseverance—more perseverance than most managers are willing to commit. It means staying the course even when other activities seem to be more important. Most important, implementing change in the near term is about instilling the *capacity* for change within an organization for the long term. In my view, this capacity for ongoing change is the ultimate source of competitive advantage. It is the capacity that separates the organizations that are good from those that are the best.

[18]

Levers for Organization Renewal

Innovation Streams, Ambidextrous Organizations, and Strategic Change

Michael L. Tushman,
Philip Anderson, and
Charles O'Reilly

I N THIS CHAPTER we present concepts and tools to help managers
manage for today's innovation requirements even as they build both
technical and organizational competencies to develop innovation that
will shape tomorrow's competitive requirements. Managers cannot
know in advance what innovations will achieve market success; but in
managing simultaneously for today and tomorrow, managers can build
organizations that are systematically both more "lucky" than the competition and more capable of shaping the direction of their markets.

Innovation Streams and the Paradox of Success

Innovation and new product development are crucial sources of competitive advantage. After cost cutting, downsizing, and reengineering
have stabilized a firm's bottom line, it is through innovation and
product development that firms can grow and reinvent themselves.

A preliminary version of this paper appears in Michael Tushman and Philip Anderson (eds.), *Managing Strategic Innovation: A Collection of Readings.* New York: Oxford
University Press, 1997.

Noika, Microsoft, Intel, Sony, Seiko, Corning, and Motorola have all generated sustained competitive advantage through continuous streams of fundamentally different types of innovation.[1]

Yet with all the attention paid to the importance of innovation and new product development, there is a curious puzzle that should concern reflective managers. Technology- and resource-rich firms often fail to sustain their competitiveness in times of technology transitions. Consider SSIH, the Swiss watch consortium, and Oticon, the Danish hearing aid firm. Both organizations dominated their respective worldwide markets, SSIH through the 1970s and Oticon through the 1980s; and both developed new technologies that had the capabilities to re-create their markets (e.g., quartz movements and in-the-ear [ITE] volume and tone control). But although SSIH and Oticon had the technology and the resources to innovate, it was smaller, more aggressive firms that initiated new technology in watches and hearing aids. SSIH and Oticon prospered until new industry standards—what we will call dominant designs—rapidly destroyed both of their market positions.

In both the watch and hearing aid markets, it was not new technology that led to the demise of the Swiss or the Danes; indeed, SSIH and Oticon were the technology leaders. Nor was the sudden loss in market share due to lack of financial resources or to governmental regulations. Rather, the sudden demise of SSIH and the huge losses at Oticon were rooted in organizational complacency and inertia. These pathologies of sustained success stunted SSIH's and Oticon's ability to renew themselves by proactively initiating streams of innovation. Innovation streams are patterns of innovations that simultaneously build on and extend prior products (e.g., mechanical watches and behind-the-ear [BTE] hearing aids) *and* destroy those very products that account for a firm's historical success. Innovation streams focus managerial attention away from isolated innovations and toward patterns of innovation over time. Those firms that are able to initiate innovation streams are able, in turn, to shape and reshape competitive markets.

SSIH and Oticon are not unique. The stultifying, innovation-numbing effects of success are a global phenomenon. Consider the recent economic performance of the firms listed in Table 18.1. Each firm on the list, whether American, French, Japanese, Dutch, German, or Swiss, dominated their respective market for years, only to be rocked by economic crisis as the markets shifted. Each firm on the list, like

Table 18.1

The Paradox of Success

Company	Product
ICI	Chemicals
IBM	Personal computers
Kodak	Photography
Sears	Retailing
General Motors	Automobiles
Ampex	Video recorders
Winchester	Disk drives
Polaroid	Photography
U.S. Steel	Steel
Syntex	Pharmaceuticals
Philips	Electronics
Volkswagen	Automobiles
SSIH	Watches
Oticon	Hearing aids
Bank of America	Financial services
Goodyear	Tires
Smith-Corona	Typewriters
Mercedes-Benz	Automobiles
Fuji Xerox	Copiers
Zenith	TVs
EMI	CT Scanners
L'Air Liquide	Industrial gas
Harley-Davidson	Motorcycles

SSIH or Oticon, was out-innovated by more nimble and foresightful (though not more resource-rich) competitors. This paradoxical pattern in which winners, with all their competencies and assets, become losers is found across industries and countries.[2] It seems that building core competencies and managing through continuous improvement are not sufficient for sustained competitive advantage. Worse, under a remarkably common set of conditions, building on core competencies (e.g., for the Swiss, precision mechanics) and engaging in continuous incremental improvement actually traps the organization in its distinguished past and leads to catastrophic failure as technologies and, in turn, markets shift. Core competencies often turn into rigidities.[3]

This success paradox is driven by historically constrained managerial action (often inaction) and organizational processes in the context of changing technological and market opportunities, not by the invisible hand of the market or by public policy. As with SSIH and Oticon, the troubles at General Motors, IBM, Xerox, Philips, or Siemens were rooted not in public policy issues but rather in these companies' failure to take advantage of technological opportunities. These firms were unable to build, extend, and in some cases even destroy their existing competencies in order to develop innovations that would create new markets (as Starkey did with ITE hearing aids) or rewrite the competitive rules in existing markets (as Seiko did with quartz watches).

The success paradox is not deterministic; core competencies need not become core rigidities. Some organizations are capable of moving from strength to strength, proactively moving to shift bases of competition through streams of innovation. These firms are able to develop incremental innovation as well as innovations that alter industry standards, substitute for existing products, or reconfigure products to fundamentally different markets. For example, in the watch industry, Seiko not only was able to compete in mechanical watches but was willing to experiment with quartz and tuning fork movements. Seiko managers made the bold decision to substitute quartz movements for their existing mechanical movements, and the switch to quartz led to fundamentally different competitive rules in the watch industry. Similarly, Starkey (a U.S. hearing aid company) was able to move beyond BTE hearing aids to ITE hearing aids by simply reconfiguring existing hearing aid components. This seemingly minor innovation—what we call an architectural innovation—led to a new industry standard and to different industry rules focusing on sound quality and fashion.

Noika, Intel, Microsoft, Sony, Hewlett-Packard, Ericsson, and Motorola are other firms that have been able to move from today's strength to tomorrow's strength.[4] These firms compete through patterns of innovation over time: incremental, competence-enhancing innovation (e.g., thinner mechanical watches); architectural innovation (e.g., Starkey's ITE hearing aid); and fundamentally new, competence-destroying innovation (e.g., Seiko's quartz movement). By actively managing these multiple streams of innovation, senior teams increase the probability that their firm will be able to shape industry standards, take advantage of new markets for existing technology, and proactively introduce substitute products that, as they cannibalize existing products, create new markets and competitive rules.[5]

Technology Cycles

Neither technology push nor market pull innovation is sufficient for sustained competitive advantage.[6] Market leadership over time can be built only through a combination of different types of innovation—the creation of product substitutes (e.g., Windows for DOS), architectural innovation (e.g., Canon's small copiers), and continuous incremental innovation (e.g., DOS versions 1.0 through 6.22).[7] In order to better understand the structure and flow of innovation streams, we need to understand technology cycles. Clarifying technology cycles helps us untangle the relative timing and importance of incremental, architectural, and discontinuous innovation.

Technology cycles are composed of technological discontinuities (for example, quartz and tuning fork movements in watches) that trigger periods of technological and competitive ferment. During eras of ferment, rival technologies compete with each other and with the existing technological regime. These turbulent innovation periods close with the emergence of an industry standard or dominant design.[8] For example, in early radio transmission, continuous-wave transmission was a technological discontinuity that threatened to replace spark-gap transmission. Continuous-wave transmission initiated competition not only between continuous-wave transmission and spark-gap transmission but among three variants of continuous-wave transmission: alternating-wave, arc, and vacuum tube transmission. This period of technological ferment led to vacuum tube transmission as the dominant design in radio transmission.

The emergence of a dominant design ushers in a period of incremental as well as architectural technological change, a period that is broken at some point by the next substitute product; for example, electronic typewriters replaced electric typewriters, which had previously replaced mechanical typewriters. The subsequent technological

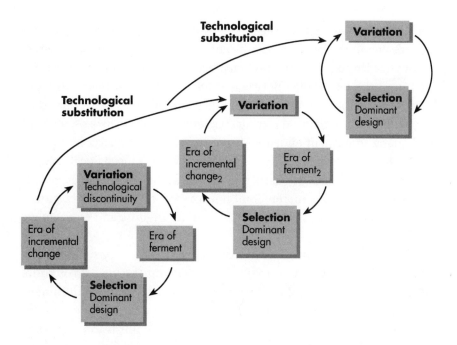

Figure 18.1 Technology cycles over time

discontinuity then triggers the next wave of technological variation, selection, and retention (see Figure 18.1).

Technology cycles are seen most directly in nonassembled or relatively simple products (e.g., glass, chemicals, skis, tennis racquets). For example, in crop fungicides, Ciba-Geigy's Tilt (propiconazol) was a new chemical entity that challenged Bayer's and BASF's products. Tilt triggered competition between chemical entities as well as between a vast number of propiconazol formulations. Ciba eventually created its EC 250 version, which became the industry standard in crop fungicides. More recently, Ciba's Crop Protection Division has initiated several product substitutes (including genetically engineered seeds) to cannibalize and replace propiconazol. These fundamentally new crop protection products will initiate the next technology cycle in the crop protection market.

In more complex assembled products (e.g., computers or watches) and systems (e.g., radio or voice mail), technology cycles apply at the subsystem level. For example, watches are assembled products made up of at least four subsystems: energy source, oscillation device, transmission, and display. Each of these subsystems has its own technology cycle. In watch oscillation, the pin–lever escapement became the dominant design in the late nineteenth century. Escapements became better and better through incremental changes in the same fundamental design until the late 1960s. Between 1968 and 1972, escapements were threatened by both tuning fork and quartz oscillation. This period of technological competition among escapements, tuning fork oscillation, and quartz movement ended with the emergence of quartz oscillation as the dominant design in the subsystem.[9] As with mechanical escapements, the emergence of quartz movements as the dominant design led, in turn, to numerous incremental improvements in the quartz movement and sharp decreases in innovation in tuning fork and escapement oscillation devices.

In the watch industry between 1970 and 1985, every subsystem of the watch, from energy source to face, was transformed through its own technology cycle of technical variation, selection of a dominant design, and subsequent period of incremental change. While watches are a unique product, they do provide a generic illustration of complex products as made up of interconnected subsystems, each of which has its own technology cycle. Further, each subsystem shifts in relative strategic importance as the industry evolves. In watches, oscillation was the key strategic battlefield through the early 1970s; then, once the quartz movement became the dominant design, the locus of strategic innovation shifted to the face, energy, and transmission subsystems. Similar dynamics of subsystem and linkage technology cycles have been documented in a variety of industries.[10]

The technological discontinuities that initiate technology cycles are rare, unpredictable events triggered by scientific advance (e.g., battery technology for watches) or through a radical recombining of existing technology (e.g., Sony's Walkman or continuous aim gunfire). Technological discontinuities rupture existing incremental innovation patterns and spawn periods of technological ferment that are confusing, uncertain, and costly to customers, suppliers, vendors, and regulatory agencies (see Figure 18.2). For such periods of variation, or eras of technological ferment, a single dominant design emerges.[11] Competing firms must switch to the new standard or risk getting locked out of the market. Table 18.2 lists some well-known dominant designs.

How do dominant designs emerge? Except for the most simple nonassembled products, the closing on a dominant design is not technologically driven, because no technology can dominate on all possible

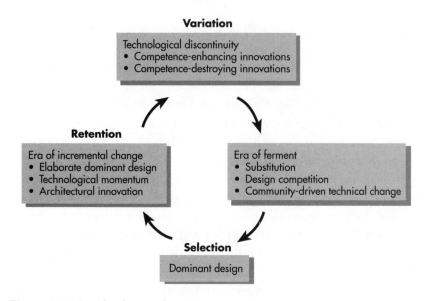

Figure 18.2 A technology cycle

dimensions of merit; nor does the closing on a dominant design take place through the invisible hand of the market. Rather, it occurs through social, political, and organizational competition among the alternative technological variants.[12] Dominant designs emerge out of the struggle between alternative technological trajectories initiated and pushed by competitors, alliance groups, and governmental regulators—each with their own political, social, and economic agendas. For example, Windows was able to dominate OS/2 and Mac operating systems, and JVC's VHS format was able to dominate Sony's Beta format,

Table 18.2

Examples of Dominant Designs

Model T: Internal combustion engine

AC Power System

DC-3

IBM 360

Smith Model 5 typewriter

VHS, ½ inch

Windows 3.1 operating system

Quartz movements

---

not because Windows and VHS were superior technologies but because they were good enough *and* were coupled to strong marketing, sales, and distribution strategies. Or, in digital videodiscs, a unified standard emerged after the two competing systems (one led by Sony and Philips, the other by Toshiba and Time) agreed on a standard.

Dominant designs are watershed events in a technology cycle. Before a dominant design has emerged, technological process is driven by competition between alternative technologies; but after a dominant design appears, subsequent technological change is driven by the logic of the selected technology itself (refer to Figure 18.2). That is, the closing on a dominant design shifts innovation from major product variation to major process innovation and, in turn, to incremental innovation—to building on, extending, and continuously improving the dominant design. These periods of incremental innovation lead to profound advances in the now standard product.[13] In contrast the consequences of betting on the "wrong" design are devastating—particularly if that design is a core subsystem (e.g., IBM's losing control of the microprocessor and operating system of PCs to Intel and Microsoft, respectively).

The emergence of a dominant design also permits the development of product platforms and families.[14] A platform is a set of core subsystems; a product family is a set of products built from the same platform. These product families share traits, architecture, components, and interface standards. For example, once Sony closed on the WM-20 platform for their Walkman, they were then able to generate more than 30 incremental versions within the same family. Over a ten-year period, Sony was able to develop four Walkman product families and more than 160 incremental versions of those four families. Devoting sustained attention to technological discontinuities at the subsystem level (e.g., the flat motor and the miniature battery), closing on a few standard platforms, and generating incremental product proliferation helped Sony control industry standards in their product class and outperform their Japanese, American, and European competitors.[15]

Subsequent product or process technological discontinuities trigger the next cycle of technological variation, selection, and incremental change (Figures 18.1 and 18.3). For example, in Ciba's Crop Protection Division, Dr. Wolfgang Samo hosted the development of fundamentally new chemical fungicides (competence enhancing) as well as biologically engineered seeds (competence destroying).

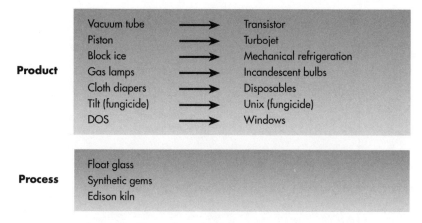

Figure 18.3 Product and process substitution driven by managerial action and organizational competencies.

Samo's point of view was that if Ciba did not substitute for its own successful product line, BASF or Bayer would. Creating substitute products or processes and cannibalizing one's product line before the competition does is an important source of competitive advantage.[16]

Finally, architectural innovations affect how a given set of core subsystems are configured or linked together.[17] Canon reconfigured existing reprographic technology and revolutionized the copier market with smaller copiers; Microsoft simply integrated several of its existing application programs into its Office product. Architectural innovations reconfigure existing core technologies and take the reconfigured product to different markets; examples are Starkey's move into the fashion hearing aid market, Honda's early move to smaller motorcycles, and the migration of disk drive technology from mainframes to personal computers. Architectural shifts may be technologically simple and can be associated with substantial economic returns; but, as we have noted, these shifts are frequently missed by incumbent firms.[18]

Technology cycles apply both for product subsystems and for linking technologies, and they apply across product classes—the only difference between high-tech (e.g., minicomputer) and low-tech (e.g., concrete) industries is the length of time between the closing on a standard design and the subsequent discontinuity.

Thus, lying behind the familiar S-shaped product life cycle curve are fundamentally different innovation requirements. Eras of ferment require discontinuous product variants. Dominant designs require

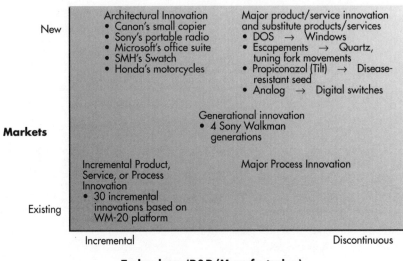

Figure 18.4 Innovation streams

fundamental process innovation. And eras of incremental change require streams of incremental and architectural innovation (refer to Figures 18.1 and 18.2). Given the nature of technology cycles, then, the roots of sustained competitive advantage lie in a firm's ability to proactively initiate all these types of innovation. Management must develop the diverse competencies and organizational capabilities to shape and take advantage of dominant designs (e.g., Windows versus OS/2), to shape architectural innovation, and to introduce substitute products before the competition does (e.g., Windows 95 versus IBM's WARP) (see Figure 18.4).

Through such proactive management of technology cycles and innovation streams, managers can maintain control over core product subsystems and extend mature technologies, while exploiting dominant designs, architectural innovation, and product substitution as windows of opportunity for technological evolution and successful competition.

Building Ambidextrous Organizations

Sustained competitiveness demands an ability to operate simultaneously in multiple modes: managing incremental and architectural as well as discontinuous innovation, and managing for short-term efficiency as well as for long-term innovation. Senior teams must be capable of building organizations that can handle such innovative and strategic diversity—that is, "ambidextrous organizations," or organizations with multiple internally inconsistent architectures.[19] Such dual organizations build in the experimentation, improvisation, and luck associated with small organizations, along with the efficiency, consistency, and reliability associated with larger organizations.[20]

Managers have hardware and software tools in building organizational architectures.[21] Hardware tools include organization structures, systems, and rewards as well as processes and flows. Software tools include the firm's human resource capabilities, its culture, its social networks, and the characteristics and competencies of the senior team (Figure 18.5). Anchored by the unit's strategy, objectives, and vision, management teams build social and technical systems, internally congruent organization arrangements, human resources, culture, and work processes to execute the unit's strategic intent.[22]

Organizational architectures for incremental innovation are fundamentally different from those for discontinuous innovation. What organizational architecture is appropriate for incremental innovation? Continuous incremental improvement in both the product and associated processes, and high-volume throughput associated with incremental innovation, require organizations with relatively formalized roles and responsibilities, centralized procedures, functional structures, efficiency-oriented cultures, highly engineered work processes, strong manufacturing and sales capabilities, and an older, experienced, relatively homogeneous workforce.[23] Efficiency-oriented units drive continuous improvement and the elimination of variability and have relatively short time horizons. Such units are often relatively large and old, with highly ingrained, taken-for-granted assumptions and knowledge systems. They are highly inertial and often have glorious histories; SSIH, Unites States Steel, IBM, and Philips are examples. Neither discontinuous nor architectural innovation is a natural outcome of efficiency-oriented organizations.[24]

What organizational architecture is appropriate for discontinuous innovation? In dramatic contrast to incremental innovation, discontinuous innovation emerges from entrepreneurial, skunk-works types of organizations. Entrepreneurial units are relatively small; they have loose, decentralized product structures, experimental cultures, loose work processes, strong entrepreneurial and technical competencies,

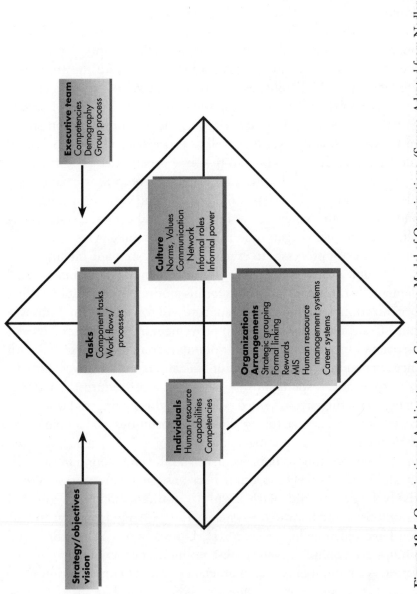

Figure 18.5 Organizational Architecture: A Congruence Model of Organizations. (Source: Adapted from Nadler and Tushman, 1997.)

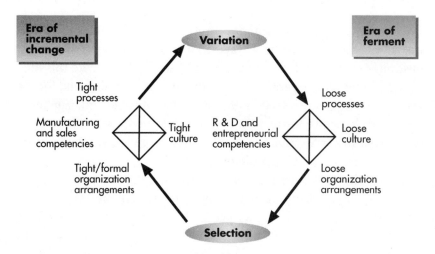

Figure 18.6 Organizational architectures and technology cycles

and relatively young and heterogeneous human resource profiles. These units generate the experiments from which the larger organization's senior team can learn about the future. They explicitly build new experience bases, knowledge systems, and networks to break from the larger organization's history. They generate the variants from which the senior team can make bets on both possible dominant designs and technological discontinuities (see Figure 18.6).[25] In contrast to the larger, more mature, efficiency-oriented units, these small entrepreneurial units are inefficient and rarely profitable and have no established histories.

What organizational architecture is appropriate for architectural innovation? Architectural innovation takes existing technologies and links these technologies in novel ways; it is built not on new technological breakthroughs, but rather on integrating competencies from both efficiency and entrepreneurial units. It calls for the construction of distinct organizational architectures to bring this new product to new markets.[26] While technologically simple, architectural innovations are often not initiated by incumbent industry leaders because of the difficulties these firms have in developing organizational linking capabilities.

In sum, incremental, architectural, and discontinuous innovation types require fundamentally different organization architectures within a single business unit. For example, Dr. Samo at Ciba Crop Protection could not afford an either/or innovation strategy. He had to continue to support incremental innovation in his mature propiconazol product even as he worked to develop fundamental product substitutes (e.g., a biologically engineered seed). To execute this dual strategy, Samo built separate units for the mature fungicide and for the genetically engineered seed. These units had different management teams and their own structures, cultures, and processes. These units were physically separated from each other—one located in Switzerland, the other in the United States.

In building this ambidextrous organization, Dr. Samo and his senior team provided the push and drive for incremental innovation even as they challenged another part of the organization to re-create the future (see Figure 18.7). More generally, senior management's challenge is to build into a single organization multiple integrated organizational architectures. A single organization must host multiple cultures, structures, processes, management teams, and human resource capabilities in order to be incrementally innovative (e.g., new and improved propiconazol) while at the same time creating products that may make the existing product line obsolete (e.g., a new seed).

Ambidextrous organizations have built-in cultural, structural, and demographic contradictions. These internal contradictions are necessary if the organization is to be able to produce streams of innovations. Yet these contradictions create instability and conflict between the different organization units—between those historically profitable, large, efficient, older, cash-generating units and the young, entrepreneurial, experimental, cash-absorbing units. Because the power, resources, and traditions of organizations are usually anchored in the older, more traditional units, these units usually work to ignore, sabotage, or otherwise trample entrepreneurial units.[27] The certainty of today's incremental advance often works to destroy the potential of tomorrow's architectural and discontinuous advance.

For example, the Swiss watch producers had all the quartz and tuning fork technology but chose to destroy those variants and reinvest in mechanical movements. Oticon had both the idea and the technology to move into ITE hearing aids, yet they were incapable of innovating until after Starkey had taken this new market. Similarly, although IBM had the software and microprocessor competencies and Xerox had the imaging competencies, IBM and Xerox chose to reinvest in mainframe and reprographic technology, respectively. Given the inertial, defensive, and political dynamics that exist in large

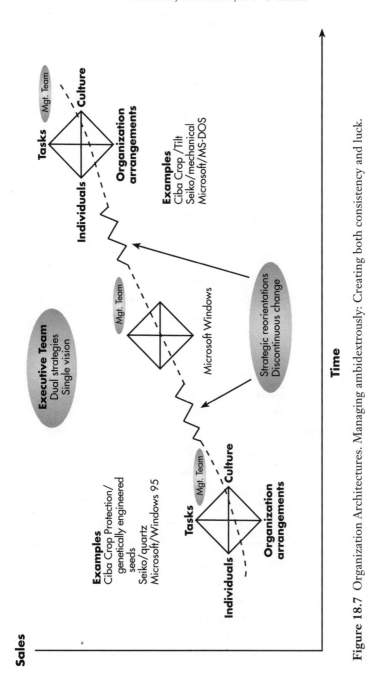

Figure 18.7 Organization Architectures. Managing ambidextrously: Creating both consistency and luck.

organizations, the senior management team must not only protect and legitimize the entrepreneurial units; they must also keep these units physically separate and culturally and structurally distinct from the more mature units. But this is difficult. In industry after industry, major firms—those with the competencies to unleash architectural or discontinuous innovation—have chosen to close off internally generated learning and to reinvest in their past. Over and over, we see core capabilities become core rigidities.

Ambidextrous Management Teams

Internal diversity provides the senior team with the ability to improvise in the present even as it experiments for the future. If these diverse capabilities can be integrated, they permit the organization to innovate for both today and tomorrow; but without integration, the potential of an ambidextrous organization is lost. The senior team must be able to both host and reconcile the paradoxical requirements of ambidextrous organizations; they must create both highly differentiated and highly integrated organizations.[28]

What levers can senior teams use to reconcile the tensions and take advantage of the opportunities of ambidextrous organizations? Perhaps most fundamentally, a clear, emotionally engaging vision provides a strategic anchor from which senior teams can balance the contrasting requirements of strategic innovation. Simple, direct competitive visions create a point of clarity within which an organization can be simultaneously incremental and discontinuous, short term and long term.[29] For example, in the mid-1980s, Seymour Cray and John Rollwagen's theme for Cray Research was "We make the world's fastest computer." With such a vision, Cray Research was able to hold onto its classic Cray business of custom-made computers as well as moving into high-volume, low-cost supercomputers. Similarly, slogans such as Motorola's "best in class in portable communication devices" or Ciba Crop Protection's "most dominant crop protection competitor, worldwide" permit these senior teams to drive incremental innovation and efficiency along with discontinuous change and experimentation.

Sustained, consistent commitment to a unit's vision, even as strategies and objectives change, further reinforces that vision. Commitment is further reinforced by senior management continuity and by their consistent behaviors in support of the vision (e.g., Gates at

Microsoft or Galvin at Motorola). Through such clarity and consistency of vision the senior team can support the internally contradictory organizational architectures associated with ambidextrous organizations and still be seen as consistent and credible.

The senior team's composition and demography and its ways of working together are also powerful tools for achieving integration in ambidextrous organizations. While there are great benefits in senior management continuity, there are also benefits in creating highly heterogeneous, demographically young senior teams. Such teams have the benefit of consistency in vision from the top along with the ability to import new team members with different competencies and expertise.[30] For example, as Microsoft grew, Bill Gates broadened his senior team with managers from outside Microsoft with marketing, organizational, and technical skills.[31]

Highly effective senior teams have diverse competencies to handle the contrasting innovation demands of ambidextrous organizations. In contrast, senior teams that have been together for extended periods and are dominated by a single competency often get stuck in their ways and are unable to deal with those contrasting demands.[32] Company leaders can develop diverse competencies by importing executives from outside the firm, by creating diverse career experiences internally, and by building heterogeneous teams within the organization.

But senior teams must have more than diverse competencies. Highly effective senior teams are able to work together in a way that can take advantage of their internal differences. Effective teams have internal processes that enable them to handle greater information and decision alternatives and to deal with diverse points of view and contrasting opinions. Diverse, self-critical senior teams with effective group processes not only get their own work accomplished but model appropriate ways to deal with conflict and cross-cutting priorities in the larger organization. In contrast, senior teams that send mixed messages, that cannot resolve their own conflicts, and that do not collaborate internally create highly unstable, politically chaotic organizations. Unclear signals from the senior team squander the potential of ambidextrous organizations.[33]

Finally, senior management teams can create roles, structures, formal processes, and rewards to facilitate integration. Particularly for architectural innovation, the development roles and formal linking mechanisms encourage integration within the senior team and across diverse parts of the organization. Team-based rewards that measure and value diverse types of innovation and collaborative team behaviors motivate team members to work together, whether to excel today through incremental innovation or to create the future through architectural or discontinuous innovation.[34]

A clear, consistent vision, diverse senior team competencies, healthy senior team group processes, and rich organization-linking mechanisms are tools to achieve integration in ambidextrous organizations. With such integration, the senior team can develop the diverse perspectives and experiences that are the great assets of truly ambidextrous organizations. These perspectives and data provide a base from which the senior team can cultivate the insight to win for today and the foresight to alter industry rules to win for tomorrow.[35] An image of a senior team managing streams of innovation is, then, that of a juggler juggling multiple balls. Most management teams juggle one ball well. But it is the rare management team that can juggle numerous balls—that can articulate a clear, compelling vision and simultaneously host multiple organizational architectures—without sounding confused or, worse, hypocritical.

Managing Strategic Innovation and Discontinuous Organization Change

Business units in ambidextrous organizations have the capability of managing in multiple time frames: managing simultaneously for today's innovation requirements and tomorrow's innovation possibilities. Entrepreneurial units provide learning-by-doing data, imagination, and luck to drive possible new dominant designs, architectural innovations, and/or product substitutions. From these entrepreneurial units the senior team can learn about possible long-term futures. In contrast, more mature units drive sustained incremental innovation and more short-term learning. The senior management team can then draw upon these diverse types of innovation and learning to make strategic decisions—when to try to create a dominant design (and what product variant to bet on), when to initiate an architectural innovation, or when to introduce a product substitute that might cannibalize the existing product line. For example, Dr. Samo and his senior team at Ciba Crop Protection must understand the options both for continued development of propiconazol and for introduction of genetically engineered seed so as to make the decision when, where, and how to initiate a substitute product.

Dominant designs, architectural innovation, and product substitution events are windows of strategic opportunity where managerial action can shape or reinvent a product class.[36] During eras of ferment, management can move to shape the closing on a dominant design. During eras of incremental change, management can act to substitute for their existing product line or to extend it through architectural innovation. For example, IBM's bet on the 360 mainframe series fundamentally shaped the evolution of that product class, just as Seiko's move on the quartz movement fundamentally changed the watch product class.

Obviously, everyone recognizes dominant designs and successful architectural or product substitutes after the fact: VHS beat Beta, quartz beat escapements. But management teams cannot know the "right" decisions on innovation streams in real time. Through building dual organizational capabilities, however, the management team maximizes the probability that they will have both the expertise and the luck from which to make industry-shaping decisions proactively rather than reactively. Further, while "correct" strategic innovation bets can be known only in retrospect, managerial action within the firm—and with collaborators, alliance partners, and governmental agencies—can affect the ultimate closing on an industry standard or the success of a product substitute.[37]

At the closing of a dominant design, strategic management within the firm shifts its focus from major product variation to major process innovation, then to sustained incremental innovation.[38] At product substitution events and for architectural innovation, strategic management shifts from incremental innovation to major product or process innovation. As strategic innovation requirements shift at these junctures, so too must the dominant organizational capabilities. Those organizational architectures—those structures, roles, cultures, processes, and competencies—so appropriate during eras of ferment are no longer appropriate during eras of incremental change, just as those organizational architectures so appropriate during eras of incremental change are no longer appropriate during eras of ferment.

At these strategic junctures, shifts in a firm's innovation stream can be executed only through concurrent discontinuous organizational change; managers can attempt to rewrite their industry's rules only if they are willing to rewrite their organization's rules. For example, IBM's 360 decision in mainframes was coupled with sweeping shifts in IBM's structure, controls, systems, and culture. In contrast, leaving bold strategic moves or great technology uncoupled from organizational capabilities leads to underperformance. Sony's superior Beta technology format was to able to counter JVC's combination of an adequate VHS technology coupled with brilliant organizational capabilities and strategic alliances. Strategic innovation, then, is rooted as much in reconfigured organizational architectures as in technological prowess.[39]

Yet the need for discontinuous organizational change runs headlong into internal forces for inertia. Patterns in organizational evolution across industries and countries suggest that sweeping organizational shifts cannot be effected through incremental change. Incremental change benefits today's organization but stunts the move to tomorrow's organization. Organization renewal and shifts in innovation streams can be executed only through strategic reorientation—discontinuous and concurrent shifts in strategy, structure, competencies, and processes. These frame-breaking organizational changes are often initiated by revised senior teams.[40]

Our model of business unit evolution is one of long periods of incremental change punctuated by discontinuous, frame-breaking, organization change (see Figure 18.8). Organizations can move from today's strength to tomorrow's strength through strategic reorientations. Strategic reorientations are coupled to shifts in the innovation stream such as moves on a dominant design, architectural innovation, or product substitution. For example, IBM's shift to the 360 series, Seiko's shift to quartz, and Starkey's shift to ITE hearing aids were all coupled with proactive strategic reorientations. If strategic reorientations are not done proactively, they have to be done reactively—as with Burroughs in mainframes, SSIH in watches, and Oticon in hearing aids. But reactive reorientations (often called turnarounds) are more risky than proactive reorientations, because they must be implemented under crisis conditions and under considerable time pressure that hinders the firm's ability to learn.[41]

The senior team, then, must develop not only their ability to conceptualize strategic reorientations but their ability to execute the strategic changes associated with going from a given present state to a

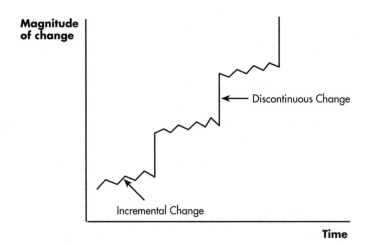

Figure 18.8 Patterns in organizational evolution

fundamentally different future state. The senior team must build their capabilities to manage not only incremental organizational change but discontinuous organizational change.[42]

Senior management's challenge in leading discontinuous change is fundamentally different from that in leading incremental change. Discontinuous change must be initiated and directed by the senior team, must be shaped by an integrated change agenda, and must be rapidly implemented—driven by the senior team's clear vision and committed actions. These challenges often necessitate shifts in the senior team and within middle management. The management of strategic reorientations must attend to the politics of the change, cope with individual resistance to change, and maintain control during the transition period. If implemented through incremental change methods, strategic reorientations run the risk of being sabotaged by the politics, structures, and competencies of the status quo.[43] For example, in Ciba's Crop Protection Division, the transition from fundamentally different fungicides to EC-50 (their bet on a dominant design) was executed through sweeping changes in the division and through a new fungicide team. In contrast, breakthrough innovation at Xerox in the late 1970s and early 1980s was not coupled with corresponding organizational shifts. The politics of stability held Xerox hostage to its past.[44]

Managing innovation streams is about managing dualities: managing and embracing efficiency *and* innovation, tactical *and* strategic, incremental *and* discontinuous, today *and* tomorrow. Managing innovation streams is about consistency and control as well as variability, learning by doing, and the cultivation of luck. It is the crucial role of the senior team to embrace these contradictions and take advantage of the tensions and synergies that emerge from juggling multiple competencies simultaneously.[45] It is the role of vision and strategy to bind these paradoxical requirements together.

Conclusion

While success seems to be hazardous, it is possible to lead a product class over time. Corning's success in ceramics, Microsoft's in software, Ciba's in crop protection, and Motorola's in mobile phones demonstrate that it is possible to build sustained competitive advantage.[46] We have emphasized building executive teams and leadership throughout the organization that can simultaneously manage short-term efficiency and create the conditions for tomorrow's strategic innovation. It is through such dual organizational capabilities that managers create both the expertise and luck from which they can shape their firm's future.

Strategic innovation is about implementation. The world is full of great visions, strategies, technologies, and innovations that were never implemented, or that were implemented after the competition led the way. Because it is the execution of vision, strategy, and innovation streams that really counts, we have highlighted the importance of effectively managing strategic change. Innovation is always associated with organizational changes, so managers must focus on managing change within their units and change across their own and other organizations. We have coupled the ideas of managing innovation streams with the dynamics of managing change.

Even if periods of incremental change do build organizational inertia, organizations can move from strength to strength. Through proactive strategic change, senior teams can manage the rhythm by which each expiring strength gives birth to its successor. Prior organizational competencies can provide a platform so that the next phase of an organization's evolution does not start from ground zero. Organizations can, then, renew themselves through a series of proactive strategic reorientations anchored by a common vision. Like a dying vine, the prior period of incremental change provides the compost for

Table 18.3

Managerial Metaphors in the Management of Strategic Innovation and Change

The Manager As	Role
Architect/Engineer	Building fit, consistency, and congruence of structures, human resources, and cultures to execute critical tasks in service of strategy, objectives, and vision. Continuous improvement.
Network Builder/Politician	Managing strategic change by building networks and shaping coalitions down, across, and outside the manager's unit.
Artist/Juggler	Building in contradictory strategies, structures, competencies, and cultures in service of both incremental and discontinuous innovation, as well as integrating these contradictions through vision and strategy.

its own seeds, its own variants, to thrive following a major reorientation, in the subsequent period of incremental change.

Our approach to strategic innovation evokes several images of managers involved in the management of innovation streams. We can see managers as simultaneously organization architects/social engineers, network builders/politicians, and artists/jugglers (see Table 18.3). The manager as architect/engineer focuses on social engineering, using the tools of strategy, structures, human resource competencies, and cultures to build a robust organization to get today's work and tomorrow's innovation accomplished. Yet at junctures in a product class, shifts in the innovation stream must be coupled with discontinuous organization change. These change requirements run counter to the dynamic conservatism found in successful firms. Therefore the second managerial metaphor is that of the manager as a network builder and politician, building coalitions in the service of innovation and change. Finally, we have considered the manager as artist, juggling the tensions and contradictions of managing both for today and for tomorrow while integrating these contradictions into an internally consistent whole. These multiple managerial and, in turn, organizational competencies seem to be necessary if a company is to achieve and sustain competitive advantage in turbulent product classes.

Notes

1. There is a burgeoning literature on the competitive importance of innovation and the linkage between innovation and organizational renewal across industries and countries. See Schoonhoven et al., 1990; Morone, 1993; Hamel and Prahalad, 1994; Burgelman, 1994; Brown and Eisenhardt, 1995; Henderson and Clark, 1990; Rosenbloom and Christensen, 1994; Utterback, 1994; Jellinek and Schoonhoven, 1990; Anderson and Tushman, 1990, Florida and Kenney, 1990; Gomory, 1991.

2. See, for example, Rosenbloom and Christensen, 1994; Miller, 1994; Henderson and Clark, 1990.

3. See Barton, 1992.

4. See, for example, Barton, 1992; Jellinek and Schoonhoven, 1990; Foster, 1987; Morone 1993; Brown and Eisenhardt, 1997.

5. See also Hurst, 1995; Foster, 1987; Hamel and Prahalad, 1994; Utterback, 1994.

6. See, for example, Morone, 1993; Deschamps and Nayak, 1995.

7. See Abernathy and Clark, 1985; Iansiti and Clark, 1994; Brown and Eisenhardt, 1995; Sanderson and Uzumeri, 1995.

8. See Tushman and Anderson, 1986; Anderson and Tushman, 1990; Utterback, 1994; Aitken, 1985; Rosenkopf and Tushman, 1994.

9. See Landes, 1983.

10. See Tushman and Rosenkopf, 1992; Henderson and Clark, 1990; Henderson, 1995; Nobel, 1984; Hughes, 1983; Van de Ven and Garud, 1994; David, 1985; Morone, 1993.

11. See Noble, 1984; Morone, 1993; Cusumano and Selby, 1995; Hughes, 1983; Cusumano et al., 1992.

12. See Henderson, 1995; Hughes, 1983; Noble, 1984; Baum and Korn, 1995; Tushman and Rosenkopf, 1992.

13. See Abernathy and Utterback, 1978; Hollander, 1965, Florida and Kenney, 1990; Tushman and Anderson, 1986; Anderson and Tushman, 1990.

14. See Morone, 1993; Sanderson and Uzumeri, 1995; Meyer and Utterback, 1993.

15. See Sanderson and Uzumeri, 1995.

16. See Foster, 1987; Iansiti and Clark, 1994; Morone, 1993.

17. See Henderson and Clark, 1990.

18. See Henderson and Clark, 1990; Henderson, 1995; Rosenbloom and Christensen, 1994.

19. See, for example, Rosenbloom and Christensen, 1994; Iansiti and Clark, 1994; Morone, 1993; Weick, 1979; Burgelman, 1994.

20. See, for example, Eisenhardt and Tabrizi, 1995; Imai et al., 1985.

21. See Nadler and Tushman, 1989, in press; Tushman and O'Reilly, in press.

22. See Tushman and O'Reilly, in press.

23. See Nadler and Tushman, 1989, in press; Eisenhardt and Tabrizi, 1995.

24. See, for example, Henderson and Clark, 1990.

25. See Burgelman, 1994; Nonaka, 1988; Eisenhardt and Tabrizi, 1995.
26. See also Iansiti and Clark's (1994) discussion of supercomputers and Brown and Eisenhardt's (1995) discussion of computers and workstations; also Henderson and Clark, 1990; Henderson, 1995.
27. See Cooper and Smith, 1992; Barton, 1992; Utterback, 1994; Kearns and Nadler, 1992; Foster, 1987; Morone, 1993; Hamel and Prahalad, 1994; Rosenbloom and Christensen, 1994.
28. See Brown and Eisenhardt, 1995; Iansiti and Clark, 1994; Lawrence and Lorsch, 1967.
29. Collins and Porras, 1994; Nonaka, 1998; Imai et al., 1985; Morone, 1983.
30. See Virany et al., 1992; O'Reilly et al., 1989.
31. See Cusumano and Selby, 1995.
32. See Cusumano and Selby, 1995; Eisenhardt and Tabrizi 1995; Katz, 1997; Ancona and Nadler, 1992; Nonaka, 1988; Miller, 1990, 1994; Hambrick and D'Aveny, 1988.
33. See Eisenhardt, 1989; Pfeffer, 1992.
34. See Nadler and Tushman, in press; Iansiti and Clark, 1994; Henderson and Clark, 1990; Brown and Eisenhardt, 1995.
35. See Hamel and Prahalad, 1994.
36. See McGrath et al., 1992; Tushman and Rosenkopf, 1992; Hamel and Prahalad, 1994.
37. See for example, Peters, 1990; Cohen and Levinthal 1990; Teece, 1987; McGrath et al., 1992.
38. Abernathy, 1978; Abernathy and Clark, 1985.
39. See Anderson and Tushman, 1990; Romanelli and Tushman, 1994; Utterback, 1994; Morone, 1993; Rosenbloom and Cusumano, 1987; Teece, 1987; Rosenbloom and Christensen, 1994.
40. See Tushman et al., 1986; Romanelli and Tushman, 1994; Miller, 1990, 1994; Meyer et al., 1990.
41. See Tushman and O'Reilly, in press; Hamel and Prahalad, 1994; Hurst, 1995; Rosenbloom and Christensen, 1994.
42. See Nadler and Tushman, 1997; Tushman and O'Reilly, in press, Hurst, 1995.
43. See, for example, Virany et al., 1992; Kearns and Nadler, 1992.
44. See Virany et al., 1992; Nadler et al., 1995; Tushman and O'Reilly, in press; Nadler and Tushman, 1997, in press; Smith and Alexander, 1990; Kearns and Nadler, 1992.
45. See Hurst, 1995; Collins and Porras, 1994; Van de Ven, Angle, and Poole, 1988.
46. See Morone, 1993; Brown and Eisenhardt, 1995.

References

Abernathy, W. *The Productivity Dilemma*. Baltimore: Johns Hopkins University Press, 1978.
Abernathy, W., and K. Clark. "Innovation: Mapping the Winds of Creative Destruction." *Research Policy*, 1985.

Abernathy, W., and J. Utterback. "Patterns of Industrial Innovation." *Technology Review*, 80, 1978, 40–47.

Aitken, H. *The Continuous Wave.* Princeton: Princeton University Press, 1985.

Ancona, D., and D. Nadler. "Top Hats and Executive Teams." *Sloan Management Review*, 1992.

Anderson, P., and M. Tushman. "Technological Discontinuities and Dominant Designs: A Cyclical Model of Technological Change." *Administrative Science Quarterly*, 1990, 35, 604–633.

Barton, D. "Core Capabilities and Core Rigidities: A Paradox in Managing New Product Development." *Strategic Management Journal*, 1992.

Baum, J., and H. Korn. "Dominant Designs and Population Dynamics in Telecommunications Services." *Social Science Research*, 1995.

Brown, S., and K. Eisenhardt. "Product Development: Past Research, Present Findings and Future Directions." *Academy of Management Review*, 1995.

Brown, S., and K. Eisenhardt. "Product Innovation As Core Capability: The Art of Dynamic Adaptation." *Administrative Science Quarterly*, 42, 1997, 1–34.

Burgelman, R. "Fading Memories: A Process Theory of Strategic Business Exit." *Administrative Science Quarterly*, 1994.

Cohen W., and D. Levinthal. "Absorptive Capacity: A New Perspective on Learning and Innovation." *Administrative Science Quarterly*, 1990.

Collins, J., and J. Porras. *Built to Last.* New York: Harper Business, 1994.

Cooper, A., and C. Smith. "How Established Firms Respond to Threatening Technologies." *Academy of Management Executive*, 6(2) 1992, 55–70.

Cusumano, M., Y. Mylonadis, and R. Rosenbloom. "Strategic Maneuvering and Mass Market Dynamics: The Triumph of VHS over Beta." *Business History Review*, 1992.

Cusumano, M., and R. Selby. *Microsoft Secrets.* New York: Free Press, 1995.

David, P. "Clio and the Economics of Qwerty." *Economics History*, 1985.

Deschamps, J., and P. Nayak. *Product Juggernauts.* Boston: Harvard Business School Press, 1995.

Eisenhardt, K. "Making Fast Strategic Decisions in High Velocity Environments. *Academy of Management Journal*, 1989.

Eisenhardt, K., and B. Tabrizi. "Acceleration Adaptive Processes." *Administrative Science Quarterly*, 1995.

Florida, R., and J. Kenney, *The Breakthrough Illusion.* New York: Basic Books, 1990.

Foster, R. *Innovation: The Attacker's Advantage.* New York: Summit Books, 1987.

Gomory, R. "The Technology–Product Relationship: Early and Late Stages." In Rosenberg, N., R. Landau, and D. Mowery (eds.), *Technology and the Wealth of Nations*, Palo Alto, Calif.: Stanford University Press, 1991.

Hambrick, D., and R. D'Aveni. "Large Corporate Failures As Downward Spirals." *Administrative Science Quarterly*, 33, 1–23, 1988.

Hamel, G., and C. Prahalad. *Competing for the Future.* Boston: Harvard Business School Press, 1994.

Henderson, R. "Of Life Cycles Real and Imaginary: The Unexpectedly Long Old Age of Optical Lithography." *Research Policy*, 1995.

Henderson, R., and K. Clark. "Architectural Innovation: The Reconfiguration of Existing Product Technologies and the Failure of Established Firms." *Administrative Science Quarterly*, 1990.

Hollander, S. *Sources of Efficiency*. Cambridge, Mass.: MIT Press, 1965.

Hughes, T. *Networks of Power*. Baltimore: Johns Hopkins Press, 1983.

Hurst, D. *Crisis and Renewal*. Boston: Harvard Business School Press, 1995.

Iansiti, M., and K. Clark. "Integration and Dynamic Capability." *Industry and Corporation Change*, 1994.

Imai, K., I. Nonaka, and H. Takeuchi. "Managing the New Product Development Process: How Japanese Firms Learn and Unlearn." In K. Clark et al., *The Uneasy Alliance*. Boston: Harvard Business School Press, 1985.

Jellinek, M., and C. Schoonhoven. *The Innovation Marathon*. London: Blackwell, 1990.

Katz, R. "Managing Professional Careers; Influence of Job Longevity and Group Age" in M. Tushman and P. Anderson (eds.), *Managing Strategic Innovation and Change*. New York: Oxford University Press, 1997.

Kearns, D., and D. Nadler. *Prophets in the Dark*. New York: Harper, 1992.

Landes, D., *Revolution in Time*. Cambridge, Mass.: Harvard University Press, 1983.

Lawrence, P., and J. Lorsch. *Organizations and Environments*. Boston: Harvard Business School Press, 1967.

McGrath, R., I MacMillan, and M. Tushman. "The Role of Executive Team Actions in Shaping Dominant Designs: Towards Shaping Technological Progress." *Strategic Management Journal*, 1992, 13, 137–161.

Meyer, A., G. Brooks, and J. Goes. "Environmental Jolts and Industry Revolutions." *Strategic Management Journal*, 1990.

Meyer, M., and J. Utterback. "Product Family and the Dynamics of Core Capability." *Sloan Management Review*, 1993.

Miller, D. *The Icarus Paradox: How Exceptional Companies Bring About Their Own Downfall*. New York: Harper, 1990.

Miller, D. "What Happens after Success: The Perils of Excellence" *Journal of Management Studies*, 31:3, 1994.

Morone, J. *Winning in High Tech Markets*. Boston: Harvard Business School Press, 1993.

Nadler, D., R. Shaw, and E. Walton, *Discontinuous Change*. San Francisco: Jossey-Bass, 1995.

Nadler, D., and M. Tushman. *Competing by Design: The Power of Organizational Architectures*. New York: Oxford University Press, 1997.

Nadler, D., and M. Tushman. *Strategic Organization Design*. New York: Oxford University Press, 1989.

Noble, D. *Forces of Production*. New York: Knopf, 1984.

Nonaka, I. "Creating Order out of Chaos: Self-Renewal in Japanese Firms." *California Management Review*, 1988.

O'Reilly, C., D. Caldwell, and W. Barnett. "Work Group Demography, Social Integration and Turnover." *Administrative Science Quarterly*, 34, 21–37, 1989.

Peters, T. "Get Innovative or Get Dead." *California Management Review*, 1990.

Pfeffer, J. *Managing with Power.* Boston: Harvard Business School Press, 1992.

Romanelli, E., and M. Tushman. "Organization Transformation as Punctuated Equilibrium." *Academy of Management Journal,* 1994, 37, 1141–1166.

Rosenbloom, D., and C. Christensen. "Technological Discontinuities, Organization Capabilities, and Strategic Commitments." *Industry and Corporate Change,* 1994.

Rosenbloom, R., and M. Cusumano. "Technological Pioneering and Competitive Advantage: The Birth of the VCR Industry." *California Management Review,* 29, 4, 1987, 3–22.

Rosenkopf, L., and M. Tushman. "The Coevolution of Technology and Organization." In J. Baum and J. Singh, *Evolutionary Dynamics of Organizations.* New York: Oxford University Press, 1994.

Sanderson, S., and M. Uzumeri. "Product Platforms and Dominant Designs: The Case of Sony's Walkman." *Research Policy,* 1995, 24, 583–607.

Schoonhoven, K., K. Eisenhardt, and K. Lyman. "Speeding Products to Market." *Administrative Science Quarterly,* 1990.

Smith, D., and R. Alexander. *Fumbling the Future.* New York: Harper, 1990.

Teece, D. "Profiting from Technological Innovation." In D. Teece (ed.), *The Competitive Challenge.* New York: Harper & Row, 1987.

Tushman, M., and P. Anderson, "Technological Discontinuities and Organization Environments." *Administrative Science Quarterly,* 1986, 31, 439–465.

Tushman, M., W. Newman, and E. Romanelli. "Convergence and Upheaval: Managing the Unsteady Pace of Organizational Evolution." *California Management Review,* 1986.

Tushman, M., and C. O'Reilly. *Evolution and Revolution: A Practical Guide to Managing Innovation and Change.* Boston: Harvard Business School Press, 1997.

Tushman, M., and L. Rosenkopf. "On the Organizational Determinants of Technological Change: Towards a Sociology of Technological Evolution." In B. Staw and L. Cummings, *Research in Organizational Behavior,* vol. 14. Greenwich, Conn: JAI Press, 1992.

Utterback, J. *Mastering the Dynamics of Innovation.* Boston: Harvard Business School Press, 1994.

Van de Ven A., and R. Garud. "The Coevolution of Technical and Institutional Events in the Development of an Innovation." In J. Baum and J. Singh, *Evolutionary Dynamics of Organization.* New York: Oxford University Press, 1994.

Van de Ven, A., H. Angle, and M. Poole. *Research on the Management of Innovation.* New York: Harper, 1988.

Virany, B., M. Tushman, and E. Romanelli. "Executive Succession and Organization Outcomes in Turbulent Environments." *Organization Science,* 1992.

Weick, K. *The Social Psychology of Organizing.* Reading, Mass.: Addison-Wesley, 1979.

[19]

Senior Leadership and Discontinuous Change

Some Themes

Elise Walton

T HE THREE CHAPTERS PRECEDING THIS ONE discuss the management of discontinuous change from the CEO and organizational perspectives. The CEOs' case studies (Chapters 16 and 17) and the theoretical essay (Chapter 18) share several themes regarding organizational change. In this chapter I will look at three of those themes and will summarize several related insights.

Specifically, the CEO papers indicate the importance of creating the change agenda: determining the need for change and making the core choices about the change direction and process. As indicated here and elsewhere, creating and executing a change agenda is a team sport—who is enlisted to define and support the transformation is important. The second theme is the question of what can be done to sequence and manage the stages of change. Timing, and the sequencing of actions and communications, influence how effective the change effort is. Last, a clear theme that emerges is the importance of focus on the organization. Robert Bauman cites the organization as hero; Michael Tushman, Philip Anderson, and Charles O'Reilly point out the importance of "ambidextrous" capabilities in an organization.

Determining the Need for a Change Agenda

As a starting point, the need for change—the need for a diversion from the status quo—must be recognized. The CEO and the senior management team must recognize that an altered course is required, and the senior team is the lens that focuses the information mandating change. An enterprise cannot act on or react to environmental change if the senior team can't see it. Also, an enterprise may need the ability to create action even without clear environmental signals. The question then is how the CEO becomes engaged in determining the need for and setting the direction of change. All these questions are easily answered in retrospect, but it is understanding and action in the face of uncertainty that create success.

The SmithKline Beecham case (Chapter 17) offers an example of change in response to clear environmental signals. Health care distribution was changing, with an increasing percentage of the population being covered by cost-oriented managed care programs. The industry was moving from providing pills (and the consequent focus on finding new drugs) to providing solutions, with a change in focus to consumers and the full health care cycle: prevention, diagnosis, treatment, and cure. Pharmaceutical companies and health care providers were undergoing consolidations, integrating forward to get access to consumers directly via services and distribution. Scale was becoming an ever more important competitive advantage.

Clearly, SmithKline Beecham had several alternatives, such as focusing on profitable niches only, exiting the business, or merging to build scale. As Bauman describes, the senior team was able to read the environmental dynamics quickly and move forward on a course of action. Fortunately, they acted ahead of the curve and achieved some first-mover advantages in the wave of pharmaceutical mergers that took place.

In other cases, such as that of Kaiser Permanente (Chapter 16), the need for change was less evident. Despite its strength in the past and a strong presence with its health care users, Kaiser Permanente recognized that its legacy of organizational complexity and consensus decision making could be a liability in a new, fast-moving health care environment. David Lawrence and his team foresaw that changes in the market environment, in purchasing decisions, and in overall demand were likely to change the selection decisions health care users made—to the detriment of Kaiser Permanente.

Twenty-twenty hindsight always tells us when changes undertaken were strategic, sensible, and timely—or misdirected, too little, and too late. The challenge is to be able to recognize the need for change in time. Typically, environmental warning signals include the following:

- *Shifts in industry structure or product class life cycle.* For every class of products, there are shifts in patterns of demand, underlying technology, and competition. In the embryonic phase of a product, competition is based on innovation and on growing consumer acceptance. Later in the life cycle, success may depend on cost, volume, efficiency, or quality. The emergence of new industry standards, or competition around new standards, present challenges. These shifts almost always involve discontinuous change.

- *Technological innovation.* Technological innovation, either in product or process, can challenge traditional competencies of an organization. The features of CDs made them preferable substitutes for tapes and LP records, and a large portion of the music industry had to adapt to change. The planar process in semiconductors and the float glass process in glass manufacturing introduced great uncertainty and changed the basis of competition.

- *Macroeconomic trends and crises.* Major economic and political events can effect an industry. The war in Kuwait changed alliances, trade relations, and, in the short term, petroleum prices. Currency valuation, inflation, and capital movements can all create significant change for enterprises.

- *Regulatory and legal changes.* Deregulation in the telecommunications industry created a wave of mergers, de-mergers, consolidations, downsizings, and layoffs. Deregulation also called for changes in culture and operating practice within many of the firms that survived. Similarly, the CAFE standards introduced by legislation created significant new demands on auto firms to find new manufacturing processes and product designs.

- *Market and competitive forces.* The entrance of new competitors, such as the Japanese entry into the U.S. car market, causes significant change. Dramatic changes in consumer demand, or the creation of excess capacity by overoptimistic industry scenarios, usually forewarn of significant change.

- *Growth.* As organizations get larger (or smaller), the systems and processes that run them must also change.

Reading environmental indicators is a complex task, however. For example, management must sometimes amplify and at other times attenuate signals in interpreting them for the firm as a whole. In a common example, revenues naturally vary from month to month within a quarter, and seasonally throughout the year. When does a month, or even a series of months, in which revenues decline provide an early warning signal? When is it within the band of normal variation, reflecting seasonality or purchasing cycles or exceptional events? Again, hindsight informs us; but the ability for management to smooth out natural variations, to reduce the noise, in environmental indicators without damping the signal is essential to effective management of the change agenda.

Setting the change agenda depends on the CEO's ability to notice and read environmental signals, and this in turn depends on the information-processing ability of the CEO and senior team. In fact, the CEO, as the final decision maker, is the final judgment point—the point at which the information is summed up and a course of action declared. How the CEO sifts through and evaluates information has everything to do with how well the organization acts and reacts to environmental signals.

The first source of information and attention for the CEO is experience, and CEOs tend to focus on the areas in which they have the most experience (Gabarro, 1992; Finklestein & Hambrick, 1996). A CEO with a background in finance may actively support cost control and may focus on managing Wall Street expectations. A CEO with a background in engineering may focus on the new product portfolio and may shield himself from the press and the Street.

A second source of information for the CEO is informants: the people the CEO surrounds himself or herself with. Clearly, at the senior level the primary source of information is through other individuals; the CEO relies on data and judgments provided by other people. The CEO is in no position to verify that 100,000 additional units were sold or that revenues were down $1,000,000. Managers have a network of relationships that provide them with information.

For a CEO the crucial factor is less the true expertise of an informant than the relationship and level of trust the CEO has with the informant. Effective CEOs gather information continuously and aggressively. Books, magazines, and reports are not primary sources of information (Kotter, 1986; Goodman, 1993).

The network of informants that surrounds the CEO, then, is vital to making the CEO an informed and rapid decision maker. If a certain perspective or expertise is missing, a CEO may make decisions in the absence of critical information. Depending on governance structure as well as on the personal relationships surrounding the CEO, information comes in some common packages. CEOs are often well advised to have informants who can provide information on the following topics:

Product/business lines: People who understand the nature of a product, consumer preferences and uses of the product, innovation interval cycles, changes in the product portfolio and maturity over time, competitors, benchmark financial performance, and so on.

Field operations: People who understand the way the product is distributed as well as the needs and behaviors of key partners (resellers, distributors, dealers, service providers), customers, and consumers.

Manufacturing: People who understand the logistics and capability of the production system, including a global perspective. People who understand the costs and benchmark targets of making the product, as well as alternative approaches. Included in this are logistics, distribution, and other enablers to making and selling the product.

Technology: People who understand future opportunities; trends in costs and capabilities of technologies; and technical alliances, consortiums, and interdependencies that may affect the business.

Financial performance: People who understand the financial and business models driving the business.

History: People who understand the history and culture of the firm, who are able to foresee organizational and personal reactions to a change, and who are able to use history to help management understand the opportunities and limitations of changes proposed.

Human resources: People who understand the skills, capabilities, and portability of the human assets of the company.

Social aspects: People who understand the human needs and interpersonal dynamics at play in the senior team and can help facilitate the discussion and acceptance of change.

Not only does the CEO need to become informed—and to inform the senior team—on these perspectives; he or she needs to be sure that the different views are heard and considered by the full group. This is the third source of information—socially constructed knowledge. That is, information and judgments are created by the dialogue between knowledgeable and influential individuals in the senior team. The group creates value-added insight above and beyond individual contributions and perspectives.

One of the dilemmas that executive groups face is that as they get to know one another better, they begin to predict (rightly or wrongly) where the other is "coming from." This often leads to executives' discounting others' information based on their own prior beliefs about the informants' agendas. Also, we all tend to re-create data to fit our own paradigm or filter. Consider the following case: Consumer products company A introduces a new, high-density liquid soap. It replaces the 50-ounce bottle with a 32-ounce bottle. At the same time, a powerful competitor adds a 40-ounce bottle of high-density liquid soap to its product line. After company A's product has been on the shelves six months, the sales VP tells the executive team that there's a problem with the 32-ounce product: Inventory is piling up, customers won't place any more orders, and consumer sales are sinking like a stone. Consumers prefer the competitors' 40-ounce product, which looks like more soap for the money, although it has the same number of washloads as company A's 32-ounce bottle. The marketing person, who recalls the strong endorsement of the focus groups for the 32-ounce product, tries to figure out how to better communicate the value proposition of the product—the fact that the 40-ounce product has more water. The financial manager figures out how to replace the margin points in the annual plan. The man in charge of manufacturing figures out how to replace the product in the production schedule; he also challenges the inventory data, because he's working from a different database. Purchasing and distribution cite the transportation and environmental benefits of a smaller bottle. Meanwhile, suppliers have tooled up for 32-ounce bottles and aren't amenable to change.

All told, each member of company A's senior team finds a reason to challenge the data brought forward by the sales VP. Some raise questions about the sales force's ability and willingness to actively push a new product. Some question the general competence of the sales force. All told, they dismiss the environmental data as a personal agenda of the sales VP. Six wasted months later, however, additional data incontrovertibly indicate the product has failed. The team failed to address the issue brought in by the sales VP, at significant cost to the company.

This small case illustrates how personal filters and needs can undermine the ability of a senior team to identify and act on a problem. People tend to recast information in terms of their individual perspectives, with little heed to what the information may imply for the whole. This case also exemplifies a general problem of humans: distaste for bad news and its implications. We usually put more effort into defending against unpleasant news than into understanding the news. This tendency is deadly when the executive team needs to identify and act rapidly on the need for change.

This problem is amplified when senior teams have limited time together. With inadequate time, team members will tend to avoid the conflict provoked by difficult issues (see Chapter 8 of this text). As the liquid soap case illustrates, each member defines his or her own position; then the meeting ends, and the same situation exists next time. The cycle continues until the environment gives an incontestable signal.

Both Bauman and Lawrence point out the importance of engaging all members of the senior team in the change agenda. Teamwork provides a countermeasure to this individual inability to identify with a common problem. There are specific actions that enhance the ability to create teamwork around the common change agenda.

Have the right team members. Most CEOs, looking back on change efforts, felt they took too long to put together the right team. CEOs are often overly reluctant to identify and remove senior team members who are unable to change. Those embedded in a mainframe world may have a hard time with distributed computing and PCs. Those who believe sales coverage is key to revenue growth may be reluctant to accept telemarketing. Those accustomed to a clublike work environment may find the style of a lean, profit-oriented company unmannerly.

Make listening a core skill. The senior team must be excellent at identifying and considering information. It must be able to sort through mounds of data to get to information. In a social sense, this is a matter of who gets heard and who gets listened to. If, as has often been asserted, key ideas come from unexpected sources, then attending to the weak and minority voices is important. Seeking ideas from outsiders, new employees, consultants, even competitors minimizes the risk of insular thinking.

Make information processing a core skill. Information-processing ability reflects a group's ability to learn and change. Most groups, including senior teams, are not skilled at reasoning together. Often, conflict is suppressed; and when it does emerge, the skills of reasoned dialogue are often weak. Even when a group can reason through a problem together, outcomes are often rejected if they imply an unpleasant or painful course of action. There are many concrete suggestions about how to manage dialogue and conversation in ways that enable learning and change (see Chapter 8 of this text; Ford & Ford, 1995; Senge, 1990). Overall, this points to the value of making the senior team a learning device (Nadler & Tushman, 1988).

Two specific information-processing skills are required. First, listening to nonroutine information is key. Organizations become skilled at dealing with routine information: monthly sales figures, turnover, earnings, orders, and so on. Whole systems are developed to deal with the flow of information around a specific process (market to collection, order to delivery, etc.). But it is often the information that doesn't fit into established processes and patterns that is so important to deal with. Information about discontinuous change comes in a nonroutine way.

Second, conflict management is vital—because it enables a team to sort through information in the most rational way possible in order to reach a reasoned judgment.

Make communication a core skill. The Kaiser Permanente and SmithKline Beecham cases illustrate the importance of enrolling the organization through communication. Stakeholders and opinion groups must be analyzed. Change readiness must be assessed. Communication is vital and it is a core element in the sequencing efforts described by the change managers.

The Importance of Timing and Sequencing Change

The most important timing action that a firm can take is to try to change early in an industry change cycle. One study found that companies that changed early in a cycle, when the disequilibrium was just beginning, had a 50 percent chance of continuing as a viable company. Those who reacted to change toward the end of the cycle had a 10 percent survival rate (Nadler, Shaw, & Walton, 1995).

Clearly, change is affected by many external and unpredictable events. AT&T, for instance, had a well-planned and well-orchestrated approach to its 1996 spin-off of Lucent and NCR. It had thought through the strategic value of spinning off core businesses. It developed a process for separating corporate overhead to the relevant new companies. It worked out a process to restaff each business that was designed to be effective, considerate, and equitable. Throughout the early stages of the change, AT&T received great press for the forethought and organization of the de-merger. Yet, midstream in this change, would-be presidential candidate Pat Buchanan raised the issue of corporate layoffs and pointed to AT&T as a villain of working people. This focus on the layoffs associated with the de-merger created a great deal of difficulty for what was an otherwise positive event. The story demonstrates how external and unpredictable events can affect the course of a change effort.

While timing and opportunism in response to external events is important, most planned change efforts undergo a common set of stages (Figure 19.1), as described in Chapters 16 and 17. Each of these stages has distinct tasks, activities, and challenges. Table 19.1 outlines the challenges in the specific areas of leadership, corporate identity, and organizational architecture in each stage. One key to the implementation of change is an ongoing assessment and learning during the acting and consolidating phases. Invariably, the organizational, strategic, and leadership choices made during the earlier phases are only partially informed. As experience and events provide feedback to the organization, adjustments are almost always called for.

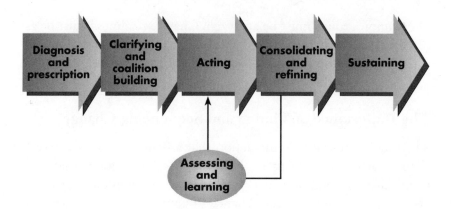

Figure 19.1 Change stages

Communications, engagement, and enrollment are vital activities throughout all the phases of change. These usually come after the change agenda has been defined by the senior team. In some cases these activities constitute a primary vehicle for clarifying and coalition building—one of the earlier stages of change. For instance, once the major strategic direction had been decided on at SmithKline Beecham, Bauman wanted to design a totally new company and get employees to buy into it quickly. To involve employees in the decision process, SmithKline Beecham split the workforce into more than 300 teams of employees, and each team was given six months to submit a plan for its respective business—where to headquarter it, what facilities it would use, what jobs it required. When the change planning process was completed, the total workforce was reduced by 14 percent. Changes were made at the executive level as well: Bauman hired Jan Leschly to run the new SmithKline Beecham.

At the same time, SmithKline Beecham was able to leverage the timing and impact of events to create a sense of urgency. Threats to profitable drug franchises such as Tagamet, as well as government and business attention to health care issues and costs, converged to give SmithKline Beecham a sense of crisis. Said Leschly, "It's a good thing; it makes people think about how to do things differently, which is absolutely necessary with health care reform" (Koselka, 1993). The SmithKline Beecham case illustrates the artful combination of planning and opportunism.

Kaiser Permanente had a major communication effort as part of the action stage. Employees were part of town meetings and broadcasts that described the changes Kaiser Permanente was undertaking. In this communication and enrollment effort, the design was already solidified and the major choices had been made; communication was part of informing and enrolling early majority support.

Focus on the Organization

Organizational architecture (structure, culture, people, etc.) is vital to managing change. As Collins and Porras (1994) put it, leaders must not see "the company as a vehicle for the products" but see "the products as a vehicle for the company." That is, companies designed for success and survival focus on building an organization that will continuously regenerate new opportunities. Organizational sustainability must be the focus of management; and only a regenerative, or ambidextrous, organization can continually re-create a sustained competitive advantage.

Companies actively work to manage the process of organizational architecture and re-creation. Bauman and Lawrence describe their efforts to manage an organization that is moving from one model to another yet all the while needing to maintain some values and identity of its past. In organizational re-creation a firm must ascertain its strengths and weaknesses and must assess its capabilities vis-à-vis its competitors.

In the SmithKline Beecham case, the company worked to assemble a set of capabilities that would qualify the firm to provide a broader range of health care solutions. This effort required thinking about existing competencies in new ways; for instance, using the sales force to get "close to the customer" and thereby compete with other pharmaceutical firms who integrated forward. The new thinking focused on pricing, testing, and prevention as increasingly important elements in the health care model. This meant that SmithKline Beecham reconstructed existing capabilities, deleted capabilities, and added capabilities in line with its new vision.

SmithKline Beecham recognized that size would be an advantage. It also saw that owning clinical labs would help it achieve its vision of becoming a full-service pharmaceutical company. And it pursued creative pricing techniques, such as providing rebates for Tagamet even

Table 19.1
The Challenges of Change

Activity Areas and Key Challenges	*Diagnosis and Prescription*	*Clarifying and Coalition Building*	*Action*	*Consolidating and Refinement*	*Sustaining*
LEADERSHIP	Build the integrated change agenda	Test and refine the change agenda	Feedback forums (focus groups, town meetings)	CEO "office visits"	Senior management forums
	Assess leadership capability (CEO, senior management)	Build engagement/enrollment plan for key opinion groups and stakeholders	Executive coaching	Feedback forums	CEO "office visits"
	Identify key informal leaders	Learn from informal leaders, support teams	Education cascades (strategy forums) executive forums, etc.	Eliminate non-support networks	Ongoing diagnosis
	Identify stakeholders/opinion groups	Select leadership team	Stakeholder and opinion group management	Build new networks/shut down old	
	Design transition management structure			Values/360° feedback	
CORPORATE IDENTITY	Scan environment	Test and refine the new identity	Go public externally	Communications "audit"	Reinforce new identity
	Design identity	Make the big moves (acquisitions, investments, divestments)	Internal broadcast communications: road shows, video and document communications	Support key new initiatives, businesses	Assess marketplace reaction
	Assess opportunity			Look for emergent learnings	

Table 19.1 (con't)

Activity Areas and Key Challenges	Diagnosis and Prescription	Clarifying and Coalition Building	Action	Consolidating and Refinement	Sustaining
ORGANIZATIONAL ARCHITECTURE/RE-CREATION	Assess organizational change capability	Define architectural vision operationally	Make major people/structure changes	Reinforce building block jobs and roles	Consolidate learnings
	Assess organizational strengths and weaknesses	Identify interventions (structure, selection, culture)	Identify required course corrections and follow-on interventions	Check functionality at interfaces and linkage points	Check for emerging organizational rigidity
	Define design intent	Build the transition plan (sequencing)	Utilize push and pull change approaches	Launch follow-on and corrective interventions	Build listening devices
				Make follow-on people changes	
KEY CHALLENGES	Realistic assessment and diagnosis	A compelling case for change	Maintaining balance (optimism vs. pessimism)	Maintaining energy	Maintaining commitment
	Strategic choices	Simplicity	Running the business	Managing information troughs	Sustaining energy
	An energizing change agenda	Early credibility tests	Project management	Making corrections	Maintaining flexibility
	Conditional buy-in	Enlisting early adopters	Late credibility tests	Enlisting late majority	
	Embrace ambiguity		Enlisting early majority		

before the drug went off-patent, to buy volume and gain consumer loyalty. Unlike Merck, which bought a mail-order drug house to get access to its distribution system and information base, SmithKline Beecham chose instead to use its existing sales force more effectively. Also, taking the view that manufacturing would become a less value-adding activity over time, SmithKline Beecham did not seek to purchase generic drug manufacturers, as some of its competitors did.

Theories of organizational re-creation focus on a "from–to" model, a model that encompasses the ideas of a past state, a desired future state, and a transition state. This model looks at change at the organizational level and conceives of change as all-encompassing. Yet organizations managing for sustainability may need to manage continuity and discontinuity simultaneously. As one business re-creates itself, another grows, and a third matures. Tushman and his colleagues put this point forward as the need for organizations to manage ambidextrously—that is, be able to handle internal inconsistency.

Duality in an organization is a known fact. Since the seminal study by Lawrence and Lorsch (1967), managers and academics have recognized that organizations must manage tensions of differentiation and integration. But it has become clear in recent years that this tension exists not only in terms of structural choices but in terms of process, culture, and people choices.

Architecture often drives the way firms "see" the environment. A product-based organization sees issues in terms of product profitability, time to market, and the product portfolio. A customer-based organization sees the environment in terms of customer or account profitability, customer retention, and the customer portfolio. Companies with a history of centralization have difficulty with empowerment and accountability at lower levels. And so on. Duality in organizations means that different lenses are being applied to the same problem. This is both an advantage and a disadvantage.

Some of the biggest, most common dualities are those driven by changes in the product life cycle. As is often noted (Hax & Majiluf, 1995), the structure, processes, and management required for start-ups, high growth, maturity, and decline are very different; but a start-up may be saddled with the same administrative costs and processes as a mature business unit. This dynamic has ruined many a Fortune 500 company's chances for real growth. The internal start-ups are burdened in ways that external competition are not—and so are doomed to failure because of slower capacity to act and higher costs.

Scientific and technological advances such as the semiconductor created a new form of duality: The world economy has changed from one in which worth is measured in the accumulation of physical capital to one in which value is increasingly defined by the store of knowledge and ideas. Although the effects of this transformation appeared most quickly in technology industries themselves, the revolution of microelectronics and software have compelled massive change across nearly every industry. These upheavals have reached out to refashion the nature of the business organization itself, mandating new approaches for the CEO who seeks to shepherd an organization through this era of accelerating change (Gilder, 1990).

The microelectronic circuit is emblematic of the shift in value away from physical goods and toward knowledge and intellectual capital. The common materials that make up a chip account for but a small fraction of its cost, which instead derives from the ideas embodied in the logical design of the chip's circuitry. But the development of the microchip has in turn accentuated the importance of information and knowledge within the enterprise—and greatly reduced the cost of their storage, manipulation, management, and communication. The microcircuit enables the decentralization of information-processing power. The decentralization of processing power compels the decentralization of information and, in turn, of decision-making structure.

The refocusing of the enterprise toward the value of knowledge and ideas poses significant new challenges for today's CEO. For example, the concept of diminishing returns of scale—the notion that production becomes inherently less efficient as it expands—has been a pillar of organization design and competitive strategy; but newer economists say the economics of ideas are different. Ideas are plentiful and infinitely replicable (Kelly, 1996)—and the result is increasing, not diminishing, returns of scale in the realm of information. Perhaps the best documented example of this phenomenon is Microsoft, which, with its Windows product line, controls nearly all of the market for desktop operating systems.

One study, in fact, argues compellingly that many industries are, or will become, hybrids of the old traditional world of production and the new world of increasing returns on information (Arthur,

1996). Hewlett-Packard, for example, holds a commanding market share in desktop printers, where low margins and fierce competition demand that they sustain excellence in their management practices in the traditional worlds of production and distribution. But closer examination reveals that HP must simultaneously manage this business in the domain of increasing returns. "The two worlds," Arthur (1996) writes, "have different economics. They differ in behavior, style, and culture. They call for different management techniques, different strategies, different understandings." In the world of production, an effective strategy requires focus on continuous improvement, development of core competencies, attention to quality processes, and constant efforts to reduce costs. But the world of ideas and information requires flatter organizations, smaller hierarchies, fewer controls, and more rapid mechanisms of adaptation.

This adds a new form of duality: two worlds driven by different economics, requiring different cultures, and necessitates distinct organizational designs. Tushman and colleagues note just how difficult large established firms in most industries have found it to manage ambidextrously. In contrast to these industries, including xerography, steel, and computers, where new competitors have exploited technological change to displace previously dominant companies, pharmaceutical companies founded in the 1940s and 1950s continue to dominate their industry. Despite their size, these firms have been able to respond effectively to much smaller challengers in their market. Henderson (1994) suggests that managerial skills have enabled these companies to leverage specialized organizational knowledge—while ensuring that the knowledge does not tie the company inextricably to its past and so leave it unable to respond to new competitive threats. In the language of Tushman, pharmaceutical firms have been able to build upon their core competencies while not becoming trapped in their distinguished past: Core competencies have not become core rigidities.

For instance, Henderson notes that research for new drug discovery has become more systematic as tools have become more sophisticated. As a result, effective management plays an increasingly significant role in guiding the search for leading-edge drugs. Management must deploy information systems that integrate information from a broad set of scientific disciplines at a time when the information intensiveness of the company is greatly increasing. On average,

Henderson finds, technical publications per pharmaceutical company rose eightfold between 1975 and 1990.

Pharmaceutical companies face the systems, cultural, and organizational challenges of managing in a digital world. They must integrate information across both the scientific fields and the network of companies that define the competitive landscape in which they operate. Such companies' success in managing in the environment, Henderson found, is synergistically linked to effectiveness of the budgeting process. That is, effective information improves the budgeting process, which in turn appears to stimulate the flow of information across organizational boundaries. This in turn diminishes the establishment of personal fiefdoms and discourages narrowness of vision.

So an organization undergoing massive change needs to create a context that embraces duality. This duality may be based in different business models, different economic models, different phases of industry development, or different stages of organizational change. But duality and differentiation mean internal differences. If one product line can be telemarketed and another requires direct sales, this is a source of difference. If Internet services and information show increasing returns of scale while copier production shows diminishing returns of scale, the two businesses must be managed differently. Yet organizations often become caught up in ideas of internal equity and fairness, even though these may be irrelevant to economic, market, product, and life cycle differences.

Managing the internal tension between a profitable but threatened business and its "cannibal" business requires great organizational skill, but it can be done. As Tushman and his colleagues describe, Ciba-Geigy actively pursued the engineering of a disease-resistant seed, knowing full well that this product offering would threaten current returns on pesticides and fungicides.

The need to manage duality leads to some very specific issues:

Complaints of favoritism. In many companies there is one core business that delivers a sizable amount of the profit. This business is usually in some market where the company is favored. This business tends to criticize the other businesses and can often be found suggesting that the other businesses should be run better or shut down or otherwise pulled up to snuff. At the same time, the weaker businesses give the core business little credit for its performance because they view the core business's success as a market and historical chance.

Lack of transparency. One reason for common processes and systems is that they promote organizational transparency—the ability to see from division to division using the same template and the same metrics. When different businesses are permitted to use different processes and there is no systems linkage, it is more difficult to make comparisons or summations between units.

Mixed messages. Ambidexterity means being able to handle duality and two types of organization simultaneously. But ambidextrous management may cause people in the organization to pick up mixed messages. They may see formal processes and thick reporting requirements coexist with simple, undersigned processes. One organization may have a clear, focused mission, while another may find itself improvising in response to rapid market changes. Some units may have a tight requirement for corporate reporting and coherence, others may have a high degree of autonomy.

Organizations are struggling with ways to manage duality, and in the process some companies are creating interesting new approaches. For instance, Thermo-Electron has developed an original approach, creating new businesses from innovative ideas. An idea that becomes a plausible business case becomes a spin-out, with the parent holding a 51 percent stake in the new company. Xerox has created a New Enterprise Board, an internal organization emulating a venture capital firm, which funds and supports new businesses that do not fit into existing business or product units. The minibusinesses are set apart from the larger organization's processes and demands and are allowed to function according to their own business models.

Henderson's (1994) research holds lessons for CEOs in a broad set of industries. CEOs in the best of Henderson's companies broke down barriers that impede the effective flow of information. By experimenting with "tiger teams" and other constructs and by ebbing and flowing between functional and product-centric architectures, CEOs in successful pharmaceutical companies have fostered the ambidextrous organization necessary to manage innovation.

Summary

The experience at the April 1996 conference and the learnings reported in Part IV of this book suggest that there are typical problems facing corporate senior leadership in their efforts to implement and manage discontinuous change. The CEO and senior team play a unique role as an information-processing and learning mechanism for the corporation. The ability to play this role effectively aids in the determination of the need for change and promotes leadership's ability to craft and sell a change agenda. Timing and opportunism plan an important role in the management of change, but so does the sequencing of change activities. In all activities, communication and enrollment are vital. Communication includes not only downward cascades of information but also the learning that occurs as organization members react to and act on messages. Last, senior leadership must effectively build an organization—which may mean a "from–to" re-creation, but which increasingly means creating a context for ongoing re-creation and cultivating the ability to manage ambidextrously.

References

Arthur, W. B. (1996). Increasing returns and the new world of business. *Harvard Business Review*, 74(4), 100–109.

Collins, J., & Porras, J. (1994). *Built to Last: Successful Habits of Visionary Companies*. New York: HarperCollins.

Finkelstein, S., & Hambrick, D. C. (1996). *Strategic Leadership: Top Executives and Their Effects on Organizations*. Minneapolis: West Publishing.

Ford, J. D., & Ford, L. W. (1995). The role of conversations in producing intentional change in organizations. *Academy of Management Review*, 20(3), 541–570.

Gabarro, J. (1992). *The Dynamics of Taking Charge*. Boston: Harvard Business School Press.

Gilder, G. (1990). *Microcosm: The Quantum Revolution in Economics and Technology*. New York: Simon and Schuster.

Goodman, S. K. (1993). Information needs for management decision making. *Records Management Quarterly*, 27(4), 12–23.

Hax, A., & Majiluf, N. (1995). *Strategy Concept and Process: A Pragmatic Approach*. New York: Prentice Hall.

Henderson, R. (1994). Managing innovation in the information age. *Harvard Business Review*, 100–105.

Kelly K. (1996). The economics of ideas. *Wired*, 148–218.

Koselka, R. (1993, Dec. 20). Heads we win, tails we win: How SmithKline Beecham will benefit from health care reform. *Forbes*, 152(14), 52.

Kotter, J. (1986). *The General Managers*. Boston: Harvard Business School Press.

Lawrence, P., & Lorsch, J. (1967). *Organization and Environment*. Homewood, Ill: Richard D. Irvin.

Nadler, D. A., Shaw, R. B., & Walton, A. E. (1995). *Discontinuous Change*. San Francisco: Jossey-Bass.

Nadler, D. A., & Tushman, M. L. (1988). *Strategic Organizational Design: Concepts, Tools, and Processes*. New York: HarperCollins.

Senge, P. (1990). *The Fifth Discipline*. New York: Currency Doubleday.

[V]
Integration

[20]

How CEOs, Top Teams, and Boards Make Successful Transformations

E. Ralph Biggadike

MANY COMPANIES featured in this book have made successful transformations. These companies have coped with major changes to their industry and rejuvenated themselves. None is settling into a new state of inertia. Having rejuvenated themselves once, they have learned in the process that they will certainly have to rejuvenate themselves again. The CEOs, top teams, and boards of these companies view change as a constant that bids them prepare for the certainty of surprise. They are striving to build firms that are adaptable above all. The picture that comes clear in these chapters is one of companies continuously evolving and experimenting. It is framed by two compelling concerns: to improve financial performance and to better serve society. Both make for a tall order.

The authors capture the essence of the organization that prospers in turbulent times with images such as that of the jazz combo as opposed to the orchestra (Kets de Vries, Chapter 3); the "individualized corporation" rather than the "organization man" corporations of the 1950s and 1960s (Bartlett and Ghoshal, Chapter 4); the "coherent" company possessing an integrated logic and basis for action (Hambrick, Chapter 7); and the "ambidextrous" corporation, able to innovate continuously as well as manage for short-term efficiency

(Tushman, Anderson, and O'Reilly, Chapter 18). Far from resembling traditional hierarchical organizations, these companies have burst the old biological metaphor that pictured a body nicely functioning according to a precise division of labor: hands held, feet walked, arms lifted, and so forth. In contrast, these organizations portray themselves as something akin to a living, sensing, thinking brain. In them, all employees are involved in trying to interpret the environment, lead change, and anticipate trends. In the words of Christopher Bartlett and Sumantra Ghoshal (Chapter 4), these companies have become able to "capture the energy, commitment, and creativity of those within the institution by treating them as valued organizational members." We have moved a long way indeed from the view that in employees "a good pair of hands can come attached to a difficult person." Where once the task of management was to "make employees as reliable and predictable as the equipment they run," the management of these successfully transformed companies has come to understand (in words that Jamie Houghton recalled) that "when you hire a pair of hands, you get a head for free."

The astonishing feature of the transformations described in this book is their diversity. They represent all kinds of industries—high-tech and low-tech, old and young, inherently slow and fast-growing, industrial and consumer, product-centered and service-oriented. The companies themselves are equally diverse: U.S. and European, regional and global, old (like GE) or young (like Virgin), profit and nonprofit. Their CEOs are different too, in personality, functional skills, and backgrounds. And yet, in the way these companies have coped with turbulent times, and in their characteristics today as transformed organizations, there is a pattern. Regardless of background, these companies are "converging on a similar posttransformational organization model that represented a major change from their traditional authority-based hierarchies" (Bartlett and Ghoshal, Chapter 4).

While, for now, it's best to regard this posttransformational model as an emergent pattern, consider what some companies have already achieved.

1. Paul Allaire became CEO of Xerox in 1989 and accelerated Xerox's recovery. He introduced "Xerox 200" to focus the company on re-creating the document services industry, achieving leadership in quality, and generating more rapid product devel-

opment. Xerox has been reorganized around 5,000 self-managed teams for greater involvement and responsiveness. Major technologies are reaching the market in a much shorter time, a far cry from the old days when Xerox's inability to bring its inventions to market were acutely embarrassing. ROE improved from 9.6 percent in 1990 to 17 percent in 1995. In the four years to 1995, Xerox's stock price rose 200 percent.

2. GE, a soundly based, methodical, slow but sure manufacturing company prior to Jack Welch, has probably contributed more ideas to scientific management than any other company. Under Welch, services have come to represent almost half of GE's revenues, operational autonomy and entrepreneurship have replaced corporate staffers, and GE is restoring instinct and passion to management. ROE improved from 16 percent in 1986 to 22 percent in 1995. The stock price in 1996 was almost four times what it was in 1986. Although not ranked first in sales revenues, GE achieved first place in stock market valuation in 1996.

3. Corning, under Jamie Houghton, is an exemplar of transformation through joint ventures. In 1991–95 ventures contributed more than $500 million to earnings and $3 billion to sales. With a unique blend of alliances, company-owned ventures, and established businesses, Corning has changed from a formal organization to a web of businesses in which, Houghton says, trust is the key. Sales growth has picked up and is around 13 percent per year; ROE has more than doubled, to 18 percent and 70 percent of Corning's profits today come from businesses that did not exist in 1980.

4. Richard Branson has built Virgin from a mail-order record company to a $2 billion plus (after selling Virgin Music for $560 million in 1992) travel, retail, and communications group with one of the best-known brand names in the world. Virgin has about it an air of virtual reality. Kets de Vries (Chapter 3) describes it as consisting of "numerous small, autonymous units, continually dividing and reproducing like an amoeba."

5. Percy Barnevik created the world's largest cross-border merger in 1987 out of two sleepy regional companies, and he is trying to transform the new entity, ASEA/Brown Boveri (ABB), into

a global power equipment and engineering group. ABB is a giant worldwide matrix with, on the one hand, 5,000 decentralized profit centers in 140 countries and, on the other, companywide coordination and monitoring. Sales grew from $22 billion in 1989 to $34 billion in 1995; return on invested capital doubled, to 17 percent; and cash flow per share tripled.

6. Facing one of the most turbulent industries of recent times, Kaiser Permanente, guided by David Lawrence, is transforming itself with a combination of decentralized health care delivery, for local customer responsiveness, and centralized administrative practices, for cost reduction and sharing of "best medical practices" to reduce variation in the delivery of care. Kaiser has achieved very high quality rankings in measures such as HEDIS, and has lowered costs of delivery significantly.

7. Bob Bauman took two ailing companies, Beecham in the United Kingdom and SmithKline in the United States and merged them in 1989 into what is now regarded as a vibrant new company, well positioned to provide total pharmaceutical care. Bauman and board chairman Henry Wendt formed more than 300 teams from the two companies to make the merger happen. Bauman said they had to get people to create and believe in a totally new company. Sales grew from $3.7 billion in 1989 to $5.3 billion in 1993, when Bauman and Wendt retired, and earnings per share were up 50 percent. Return on equity improved from 23 percent in 1990 to 51 percent in 1993.

The particular focus of this book is the part played by CEOs, top teams, and boards in making these transformations happen. Clearly, the role of the CEO is central in all these companies (Nadler and Heilpern, Chapter 1). But it is central for a new reason. Gone is the old "information up/orders down" model, in which the board was kept at a distance and the top team was convened only to deal with a crisis or to report quarterly results. Instead, these CEOs are central because they disseminate energy, encouragement, and support. They help their organizations to cope with ambiguity, uncertainty, and paradox, even as they focus their people on clear goals and tasks. They value the individual; they look for the traits of self-starters to make their vision of a self-driven, self-renewing organization come

alive. They involve their boards as partners in the transformation effort—partners who will both stretch their own talent and help them
to stay alert for continuous change (Houghton; Lawrence, Chapter
16). And they work together with their top team to develop vision,
strategy, and organization.

Among these leaders' ideas for coping with turbulent times, six
stand out: (1) Master the and/also; (2) believe in the individual and
value diversity; (3) look for embedded traits; (4) stimulate constructive conflict; (5) CEO's top teams, and boards work together; and (6)
vision and information management hold everything together.

Master the And/Also

Only mastery of the "and/also" helps companies lead in turbulent
times. Tushman and colleagues (Chapter 18) believe that companies
have to be efficient and innovative, strategic and tactical at the same
time. Indeed, Tushman's concept of the "ambidextrous organization"
is the epitome of and/also. Percy Barnevik has the same idea when he
says, "We want to be centralized and decentralized, big and small,
global and local (Kets de Vries, Chapter 3).

CEOs who lead successful transformations are assertive and inclusive at the same time. They take responsibility for establishing vision,
but they involve others in the process of shaping it. They exercise
their power by sharing it with employees (Kets de Vries, Chapter 3)
in order to mobilize latent energy and creativity and to foster a sense
of ownership at all levels of the organization. They are unequivocally
bosses; but, as 3M CEO Livio "Desi" DeSimone reminds his managers, bosses must always ask their subordinates, "What do *you* see that
I am missing?" (Bartlett and Ghoshal, Chapter 4; emphasis added).
For Barnevik, Branson, and Welch, being in charge means being willing to let others shine (Kets de Vries, Chapter 3). Houghton is also
clearly in charge but says that leaders must recognize that "personal
success can come only from group success" (Chapter 2). If CEOs still
appear to some as icons, just as CEOs have always been, the CEOs in
these transformed organizations are icons recast as coaches.

For many employees of the old, highly structured corporate organizations, one considerable benefit was the structure's simplicity:
You came to work; you carried out instructions to a specified performance level; and then, at the end of the day, you went home. Life is

different in the posttransformational organization, which mixes elements from the traditional organization with the new ways of the transformed companies. Employees are free to act, and indeed are expected to do so. They are also accountable for results. They are expected to be self-starters, and to produce superior individual performance, but they are also expected to work cooperatively for team success. They are expected to plan and budget but are also encouraged to experiment. They are expected to think things through deliberately, but also to act with dispatch. Mistakes are expected and tolerated. (Barnevik looks for a 70 percent batting average; Kets de Vries, Chapter 3.)

These companies focus on the "hard" and "soft" simultaneously. They are as focused (if not more focused) on financial performance as any of their predecessors. To "come off your numbers," in the famous GE phrase, is still as perilous as ever. But Jack Welch believes that it is only with a combination of hard and soft approaches to making those numbers that he can surmount turbulent times and in fact produce superior performance. In the new course of things, he promotes teamwork; individual initiative; and managerial innovations, such as "workouts," that encourage employees to present what might be counterculture solutions to their bosses.

In the and/also mode of thinking, ambitious goals are presented as exciting challenges, as a way to gain personal respect and pride (Kets de Vries, Chapter 3), and as the instrument that, as 3M expresses it, "stimulates ordinary people to produce extraordinary performance" (Bartlett and Ghoshal, Chapter 4). This emphasis on both corporate performance and individual autonomy produces organizations that are centralized and decentralized at once. Top management tracks performance very thoroughly. It also yields much operational freedom to the frontline units.

Believe in the Individual and Value Diversity

Successful company transformations and a sustained ability for continuous change depend on the individual. The CEOs in this book believe that a company can deal with turbulent times only if all employees are fully alert: sensing, thinking, creating, and acting. They treat employees as responsible human beings. Manfred Kets de Vries tells us that Barnevik, Branson, and Welch are adamant about releasing the creative energy at all levels of their organizations. Branson says company success depends on individual enthusiasm, dependability, and effectiveness. Barnevik insists that jobs be designed to fit the individual, not the other way around. Houghton (Chapter 2) argues that if you believe knowledge is the only true competitive advantage, then you must value the individual as the true repository of knowledge. Instead of building on the basis of company loyalty, these companies build on the basis of employee "employability"—providing opportunities for continued individual growth from which organizational growth can follow (Houghton, Chapter 2; Kets de Vries, Chapter 3; Bartlett and Ghoshal, Chapter 4).

These CEOs try to create in each individual a sense of ownership, in the conviction that the resulting higher feeling of personal control will increase creativity and energy. Branson believes in the individual to the degree that he gives all employees his home address. He answers their letters first: In the stakeholder hierarchy at Virgin, he ranks employees first, customers second, and shareholders third. His reasoning is that shareholder value depends on satisfied customers and that customer satisfaction depends on employees who have pride in their work and their company. Houghton (Chapter 2) says that "we need to entrust employees with strategic ownership of the business." This makes for a more "inventive company," which is needed to deal with today's environment. Barnevik, Branson, and Welch push strategic awareness down into the organization. Bob Bauman (Chapter 17) says that the employees have to believe that they are the "heroes" in the company's success; they have to be able to look back and say, "Look at what has been accomplished—we did that." Under Welch, Kets de Vries comments, there has been a huge increase in the number of GE employees who have been granted stock options. The explicit objective is to contribute to workers' sense of ownership.

Ironically, profession of belief in the individual suggests a return of an older pattern in business life. Earlier in this century, the independent frontier spirit that helped build this country was reflected in the many small, individually owned businesses that dominated commercial activity. Then, as organizations grew larger and larger, they succeeded by stressing company loyalty and standardizing company operating procedures. The "organization man" of the 1950s and '60s became the model of the ideal employee. Profitability was based on what Bartlett and Ghoshal (Chapter 4) call the Russian doll model of management. That is, the knowledge and skills gained at lower management levels were considered adequate preparation for promotion to the next level and to the next, until a few reached the top, still managing in essentially the same way as at the lowest levels.

But in turbulent times, the Russian doll model is hopelessly inappropriate and the organization man a liability. Instead, Bartlett and Ghoshal argue, transformed companies have moved to the "individualized corporation" model, in which the required knowledge and skills are different at each level and people work at the level that best suits their capabilities and interests. The individualized corporation "capitalizes on the idiosyncrasies and even the eccentricities of exceptional people by recognizing and making the most of their unique capabilities."

There is a recognition, too, that diversity in employees' perspectives helps companies navigate turbulent times and cope with continuous change. Barnevik sees great value in different nationalities, functional backgrounds, personalities, and life experiences. Without these, he asks, how can you understand the issues that are causing continuous change? And how can you be sure that your assumptions are continually tested and reframed? Houghton (Chapter 2) adds that companies need to tap the best talent and "cannot rely only on white males."

This emphasis on the autonomy of the individual and on the diversity of the group conforms with attitudes and aspirations that many of today's employees bring with them to work. Such high expectations create significant management challenges. Branson, Barnevik, and Welch realize that today's high performers are like frogs in a wheelbarrow; they can jump out any time (Kets de Vries, Chapter 3). Employees must be given opportunities to spread their wings. Houghton says that in 1972 one third of Corning's workforce consisted of conceptual workers, while two thirds were people who basically worked with their hands. Today, this ratio is completely reversed. But conceptual workers can move anywhere; as Houghton (Chapter 2) says, "businesses need this group of mobile workers more than they need us." The traditional command-and-control company was designed for an unskilled labor force in simpler times. Transformed companies must speak to a vastly different skill base and must design their organizations so the people can expect, in addition to their pay, appreciation, independence, and the flexibility to make decisions at the level where work is being done.

Look for Embedded Traits

People lead transformations, and people implement transformations. But what kind of people? This book suggests that successful companies have been transformed by people who are very different from traditional managers in traditional companies. The difference springs from their embedded traits. Embedded traits, several authors argue, have more influence on the ability to lead successfully in turbulent times than do knowledge, experience, or skills. Bartlett and Ghoshal (Chapter 4) cite Goran Lindahl of ABB, who thinks that an individual's natural characteristics should be the dominant factor in selection: "I will always pick a person with tenacity over one with just experience."

Obviously, certain kinds of people are better than others at creating and working in posttransformational organizations. Bartlett and Ghoshal point to Poul Andreassen, who questions and challenges everything and who became CEO of ISS primarily on the strength of his personal traits. To CEOs Barnevik, Branson, and Welch, Kets de Vries ascribes practicality, openness, independence, competitiveness, toughness, trustworthiness, reliability, unpretentiousness, and instincts for managing conflict and deal making. Employees in these CEOs' organizations should be self-starters who can help build an organization capable of continuous change more quickly. They should be people who set their own high standards and who criticize themselves when they fall short. They should be people who are inner-driven, eager to learn, adaptable, and possessing high tolerance for ambiguity.

Another reason to pay close attention to embedded traits is that managers are beginning to realize that "it is much more difficult to convince an authoritarian industry expert to adopt a more people-sensitive style than to develop industry expertise in a strong people manager" (Bartlett and Ghoshal, Chapter 4). Kets de Vries (Chapter 3) observes that weaning traditional managers away from their need for authority, structure, and control is not easy. Some evidence of the difficulty comes from Bartlett and Ghoshal, who report that a notable 40 percent of the original top 300 managers in ABB, all carefully selected at the time of the merger, are no longer with the company.

A third reason why embedded traits are key derives from the view that the individualized corporation needs people with different traits for different levels of management (Bartlett and Ghoshal, Chapter 4).

Operating-level entrepreneurs need traits of creativity, persuasiveness, and competitiveness. Senior-level managers need patience, flexibility, and the ability to be both supportive and demanding. The traits Bartlett and Ghoshal suggest for top-level leaders are similar to those outlined by Kets de Vries. It is these personal characteristics that primarily determine whether an individual can perform at a given level. Few people will, in Bartlett and Ghoshal's words, have the "temperamental range" to perform at all levels of management in the posttransformational company.

Given the importance of embedded traits in both executives and employees, it is important to know where they come from and how they are enhanced and developed. Kets de Vries (Chapter 3) argues that people's approaches to organization, power, and authority are formed in the family, this being the first organizational entity that we encounter as children. He discusses the upbringing of Branson, Barnevik, and Welch and relates these experiences to the organizations they have shaped. Jack Welch, an only child, grew up playing competitive team sports, particularly street hockey. His father was pleasant enough but away most of the day; essentially, Welch was raised by his mother. She continuously told him that he could do anything he set his mind to. Percy Barnevik worked as a child in his parents' small print shop in Sweden. From that experience Barnevik took away lessons about the motivational power of small units and about the importance of responsiveness to customers, cooperation with fellow workers, and the shared willingness to work long and hard. From the culture of Lutheran Sweden, Barnevik learned the strict Protestant work ethic of fishermen and boat builders. Branson was raised by a supportive but relatively unambitious father and an independent, adventurous mother. She pushed Branson to be self-reliant and competitive and to take control of his life; when Branson was four, she put him out of the car and told him to find his way home. The family's financial situation was usually precarious, and Branson's mother came up with "one mad idea after another" to make some money. Branson himself, at age eleven, planted a thousand seedlings, convinced he would make a killing selling Christmas trees. (Rabbits ate the seedlings while he was away at school.)

An executive's type of narcissism—or simply one's manner of self-regard—is very much influenced by these early life experiences, Kets de Vries suggests. Narcissism can be positive, if it leads to a secure sense of personal identity and reasonable judgment of what one is able to do. But it can also, and more likely, be negative, if it provokes emotions of envy, spite, and vengefulness. Such reactive narcissism can be a key element in defective leadership, as observation of the link between individual and organizational pathologies suggests. Because of their increasingly dysfunctional personal behavior, Ford, Delorean, Geneen, Maxwell, Olson, and Tapie maimed or destroyed their organizations. In contrast, constructive narcissists have the capacity for self-reflection and empathy; they are able to accept dissenters. These are the leaders who build learning organizations from which they themselves can learn and that will last long after they have gone.

But what do you do if your early family experiences did not endow you with the embedded traits and values of these enlightened CEOs? Can you develop these characteristics in a different way? Or can you succeed with a different set? What matters more: nature or nurture? How do they work together? How is it that some leaders manage to transcend embedded traits that brought success at one level but are unhelpful at the next level? For example, early success typically comes from working hard; performing limited tasks very well; and, usually, being a specialist. Somehow, some people change and grow through their careers and become more adaptable, more able to see the larger picture, and thus more fit for broader responsibilities. Those who become enlightened CEOs somehow learn how to avoid "overfunctioning" and to allow other people to take control and to be part of a team.

Stimulate Constructive Conflict

Perhaps it's ironic, but the kind of organization that has most successfully handled tumultuous change is also the organization where the potential for conflict is high. The open, candid, and ambidextrous organizations described in this book invite blurring of traditional roles, processes, and procedures. Blurred responsibilities, ambiguity, and instability create opportunities for conflict (Raben and Spencer, Chapter 9). And "opportunities" is the right word here. As Paul Allaire put it, "There is a conflict between getting a decision and stimulating conflict in the group." Moreover, turbulent times provoke widely differing—and deeply held—personal views about what strategies and organization forms are most appropriate (Raben and

Spencer). Tushman and his colleagues (Chapter 18) point out that companies can respond successfully to major industry changes only if managers are willing to rewrite their organization's rules. Yet such action will "always face entrenched resistance from the status quo," and there will always be conflict between large, older, cash-generating units and entrepreneurial, younger, cash-absorbing units. Andrew Pettigrew and Terry McNulty (Chapter 13) worry that there is little help available to board members as they wrestle with the conflicts inherent in efforts to both exercise control and stimulate creativity.

But potential for conflict may not mean that necessary and constructive conflict will actually occur. Kets de Vries (Chapter 3) points out that employees with low self-esteem may try excessively to please their leaders. The leaders may eventually find themselves in "a hall of mirrors, hearing and seeing only what they want to hear and see." Kathleen Eisenhardt and her colleagues (Chapter 8) and Edward Zajac and James Westphal (Chapter 14) point out that groupthink is an ever present risk (as demonstrated in the well-known Abilene paradox). John Vogelstein (Chapter 11) believes that conflict avoidance among boards of directors is at the heart of what he calls "the General Motors problem": "decline in one of the United States' largest companies that continued for more than a decade before the board acted." In many cases, says Donald Hambrick (Chapter 7), conflict doesn't break out because the members of the top team "rarely collaborate" and "focus almost entirely on their own pieces of the enterprise."

To many people, conflict is disruptive, energy-sapping, and unpleasant. "In its raw, unmanaged form, it can be ugly and ultimately destructive" (Raben and Spencer, Chapter 9). Most of us get instinctively good at defensive routines (Argyris, 1990) that help avoid this kind of outcome. We have an in-built tendency to avoid embarrassing people. The result, to use another Argyris term, is that every company has "undiscussables": issues about crucial topics—such as strategy, performance, and organization—that somehow never make it onto the agenda.

On the other hand, conflict may break out but in an unconstructive way. Eisenhardt, Kahwajy, and Bourgeois (Chapter 8) draw a distinction between issue-oriented conflict and interpersonal conflict. The former centers on issues and can be constructive. The latter becomes personal and creates animosity and distrust no matter what the larger issues may be. For Kets de Vries's narcissists this distinction is not easy, because they tend to get overinvested in the issues and experience debate on issues as personal attacks. Failure to agree with such a leader can cause unconstructive conflict because of "group revenge" behavior (Kets de Vries, Chapter 3). Hostile acts instigated by a narcissistic leader are committed against those who do not share the leader's vision: Such people get made into "evildoers," villains, or scapegoats. Paradoxically, scapegoats provide a sense of stability—a sense they are the reason everything is bad in the first place. The issues, however, do not get addressed; and in extreme cases the organization self-destructs. Tushman and colleagues (Chapter 18) remind us that there is strong evidence that older, historically profitable units perversely "work to ignore, sabotage, or otherwise trample entrepreneurial units."

Yet conflict can have real value. It sharpens debate, questions assumptions, creates more options, and energizes the entire organization. As Eisenhardt and her colleagues (Chapter 8) put it, the lack of conflict suggests apathy, not harmony. High-conflict discussions can enrich understanding of the issues; low-conflict discussions are superficial. Charles Raben and Janet Spencer (Chapter 9) assert that "the best strategic decisions always emerge from a vigorous, candid consideration of the widest possible range of plausible alternatives." And for Tushman and colleagues (Chapter 18), the conflict inherent in multiple units' pursuing different forms of innovation in the same product area is a fundamental requirement if a company is to remain a technological leader. Allaire, Andreassen, Barnevik, Bauman, Branson, DeSimone, Houghton, Lawrence, Vogelstein, and Welch all believe that conflict, properly encouraged and managed, contributes to high performance.

All of these CEOs pay a lot of attention to encouraging and then managing conflict. One of Welch's rules is "Be candid with everyone," and GE's "workout" is a way to get the "undiscussables" on the table and acted on. Barnevik goes to great lengths to encourage people to speak their minds. Branson keeps an open door to invite critical comments about ways to improve operations. The contributors to this book point to numerous structural aids to conflict, such as regular meetings, frequent interaction, agendas detailing real work, clear roles for team members, group incentives to provide tangible evidence of support for teamwork, and mechanisms such as scenario planning to create multiple solutions. These aids can help deal with the natural tendency for conflict avoidance. In addition, Jay Lorsch (Chapter 12) suggests that corporate governance principles can legitimate the expression of board opinions, and John Vogelstein (Chapter 11) believes that making board members more like owners would help promote active discussion. Specifically, he suggests eliminating "hundred-share" directors and requiring directors to put some of their own net worth on the line.

But all the CEOs and researchers in this book think that the most important aid to encouraging and managing conflict is behavioral skills. Kets de Vries's (Chapter 3) three CEOs, Barnevik, Branson, and Welch, all try to react constructively to bearers of bad news. They practice "active listening as well as talking." Eisenhardt and her colleagues (Chapter 8) advise seeking first to be influenced before trying to influence. They suggest phrasing such as "I feel this way" rather than "the situation is this way." In particular, the role of the CEO in helping members of the top team differentiate disagreement on issues from personal disagreement is crucial. Hambrick (Chapter 7) describes the CEO of the company he calls "MediaTech" as adept at moderating and pacing discussions, wrapping up and synthesizing, and soothing the psyches of executives whose views did not prevail. Raben and Spencer (Chapter 9) stress, among many skills, the ability of CEOs to respond appropriately with different conflict resolution approaches tailored to the specific situations.

Unfortunately, the behavioral skills needed to encourage and then manage conflict "are often absent from, and sometimes clearly at odds with, the managerial repertoire of many CEOs" (Raben and Spencer, Chapter 9). An ability to get things done in the authority-based, hierarchical, "command-and-control" organizations that will have been the training ground of most senior managers is scant preparation for turbulent times and delayered, autonomous, individualized corporations. In this new setting, encouraging and managing conflict requires CEOs to be as behaviorally deft as they are skilled in the functions of their business and their industry. The CEOs in this book have achieved this duality of excellence. This skill is another example of their mastery of the "and/also."

CEOs, Top Teams, and Boards Work Together

New relationships between the CEO and the board and between the CEO and the top team have been important ingredients of the successful transformations described in this book. David Lawrence, in relating his lessons from dealing with tumultuous change in the health care industry, commented at the April 1996 conference that he needed a top team on whom "I could be 100 percent dependent" and who "would be fighting in the same way that I was in trying to make the changes." Regarding Kaiser Permanente's board, Lawrence observed that "the board has been absolutely essential" and that "they have been an important source of stability and support; at the same time, by being better educated, they are placing higher demands on me." Throughout this book there is a clear theme of sharing the task of transformation among CEOs, top teams, and boards. I will review each of these relationships in turn.

CEOs and Top Teams

All the CEOs echo Lawrence in their judgment of the importance of a good working relationship with their top team. Paul Allaire (Chapter 6) for example, has stated that top teams are necessary partners to help set strategic direction, redesign organization architecture, and improve business processes. It's easy to see why the top team can be so valuable in organizational change: All the CEOs and researchers talk about the sheer scale and scope of effort that is needed to respond to turbulent times. Nothing less than an "integrated change agenda" (Nadler and Heilpern, Chapter 1) will suffice. The whole organization has to be galvanized into action. No CEO can bring about change of this magnitude and comprehensiveness single-handedly (Raben and Spencer, Chapter 9).

Members of the top team represent different parts of the company. The integrated change agenda is likely to be more thoughtful and perceptive if it includes points of view from all parts of the organization. And in implementing the changes, members of the top team can articulate and lead the transformation efforts in their area of responsibility. Furthermore, as Hambrick (Chapter 7) points out, the top team is the only entity that can leverage the company's core competencies, exercise global clout, and respond fast. Tushman and colleagues (Chapter 18) argue that the top team is also the only entity that can successfully help the entire organization handle the conflicts and tensions inherent in the ambidextrous organization. Additionally, members of the top team can provide strengths in areas where the CEO is weak (Nadler and Heilpern, Chapter 1; Kets de Vries, Chapter 3). Kets de Vries points out that Barnevik, Branson, and Welch have always looked for senior managers to balance their own shortcomings. Branson's choice of managing director Trevor Abbot for his skill in finance is an example. (Branson does not read financial statements.)

David Lawrence's experience in leading Kaiser Permanente demonstrated what can happen if the top team and CEO are not working together. His initial top team included some people who were "not committed to our basic ideas of change but instead had their own priorities and agendas" (Chapter 16). The constant dissension "began to sap our energy, our focus, and our will to move forward." Bartlett and Ghoshal (Chapter 4) also comment that senior managers "can become the silent subverters of change; and their invisible yet persistent resistance can derail even the most carefully planned transformation program." Hambrick (Chapter 7), the leading researcher on top teams, comments on their role in selling the change programs to the whole organization: "If any of these key executives drag their feet or emit mixed signals to their subunits, the change effort is doomed."

Unfortunately, an effective working relationship between the CEO and the top team members is not the rule. Hambrick points out that some CEOs fear that cooperation is "an abdication of their leadership role or that it runs counter to their company culture of subunit accountability and initiative." Allaire (Chapter 6) cites a call on a customer that was the first time the CEO and all "direct reports had ever been in the same room together." Hambrick goes so far as to say that the term *top management team* is a misnomer for most companies. Raben and Spencer (Chapter 9) also point out the " 'horse-race' phenomenon of executive succession," which can be a distraction—sometimes a destructive one. These are not easy issues. But the CEO–top team working relationship is so crucial to the transformation task that it must be addressed.

Chapters 6 through 10 offer advice on how to achieve effective teams. Here, I will concentrate on the conceptualization of the relationship between the CEO and the top team. Some authors suggest that the top team is an extension of the CEO (Nadler and Heilpern, Chapter 1; Hambrick, Chapter 7; Raben and Spencer, Chapter 9). At the same time they, and others, were not so sure. Kets de Vries (Chapter 3), in discussing human development, argues that unless we are careful people can be turned into narcissistic extensions of others, "thus becoming confused about what kind of life they are supposed to lead." After some missteps with his top team, Lawrence settled on a team of four who meet one full day each week and make decisions; there is a sense of both collective and individual responsibility in this team. Dual responsibility is part of Hambrick's (Chapter 7) concept of "behavioral integration" and his advocacy of a top team that "shares information, shares resources, and shares decisions." David Nadler and Jeffrey Heilpern (Chapter 1) advocate that the top team "become partners with the CEO in articulating the team's collective vision" and implementing it. Houghton has spoken of the importance of top team members contributing their own expertise and insights to discussions; but at the end of the day, the CEO still must make the decisions. Allaire (Chapter 6) agrees: "laissez faire or consensus leadership doesn't work" but, while being a strong leader "the CEO must be a team player also."

Rather than an extension, perhaps we are striving for a CEO-top team relationship that is a partnership, with the CEO as head partner. In this view, while the CEO is a member of the team, he or she does not get lost in the team. The CEO remains an individual, maintaining power of leadership and the right to delegate responsibilities to top team members and, in cases of poor performance, to reassign them to somebody else. Similarly, each member of the top team remains an individual, representing the part of the organization for which he or she is responsible. In this notion of partnership, the CEO and the members of the top team contribute their distinctive perspectives for the good of the whole. If they fail in this role, then the whole notion of the delayered company made up of autonomous, freestanding business units also fails at the point of the creation and implementation of corporate policy. We are back to command and control: orders down from the top. But the quality of data about turbulent times being fed into top team discussions will be weak, and the ability of the top team to discuss tough issues candidly will be impaired.

Overall, viewing the top team as an extension of the CEO seems likely to exacerbate the problem of "undiscussable" data remaining undiscussed. The partnership concept—in which the team works together while expressing individuality of viewpoint, action, and accountability—may best capture the spirit of the leadership teams of successfully transformed companies.

CEOs and Boards

Working together in partnership is also the essence of the CEO–board relationship in successfully transformed companies. Lawrence's comments about the Kaiser board's providing "stability and support," as well as demanding more of him, exemplify this relationship. Houghton values the different perspectives of board members and wants their full involvement in company issues; but he wants them as advisors, not as managers. Lorsch (Chapter 12) points to "the increasingly activist role directors are taking to create more adaptive companies." Vogelstein (Chapter 11) is convinced that the decline of America's great companies can be slowed by "owner–directors" who align themselves with shareholder interests and who can thus achieve greater balance in their relationship with the CEO. Pettigrew and McNulty (Chapter 13) cite a United Kingdom report that advocates an advisory and supportive role for directors.

Unfortunately, examples of CEOs and board members working effectively together, like examples of CEOs and top teams working in genuine partnership, are too rare. An "all-powerful and all-knowing CEO" (Lorsch, Chapter 12) is still the rule, as is a board that does not have the information, power, time, or leadership capacity to bring about timely change. Vogelstein (Chapter 11) sees too many professional directors who do "very little other than not rocking the CEO's boat." Pettigrew and McNulty's data in Chapter 13 show the proclivity of nonexecutive board members toward involvement in personnel matters and what might generally be classified as "control" issues. They are less involved in strategic matters, probably because "you do not need a very profound database to make a judgment of people, whereas in financial or technical matters you may require skills and a depth of knowledge that nonexecutives do not have." The attitudinal distance between most CEOs and board members is captured in the language each commonly uses when speaking of the other: "*my* board; *our* chairman."

Several factors impede CEOs and board members from developing a more productive working relationship. These include CEOs co-opting the board by appointing sympathetic directors; asymmetry in information between the CEO and the board members; insufficient time and opportunity for board members to understand the company's problems; absence of a clear leader other than the CEO (an acute problem in the United States, where chairman and CEO jobs are usually combined); and behavioral norms, such as disapproval of board members' criticizing the CEO in board meetings (Nadler and Heilpern, Chapter 1; Vogelstein, Chapter 11; Zajac and Westphal, Chapter 14; Lorsch, Chapter 12; Pettigrew and McNulty, Chapter 13).

Successfully transformed companies have worked hard to overcome these factors. For example, Lawrence tells us in Chapter 16 that he has added a fair amount of diversity to the Kaiser Permanente board and "provided the board with systematic exposure to the major issues, developments, and trends within our organization and in the health care field in general." He concludes that "They have become not only my sounding board but a crucial source of support on difficult decisions." Here is a refreshing, nontraditional CEO–board relationship. And Lorsch observes that this kind of relationship is common in adaptive companies. He says it is a relationship based on "sharing influence": CEOs and directors act more "as peers, with the CEO being primarily concerned with the leadership of the company and the directors with their oversight functions." Lorsch believes that the resulting clearer delineation of responsibilities and better-informed directors help to distribute power and facilitate more open and candid discussion. It is important to note that making directors independent is not precisely the essence of this new relationship. Pettigrew and McNulty (Chapter 13) cite two former UK chairmen who "bridle against overemphasis on the monitoring and independent role of nonexecutive directors." One of these chairmen argues "for power equivalence and a climate of quality thinking and debate between nonexecutives and executives" on the board. These words seem to capture exactly what Lawrence has achieved at Kaiser Permanente and what Lorsch has observed in adaptive companies. Lorsch reminds us that it is not easy to achieve this kind of relationship; the very prescription for producing it makes the possibility of misunderstanding and conflict between the parties more likely. Pettigrew and McNulty point out that political processes are at the heart of all CEO–board relationships and that these remain relatively "unstudied and unreported."

Zajac and Westphal in Chapter 14 make a start by suggesting an outline of a behavioral theory of CEO–board relations. For instance, they cite social psychological studies that tend to support what Lawrence did when he added diverse points of view to the board to strengthen and enrich its perceptions of the environment. Similarly, in looking at the interaction of economic and social factors, Zajac and Westphal appear to find support for Vogelstein's view that tying director compensation to company performance can help directors be more objective when assessing the CEO's performance and the need for change. They also see the possibility that this new relationship can be "catching," in that CEO/directors "who have experienced increased board control at their home companies should increase the likelihood of greater board control" at other firms where they serve. They also caution us about CEOs' announcing actions that seem to tie them to shareholder goals but then not actually implementing them (long-term incentive plans, for instance). Zajac and Westphal term this "symbolic management" and point out that it can be valuable only if it is genuine (for example, in showing employees that senior management is subject to the same performance-linked compensation systems that they are). If it is not, then the CEO will appear involved in an "entrenchment tactic," and an improved working relationship with the board will be unlikely. There is also the problem that a heightened emphasis by the board on short-term performance can lead to a climate of mistrust, which in turn can "lower the quality of CEO–board interaction on important strategic matters."

While CEO–board cooperation is fraught with both structural and behavioral barriers, there is much to be gained from overcoming these barriers. The key seems to be, as Lorsch (Chapter 12) suggests, establishing a commonality of goals and a relationship based on trust and mutual respect. Self-confident CEOs who "feel good in their skin," who are "able to accept dissenters," and who "plan for continuity" (Kets de Vries, Chapter 3) have to make the first move in establishing trust, respect, and commonality of goals. They must lead.

Vision and Information Management Hold Everything Together

Successful companies built their transformations on both individual responsibility and cooperation. Simultaneously, they fostered individual freedom to act and promoted people's working together in teams. Their freestanding businesses move with the agility and responsiveness of small companies but try to act in unison like large companies when faced with, for example, national customers. How have these companies managed all these dualities, particularly when they have all drastically reduced the role and size of their centralized corporate management? It's all very well to eliminate sectors or groups, change the role of corporate departments from control to support, and design the organization around principles such as "small is beautiful" and operational autonomy (Kets de Vries, Chapter 3; Bartlett and Ghoshal, Chapter 4); but what provides unity to the whole? For example, what makes the delayered, decentralized $30 billion ABB, with its 5,000 autonomous business units and minimalist head office staff of 150, one company? How does Jack Welch keep GE from becoming a holding company? How does Ciba-Geigy support incremental innovation in their mature crop fungicides even as they develop biologically engineered seeds that will never need fungicides (Tushman et al., Chapter 18)?

Vision is the first answer given by the CEOs and researchers in this book. (Executives and researchers at the April 1996 conference used the terms *vision*, *purpose*, and *values* interchangeably. I use the Collins and Porras [1994] definition of vision: Core ideology, consisting of core values and core purpose; and envisioned future, consisting of "big, hairy, audacious goals" and vivid descriptions of the envisioned future.) David Lawrence, in commenting on the "power of vision," has observed that "to be clear about the values [and] to be unambiguous about the strategic principals became absolutely important, because our tactics changed so much; the source of coherence became our mission and our strategic principals. Those are the kind of handholds that we grab onto as we make our way across the operational minefield." Eisenhardt and her colleagues have quoted Steve Jobs, describing the single most valuable lesson he gained from starting up Apple, Next, and Pixar: "Make sure that the people you're working with have the same long-range values. It's okay to spend a lot of time arguing about which route to take to San Francisco, when everyone wants to end up there. But a lot of time gets wasted in such arguments if one person wants to go to San Francisco and another secretly wants to go to San Diego."

Vision provides a context in which the apparently contradictory gain coherence. It "creates order out of chaos" and reduces the need for external controls (Kets de Vries, Chapter 3), and it provides help to integrate the disparate units of the ambidextrous organization and to make sense of the tensions they create (Tushman et al., Chapter 18). Perhaps most importantly, vision provides employees with a sense of purpose and direction. As Bob Bauman commented, a company needs to have a purpose; "it is well proven that an organization with a purpose to which individuals can feel aligned is going to give people more of a sense of success than one that doesn't" (Chapter 17). Vision seems particularly necessary in the paradoxical "and/also" world of the continually adaptive companies that prosper in times of turbulent change.

Vision, to these CEOs and companies, is also motivational. Percy Barnevik, for example, wants to make people "proud to belong to, and motivated to work for, the company" (Bartlett and Ghoshal, Chapter 4). Barnevik's mission for ABB is expressed in terms of economic growth, world development, environmental protection, and raising living standards. Kets de Vries (Chapter 3) believes that vision for Barnevik, Branson, and Welch extends beyond bottom-line success. Their visions "reveal a kind of pragmatic idealism" and of social concern for "doing good works"; these leaders go to great lengths to make life in their organizations a meaningful and enjoyable experience. For Welch, vision is the key element in making transformations successful: "If you can't articulate your business vision, if you can't get people to buy in, forget it. You won't be successful. It won't come from power and title" (Tichy and Sherman, 1994).

Vision uncommunicated, however, is no vision at all. Simply holding the faith is not enough: Evangelizing it is the true charge. David Lawrence has described the whole process of transforming an organization as akin to a political campaign: "Our assumption was that once we had the strategy, the mission, and the values and some tactics worked out, we could then execute. Wrong. This is really about enrolling almost a political campaign inside an organization, and it goes on for several years." Bob Bauman (Chapter 17) also sees communication as a campaign and advises: "management must communicate the plan strategically to help employees understand their role, get excited about the opportunities presented by change, and take ownership of its implementation." Kets de Vries (Chapter 3) refers to setting and communicating vision and getting commitment to it as the CEO's "charismatic role." He judges that Barnevik, Branson, and Welch are very effective in this role. Zajac and Westphal (Chapter 14) suggest that incentives are an important vehicle for importing "normative values" into the organization. Nadler and Heilpern (Chapter 1) argue that the CEO has to articulate the change agenda in simple, memorable terms that challenge, inspire, energize, and re-assure the people employed by the organization. Hambrick (Chapter 7) reports that Jack Welch sent the entire top team to "visit all major GE operations around the world and persuasively and energetically spread the message" over a period of several months. Hambrick con-cludes, "the role of the entire senior management team in mounting a unified campaign in support of the new direction was probably a key factor in the successful transition that GE experienced."

All the CEOs in this book stress the importance of living by the vision in every action and decision. Jamie Houghton warns that "you'll be judged not by your talk but by your walk." Barnevik re-minds his executives that they have to be role models for the organization's value system (Kets de Vries, Chapter 3). Jack Welch judges GE managers on two crucial dimensions: They must share GE values, and they must meet its commitments (the numbers). The or-der is important; managers who do not share the values but do meet numbers are given an opportunity to change, but if no change occurs they will be let go.

In addition to vision, a second factor is vital in keeping these delayered, decentralized companies with autonomous entrepreneurial business units together: management information systems (MIS). It is not an exaggeration to say that the posttransformational organization "has become feasible only with the revolution in information technol-ogy" (Kets de Vries, Chapter 3). In the "and/also" world of individual and business unit freedom to act combined with unremitting attention to raised corporate performance expectations, MIS is the only way freedom and control can be balanced. ABB's system, called ABACUS, is a well-known example. Barnevik explains: "We have the glue of transparent, centralized reporting. . . . Every month, ABACUS collects performance data on our [5,000] profit centers and compares perfor-mance with budgets and forecasts—you can aggregate and disaggre-gate results by business segment, countries, and companies within countries" (Simons & Bartlett, Asea Brown Boveri case 9-191-139).

Summary

What is being proposed in this book is that the successful company in turbulent times is a social institution of free-willed individuals joining together in the pursuit of organizational and individual excellence and fulfillment. Experimentation is encouraged; mistakes are permissible; and employees are expected to act, individually and collectively, within a context set by vision and monitored by MIS. The CEO, top team, and board all have to work together to make this happen.

Between this new kind of organization and its predecessors, the gap is deep and wide. Those old, inflexible, command-and-control organizations resembled creatures known to zoologists as "processionary caterpillars" (Kets de Vries, Chapter 3) which take their name from the peculiar way leaders and followers among them interact. After one caterpillar sets the direction, all others line up lock-step behind them, in what appears to be an automatic response pattern. Scientists who have watched them closely note that the eyes of the caterpillars in the following mode are half-closed. Companies that sleep-walk in today's less-than-benign business environment—whose people are not permanently on alert but prefer half-blindly to follow the leader—likely will not be here tomorrow.

The record of the new organizations is still short. Such companies still constitute, at best, an emergent model. Paradoxes abound. Consider, for example, that while the companies in this book are built on a sharing of power, this is happening only because of powerful CEOs. These CEOs are strong individuals, but secure enough in themselves that they can distribute power and sustain their top team and lower managers when they get into conflict and make mistakes. These CEOs make choices and share their power—and take it back and redistribute it if performances deteriorate.

Another paradox is the apparent return of individualism to corporate life. While work in these transformed companies is more rewarding in terms of opportunities to contribute fully, personal risk is also much higher. Long-term guarantees of employment, company pensions, and all manner of benefits are fading. "Employability" has a nice ring to it, but let employees be under no illusions: The responsibility for their "employability" is theirs and theirs alone.

Perhaps the ultimate paradox is that this autonomous, open, candid, supportive, ambidextrous organizational form has emerged at a time of higher-than-ever demands for short-term economic performance. Again, we should not delude ourselves: If ever one of the characteristics of these transformed companies—for example, teams—were to disappoint in helping performance, we would soon hear no more of it. While these companies seem to prosper by creating "learning environments" while also demanding and getting high performance, they are not in the teaching business.

An unusual confluence of trends may have conspired to bring forth this emergent model. First, there is the uncertainty of the external environment; the future seems more ambiguous than a few years ago. Second, there is the emphasis on high performance, which has seldom been more pronounced. Third, there is a realization that people productivity is the last productivity frontier. Compared to the productivity potential in fixed assets and reengineering, it is people who now offer by far the most potential for improving productivity; and transformed companies are starting to use the head and, one might add, the heart of employees. Fourth, there is a recognition that many employees themselves are seeking a new relationship with their employer: They want a more professional relationship, one in which their ideas are valued, rather than an "information up/orders down" relationship. It is not just happenstance that an increasing percentage of these employees are knowledge workers or, to use Houghton's term, conceptual workers.

These workers also want continued opportunities to learn. They know the act of transformation brings about layoffs (for example, 170,000 at GE) and dramatic revisions in job responsibilities, and they know their current knowledge alone will not maintain their employability; so they seek to continuously expand and grow. The leaders of transformed companies provide learning opportunities, not only to hold onto valued employees but also to ensure that everybody stays in a continually adaptive mode.

One promise made by institutional leadership represented in this book is that the long conflict between being a well-integrated individual with a whole life and being a company person may be easing. But it is a very large promise, inevitably difficult to keep. Just how difficult is suggested by the similarity between the characteristics of these transformed companies and the traits of what we like to think of as healthy human individuals: Both are autonomous, self-aware, open, and flexible; they are able to express conflict constructively, engage in meaningful endeavors, and have fun. Not all people manage to lead such balanced lives, however; and not all companies will be able to transform themselves. But in the examples of those that have succeeded (or have begun to succeed) thus far, there are useful guideposts for us all.

References

Argyris, C. (1990). *Overcoming Organizational Defenses*. Englewood Cliffs, NJ: Prentice Hall.

Collins, J. C., & Porras, J. I. (1994). *Built to Last*, p. 73 and Chapter 5. New York: Harper Business.

Simons, R., & Bartlett, C. (1992). Asea Brown Boveri Case Study 9-191-139. Boston: Harvard Business School.

Tichy, N., & Sherman, S. (1993). *Control Your Own Destiny or Someone Else Will*. New York: Doubleday.

Index

About the Contributors

Paul A. Allaire is chairman and CEO of Xerox Corporation in Stamford, Connecticut. He joined Xerox in 1966 as a financial analyst in Rochester, New York. He was with Rank Xerox Limited in London for 11 years and held the position of managing director from 1980 to 1983. Allaire was named senior vice president and chief staff officer of Xerox in July 1983, was elected president and a member of the board in August 1986, and chairman in May 1991.

Deborah Ancona is an associate professor of organizational studies at the Sloan School of Management at MIT. Her work has been published in the *Administrative Science Quarterly*, the *Academy of Management Journal*, and *Organizational Science*. She received her Ph.D. from Columbia University and taught at the Amos Tuck School of Business at Dartmouth College before joining the faculty at MIT. She has consulted to numerous corporations in the areas of team effectiveness, professional development, and organizational change.

Philip Anderson is an associate professor of business administration at the Amos Tuck School of Business, Dartmouth College. A former Army officer, Professor Anderson has also worked as an independent computer consultant, and an MIS manager and assistant to the president of a large nonprofit organization and an entrepreneurial start-up organization. From 1987 to1993, he was an assistant professor at Cornell University's Johnson Graduate School of Management. Professor Anderson is on the editorial boards of four academic journals, and is also the editor of the "Organization Science Electronic Letters," the first department of a major academic business journal to be published via the Internet. He is co-author, with Michael Tushman, of *Managing Strategic Innovation and Change: A Collection of Readings*, and of *Inside the Kaisha: Demystifying Japanese Business Behavior*, which he wrote with Noboru Yoshimura.

Christopher A. Bartlett has been a professor at Harvard Business School since 1979. Prior to joining the Harvard faculty, he was a marketing manager with Alcoa, a management consultant at McKinsey and Company in their London office, and general manager at Baxter Laboratories' subsidiary in France. He is the author of five books, including *Managing Across Borders: The Transnational Solution*, which he co-authored with Sumantra Ghoshal.

Retired CEO of SmithKline Beecham, **Robert P. Bauman** is currently the non-executive chairman of British Aerospace PLC. His experience includes more than 20 years at General Foods, where he was president of the International Division. In addition, he was chairman and CEO of Avco Corporation, and vice chairman of Textron, Incorporated. Bauman is a board member of ABC/Capital Cities, Union Pacific, Russell Reynolds, CIGNA, and Reuter Holdings.

Prior to joining Columbia University in 1996 as Professor of Business, **E. Ralph Biggadike** was vice president of strategic management at Becton, Dickinson and Company, a manufacturer of medical supplies, devices, and diagnostic systems. His responsibilities included strategic planning, business development, and organizational effectiveness activities. Previously he held worldwide responsibility for strategy, human resources, and organizational development. In addition, Biggadike served as the Paul M. Hammaker Professor of Business Administration at the Darden Graduate School of Business, University of Virginia.

L.J. Bourgeois III received his Ph.D. in strategic management from the University of Washington in 1978, where he wrote an award-winning dissertation about strategic decision making in companies operating in volatile environments. He has been teaching strategic management at the University of Virginia's Darden Graduate School of

Business in Charlottesville since 1986. Prior to joining the Darden faculty, Professor Bourgeois taught at the Stanford Business School. He is the author of *Strategic Management: From Concept to Implementation*, as well as more than two dozen articles in various management journals.

Gerald F. Davis is the David W. Zalaznick Jr. Associate Professor of Business at the Graduate School of Business, Columbia University. Davis's research focuses on corporate governance: boards of directors, takeovers, acquisitions, divestitures, and institutional investor influences on management. He has been published in *Administrative Science Quarterly*, *American Sociological Review*, and the *Journal of Personality and Social Psychology*.

Kathleen M. Eisenhardt is professor of strategy and organization in the department of industrial engineering and engineering management at Stanford University and is associate director of Stanford's Computer Industry Project. She is co-author, with Shona L. Brown, of the forthcoming book, *Competing on the Edge: Strategy as Structured Chaos*, and her work on strategic decision making, alliances, and other topics has been published in *Administrative Science Quarterly*, *Academy of Management Journal*, *Academy of Management Review*, *Organization Science*, and *Strategic Management Journal*.

Holder of the Robert P. Bauman Chair in Strategic Leadership, **Sumantra Ghoshal** joined the faculty of London Business School in 1994. Prior to this, he was professor of business policy at the European Institute of Business Administration (INSEAD), and taught international business at the Sloan School of Management at MIT. His publications include *The Strategy Process: European Perspective*, which he co-authored with Henry Mintzberg and J.B. Quinn; *Managing Across Borders: The Transnational Solution*, with Christopher Bartlett; and *Organization Theory and the Multinational Corporation*, with Eleanor Westney.

Donald C. Hambrick is the Samuel Bronfman Professor of Democratic Business Enterprise and chair of the Management of Organizations Division at the Graduate School of Business, Columbia University. He is the editor of *The Executive Effect: Concepts and Methods for Studying Top Managers*, and co-author, with Sydney

Finkelstein, of *Strategic Leadership: Top Executives and their Effects on Organization*. His article, "Top Management Teams: Key to Strategic Success," won the Pacific Telesis award for best article in *California Management Review*. In addition, Hambrick's work has appeared in numerous professional and scholarly journals, including *Administrative Science Quarterly*, *Academy of Management Journal*, *Academy of Management Review*, and *Strategic Management Journal*.

A managing director of the Delta Consulting Group Inc., **Jeffrey D. Heilpern** specializes in working with CEOs and senior management teams on improving their leadership effectiveness in designing and implementing an integrated change agenda. Heilpern has served as leader at Delta for practice teams in both the CEO/Governance and total quality management areas. His clients have included Weyerhaeuser, the new Chase, the U.S. Postmaster General, Pacific Telesis, Xerox, Corning, Seagram, and Nestle Foods.

James R. Houghton is retired chairman of the board of Corning Incorporated. He joined Corning in 1962 and served in production, financial, and sales positions until 1965 when he was named vice president and European area manager of Corning Glass International. In 1968, Houghton returned to the U.S., where he was appointed general manager of the Consumer Products Division and elected a vice president of Corning. He was elected chairman in 1983.

Jean L. Kahwajy is currently pursuing a doctorate in organizational behavior at Stanford University. She is also a senior associate at Strategic Decisions Group, a California-based management consulting firm serving Fortune 200 clients in the areas of strategy development, decision analysis, implementation, and executive education, and has led over 80 corporate seminars worldwide. The author of several articles concerning organizational design, interpersonal conflict mitigation, and decision making in top-level management teams, her current research explores how social and psychological forces influence decision making and mobility within organizations.

The Raoul de Vitry d'Avaucourt Chair of Human Resource Management at the European Institute of Business Administration (INSEAD), **Manfred F. R. Kets de Vries** is a clinical professor of management and leadership. He is the author of numerous books, including *Life and Death in the Executive Fast Lane*, *Family Business: Human Dilemmas in the Family Firm*, and *Leaders, Fools, and Imposters*. In addition, Kets de Vries has written many case studies, three of which won the ECCH Best Case of the Year Award. He has published more than 120 scientific papers as chapters in books and as articles in such journals as *Behavioral Science*, *Journal of Management Studies*, *Strategic Management Journal*, *Academy of Management Journal*, *Academy of Management Review*, *California Management Review*, and *Harvard Business Review*.

David M. Lawrence, M.D., is CEO and chairman of the boards of Kaiser Foundation Health Plan, Inc. and Kaiser Foundation Hospitals. During his tenure with the organization, he has served as area medical director and vice president of operations for the Northwest Permanente Medical Group, and as regional manager of the Colorado and northern California regions. Prior to joining the program, Dr. Lawrence served as health officer and director of human services for Multnomah County, Oregon; he was on the faculty of the School of Public Health and Community Medicine and the School of Medicine at the University of Washington. He served as an advisor to the Ministry of Health of Chile under the aegis of Johns Hopkins University and as a Peace Corps physician in the Dominican Republic and Washington, D.C.

Jay W. Lorsch is the Louis Kirstein Professor of Human Relations, and chairman of the doctoral programs, and director of research at the Harvard Business School. He has served as senior associate dean and chair of the Executive Education Program, as senior associate dean and director of research, as chairman of the Advanced Management Programs, and as chairman of the Organizational Behavior Area. He is the author of more than a dozen books, the most recent of which is *Pawns or Potentates: The Reality of America's Corporate Boards*. He co-authored, with Paul R. Lawrence, *Organization and Environment*, which won the Academy of Management's Best Management Book of the Year Award and the James A. Hamilton Book Award of the College of Hospital Administrators in 1969.

Terry McNulty is a senior research fellow with the Centre for Corporate Strategy and Change at the Warwick Business School. His research and expertise centers on the behavior of boards and directors, organizational change in the U.K. National Health Services, and other professional service contexts. McNulty was previously employed by Nottingham Health Authority and the Institute of Health Services Management.

Founder and chairman of Delta Consulting Group, **David A. Nadler** is an internationally recognized leader in the field of strategic organizational change. He advises CEOs and other senior corporate leaders on a range of issues related to the design and management of organizational change, including strategy, organizational architecture, operating environment and leadership. Prior to launching Delta, Nadler served for six years on the faculty of the Graduate School of Business, Columbia University, and was on the staff of the Survey Research Center Institute for Social Research at the University of Michigan. He has been published extensively in the field of organizational behavior and change management, and has authored or edited more than a dozen books, including *Champions of Change*, and, with Michael Tushman, *Competing by Design: The Power of Organizational Architecture*.

Charles A. O'Reilly III is the Frank E. Buck Professor of Human Resources Management and Organizational Behavior and director of the Human Resource Executive Program at the Stanford Graduate School of Business. Previously he taught at the Haas School of Business and the Institute of Personality Research at the University of California at Berkeley and the Anderson Graduate School of Management at UCLA. He is the co-author, with Michael Tushman, of *Winning through Innovation: A Practical Guide to Leading Organizational Change and Renewal*, and he has published more than 60 articles in academic and professional journals.

A professor of organizational behavior at Warwick Business School, **Andrew M. Pettigrew** founded the Centre for Corporate Strategy and Change (CCSC) at the University of Warwick. He directed CCSC from 1985 to 1995. He has taught and researched at Yale University, London Business School, Harvard Business School, and the European Institute for Advanced Studies in Management. He has written, co-authored, or edited 10 books, including, with Ewan Ferlie and Lorna McKee, *Shaping Strategic Change*.

Charles S. Raben is a managing director of the Delta Consulting Group and head of the firm's San Francisco office. A management consultant for more than 20 years, Raben works with CEOs of major U.S. companies to help them manage the complexities of change. He has worked with companies such as Sun Microsystems, KPMG Peat Marwick, and Chase Manhattan Bank. Prior to joining Delta, Dr. Raben was associated with Arco Oil and Gas Company, where he managed a consulting group responsible for organizational planning and development. He has served on the faculties of the University of California, Berkeley, and the University of Maryland.

Jeffrey A. Sonnenfeld is a professor of organization and management and the director of the Center for Leadership and Career Studies (CLCS) of the Goizueta Business School at Emory University. Founded in 1989, CLCS is the nation's first and only school for chief executives. Prior to joining the Emory faculty, Sonnenfeld was a professor at the Harvard Business School. He has published five books, including *The Hero's Farewell: What Happens When CEOs Retire*, and numerous articles in the areas of career management, executive training and development, and the management of corporate social performance. His articles have appeared in the *Academy of Management Journal*, the *Academy of Management Review*, *American Psychologist*, *Harvard Business Review*, and *Human Resource Management*.

A senior director with Delta Consulting Group, **Janet L. Spencer, Ph.D.**, works in the areas of senior team development, executive leadership, and strategy formulation. As an executive-level management consultant, she assists CEOs and senior managers on strategic implementation of large-scale organizational change. Prior to her association with Delta, Dr. Spencer worked for AT&T, specializing in assessment center design and implementation.

The Phillip Hettleman Professor and Director of the Center for Studies in Innovation and Entrepreneurship at the Graduate School of Business at Columbia University, **Michael L. Tushman** is internationally recognized for his work on the relations between technological change, executive leadership and organization adaptation, and for his work on managing R&D laboratories. He has been a visiting professor at the Sloan School of Management at MIT and at INSEAD and has served on the boards of many scholarly journals, including *Administrative Science Quarterly*, *Management Science*, and the *Academy of Management Journal*. Tushman is co-author, with Charles A. O'Reilly III, of *Winning through Innovation: A Practical Guide to Leading Organizational Change and Renewal*, and with David Nadler, *Competing by Design : The Power of Organizational Architectures*.

John L. Vogelstein is vice chairman of the board and president of Warburg, Pincus. He has been with the company since 1967 and has been in the investment business for more than 40 years. Prior to joining Warburg, Pincus, he was a partner of Lazard Freres & Co. Vogelstein serves on numbers boards of directors, and he is vice chairman of the Board of Trustees of The Taft School.

A senior director at Delta Consulting Group, **Elise Walton** specializes in change management, global strategy, organization design, and quality. Prior to joining Delta, she was an independent consultant working with clients such as Merrill Lynch, Becton, Dickinson and Company, BBDO, and Citibank. She also participated in a joint venture between Harvard Business School and the Soviet Institute for International Economics to assess and compare management practices.

James D. Westphal is an assistant professor at the College of Business Administration at the University of Texas at Austin. His current research and teaching interests include corporate governance, boards of directors, top management compensation, and strategic change. He has published articles in such journals as *Administrative Science Quarterly*, and he received his Ph.D. in organization behavior from Northwestern University.

Edward J. Zajac is the James F. Beré Professor of Organization Behavior at the J.L. Kellogg Graduate School of Management at Northwestern University. He joined Kellogg in 1986 upon completion of his Ph.D. in organization and strategy at The Wharton School. In addition, he was a Fulbright Scholar at the University of Cologne, Germany, and he has been a visiting professor at the Free University of Berlin. Zajac's work has been published widely in such journals as *Strategic Management Journal*, *Administrative Science Quarterly*, and *Organization Science*.